OCR
PSYCHOLOGY
FOR AS

OCR
PSYCHOLOGY
FOR AS

KARON OLIVER
LOUISE ELLERBY-JONES

DYNAMIC LEARNING
Innovate • Motivate • Personalise
CD-ROM INSIDE

HODDER
EDUCATION
PART OF HACHETTE LIVRE UK

A Dynamic Learning disk is included with this book giving access to a wealth of free electronic resources. The disk is designed and licensed for home use only. It will not run on a network. For further support, visit www.dynamic-learning.co.uk/studentsupport.

Orders: please contact Bookpoint Ltd, 130 Milton Park, Abingdon, Oxon OX14 4SB. Telephone: (44) 01235 827720. Fax: (44) 01235 400454. Lines are open from 9.00–5.00, Monday to Saturday, with a 24 hour message answering service. You can also order through our website www.hoddereducation.co.uk

If you have any comments to make about this, or any of our other titles, please send them to educationenquiries@hodder.co.uk

British Library Cataloguing in Publication Data
A catalogue record for this title is available from the British Library

ISBN: 978 0 340 96812 3

First Edition Published 2008

Impression number   10 9 8 7 6 5 4 3 2

Year   2012 2011 2010 2009 2008

Copyright © 2008 Karon Oliver and Louise Ellerby-Jones

Hachette's policy is to use papers that are natural, renewable and recyclable products and made from wood grown in sustainable forests. The logging and manufacturing processes are expected to conform to the environmental regulations of the country of origin.

Artwork by Barking Dog Art
Cover photo © Andrew Johnson/ iStockphoto.com

Typeset in 10.5/12 Minion by Charon Tec Ltd (A Macmillan Company), Chennai, India
www.charontec.com

Printed and bound in Italy

Contents

ACC No.

CAT No.

V

What does 'the expert choice' mean for you?

**HODDER
EDUCATION**
The Expert Choice

We work with more examiners and experts than any other publisher

● Because we work with more experts and examiners than any other publisher, the very latest curriculum requirements are built into this course and there is a perfect match between your course and the resources that you need to succeed. We make it easier for you to gain the skills and knowledge that you need for the best results.

● We have chosen the best team of experts – including the people that mark the exams – to give you the very best chance of success; look out for their advice throughout this book: this is content that you can trust.

Innovate • Motivate • Personalise

Welcome to Dynamic Learning

Dynamic Learning is a simple and powerful way of integrating this text with digital resources to help you succeed, by bringing learning to life. Whatever your learning style, Dynamic Learning will help boost your understanding.

1

● Boost your understanding through interactive activities, quizzes, web links and a full Glossary for each chapter.

2

● Activities for each case study, allowing students to test their knowledge and understanding of all key areas.

More direct contact with teachers and students than any other publisher

- We talk with more than 100 000 students every year through our student conferences, run by Philip Allan Updates. We hear at first hand what you need to make a success of your A-level studies and build what we learn into every new course. Learn more about our conferences at **www.philipallan.co.uk**

- Our new materials are trialled in classrooms as we develop them, and the feedback built into every new book or resource that we publish. You can be part of that. If you have comments that you would like to make about this book, please email us at: **feedback@hodder.co.uk**

More collaboration with Subject Associations than any other publisher

- Subject Associations sit at the heart of education. We work closely with more Associations than any other publisher. This means that our resources support the most creative teaching and learning, using the skills of the best teachers in their field to create resources for you.

More opportunities for your teachers to stay ahead than with any other publisher

- Through our Philip Allan Updates Conferences, we offer teachers access to Continuing Professional Development. Our focused and practical conferences ensure that your teachers have access to the best presenters, teaching materials and training resources. Our presenters include experienced teachers, Chief and Principal Examiners, leading educationalists, authors and consultants. This course is built on all of this expertise.

 ## RESULTS

- All 40 subjects gave shocks up to 300 volts, with five refusing to go beyond this point.
- Between 315 volts and 375 volts a further nine Ss stopped obeying.
- This meant that 26/40, a staggering 65% of Ss tested, went all the way up to 450 volts.

 The Network Edition (ISBN: 9780340968130) includes PowerPoint slides which provide an in-depth summary of each case study and additional activities and learning materials.

- A Dynamic Learning disk is included with this book giving access to a wealth of free electronic resources. The disk is designed and licensed for home use only. It will not run on a network. For further support, visit www.dynamic-learning.co.uk/studentsupport.

To start up Dynamic Learning now insert the disk into your CD ROM drive. Dynamic Learning should run automatically if you have 'Auto Run' enabled. Full installation instructions are printed on the disk label.

Basic system requirements for your Student Edition: **PC** Windows 2000 (SP4), XP SP2 (Home & Pro), Vista; **PC (Server)** Windows 2000 and 2003; **Mac** Mac OS X 10.3 or 10.4; G4, G5 or Intel processor. Up to 1.4Gb hard disc space per title. Minimum screen resolution 1024 x 768. Sound card. A fast processor (PC, 1GHz; Mac, 1.25 GHz) and good graphics card. Copyright restrictions mean that some materials may not be accessible from within the Dynamic Learning edition. Full details of your one standalone licence can be found on the disk under 'Contents'.

You can find out more at www.dynamic-learning.co.uk

Introduction

The third edition of this textbook is written to match the 2008 specification of the OCR AS syllabus, but don't let this put you off if you are a new reader to the subject of psychology. We really hope that you will find the topics we have covered will inspire you to read more about what is really the most brilliant subject. In fact both of us have been involved in the study of psychology for a large number of years and neither of us have, as yet, grown tired of learning about a subject which is dynamic, relevant and never boring!

The book covers five areas of psychology: social psychology, cognitive psychology, developmental psychology, physiological psychology and individual differences. This will give you a broad introduction to most of the topics that go to make up the subject. Within each area we have written about three studies, some of which are relatively old but remain key to our understanding, and some which are much more contemporary. This gives a total of fifteen studies in all.

Each study is preceded by some background information in order to provide a context and understanding as to why the research was conducted. This background information is often illustrated by short stories (or vignettes) which will make the information link to the things that you, as humans, are probably very familiar with. For example, in the chapter about Social Psychology, we talk about how going out with a large crowd will give you the kind of anonymity to behave in a slightly different way to the way you would behave when you are on your own.

You will find in the studies themselves evaluative points or comments which are intended to help you think more about the wider issues which come from the study itself. Linking with this you will have a CD-ROM which gives first of all a really good basic introduction into the way psychological research is conducted. You will find suggestions for further reading including lots of weblinks. Also there are other sections called 'Additional Reading' which are intended to provide further information on the background to the studies.

The final chapter in the book is intended to help those of you who are planning to take this subject as an AS Level examination with OCR. The purpose of this chapter is to tell you what you need to learn, give you some insight into ways you can learn, and give you some ways to test your learning. In order to support your learning, there are numerous tests, puzzles and activities also on the CD-ROM.

We do hope you enjoy reading as much as we have enjoyed preparing the information for you and wish you every success in your endeavours.

Karon Oliver and Louise Ellerby-Jones

Acknowledgements

The authors and publishers should like to think the following for permission to repro-duce illustrative copyright material:

Picture on page 12 © Bettmann/Corbis; page 48 © Tom Kidd / Alamy; page 54 © AP/PA Photos; page 68 © BBC; page 89 © John Dee / Rex Features; page 100 © United Artists / The Kobal Collection; page 113 © Tina Manley/North America / Alamy; page 138 © Yvonne Hemsey/Getty Images; page 139 © Christopher Felver/Corbis; page 148 © Anna Clopet/Corbis; page 154 © Great Ape Trust of Iowa; page 194(a) © Hulton-Deutsch Collection/Corbis; page 194(b) © Gideon Mendel/Corbis; page 198 © Bettmann/Corbis; page 209 © Albert Bandura, Stanford University; page 217 © Hulton-Deutsch Collection/Corbis; page 243 © CNRI/Science Photo Library Photo Library; page 249 © ER Productions/Corbis; page 250(a) © Sovereign, ISM/Science Photo Library; page 250(b) © Roger Ressmeyer/Corbis; page 252 © Mauro Fermariello/Science Photo Library; page 266 © J.C. Revy/Science Photo Library page 296 © AP/PA Photos; page 332 © Science Museum/Science & Society PL; page 352 © David Crausby/Alamy.

Every effort has been made to trace and acknowledge ownership of copyright. The pub-lishers will be glad to make suitable arrangements with any copyright holders whom it has not been possible to contact.

Introduction to psychology

Why do people do what they do, and why don't they do the same things that I do? How can they do things that I would never do, or would never want to do? Why do they think the way they do, and why don't they seem to think the same way that I do? How can people believe in things that I don't believe in? Do people feel the same things that I'm feeling?

If these are the kind of questions that interest you, then you have chosen the right subject – psychology. What psychology actually is, however, is not commonly understood. Here is a psychology teacher's story:

> When I meet new people, one of the questions they ask is, 'What do you do?' I hate this question, so I try to avoid telling them, and go for half the story: 'I'm a teacher,' I say. Then, of course, their next question is, 'What do you teach?' Well, I can hold them off with the facetious answer, 'Students', but that's a bit rude, so I have to admit it: 'Psychology,' I say eventually. This is then, as often as not, followed by them saying, 'Ooh! I'll have to be careful what I say now, won't I? You're going to be reading my mind,' or they say, 'You're going to be analysing me now, aren't you?'
>
> Typically they might ask me something along the lines of: 'I had this dream about being chased by a giant snail round a 400 m running track and it was wearing a baseball cap and calling out my name. What does it mean, then?' or 'I must introduce you to my brother, Rick. We think he's bipolar. Maybe you could confirm it for us?'

Psychologists don't tell you what your dreams mean. Psychologists don't diagnose mental disorders: that's the job of psychiatrists – medical doctors who have specialist psychiatric training. They don't offer you therapy or counselling: that's the job of psychotherapists, not psychologists. Psychologists don't read your mind. No one can do that.

What psychologists actually do is systematically investigate human behaviour and experience, with the aim of trying to explain, understand, predict or manage behaviour. It is to be hoped that what they discover helps us to live better, happier lives and makes a positive contribution to human welfare. Psychologists, then, are best thought of as researchers or scientists, and never as therapists, doctors, gurus or magicians.

Psychology is considered to have begun in the 1870s in Leipzig, in modern Germany, when Wilhelm Wundt and his colleagues opened their 'psychology laboratory'. Their method of studying psychology was to take an introspective approach – asking themselves: What do I feel? Why do I feel like this? How do I behave? How does my memory work? and so on.

However, this was rejected as a way of studying behaviour on the grounds that it was too subjective, and despite Wundt and his colleagues focusing on collecting data about behaviour, their attempts to understand psychology were always going to be limited by the fact that they were just a handful of people and their interpretations of their own behaviour were always going to be biased.

Modern psychology, on the other hand, tries to follow an objective scientific methodology when investigating human behaviour. This means that theories are generated, which are then tested by gathering empirical evidence. To be taken seriously as an academic discipline, psychology has, for the most part, taken a scientific approach to studying behaviour. The aim of science is to determine causality by carrying out controlled experiments to test hypotheses. The findings from experiments provide proof for or against a theory. The findings need to stand up on replication, that is, if you do the study again you must get similar results. These features of science are important in psychological investigations and you will learn a great deal about how data is gathered and analysed as you progress through this book or through your programme of study. In fact, if you are following the OCR examination for AS level, you will do a whole exam paper on research methodology called the Psychological Investigations paper.

In general terms, psychologists have investigated aspects of human behaviour under five headings or 'approaches'. These are:

- The **social approach**, which investigates how the social context, including the presence and behaviour of other people, impacts on how people behave.

- The **cognitive approach**, which investigates how we think, perceive, pay attention, problem-solve and remember.

- The **developmental approach**, which investigates how our thinking changes as we mature and grow older; the development of personality – for example, Freud's psychoanalytic perspective; and how we learn – for example, the behaviourist perspective.

- The **physiological approach**, which investigates how biology, especially neurobiology, the biology of the brain, impacts on people's behaviour.

- The **individual differences approach**, which investigates the differences between people, such as abnormality and mental illness.

In reality, these approaches overlap, but in terms of developing an understanding of what psychologists do, they provide you with a useful starting point.

The aim of the OCR AS level, and therefore of this book, is to give you a grounding in these key approaches to psychology. In order to do this, three studies from each approach have been included for you to study:

Approaches	Studies		
SOCIAL PSYCHOLOGY	Milgram – obedience	Piliavin, Rodin and Piliavin – subway Samaritan	Reicher and Haslam – BBC prison experiment
COGNITIVE PSYCHOLOGY	Loftus and Palmer – eyewitness testimony	Baron-Cohen et al. – theory of mind	Savage-Rumbaugh et al. – ape language
DEVELOPMENTAL PSYCHOLOGY	Samuel and Bryant – conservation	Bandura, Ross and Ross – imitating aggression	Freud – little Hans
PHYSIOLOGICAL PSYCHOLOGY	Maguire et al. – taxi drivers' brains	Dement and Kleitman – dreaming	Sperry – split brains
PSYCHOLOGY OF INDIVIDUAL DIFFERENCES	Rosenhan – being sane in insane places	Thigpen and Cleckley – multiple personality	Griffiths – gambling

The 15 core studies and the five approaches

You also have to study methods and issues and relate these to the 15 core studies:

Methods	Issues
• Experimental method (laboratory and field) • Case study • Self-report • Observation • Methodological issues such as reliability and validity	• Ethics • Ecological validity • Longitudinal and snapshot • Qualitative and quantitative data

Much of the psychological terminology that you will have to get to grips with will be in relation to research methodology. To help with this we have explained key research methods concepts for you as each one crops up. We have also explained key concepts that relate to specific studies in a similar way.

There is a list of 50 key methodological concepts and issues on the CD-ROM for you to refer to. You will also find a section on the CD-ROM called 'Investigating people', which gives examples of how psychologists investigate behaviour.

Well, we have told you that as psychologists we cannot read your mind. However, we can infer what is going on in your mind from your behaviour. That is, if you are reading this book, then either you must be interested in finding out about psychology or you have already started to study psychology for AS or A level.

And if you want a bit of magic, then we can definitely predict the future for you: you are going to love psychology. Why? Psychology is fascinating because it is all about people, and what could be more fascinating than us?

Social psychology

Introduction

Some species live a solitary existence whilst others prefer to live in social groups. Humans are just such a species and as part of the human race, we will recognise how important social relationships are to us. In fact, the relationships we have with others probably cause us more joy or heartache than any other aspect of our lives. You will know by now that when we have good friends or partners and the relationships are going well, we generally feel more positive and motivated than when things are going wrong. It is because of the relevance of social relationships in our lives that we have chosen to begin with the three social psychology studies on the OCR syllabus.

As psychologists are interested in understanding human beings, it makes sense that they would be interested in the types of relationships we have with other human beings, how these relationships work and the way they impact on our thoughts and behaviour. Even more interesting is the fact that we do not always behave rationally when it comes to other people; hopefully, the reasons for this will become more obvious as you read this chapter.

Humans are innately social creatures who actually *need* to interact with other people. Research has indicated that one of the cruellest types of punishment is to keep someone in solitary confinement. This is not only because we enjoy the company of others; it seems also that we are biologically programmed to be sociable. Deprivation studies have shown that if we are kept apart from other people our brain 'manufactures' them in the form of dreams or hallucinations (many of the main psychology textbooks give information about sensory deprivation studies). You may argue that some people actually choose to live a life of social isolation, avoiding any kind of unnecessary interaction, but even people who are antisocial have to have some form of contact with others (for work or shopping, for example) in order to survive, and perhaps this level of social interaction, for them, is enough to fulfil that biological need.

It will probably be clear by now that if humans need to interact with each other, this will guide their behaviour. If you need something enough, you will sometimes do things which go against what you actually feel or believe in order to get what you want. An example of this would be being nice to or doing things for people who you do not really like, because you would rather have their company than be on your own. This is the basis of much of our social interaction – we need something from others and will do what is necessary to get it.

The topic of social psychology is divided into two sub-areas. **Social interaction** is concerned with how we interact with each other and how our position in society has a strong effect on the type of behaviour we demonstrate. It also takes into account the factors which affect this behaviour, such as our past experiences, the roles we are playing or our perceived vulnerability. You might think that the way you behave is entirely unique to you, but the truth is that we all tend to follow certain patterns of behaviour, and in some cases these patterns are entirely predictable. The two studies which focus on this area of psychology are the study by Milgram, which investigates obedience, and the study undertaken by Reicher and Haslam, who investigated the effect that roles have on our behaviour.

Social cognition involves how we think and feel about current social experiences and how we try to make sense of them, much of which is affected by memories. It also considers how we use stored information to predict the course of interactions and their possible outcomes. The study which relates to social cognition is the Piliavin et al. study, which looks at the factors which make us willing to help another person.

Social animals

How does all this fit into real life? Part of being a social animal is that our lives involve numerous social relationships. Many of these relationships follow consistent patterns or are predictable, but what happens when we don't know the person very well or someone close to us behaves in a way which is unexpected or out of character? We are left feeling confused or anxious, and consequently devote much of our time to thinking about these relationships and trying to work out why certain things have happened. In fact, one of the reasons people give when explaining why they have chosen to study psychology is to help them understand their own and other people's behaviour. To explain the point further, here is an example of a situation you may have experienced in some form.

> On one particular day my best friend was absolutely foul to me. I was really hurt and spent some time trying to work out why she had been so horrible, because it wasn't like her. It turned out that her boyfriend had dumped her that day and she was extremely upset and just couldn't bear to talk about it, so she snapped at me, almost as a way of making me leave her alone. The trouble was that I didn't know this at the time and I was concerned about the cause of her behaviour. Had she turned into a monster or was there another reason for her being so snappy?

The knowledge that social behaviour usually has a cause, even if it is not easily identifiable, is the basis of social understanding (or social cognition). The situation above would be analysed in terms of trying to work out why my best friend reacted like this. Here I would have to refer to my memory of what she was like normally and think about what had happened recently, using the two factors to interpret the current situation. Another question might be whether I had done anything wrong; this could only be assessed by going back over my own behaviour and trying to work out if I had been nasty to her or forgotten her birthday or given her some kind of just cause to be so horrible.

It appears that we need to have answers to the questions we may pose, because if we cannot come up with a reasonable answer it causes us anxiety. This means that our biological arousal levels increase, and increased arousal tends to lead to anxiety. People hate anxiety. In fact, we tend to do anything rather than allow ourselves to remain anxious for a long period of time. This means that one of the needs we have to satisfy is that of reducing the level of arousal we experience, and we shall see how the study by Piliavin et al. (see page 34) uses arousal reduction as an explanation of our motivation in deciding whether or not to help in emergency situations. Be aware, in the future, if you find yourself in a situation which makes you feel uncomfortable, that you will do something to change that situation. The problem is that we do not always behave in the most logical way and we do not always behave according to our feelings.

> My best friend hates Joan. She thinks she is the most boring and opinionated person she has ever met. In fact, she has just spent half an hour telling me why she dislikes her so much. Suddenly, Joan comes round the corner.
>
> 'Hello, sweetie, how are you? We have missed you and were wondering when we would see you again,' says my friend in the most annoying way.

Why is she saying this when she hates Joan? The obvious reason is that she is two-faced. Well, yes, she is, but there is a reason for her behaviour. Is it because she does not want to hurt Joan's feelings? Is it because she wants something from Joan? Or is it simply because she has been socialised to behave in a polite way and not to indicate how she feels?

We will now look in more detail at the often unconscious reasoning which influences our behaviour.

Conformity and obedience

The first study in this section focuses on obedience, but we are going to consider the topics of conformity and obedience. These two are very closely interlinked and we often use one term when we really mean the other. Let's begin by considering what we mean by conformity.

What is conformity?

During your childhood, there will have been some kind of craze which affected all the people in your school. It may have been to do with a particular toy or possibly a must-have item of clothing. It may have been something as simple as a type of pen or as expensive as an electronic games console.

Such crazes are often linked to toys, such as Transformers, Trolls, My Little Pony, Barbie, Pokemon or Harry Potter memorabilia. Fashion designers, toy manufacturers and anyone else involved in the retail trade love conformity. Set up a craze, especially among the young, and everyone will go for it. In fact, it's an ideal way to sell huge quantities of merchandise. The levels of conformity in consumerism are phenomenal. When you actually stand back from it and realise how easily we are convinced that having one of these items is the only way we can ensure peace of mind, you see what an important concept conformity is.

Conformity has been described as 'yielding to group pressure' (Crutchfield 1962). However, this implies that other people put pressure on us to make us conform and this is not always the case. After all, how many people pressurised you into buying whatever it was you bought that seemed at the time to be a must-have item? A better definition is given by Aronson (1976), who said it was a 'change in a person's behaviour or opinions as a result of real or imagined pressure from a person or group of people'. This would make more sense, as often the pressure we feel is imagined. The person or group he refers to would have to be important to the person at the time, irrelevant of their status.

There has been considerable research on conformity. One of the first studies looked at the answers people gave when asked to estimate the number of beans in a bottle (Jenness 1932). If you have ever entered a 'guess the number' competition, you probably looked at the previous estimates made and based your judgement on what other people had guessed. This is more or less what happened in the Jenness study. First of all, he asked the students to give their own estimates individually, and then he asked them to decide on a group estimate. Finally, he asked them alone again and discovered that they stayed with the group answer.

Probably the most famous study on conformity was undertaken by Asch (1951), when he created a situation where many of his participants gave answers which were blatantly untrue rather than contradict the people they were with. He did this by getting his participant to sit at a table with six stooges (confederates of the experimenter). He then showed them a card with a single line drawn on it, and another card which had three lines of different lengths drawn on it, labelled A, B and C, and asked them to say which line length matched that on the original card. The participant was always second to last.

Examples of cards

The stooges gave blatantly incorrect responses in a number of the trials and the participants were left in the situation where they either reported what they saw with their own eyes or conformed to the norm of the group. When the results were assessed, Asch found that in one out of every three trials where the wrong answer was given, the participant gave the same wrong answer as the stooges. This led to an average level of conformity of 32 per cent, although 75 per cent of participants conformed to the wrong answer at least once.

Asch interviewed his participants after the trials to try to find out why they had conformed to an answer which was so blatantly wrong. Most of them said that they did not want to cause problems within the group, although they also reported that when they did give wrong answers it made them feel very anxious. We all know that having some moral support makes it easier to tell the truth, and Asch found that when there was just one other person present who did not go along with the majority, no matter how many others there were, it was sufficient to make the participant give the right answer.

Each of us is under different pressures, both actual and perceived, and each of us varies from day to day in how confident we feel, depending on the situation we are in, and this can influence our behaviour. So on one occasion you might conform to the group, even if you believe they are wrong (especially if you feel threatened by them), and on another occasion you would speak out against the group consensus (usually if you feel relatively secure). The nature of the disagreement and the actual consequences of disagreeing may also sway your decision. Some people feel confident most of the time and it is these people, people with high self-esteem, who feel that they do not have to go along with the majority. They are confident enough in their judgement to go against the rest without feeling threatened or uncomfortable (Stang 1973).

Why do we conform?

Kelman (1958) outlined three processes which can explain social conformity.

1. **Compliance**
   Where participants go along with the crowd to prevent any in-group hostility or bad feeling and to maintain group harmony. However, they do not change their own private belief.

2. **Internalisation**
   Where participants come to internalise the view of the group and see its view as the more valid one. They may be able to do this, for example, by convincing themselves that their eyesight is poor.

3. **Identification**
   Where participants actually seem to change their beliefs because they want to become more like their heroes. If they really want to become part of an in-group, they will start to identify with that group and take on the group's values and beliefs, even if they are different to their own original values and beliefs. This can also happen if they want to become more like a person they respect or admire – they will change their attitudes to become more like them. This happens frequently with teenagers who want to become more like a peer group in order to be accepted and suddenly seem to go against all the values and beliefs of their parents.

If we relate these back to the Asch study, we can begin to see what was happening for the participants. Asch's participants were simply complying with the demands of the experimental situation, but they had not actually internalised the group's norms. They agreed in public, but dissented in private.

What is obedience?

Having looked at conformity, we are now going to turn to obedience. Both these topics seem to involve people renouncing their personal responsibility in a given situation. With conformity, we give up our individual responsibility when we go along with others in order to be accepted by the group. With obedience, we give up our personal responsibility to make decisions and go along with the decisions of others as to how we should act and what we should do. However, there are different reasons why we are obedient.

Self-preservation

First, obedience may be a form of self-preservation, especially if the authority figure who is telling us what to do has some kind of power. In such situations we do not necessarily have to see the authority figure as being legitimate (although it helps), because no matter what we feel, we are looking after our own welfare. This can be taken to extremes. In the army, soldiers may be court-martialled if they do not do as they are told. At home, if we do not do as we are told by our parents, we may face being grounded or having our allowance stopped.

Socialisation

The second reason that we are inclined to obey is that we have been taught to be obedient. We have been socialised to toe the line, and it is more acceptable for us to be obedient than to go against the orders or rules, especially when these are set by someone perceived as being a legitimate authority figure.

Imagine you are sitting in the classroom in a psychology lesson. The lesson has been going for 10 minutes, and will go on for another 50 minutes. You are bored out of your brain. So why don't you leave? You have finished your compulsory education so you do not have to be there; you could just get up and walk out of the door. How easy do you think this would be? What is there to stop you from leaving? How might you feel? Who has the authority in this situation?

When we are very young, we are trained to be obedient by our parents/carers and our teachers, and we are taught that these forms of authority are legitimate and have our best interests at heart. We can all remember the many occasions that our parents/carers said to us, 'Do as you are told.' This will often have been backed up with threats if you were naughty, and praise if you were obedient. What happens is that we internalise the need for obedience and therefore become conditioned to obey voluntarily in most situations (we will talk more about the process of conditioning in Chapter 4, Developmental

Psychology). This seems to become set as a default position, which means that eventually disobeying becomes the difficult action. Obedience therefore becomes the norm and to be defiant or disobedient is perceived as abnormal, drawing the disapproval of others.

Psychology teachers have been known to demonstrate how this works by selecting a particular student and asking them to do something like standing up in the classroom or standing outside the door for no apparent reason. Even though they might question why they are being asked to do this, the likelihood is that the student will obey the teacher's command. One particular student who obeyed just such a command talked about his experience. He seemed quite shocked that he had obeyed and had thought the order was unfair. He said that he knew the teacher could not really do anything to harm him, but teachers tell students to do things, so he did as he was told.

What is wrong with being obedient?

Most of the time there is nothing wrong with being obedient. Obedience fulfils an important function for us. It is necessary to maintain social harmony, for without some form of obedience to an authority we would end up with a state of anarchy. Stanley Milgram (1963) wrote: 'It must not be thought all obedience entails acts of aggression against others. Obedience serves numerous productive functions. . . Obedience may be ennobling and educative and refer to acts of charity and kindness as well as to destruction.'

On the other hand, we also have to remember that blind obedience is an undesirable state and can result in acts of destruction and damage to others. This brings us to why obedience has been studied by psychologists. What kind of person could obey orders or instructions that would lead to the injury or death of innocent people? Examples often cited are the Holocaust and the Vietnam War, where innocent civilians were slaughtered as a result of orders given by authority figures. However, research has suggested that the people who committed these atrocities were not always amoral monsters.

Eichmann was perhaps one of the worst offenders in the Second World War. He was responsible for arranging the transportation of six million Jews to their deaths. Following the war he escaped to Buenos Aires, but he was caught in 1961 and put on trial for his part in the killing of millions of Jews. While the case was being prepared he was interrogated for a total of 275 hours, as it was believed he must have been some kind of monster to have allowed this genocide to occur. Captain Avner W. Less, who interrogated Eichmann for the duration of the 275 hours, wrote:

> My first reaction when the prisoner finally stood facing us in the khaki shirt and trousers and open sandals was one of disappointment. I no longer know what I had expected – probably the sort of Nazi you see in the movies: tall, blonde, with piercing blue eyes and brutal features expressive of domineering arrogance. Whereas this rather thin, balding man not much taller than myself looked utterly ordinary.

(Von Lang and Sibyll (eds) 1983, in R. Brown 1986: 3)

Eichmann was described by the man who interrogated him for war crimes as looking 'utterly ordinary' and not a monster at all

In fact, Hannah Arendt (1965), who reported on the trial of Eichmann, concluded that he was simply a commonplace bureaucrat like any other, who obeyed orders given to him without question.

The other frequently cited evidence of how obedience to authority can be destructive comes from the case of Lieutenant William Calley's part in the My Lai massacre during the Vietnam War in 1970. Calley was the commander of a platoon of American soldiers when he received orders to round up all the inhabitants of a village called My Lai. He was told that there were Vietcong in the village, and that the soldiers should round up all the members of the village and 'waste them' (shoot them dead). The inhabitants were mainly women, old men and children and yet they were all wiped out.

Again, the nature of the man who was at fault was questioned. How could a normal person agree to order his men to shoot obviously innocent children? However, Calley had shown no criminal tendencies before My Lai, and after his sentence he continued to live quietly as an average American civilian. In 1972 a survey was carried out in the USA to gauge the reaction of the public to Calley's trial. The results were that 51 per cent of the sample said they would follow the same orders by killing the inhabitants of the village if that was what they had been instructed to do, because the orders came from a legitimate authority.

Whether or not we agree with Eichmann's or Calley's actions, the reasons for their obedience are perhaps easy to understand. First, the consequences of disobedience were perhaps too high – court martial and imprisonment or execution. Everyone else was obeying orders at the time, so they were conforming to group norms. It therefore becomes evident that there is more than one simple reason why people are obedient, and often the reasons involve conformity too.

THE STUDY

Stanley Milgram (1963) 'Behavioural study of obedience'

Journal of Abnormal and Social Psychology, 67: 371–8

BACKGROUND

Is the type of person who is seemingly blindly obedient really very different to the rest of the population, representing perhaps a few in every thousand? Perhaps there is just a sadistic minority who get drawn into situations which enable them to gratify their impulses to injure others? Or is it possible that in certain circumstances it is in fact the majority of us who would obey orders, behaving in cruel ways which we would normally like to believe we were incapable of?

Stanley Milgram is the author of the core study which focuses on obedience. Milgram began his career working at Princeton University (USA) as a research assistant to Asch, and moved on to Yale University (USA) where he took up his first teaching position. Having studied conformity with Asch, Milgram became interested in obedience to authority. One question he considered was that perhaps there was something unique about certain members of the German nation who were prepared to commit what could be seen as mass murders during the Holocaust. If this were the case, maybe other members of society, like William Calley, shared the same characteristics. On the other hand, Milgram pointed out that the inhumane policies of the Nazis 'could only be carried out on a massive scale if a very large number of persons obeyed orders', so perhaps the unquestioning obedience to authority of the thousands who took part in administering the policies may have demonstrated what most ordinary people would do when subjected to extraordinary social influences.

KEY CONCEPTS

Individual and situational explanations of behaviour and determinism
Is it the characteristics of individuals that make them behave the way they do, or is it the situation in which they find themselves that influences their behaviour? This is an important question in social psychology. Its origins lie in philosophy and the question of determinism: how far our behaviour is a result of our own free will and how far it is outside our control, being governed, or determined, by outside forces, such as society and culture, or by internal forces, such as our genes and personality.

Milgram's study attempted to show whether there is an 'obedient type' – someone who follows orders to be cruel to others – or whether this type of obedience is something of which we are all capable in certain circumstances, therefore contributing to the debate on individual vs situation explanations.

AIMS

The aim of the study was to investigate what level of obedience would be shown when subjects were told by an authority figure to administer electric shocks to another person.

METHOD

Method and design

The study was carried out in the laboratory, using observation to collect data. The data consisted of a record of the maximum level of shock the subject administered to the 'victim', together with recordings of the sessions, occasional photographs through a one-way mirror and notes of any unusual behaviour.

Subjects

The subjects who took part in Milgram's study were 40 males between the ages of 20 and 50, who came from the New Haven (Connecticut) area of the USA, from a range of occupations and educational backgrounds. They were recruited by a newspaper article and direct mail advertising, which asked for volunteers to take part in a study of memory and learning at Yale University. This was, therefore, a volunteer or self-selected sample. They were to be paid $4.50 and were told this was simply for turning up at the university and was theirs to keep whatever happened.

KEY CONCEPTS

Subjects/participants and samples

'Subject' means a person whose behaviour is being studied. The standard abbreviation is S, and Ss for the plural, 'subjects'. You will also see 'participant' (P) and 'participants' (Ps). These terms are interchangeable, but ethical guidelines (see below) suggest that we should refer to those who take part as 'participants', and modern studies do this. Where the original studies use 'subjects', as is the case in Milgram's study, we have also referred to those taking part as 'subjects'.

'Sample' refers to the whole group of participants being studied. A sample should be selected so that it is representative of the group, or target population, from which it has been drawn. If a sample is biased (e.g. all-male or all-female), represents only a narrow age range, is very small or represents only one culture or group (that is, it has an ethnocentric bias), this limits the ability of the researchers to generalise the findings from the study. There are various ways of selecting a sample and we shall come across some of these as we go through the core studies.

Volunteer or self-selected samples

As its name suggests, this type of sample is formed when participants are asked to volunteer to take part in the study. Typical ways of obtaining such a sample include putting an advert in a newspaper or a notice on a noticeboard, and sending out postal questionnaires. Those who respond to the ad or notice, and those who fill in and return the questionnaires, are volunteering to take part in the study.

This can be a cost-effective and convenient way for researchers to obtain participants to take part in their research, but the drawback is that since the vast majority of people do not volunteer (for example, the return rate for a postal questionnaire is only about 30 per cent), the sample is fundamentally biased. It is only representative of those people who volunteer, and since they are atypical, this limits the usefulness of findings of studies which use self-selected samples.

Apparatus and setting

Two rooms were used within Yale University. One room contained what looked like an electric-shock generator, which had a row of 30 switches ranging from 15 to 450 volts in 15-volt increments. There were also descriptions about the type of shocks (e.g. slight shock, strong shock, intense shock, danger: severe shock, and, finally, the last switches were marked XXX). In the other room was a chair with restraining straps where the learner was to receive the shocks via his wrist. There was also a tape recording of responses which were played according to which switch was depressed, ensuring that all subjects heard the same responses in the same order from the learner.

Two male confederates took part in the study:

● The experimenter (standard abbreviation: E) – a 31-year-old 'stern' biology teacher who wore a grey lab technician's coat.
● The learner – a 47-year-old accountant who appeared mild-mannered and likeable.

Procedure

The subject was introduced to the learner and told the cover story that the study was about the effects of punishment on learning. The subject and the confederate drew lots to see who was to be teacher or learner, although the situation was rigged: both slips of paper said 'teacher'. The teacher then saw the learner taken to the other room and strapped into the chair, and his wrist attached to the equipment that would deliver the shocks. At this point the learner explained that he had a slight heart condition and asked if the shocks were dangerous. He was told by the experimenter that although the shocks could be extremely painful, they caused no permanent tissue damage.

The teacher and experimenter returned to the first room and the teacher sat at the desk with the shock generator before him. Since the learner was located in the anteroom, neither the teacher nor the experimenter would be able to see him during the study. The teacher was then told that the learner had to learn word pairs. (Note: examples of the word pairs are **not** provided in the study although examples can be seen in the original video of Milgram's experiment. In the video the word pairs used were 'fat neck', 'blue box' and 'nice day'). The teacher had to read out the first word of the word pair and another four words, one of which was correct, and the subject had to choose the correct word. The teacher was told that the way the learner would indicate the correct answer to the teacher was by pressing one of four switches in front of him, which lit up one of four corresponding lights on the top of the shock generator. If the subject got the answer wrong, the teacher was told to give the subject an electric shock by flicking a switch on the shock generator.

The teacher was then told that for each mistake the shocks would increase; in order to do this the subject was instructed to 'move one level higher on the shock generator each time the learner flashes a wrong answer' (Milgram 1963: 374). Although no shocks were actually given to the learner, the teacher was always given a 'test shock' of 45 volts (switch 3). A battery was installed in the shock generator for this purpose – it was not really plugged in to the electrical supply! This added to the authenticity of the study and made the teacher believe the learner was truly being given shocks.

As the teacher administered the 'shocks', all subjects experienced the same feedback from the 'learner'. This consisted of standardised answers which came through the 'answer box' (a buzzer showed which answer the learner had selected), always in the same sequence. No vocal protest was made by the learner in this version of Milgram's study (although in later versions Milgram introduced a tape recording of the learner crying out in pain, and you may have seen this on a video of the study). The only response from the learner in this version was the predetermined set of answers which implied that he was taking part in the experiment, then, at 300 v (the twentieth switch on the shock generator), the learner pounded heavily on the wall and no answer came through the answer box. The teacher was told to treat no answer as a wrong answer and

The layout of the laboratory

to use the shock generator in the same way. The learner again gave no answer and after the shock at 315 v he pounded on the wall again. After this, the teacher found that when he continued with the task he received no more answers, nor heard any more pounding from the learner, leaving him to assume that the learner might be unconscious, or even dead!

When the teacher protested that he did not want to continue if the learner might be hurt, it was the experimenter's task to instruct the teacher to carry on. He used four verbal 'prods' to pressurise the subject to continue with the experiment. If the subject disobeyed all four prods the experiment was ended. The prods used by the experimenter were:

- Prod 1: Please continue/Please go on.
- Prod 2: The experiment requires that you continue.
- Prod 3: It is absolutely essential that you continue.
- Prod 4: You have no other choice, you must go on.

KEY CONCEPTS

Standardising instructions and procedures

Standardisation means keeping the test conditions the same for every partici-pant. It is a method of controlling situational variables, or environmental factors, which might have an influence on the participants' behaviour. If participants were treated differently, this would mean that fair comparisons between their responses could not be made. Standardisation of the instructions, the learner's taped responses and the sequence of prods used by the experimenter are examples of how Milgram controlled situational variables in this study.

Further prods used by the experimenter if the subject questioned the welfare of the learner were: 'Although the shocks may be painful, there is no permanent tissue damage, so please go on', and, 'Whether the learner likes it or not, you must go on until he has learned all the words correctly. So please go on'.

At the end of the study, the teacher was reunited with the learner, assured that no shocks had been given, and was thoroughly debriefed about the true nature and purpose of the experiment. Milgram also interviewed the subjects using open-ended questions, projective measures (tests intended to predict whether the experience may result in any possible long-term consequences), and attitude scales to ensure (as far as possible) that the subject left the laboratory 'in a state of well-being'.

RESULTS

The dependent variable being measured in this study was obedience. This was measured quantitatively by recording how far the subject was prepared to go on the shock generator.

KEY CONCEPTS

Quantitative and qualitative data

When we think of measurement, we tend to assume this means that numbers will be used to tell us how much or how many of something there is. This is precisely what you get with quantitative data. An advantage of using numbers to measure variables is that it allows for easy comparisons to be made between subjects (e.g. on a memory test, subject one scored 10 out of 100 and subject two scored 90). We can also summarise quantitative data easily, using averages or percentages. For example, Milgram found that 65 per cent of his subjects went up to 450 volts.

Another advantage of quantitative data is that it allows for inferential statistics to be used and hypotheses to be tested, as you will see when you are doing your practical folder. It is also easier to establish the reliability of results when quantitative data are collected, as you can repeat the test to see if the findings are replicable.

Quantitative data alone can be quite narrow, however, and can also lack ecological validity. For example, if you ask someone, 'How are things with you?', they are more likely to say, 'Pretty good, thanks' than 'On a scale of 0 to 100, where 0 is terrible and 100 is unqualified bliss, I'd say today I am scoring 65'.

In order to increase the level of detail and the validity of findings, qualitative data can be gathered. These usually consist of descriptions in words of what was observed. For example, Milgram tells us subjects were seen 'to sweat, tremble, stutter, bite their lips. . .[and] these were characteristic rather than exceptional responses to the experiment' (Milgram 1963: 375). This tells us a lot more about the experience of subjects in the experiment than just the fact that 65 per cent of them went to the end on the shock generator.

Qualitative data can also be reports of interviews, responses to open questions in questionnaires and reports of what subjects said and did during a study. Using this type of information gives a richness and detail to the findings and is more valid. However, it is harder to make comparisons between subjects' responses or to summarise qualitative data.

Prior to the commencement of the study, Milgram had questioned a number of psychology students, adults and psychiatrists as to how many people would administer fatal electric shocks to others as part of a psychology experiment, and the estimate from all groups was 0–3 per cent of subjects (mean 1.2 per cent). In the context of these predictions, Milgram's results were surprising. This illustrates well that what we think we might do is not what we actually do when faced with a situation.

All 40 subjects gave shocks up to 300 volts, with 5 refusing to go beyond this point. Between 315 volts and 375 volts a further 9 subjects stopped obeying. This meant that 26/40, a staggering 65 per cent of subjects tested, went all the way up to 450 volts.

In addition to these statistics, Milgram had invited objective observers to record what they observed during the study. Their reports provide qualitative data.

He reported that although 26 of the subjects had been obedient to the experimenter's authority right up to 450 volts, they displayed signs of extreme stress. They sweated, trembled, stuttered in their speech, bit their lips, groaned, dug their fingernails into their hands or appeared to be crying; many laughed, not in amusement, but as a nervous reaction; three subjects had violent convulsions. Milgram says that the results were also surprising to the observers, who expressed disbelief at the behaviour of the subjects. Milgram quotes one observer:

> I observed a mature and initially poised businessman enter the laboratory smiling and confident. Within 20 minutes he was reduced to a twitching, stuttering wreck, who was rapidly approaching a point of collapse. He constantly pulled on his earlobe and twisted his hands. At one point he pushed his fist into his forehead and muttered 'Oh God, let's stop it'. And yet he continued to respond to every word of the experimenter, and obeyed to the end.

> *(Milgram 1963: 377)*

DISCUSSION

The level of obedience was totally unexpected. Apparently normal men had obeyed to the point where they believed they might have seriously injured a man just like themselves – the power of obedience outweighing their personal moral beliefs that it was wrong to injure others.

Milgram suggested a number of reasons to explain why the obedience rate was so high in these circumstances:

- The fact that the study was carried out at a prestigious university influenced subjects as to the worthiness of the study and the competence of the experimenter.
- The subjects believed that the learner had also volunteered and that the allocation of roles was due to chance.
- The subjects had agreed to an implicit social contract by agreeing to take part and being paid for their participation, and therefore they felt obliged to continue.
- The subjects were told that the shocks were not harmful.
- The situation was entirely new for the subjects, so they had no past experience to guide their behaviour.
- There was no obvious point at which the subjects could stop administering shocks, because each shock was only a small amount more than the previous shock.
- The subjects who did withdraw from the study did so when the 'natural break' occurred – when the subject ceased to reply.

Milgram suggested that the subjects in his study faced a number of conflicts. First, there was the conflict which arose from being asked to meet the competing demands of the experimenter and the learner. To meet the demands of one was to fail to meet the demands of the other. The teacher was forced into making a decision, to stop or continue, and this put him in a public conflict with no satisfactory solution.

More generally, there is the conflict the subjects experienced internally: which of two ingrained behaviour dispositions should they respond to? Should they respond to their belief that one should not harm others and therefore refuse to go on with the study? Or should they respond to their equally ingrained tendency to obey authority figures, and therefore continue?

COMMENTARY: METHODS AND ISSUES

Research method, design and data gathering

Milgram carried out his research under the controlled conditions of a laboratory setting. Although it is referred to as the 'obedience experiment', it does not qualify as an 'experiment' in the true sense. (Details of what is meant by an experiment can be found in the next core study, by Piliavin et al., page 35.)

Milgram collected both quantitative data, measuring obedience by how far people were willing to go on the shock generator, and qualitative data, obtained by observing their behaviour and reactions during the study.

Does the study raise any ethical concerns?

Milgram's study has been one of the most highly criticised in the whole of psychological research and provoked an investigation after it was published, during which time Milgram's membership of the American Psychological Association was suspended.

Milgram justified his work by saying that he had not anticipated his results. Although subjects were deceived by the cover story, and therefore informed consent was not obtained, this was necessary in order for the study to be carried out. He argued that although the study did encourage the subjects to continue, as that was its purpose, the fact that some subjects could and did withdraw illustrates that this was always a choice for those taking part. Milgram denied that his subjects had been harmed by the study – either by the stress they experienced at the time, or as a result of any self-knowledge they gained through their participation in the study. This second point was confirmed by an independent psychiatrist, who followed up with subjects a year after the study.

Milgram thoroughly debriefed his subjects at the end of the study, introducing them to the learner and telling the 'obedient' ones that their behaviour was normal. All subjects received a report on the findings of this and subsequent studies, and 92 per cent responded to a questionnaire regarding their feelings about having taken part. Less than 2 per cent said they were sorry to have taken part, with 84 per cent saying they were glad to have been involved. Milgram himself saw this point as a key defence. If those who had taken part in the study were glad to have done so and felt it was worthwhile, this justified the study on ethical grounds. However, the participants' enthusiasm for the study may simply have been a way of reducing their cognitive dissonance. **Cognitive dissonance** is a state of discomfort or anxiety, caused by holding two opposing attitudes or beliefs about a situation (e.g. I smoke and smoking is bad for me, or, I am giving electric shocks and I shouldn't be giving another person electric shocks for something as silly as a memory test). To claim that they had learned something of personal significance from the study and that it had high scientific value would have reduced the subjects' dissonance.

In the end, Milgram's work was deemed to be ethical and it is regarded as one of the most significant pieces of social psychological research to date.

Is the study useful?

For a quick summary of the current BPS Ethical Guidelines, see the Ethics Spider Diagram on the CD-ROM.

KEY CONCEPTS

Usefulness of psychological research
Are the findings of a study useful? The questions we must ask are: useful *for what* and *to whom*? Findings may be useful to psychologists in that they help to explain or predict behaviour, or useful generally in helping to explain behaviours and solve problems in the real world.

- **Studies can be useful to psychology itself.**
  A study or theory may be highly **generative**, that is, it leads to a great deal of further research, both testing and refining the conclusions drawn in a particular area of study. Examples include Freud's theory of psychosexual development, and Piaget's theory of cognitive development (which we will look at later in this book).

  It follows that studies which contribute to the debate in a particular area are also useful to psychology (e.g. Samuel and Bryant's work contributes to the debate concerning children's cognitive development by providing support for the sequence of Piaget's stages, but also suggesting refinements to the timing of the stages, as their work proposes that he underestimated young children's abilities).
- **Usefulness can be assessed by asking: Are the conclusions/findings from the study of any use in helping to solve problems in the real world?**

  Note: The usefulness of a study will be reduced if:

- The study is low in ecological validity and therefore findings cannot be easily generalised to a real-life setting.
- The study is reductionist and ignores other important factors or variables which affect behaviour.
- The findings of the study are not valid (e.g. if demand characteristics could have affected the findings, if sample biases mean the findings are not generalisable to a broad population).

Milgram's study is useful to psychology as an explanation of why people obey in certain situations. In terms of the influences on our behaviour, Milgram's study shows us that we do not always act in the way we might predict. He argues that obedience 'comes easily and often', and that if we are in a situation where obedience is demanded of us by a legitimate authority, we can be encouraged by that authority to act in a way that may harm another person, even though this means acting in opposition to our personal morality.

In terms of individual and situational explanations of behaviour, Milgram's study demonstrates how it can be the situation you are in which influences your behaviour, and that we abdicate control when we are in the 'agentic state'. We are socialised to obey.

Are the conclusions we can draw from this study useful in helping to solve problems in the real world? Many writers see Milgram's work as illustrating the inevitability of good people being drawn into malevolent systems and the likely repetition of events such as the Holocaust in Nazi Germany. However, by knowing that we are socialised to obey, we are armed with the knowledge which suggests that another holocaust is far from inevitable. In terms of politics, we have the power to choose whom we obey. Good people are easily integrated into a malevolent system, and therefore it is up to us to ensure that such a system is not put into place. Use your vote wisely!

Validity and reliability of the study

KEY CONCEPTS

Internal validity (design validity)

When we ask, 'Are the findings of a study valid?', what we are really asking is, 'Can we trust the findings? Are there any reasons to believe that they might not be true?'

Internal validity is determined by the extent to which a study is free of design faults which might affect the result, meaning that the test is not a true test of what it intended to measure.

Factors which reduce the validity (internal validity) of findings include the following:

- Low generalisability of findings (e.g. sample biases, ethnocentric bias, difficulty extrapolating to other groups of people/settings). If the findings are not generalisable, they are not valid.
- If demand characteristics might have affected the study (see Key concepts: demand characteristics, below).
- If the findings of the study do not prove to be reliable (see Key concepts: reliability, below).
- If it is possible that a confounding variable has operated systematically alongside the independent variable this might affect the validity of the findings (we will look at this in more detail in later chapters).
- If it is possible that the study is out of date or has lost validity over time. This is a particular problem for studies in social psychology. Social, political, cultural and technological changes can mean that a study only represents the time and place in which it was carried out. We cannot generalise the findings to the present day.

Is this study valid? In terms of the generalisability of Milgram's sample, we might question whether conclusions could be drawn about a broader population of people's obedience to authority. It contains a number of ethnocentric biases, such as age, gender, all being from New Haven, and so on, and it is also a volunteer sample. These give us reason to question the generalisability and therefore the validity of his findings.

Did the subjects really believe they were administering shocks? It has been claimed that subjects were not really deceived by the study and did not genuinely believe that they were administering electric shocks to another person, that their behaviour was simply a response to demand characteristics present in the study.

> A diagram summarising the factors that affect validity is included on the CD-ROM

KEY CONCEPTS

Demand characteristics

Demand characteristics are the clues or cues given consciously or unconsciously by the researcher, or elements in the procedure of the study that reveal the purpose of the study. If subjects can work out what the researcher is trying to investigate, it is possible for them to falsify their results to please the researcher, to make sure that the study 'works'. Alternatively, subjects may adopt the 'screw you' approach, making sure they do not behave in the way they believe they are expected to, thus spoiling the study.

If results have been affected by subjects responding to demand characteristics, this will mean that they are not valid (i.e. they have not tested what they intended to test), which reduces the scientific value and usefulness of the research. However, when Milgram asked his subjects whether they believed they were administering real shocks in the questionnaire they completed a year after the study, only 2.4 per cent claimed to be 'certain' the learner was not receiving shocks. Unless they were all talented actors, the signs of tension shown by the teachers suggested they really did believe in the study at the time. Also, if they did not believe shocks were actually being given, why did some of the teachers feel it necessary to stop before they reached 450 volts?

In social psychological studies researchers can often justify the use of deception, telling participants a cover story to hide the true purpose of the study, as this is essential in order to avoid demand characteristics influencing participants' responses. Imagine how Milgram's results would have differed if he had told subjects that he was trying to see how far the experimenter could coerce them into going on the shock generator.

KEY CONCEPTS

Ecological validity

Is the behaviour that the participants are being asked to perform in the study comparable with behaviours that people might carry out in the course of their everyday life? In other words, how realistic is the study? If the behaviour in a study is very like real-life behaviours, the study is said to be high in ecological validity. If the behaviours required of participants in a study are not like real-life behaviours, the study is low in ecological validity and this limits its usefulness.

Since people tend to behave differently in a lab when they know they are being tested, and due to the artificial nature of the laboratory environment itself, social psychological studies carried out in the lab tend to be low in ecological validity.

This study took place in a laboratory, which was essential to convince subjects that it was a valid piece of research. However, this may mean that the subjects' behaviour was only typical of the behaviour they would display in a laboratory, so the study lacks ecological validity on this count.

KEY CONCEPTS

Reliability

Reliability refers to the consistency of a measurement. A test or measure is reliable if it gives similar results when carried out again in similar circumstances. In other words, if the findings prove to be replicable (consistent) when the same or a similar researcher carries out the study again, the test or measure is reliable. If the study is not reliable, that is, if the repeat of the study gives different results from the original, this gives us reason to question the validity of the original research. Reliable findings can help to support the validity of research.

However, the relationship between reliability and validity is not straightforward, as a test could prove to be reliable but still not be valid. For example, if a researcher decided that the cleverest people in the world had two or more 'h's in their name, Stephen Hawking (with two 'h's) would be cleverer than Albert Einstein (no 'h's!). We could count the hs again and find that the result is reliable: two 'h's for Stephen Hawking and none for Einstein is a consistent finding. However, it is not true that 'h's in your name make you clever, so the finding is not valid.

Validity over time is related to reliability; what it means is that the findings remain consistent when the study is replicated after the passage of time. Milgram's study was carried out more than 40 years ago. Do you think this study would give the same results if we carried it out in, say, Blackpool, on a sample of similar men today?

Terms in bold are included in the Glossary for Chapter 2 on the CD-ROM.

Altruism

Is there such a thing as altruism?

The definition of **altruism** is when you do something for someone else without gaining anything for yourself. But do you think we ever do anything to help another person without getting back something for ourselves? If you think about it honestly, how many times have you really done something for another person without thinking that it might be to your benefit in the future?

1. You go to have tea with your grandma, who is a bit crotchety and smells of moth-balls, when you would rather go out with your mates.

2. You wash up and clean the house while your mum is out.

3. You help your friend with his/her homework.

4. You help to decorate a friend's bedroom/house.

5. You collect money for a charity.

6. You help your teacher on open evenings at college.

7. You volunteer to stay behind at work to finish something, even though you are not getting paid for it.

All these activities are possible acts of altruism, but even though it may appear at first glance that they are being done for someone else, all of them may have ulterior motives.

1. Grandma may appreciate the visit so much that:

    ● she may give you a small amount of money when you leave, or leave you a huge amount of money in her will;

    ● maybe it will stop your mum from moaning at you for never visiting (the pay-off here is lack of moaning);

    ● it might make you feel good because you have brought some joy into her life, in which case you are rewarding yourself.

2. Your mother won't nag you and will probably let you stay out for longer or give you extra pocket money.

3. Your friend may help you in the future when you are stuck with your homework.

4. S/he may help you with your decorating at some time in the future.

5. You no longer feel guilty about all the charity boxes you did not contribute to in the past (and if you are a student it will look good on a UCAS statement or CV for an interview).

6. Your help on open evenings is rewarded by a better reference from your college.

7. Your boss bears you in mind for promotion, or finishing the tasks makes life easier for you the next day.

This should give you some idea of how acts of human altruism are often really selfish acts.

Research into animal behaviour has also shown that apparent acts of altruism are also basically extremely selfish and have more to do with the transmission of genes from one generation to the next. If we think of the example of the rabbit who thumps his foot to warn all other rabbits of impending danger, it appears that this rabbit is putting itself at risk for the sake of the rest of the group, but what it is doing is allowing others from its 'family' to survive and carry the family genes into the next generation.

Returning to human altruism, we cannot be quite so objective, because many seemingly altruistic acts have no relationship to genes although they still have a selfish element. An example of this is where adoptive parents are as protective of their children as biological parents – what would it cost them in terms of pain and misery if they were not protective? After all, the 'cost' of adoption in terms of time, emotion and organisation means that they have a vested interest in the welfare of that adopted child. However, other evidence shows that kin selection does operate in human beings. Burnstein, Crandall and Kitayama (1994) discovered that people claimed they would help others most closely related to them if the situation was life-threatening, but also said that if it was less serious they would help anyone.

Let's return to having tea with Grandma. There are two ways we can be rewarded for giving up our time: one is **extrinsically** (or externally), that is, we get praised and shown gratitude either verbally or by being left her entire fortune; the other is **intrinsically** (or internally), by having a degree of self-satisfaction, in effect rewarding ourselves.

At this point, you might have started to think that perhaps altruism does not exist and that is quite a reasonable belief. There are others, however, who strongly believe that altruism does exist, such as Daniel Batson (1991). He agrees that often people help for selfish reasons, but suggests that at other times they are willing to do something for someone else with no apparent gain for themselves, but this is usually because we feel empathy for the person in need of help. This means that we identify with the person and can almost feel the pain and heartache they are experiencing.

> Penny's coursework was finally completed. Everything had gone wrong for her, from the college computer being shut down with a virus, to her supervising teacher going off on long-term sickness. Penny braced herself against the rain as she ran over the yard to finally hand in the finished work. Just before she got to the door, she tripped and fell over, dropping the folder and spreading its contents over the wet ground.

If Batson is correct, we would probably run to help Penny, despite the rain, as most of us could identify with how devastated she would feel.

Kitty Genovese and the altruism debate

The debate surrounding the existence of altruism alone would be sufficient to provoke research into the area, but perhaps a greater provocation occurred in America in 1964, with the murder of a 28-year-old woman called Kitty Genovese.

Kitty was attacked on three separate occasions, within a 35-minute period, by a man carrying a knife, although it was not until the third attack that he actually succeeded in killing her. What made it worse was that 38 people actually saw the killer from the windows of their homes, but none of them reported the incident to the police. No one was prepared to come forward and help, either by intervening or by telephoning the police until, finally, one man got a neighbour to call after phoning a friend in a different county for advice.

The incident was reported in the *New York Times* in March 1964 and contained the following condensed extracts:

> Twice the sound of their voices and the sudden glow of their bedroom lights interrupted him and frightened him off. Each time he returned, sought her out and stabbed her again. Not one person telephoned the police during the assault; one witness called after the woman was dead.

> Kitty Genovese was returning home from her job as manager of a bar in Hollis. She parked her red Fiat in a lot adjacent to the Kew Gardens Long Island Rail Road Station. . . She turned off the lights of her car, locked the door and started to walk the 100 feet to the entrance of her apartment. . . She got as far as a street light in front of a bookstore before the man grabbed her. She screamed. Lights went on in the ten-storey apartment house. . . Windows slid open and voices punctured the early morning stillness.

> Miss Genovese screamed: 'Oh, my God, he stabbed me! Please help me! Please help me!'

> From one of the upper windows in the apartment house, a man called down: 'Let that girl alone!'

> The assailant looked up at him, shrugged and walked down Austin Street toward a white sedan parked a short distance away. Miss Genovese struggled to her feet.

> Lights went out. The killer returned to Miss Genovese, now trying to make her way around the side of the building by the parking lot to get to her apartment. The assailant grabbed her again. 'I'm dying!' she shrieked. 'I'm dying!'

> Windows opened again, and lights went on in many apartments. The assailant got into his car and drove away. Miss Genovese staggered to her feet. . .

> The assailant returned. By then, Miss Genovese had crawled to the back of the building where the freshly painted brown doors to the apartment house held out hope of safety. The killer tried the first door; she wasn't there. At the second door . . . he saw her slumped on the floor at the foot of the stairs. He stabbed her a third time – fatally.

> . . .the police received their first call from a man who was a neighbour of Miss Genovese. In two minutes they were at the scene. . . The man explained. . . 'I didn't want to get involved.'

How many times have you heard a child screaming in the street and simply assumed that the child is playing? How many times have you rationalised the situation to yourself and decided that you should not get involved? In fact, if you think about many of the criminal activities that go on in our world, it makes you realise that it is probably almost normal not to get involved. You may remember the events of Friday 12 February 1993, when the security cameras at the Bootle Strand Shopping Centre near Liverpool caught the abduction of two-year-old Jamie Bulger by two ten-year-old boys who later murdered him. But imagine how you would have interpreted the situation if you had seen these two boys marching a small child out of a shopping centre. You would probably think that they were the child's older brothers rather than murderers. You would justify your lack of involvement by seeing the situation as nothing untoward.

There are numerous cases where bystanders did nothing to help victims of varying crimes. Just typing 'bystanders did nothing' into Google, you will find example after example of cases where people have not responded to cries for help. It is very easy to criticise, but imagine that you saw a woman screaming at a small tearful child, possibly even hitting the child. Would you go up to the woman and stick up for the small child? If not, why not? Now imagine you are walking along a street, you turn the corner and see a man holding on to a woman's arm and shouting at her, while she screams back at him and looks as if she is pulling away. Would you feel that you could 'interfere' in this situation?

If we decide to intervene in such situations, we would have to consider the circumstances carefully because both of these are ambiguous – that is, we have no idea what is really happening here because we do not have all the facts. We would therefore have to make attributions about the nature of the situation and decide who was to blame (if anyone) or whether the person actually needed help or not.

This is the basis of what is known as **attribution theory**, a theory which helps to explain how people attribute causes to their own and other people's behaviour. Although we are really concerned with altruistic behaviour, attribution theory is relevant here because it is part of the basis on which we decide to intervene, or not, in different situations. If we believe that it is someone's fault that they are in a certain situation, we may be less likely to help than if we attribute the situation to an accident. For example, if a man were drunk and therefore fell over in the snow, we might be less likely to help him up than we would a little old lady who had fallen over. We would make the attribution that it was his own fault he had fallen over and that he should not have drunk so much, whereas being old and perhaps a little unsteady is not the little old lady's fault.

We should also be aware of what might happen if we got our interpretation wrong in the situations mentioned earlier. The woman with the small child might be furious and tell us to mind our own business. The man and woman might do the same. The cost of getting involved might far outweigh the benefits, so we would decide not to risk it.

Considerations such as these, together with the Kitty Genovese incident, have resulted in researchers becoming interested in investigating the existence of altruism. We have already considered some of the factors which might influence a person's likelihood of becoming involved, but let us now put them into some kind of framework:

1. **The nature of the situation**
    If you were in a dark street in the middle of the night, you would be less likely to go to the aid of someone lying in the gutter than if you were in the middle of a street on a summer's day and found someone who had seemingly collapsed. If there were lots of other people around, would that make you more or less likely to help? If everyone else was ignoring the situation, would you feel it was not critical?

2. **The nature of the potential or actual helper**
    If you were a doctor, would this make you more willing to help than if you had no medical training? If there were people watching and you did not think you were very competent, would this affect whether or not you intervened?

3. **The cost of helping**
    If you were on your way to an interview for a job that you really wanted, would this make you more or less likely to stop and help?

4. **The nature of the victim**
    If the person who had collapsed was drunk, would this make you more or less likely to help than if they were sober?

The nature of the situation

Latané and Darley (1968) were social psychologists teaching in New York at the time of the Kitty Genovese incident. They were interested in whether the presence of other people affected helping behaviour. Using the Kitty Genovese incident as a stimulus, they decided to look at the idea of the 'unresponsive bystander'. They thought that it was because there were so many witnesses to her murder that she was not helped.

Latané and Darley asked male college students to sit in a waiting room and fill in a questionnaire before taking part in a study of people's attitudes toward the problems of urban life. They were sitting either alone or in groups of three. The researchers arranged for smoke to pour in through a small ventilation grille and secretly watched the students' behaviour over the next 6 minutes.

You would expect that the moment smoke started coming through the vent they would feel very uncomfortable and become concerned that the building was on fire. When they were on their own, this was what happened, with students in 50 per cent of cases reporting the smoke within 2 minutes, and 75 per cent reporting it within the 6-minute period. However, what happened with the participants waiting together was quite different. Only 12 per cent of these students reported the smoke within 2 minutes, and only 38 per cent reported the smoke within the 6-minute period, which meant that the other 62 per cent carried on working for the full 6 minutes, even though the room was completely full of smoke.

The participants later explained their actions. The ones who were waiting together had looked to each other for guidance as to how to behave. As none of them knew what to do, and no one moved, they redefined the situation as harmless. Latané and Darley called this redefinition **pluralistic ignorance**, although this situation can only occur when people are not actually aware of *all* the facts.

Another possible explanation of why the effects occurred was that none of the participants wanted to look like a wimp in front of the others. Latané and Rodin (1969) decided to investigate the 'macho' ingredient by having participants wait outside a room. They suddenly heard a female researcher cry out for help after apparently falling in the next room. Obviously it would not affect the 'street cred' of our potential helpers this time, but again the participants appeared to be suffering from some kind of problem. This time 70 per cent of participants waiting on their own went to help the woman, but only 40 per cent of the participants waiting with other people bothered to help. This was an improvement, but still suggested that the presence of others was having a considerable influence. Participants showed once more that they had redefined the situation as not being serious. They had also been influenced by each other's apparent calmness, again producing a situation of pluralistic ignorance.

Another factor which influences whether others are prepared to help or not is when **diffusion of responsibility** occurs. Diffusion of responsibility is where the responsibility for the situation is actually spread, or diffused, among the people present. This means that the person's lack of action is actually not so bad because no one else is doing anything to help either, so all are equally to blame. Here is an example of how this works:

> Okay Class 4B, I know that some of you wrote those obscenities on the board. I want the culprits to own up or the whole class will stay in after school tonight.

It doesn't feel so bad when you are part of the group, does it? You have shared the responsibility among all of you, rather than just one person taking the blame.

Darley and Latané (1968) thought that if there were lots of people present this might decrease the likelihood of helping behaviour. They decided to investigate this by manipulating the size of a group again. In this case, however, none of the group could see each other, yet all were apparently aware of exactly what was happening.

They recruited their participants from a group of students and told them they were to take part in a discussion group where college students were to talk about the kinds of personal problems they were experiencing. They were told that the way they would be assured of anonymity was to stay in separate cubicles and talk over a kind of intercom. It was also explained that this was to ensure that they could talk openly without embarrassment.

At the beginning of the discussion students were led to believe that they were taking part in the discussion with either five other students, three other students or one other student. They were also told that they would each have a chance to speak for 2 minutes and that the other members of the group would then each have a turn to comment on what they had just said. The reason for this was in fact because there was only one participants per group, and all the other 'participants' were actually pre-recorded voices.

Soon after they started the discussion, the stooge would explain that he had epilepsy and would imply that he was prone to seizures as he was quite stressed by urban living. Shortly afterwards he could be heard to make a series of noises and gasps for help, crying out that he was having a seizure and then falling silent.

Darley and Latané noted the number of participants who actually left their cubicle to find out what was happening to the victim or to find someone to help.

- When they believed they were the only ones present, 85 per cent helped within 60 seconds.

- When they thought there was one other person besides themselves hearing the 'victim', the speed of response was slower, and only 62 per cent helped within 60 seconds.

- When the participants thought there were four other students besides themselves and the seizure victim, only 31 per cent helped in the first 60 seconds.

The conclusion was that the likelihood of people helping in an emergency situation will go down as the number of people who witness the situation goes up. This is the **bystander effect**, where the responsibility is diffused among the people present, and the more people there are, the less responsibility each one takes. But is this really diffusion of responsibility?

Piliavin et al. (1981) said that we should clarify what is meant by diffusion of responsibility. Diffusion is where everyone knows what is going on, but all the people present share responsibility for the event. They claim that it is often confused with **dissolution of responsibility**, which is where we know there are other witnesses but their behaviour cannot be observed, so we can rationalise that someone else will have done something. This is probably what happened in the Darley and Latané (1968) study above.

Other research looking at the effects of being assessed either as an individual or as part of a crowd has confirmed these findings. Ringelmann (1913) discovered that a group of men pulling on a rope exerted less individual effort than when they did it on their own. This lack of effort made when we are part of a group is known as **social loafing**, which is another way of stating that when a number of people are performing an action an individual will put less effort into it than if acting alone. It seems, however, that social loafing only occurs when people feel that their individual performances cannot be evaluated. If they are in a situation where it could be assessed, this phenomenon does not occur.

The nature of the potential or actual helper

As we mentioned earlier, the type of person who is on hand to help will have to make the decision as to whether they are competent or confident enough to help. There are a number of factors which will decide whether or not they will intervene.

According to Eagly and Crowley (1986), in their review of more than 170 studies, if you are a male and the situation requires some kind of heroic deed, you are more likely to help than if you are female. This is especially evident in western cultures, where men are socialised to be chivalrous and heroic. Although there are only a few studies looking at gender differences in situations that require more caring and nurturing, or involve a longer time commitment, it has been found that women are more willing to help in such situations. This is supported by the fact that the majority of carers of elderly parents in the UK are women.

Perceived competence also plays a part. If you think you are experienced at dealing with a situation you will be far more willing to intervene than if you feel you do not really know what you are doing. Huston et al. (1981) investigated what sort of people helped in an emergency situation and discovered that people who are most likely to assist would be those who have the relevant skills, such as first-aid knowledge or life-saving skills. This is even more likely to be the case if you are being watched. If you think that someone is there, assessing your performance (even if they are not doing so), you will be far less likely to help if you do not feel very competent, but if you feel confident in your ability you will not mind being observed.

The cost of helping

Have you ever been in a car and witnessed an accident? Did you stop and offer to be a witness? If not, why not?

> 'I saw a dreadful smash-up on the way to work this morning. The bloke driving the lorry was on the phone and he just ploughed into this car. It was a real mess. I felt so sorry for the little old lady in the car.'
>
> 'Was she all right?'
>
> 'I don't know. I didn't stop.'
>
> 'Why on earth not?'
>
> 'Because I would have been late for work.'

People who witness accidents often admit that they did not stop because it would have taken time and they would have had to fill in lengthy forms or even go to court. It seems that everyone weighs up the cost of helping, often unconsciously, and usually instantaneously, and this will have a huge influence on whether they are willing to get involved.

This cost–benefit analysis is known as **social exchange theory** and was proposed by Thibaut and Kelley in 1959. This theory can be used to interpret studies of bystander intervention. What it is stating is that we may decide to help if there is some kind of profit in the situation for us. We calculate this profit by looking at the rewards minus the cost of helping. Rewards could be things like feeling good about ourselves, not worrying, striking up a new relationship or gaining some kind of payment. Costs could be things like being late to an appointment, looking a complete idiot in front of other people, getting dirty, catching something or being in danger, especially if the person is drunk or the area is one with a high crime rate. Remember, too, that women may perceive themselves as being in greater danger than men, even though they are in the same situation – this might help to explain some of the differences in helping behaviours between the genders.

According to social exchange theory, we only get involved in some kind of pro-social behaviour as the likelihood of making a profit increases. Where there is too much to lose and very little to gain, we would decide not to help. Basically, this points to the fact that acts may look altruistic, but actually are not altruistic at all.

The nature of the victim

If you saw a really unpleasant-looking, smelly, dirty old tramp trip over something in front of you, would you immediately rush to him and try to help him up? What about the fact that it might be a frail old lady, who smelt of lavender and had a walking stick in her hand? Would that make a difference? It seems that the nature of the victim has a huge effect on whether or not we are willing to act in an altruistic way.

First of all, as you know, we have to make attributions about the type of situation we find ourselves in. We have to decide, on the basis of the available information, whether or not the person really needs help. Kelley (1973) devised the **causal schemata model**, which is one of several models that help to explain how we frequently make attributions about a situation (and why these attributions are often wrong). We will use an example to look at how this model works.

Ruth is walking down the road when she comes across a man lying in the gutter. He stinks of alcohol and he is holding a paper bag containing what is left of a broken bottle. Her initial thought is what a state for a drunk to get into, and she passes by on the other side of the road.

What Ruth does not know is that the man is a priest who is extremely fond of his elderly mother. He also suffers with high cholesterol levels and has been told that he has to take things easy as he has a weak heart. It is his mother's eightieth birthday and he decided to buy her a bottle of her favourite spirit as a birthday present. He was just on his way to the off-licence to get the bottle when he was stopped by a parishioner. Consequently he was late and was extremely concerned that the off-licence would close, so he had hurried all the way there and was now on his way to buy his mother a card. Because he had become so anxious, and because he had put his heart under such pressure when running, he had had a heart attack and had fallen down in the gutter, and the bottle had smashed as he hit the ground.

What a mistake for Ruth to make!

What is happening here is that we are actually using information we have stored in our memories from previous experiences to help us make sense of the situation (you will learn more about schemas in Chapter 3, when we consider the nature of memory). Experience would suggest that if someone has collapsed and smells of alcohol, it is the alcohol that is responsible and the likelihood is that it is their fault. We will therefore take the 'obvious' explanation for the situation without considering other possible causes. We seem to use what is known as the 'discounting principle', which means that we discount other possible explanations in favour of what to us is a more familiar explanation. In fact, what we are using is a kind of 'causal shorthand' (Fiske and Taylor 1991) to explain behaviour quickly.

Darley and Latané (1970) illustrated how this happens with a study looking at how many people would be willing to give money to someone in the street, and whether the person's reason for asking affected the amount of giving. In the first condition the actor asked for some money for no reason, and in this case 34 per cent of people gave money. I suppose they figured that there must have been a good reason for him to ask in the first place! In the second condition he said it was to make a telephone call, and this resulted in 64 per cent of people giving money. In the third condition the man said his wallet had been stolen (a more worthy cause?), and in this condition 70 per cent of people helped. It seems that the perceived nature of the victim's need is another factor which can influence helping behaviour.

THE STUDY

Irving M. Piliavin, Judith A. Rodin and Jane Allyn Piliavin (1969) 'Good Samaritanism, an underground phenomenon?'

Journal of Personality and Social Psychology, 13: 289–99

BACKGROUND

Prior to this study, research had already suggested that there were a number of factors which would influence the likelihood of helping behaviour occurring. However, many of the past studies had confounding factors which may have influenced the results, such as ambiguity or a lack of ecological validity. Where the 'accident' occurred out of sight there was ambiguity: had someone else helped? Was the emergency over now? Where the incident was set up under laboratory conditions within a controlled setting there might be low ecological validity, especially where a large number of confederates had been told to do nothing, as in real life we are not in a situation where most of the potential helpers or responders present have been primed from the outset not to react.

Piliavin et al. (1969) designed their study to take place in a natural environment, to improve ecological validity, and to stage an incident where the ambiguity of the situation was reduced to a minimum so that pluralistic ignorance should not enter the equation. People would be able to see the 'emergency' face to face, so the person's need for help, and whether or not he had already been helped, would be obvious as it was happening right in front of the subjects.

AIMS AND HYPOTHESES

The aims of the study were to see, in a face-to-face situation in a real-life setting, from which there would be no clear escape route:

- whether an ill person would get more help than a drunk person;
- whether there would be ethnocentric behaviour in helping (i.e. people would help someone of their own race more than someone of another race);
- whether the intervention of a model (a confederate of the experimenters, who would step in and offer help) would influence others' helping behaviour.

35

METHOD

Method and design

For this study the experimental method was used.

See the CD-ROM for more about experiments.

> **KEY CONCEPTS**
>
> **Experimental method**
> The experimental method (or scientific method, as it is also known) is a research method which can establish causal relationships between variables. A hypothesis is formulated to predict the effect of one variable, known as the independent variable (IV), on another variable, known as the dependent variable (DV). Usually two conditions are operated, with one testing subjects in the experimental condition, where the IV is introduced, and one testing subjects in the control condition. The control condition is used for comparison to see if the IV has affected the DV.

A field experiment was carried out using covert observation techniques to gather data (see Commentary, below, for explanations of these concepts).

Piliavin et al. engaged 16 General Studies students from the University of Columbia (USA) to carry out the study and gather the data. These 16 were split into four teams of researchers, giving four members in each team, two of whom were female. Each team member was given a role; they always performed the same role in each trial and they always worked in the same teams over 103 trials.

Below is a description of the roles played by the team members.

Team member	Role, appearance and behaviour
Victim	• The victims were standardised in their appearance and behaviour across the four teams. • They were always male, between the ages of 26 and 35. • Their dress was identical: Eisenhower jacket, old trousers, no tie. • They got on the train and went to stand near the pole in the centre of the carriage (critical area), waited 70 seconds, then staggered forwards and collapsed on the floor, looking up at the ceiling. • In order to operationalise the IV 'drunk' or 'ill', the victim played these two roles on alternate days. On the drunk day he smelled of alcohol and carried a liquor bottle in a brown paper bag. On the ill days he carried a black cane (walking stick). • In order to test whether same-race helping occurred, one of the victims was black and three were white (the only black

Team member	Role, appearance and behaviour
	male student who had volunteered to carry out the study was allocated to the role of victim).
Observer 1 and Observer 2	• These were female, and appeared to be just ordinary passengers on the train. They would get on with the other team members and make their way to be as close to their allotted position in the adjacent areas as possible. • Observer 1 would then observe and record: the race, sex and location of passengers in the critical area, the total number of passengers in the whole carriage and the total number of helpers who assisted the victim, and their race, sex and original position in the carriage. • Observer 2 would observe and record: the race, sex and location of passengers in the critical area, the total number of passengers in the whole carriage and the total number of helpers who assisted the victim. She also measured how long it took for the first helper to assist and, in the model conditions, how long it took for a subsequent helper to assist. • Both spoke to the person immediately next to them after the event took place, noting down what they responded and also making a note of any other spontaneous comments made by passengers.
Model	• Since laboratory studies had suggested that people did not help, a further team member was used who was to step in and help to see if his actions would bring in others to assist. The model was always male, aged 24–29, and casually dressed. The model was to help by getting the victim to a seated position and staying with him until the train stopped, when they would both disembark. • To see if the model had any effect, and whether which side of the carriage he was in or how long it took him to help would affect others helping, five model conditions were devised: – Critical area, early help (i.e. he stood in the critical area when he got on the train and helped approximately 70 seconds after the victim fell). – Critical area, late help (late meant after approximately 150 seconds). – Adjacent area, early help. – Adjacent area, late help (for both 'adjacent area' conditions he would have to cross the carriage to help). – No model: this was to act as a control condition to see what would happen with no model intervention.

Location

The study took place in the New York subway, between 59th and 125th Street stations on the 8th Avenue line. This particular run of track was selected as there was a non-stop ride of $7\frac{1}{2}$ minutes, giving enough time for the procedure to be carried out. The trials took place between April and June 1968, between the hours of 11 a.m. and 3 p.m. The teams only selected the old-style trains with two-seater seats. The 'experimental' carriage was varied from trial to trial.

Subjects

Over the 3-month period approximately 4,450 unsolicited subjects were observed over the trials. The racial mix was about 55 per cent white and 45 per cent black, and the mean number of people present in the whole carriage was 43, with a mean of 8.5 for the critical area where the incident took place.

Variables

There were three independent variables:

1 whether the victim appeared drunk or ill;
2 whether the victim was black or white;
3 the manipulation of the actions of the model (the effect of the presence or absence of the model, manipulations in the time delay before the model helped and which side of the carriage the model was originally standing in).

The dependent variables measured included:

1 the number of helpers and the speed at which they offered help;
2 the race and gender of helpers;
3 if anyone moved out of the critical area;
4 the comments made by passengers during the incident.

Procedure

The teams entered the train through different doors and the victim enacted his 'collapse' after 70 seconds. By consulting a random number table drawn up before the trials, the model would have worked out which condition he was in and he would stand on the appropriate side of the carriage and time himself ready to step in. The observers made their recordings as unobtrusively as possible. They were participant observers.

At the end of the 'no model' trials the model was to get the victim to his feet and get him off the train. The four team members would get off at the next stop and then cross over to the opposite platform and carry out another trial, this time in the other direction.

The teams were supposed to alternate the victim condition daily (drunk or ill), but the victim for team 2 did not like performing the drunk condition, which meant that the ill condition was carried out more often. A total of 103 trials were recorded, 65 in the ill condition and 38 in the drunk condition.

RESULTS

One of the main findings was that people generally helped and were quick to help, which contrasted with the results of previous laboratory experiments. In fact there were only 6 occasions in 103 trials where the victims were not helped.

The following table shows the total number of trials run with and without models:

	White victims		Black victims	
	Cane	Drunk	Cane	Drunk
No model	54	11	8	11
Model	3	13	0	3
Total	57	24	8	14

The nature of the victim influenced levels of helping. The cane (ill) victim received spontaneous help (that is, help without the model intervention) from a fellow passenger after his collapse in 62 out of 65 trials and the drunk victim in 19 out of 38 trials.

This confirmed that someone who appears ill is more likely to receive help than someone who appears drunk. Not only was there more help for the ill victim, but help also came more quickly (a median of 5 seconds rather than the 109 seconds for the drunk condition).

The table below indicates time taken to help for both conditions (includes those trials requiring 'model' intervention).

		White	Black
Before 70 seconds	Cane	52	7
	Drunk	5	4
	Total	57	11
After 70 seconds	Cane	5	1
	Drunk	19	10
	Total	24	11

The following table shows the percentage of helping with and without models:

	White victims		Black victims	
	Cane	Drunk	Cane	Drunk
	No of times helped (and %)	No of times helped (and %)	No of times helped (and %)	No of times helped (and %)
No model	54/54 (100%)	11/11 (100%)	8/8 (100%)	8/11 (73%)
Model	3/3 (100%)	10/13 (77%)	None run	2/3 (67%)
Total	57/57	21/24	8/8	10/14

This table shows the high level of helping for the cane (ill) condition with 100% of victims being helped. It also shows the slightly lower level of helping for the black drunk victim in the 'No model' trials and the lower level of helping in the drunk 'Model' trials with both white and black victims.

Of the 81 first helpers, 90% were males (even though gender breakdown for the critical areas was 60% male and 40% female); this leads to the conclusion that men were more likely to help in this sort of scenario than women.

No one left the compartment during any of the trials but in 21 of the 103 trials, 34 people moved from the critical area to the adjacent area, with more leaving in the drunk than the ill trials.

No significant tendency for same race helping was seen, although there was a slight tendency for same-race helping to occur more in the drunk condition than the ill condition.

There was no evidence of diffusion of responsibility. Remember this was the hypothesis derived from laboratory studies, that the more people there are present, the less help would be offered. This was supposed to be because each person would feel less personally responsible the more people there were available to share the responsibility. In fact a slight trend was shown in the opposite direction with more help being offered when the carriage was fuller.

What explanation do Piliavin et al. offer for the findings?

Piliavin et al. propose a model of helping which included the assumptions that observation of an emergency creates an emotional state in the bystander, that is, it induces a state of arousal (interpreted negatively in this instance as either disgust, fear or sympathy), and that we are motivated to reduce this negative arousal. This can be achieved by the following actions:

- helping directly;
- going to get help;
- leaving;
- not offering help because you have decided the victim does not deserve it.

Additionally, the action we choose in order to reduce arousal will depend on us carrying out a cost–benefit analysis. This means we will carry out the action that we assess as giving us the greatest benefit and the least cost. Costs of helping include effort, disgust and embarrassment; and there are also the costs of not helping to weigh up, such as self-blame and our worry about what others will think of us if we do not help. Benefits might include self-praise or the praise of others.

Piliavin et al. suggested that this model is consistent with all their findings. For example, the drunk is helped less because the costs of helping are higher – he may get angry, over-friendly or may even vomit! – and the costs of not helping are lower, as we may feel less guilt for not helping because we believe he is at least partially to blame for the position he is in.

Women help less in this study because the costs of helping (effort) are high, and the costs of not helping are low – as it is not a woman's place to help in such a situation, she will feel less self-blame or have less fear of judgement by others.

Why was no diffusion of responsibility recorded in this study?

Piliavin et al. suggested that this may be because the subjects on the train were face to face with the victim and could not conclude either that there was no emergency, or, if no helper came along, that the emergency was over. These are two possible assumptions which might have led the subjects in the earlier laboratory-based studies not to offer help.

Perhaps the reason why diffusion of responsibility was not evident in the subway study was because there were more potential helpers present here than in laboratory experiments. All past research had involved the use of only one subject, with the rest being stooges of the experimenter. Therefore, there was only one potential helper and that potential helper may have been looking to everyone else to guide them as to what they should do. Bearing in mind that all the other people 'taking part' did nothing as part of the study, perhaps the phenomenon of pluralistic ignorance could explain the results of past research in this area. In the subway study there were large numbers of potential helpers, and this may have resulted in more helping behaviour rather than less, and as the group size increased, the potential number of helpers grew.

It may therefore be that diffusion of responsibility is only an artefact of laboratory-based studies with one potential helper, the naive subject.

COMMENTARY: METHODS AND ISSUES

Research method, design and data gathering

The study used the experimental method. It was a field experiment, using an independent groups design comparing, for example, the helping response to an ill or drunk victim, the helping response to a victim of the same or a different race, and so on.

KEY CONCEPTS

Laboratory vs field experiments
The following table provides a breakdown of the strengths and weaknesses of each experimental setting.

Location	Strengths	Weaknesses
Laboratory	• In the controlled environment of the lab it is easier to isolate the IV as a causal factor and keep all extraneous variables constant or controlled. • In the lab, technical equipment can be used to measure variables (e.g. EEG machine).	• One problem with the lab setting is that subjects have consented to attend and be studied. This means that all lab studies can be affected by subject reactivity, with subjects responding to demand characteristics. This leads us to question the internal validity of lab-based studies. • Since the lab setting is often constrained and unlike real-life settings, lab studies also tend to lack ecological validity.

Location	Strengths	Weaknesses
Field (natural or real-life setting)	• By carrying out a study in a real-life setting, the ecological validity of a study can be improved. (**Note:** Be careful not to assume that all studies carried out in a real-life setting are ecologically valid. For example, if the study involved 300 clowns riding bikes through a supermarket to see how people react, this would not be ecologically valid, as the experience of subjects would not be realistic!)	• In the field it is harder to isolate the IV as a causal factor and keep all extraneous variables constant or controlled, so the possibility of other variables affecting the DV, becoming confounding variables, is higher in the field. • It can be harder to transport and set up sensitive technical equipment in the field.

The data-gathering method used in this study was participant, covert observation.

KEY CONCEPTS

Observation as a data-gathering technique

Observation can be carried out either covertly, that is, undercover and without the knowledge of those being observed, or overtly, where subjects are either aware or have been informed of the fact that they are being observed.

The advantage of covert observation is that you are sampling 'real' behaviour, uncontaminated by the subjects' desire to respond to demand characteristics. Some researchers believe that the only valid way to sample typical human behaviour is by covert observation in a field setting, the method used by Piliavin et al. in this study.

Observation can also be carried out as participant or non-participant observation. This means that the researcher is either a part of the setting/event s/he is observing (participant), or is outside the setting (non-participant). The advantage of being a participant, as in the Piliavin et al. study, is that you get an insight into the experience yourself, and also you have a good vantage point for your observations. However, your mere presence may change the course of the events you are observing. It could be that the inactivity of some potential helpers in the adjacent area in the trials was because of the inactivity of the two observers; we cannot know for sure.

It is also possible that if you are observing as a participant for a longer period of time, you may become too involved in the setting to be objective about your observations.

Does the study raise any ethical concerns?

There is a problem with carrying out the study using covert observation techniques. An unsolicited subject cannot be briefed about the nature of the study and give their informed consent. Nor is it always possible for the subject to be debriefed and later asked for permission to use their data. This means that this study raises ethical concerns about consent and invading people's privacy. Don't we have the right to go about our daily business without being monitored for the purposes of scientific research without our knowledge?

Also, deception is used in the study. The victim is not really in need of help, just play-acting a role for the purposes of the study. Seeing someone fall, and the anxiety such an event can arouse, may have upset some of the passengers on the train, who would never know that this was not a real collapse. They might also have to confront their conscience about their lack of willingness to help, and this self-knowledge might have caused distress to some subjects.

Is the study useful?

The study offers a useful model where helping behaviour is described in terms of the emotional and cognitive processes which a person responds to in making a decision to offer assistance. The study is also useful in that it shows the care that must be taken when trying to generalise findings from the social psychology laboratory to real-life settings.

Even though the study does contradict the earlier laboratory studies, and shows a much higher level of helping than the laboratory studies would have predicted, there is still no suggestion that people act out of pure altruistic motives. Piliavin et al. see them as acting out of 'a selfish desire to rid oneself of an unpleasant emotional state'.

Validity and reliability of the study

Given that the study took place on a real train in a real setting, and that the behaviour enacted by the victim, although uncommon, is a possible scenario people may encounter, the study is high in ecological validity. The internal validity of the study is also increased by the fact that the subjects were unaware that they were being observed, which would suggest that their behaviour was as it would have been if the event were actually real and not part of a psychological investigation. In other words, demand characteristics were less likely to be a threat to the validity of the findings.

It is possible to question the generalisability of the sample, however, and this means that the validity of the study's findings may be affected. The study is now around 40 years old – do you think people would be as helpful today as they were back then? Is it possible that the study's findings have lost validity over time? As this study was a field experiment and used an independent groups design, it is also possible that the behaviour of the subjects was affected by variables other than those tested by the researcher, and these extraneous variables may have confounded the study.

> **KEY CONCEPTS**
>
> **Extraneous and confounding variables**
> For an experiment to establish that it is the IV causing any observed change in the DV, all other variables, known as extraneous variables, need to be controlled or kept constant. The experimenter has to make sure the subjects are not too dissimilar from each other, and must control situational variables, for example by standardising procedures and instructions.
>
> Variables which are not controlled operate alongside the IV, making it impossible to establish whether it is the IV or this second variable, that has become a confounding variable, that has caused any change in the DV. If it is possible that the study has been affected by confounding variables then the study's validity can be questioned. Field experiments and studies which employ an independent groups design are most likely to be affected by extraneous and confounding variables.

Roles

We have considered so far the social influence that can be exerted by one person on another in the form of **obedience** to authority. We have mentioned, too, that **conformity** also affects the behaviour of others because they will adjust their behaviour in order to fit in with the desired person or group in order to be accepted by that group.

Social influence also comes into play when we take on one of the many roles that are part of our daily lives: daughter or son, student, grandchild, employee, and so on. Our behaviour is influenced by the role we adopt, and the role may also change the status we have in relation to others. In fact, a role does not exist unless it involves some kind of interaction with others. You cannot be a nurse unless you have a patient, or a teacher unless you have a student.

A role is usually defined as 'the behaviours expected of a person occupying a certain position in a group'. These behaviours are expected by people seeing us in that position – you would be considered very strange if you dressed in a nurse's uniform and then went out and started directing traffic.

Deindividuation and mob psychology

Think of the roles you have to undertake and the fact that each of those requires a slightly different type of behaviour. You would not act with your grandparents in the same way as you would with a group of friends, so the two roles are completely different and involve different norms of behaviour. One important psychological effect of taking on a role is that your individual identity may be replaced by a group or role identity, which could offer you a different status and also, perhaps, anonymity.

The following story illustrates this point.

45

> George had just completed his initial training for the police and it was his first day on the beat. He was standing by the entrance to Tesco's car park when he saw a car driving out in which the driver had not put on his seat belt. Here goes, he thought, and he could feel the butterflies in his stomach. He raised his hand, indicating to the driver to pull over, thinking to himself, I wonder if he will stop? What will I do if he doesn't? This seems really mean – he was only just leaving the car park, but then if I don't stop him, I would not be doing my duty.
>
> As he walked up to the car, the driver wound down the window.
>
> 'Excuse me, sir, but I have had to stop you as you weren't wearing your seat belt.'
>
> 'But I'm only just coming out of the car park,' said the driver, looking both shocked and annoyed.
>
> 'I know, sir, but you have just joined a public highway and it's my duty to stop you as you are in breach of the law.' George got out his pad to issue a ticket to the driver. 'I am afraid I will have to ask you to take your documents to the local police station and you will be fined £30.'

The role George had taken dictated that he should exert his authority in a situation where he was obviously in slight conflict about what he was doing. You can also imagine that as an individual he would probably find his behaviour a little over the top and would have been just as angry if someone else had done this to him. George stopped being George and instead became a policeman, which in turn affected the usual constraints on his behaviour and led to him losing some of his individuality. This phenomenon is known as **deindividuation**.

There may have been times when you have been in a role that has had a specific influence on your behaviour. If you work in a shop, for example, you take on a different authority over the customers than another customer would. You can ask people to move, or tell them to go to the checkout, for example. Imagine doing this with a uniform on; here it is harder to be identified as an individual, which increases the feeling of anonymity, and this may make your behaviour more extreme.

One of the topics which inspired the development of the theory of deindividuation was **mob psychology**, which considered the effects on people of being in a large crowd. As you can imagine, when you become part of a large crowd, you feel that you are less likely to be singled out as an individual and held responsible for your possibly extreme behaviour. Le Bon, writing in 1895 about the behaviours of crowds, suggested that crowds were dangerous. He indicated that when a crowd develops, it seems to act in accordance with primitive impulses and lacks any sort of rationality. He continued by saying that a crowd can be induced to commit irrational acts that its individual members would not normally engage in. Le Bon suggested that crowd members act according to the 'law of mental unity', that is, they become as one person, without thinking for themselves. He also explained that this occurs because when individuals become 'submerged' in a crowd, they lose their personal identity and sense of moral responsibility and become extremely suggestible, and an overriding and frequently irrational mentality can spread among the crowd members which he called the process of **social contagion**. This process implies that people do not actually think about their feelings, but simply 'catch' the beliefs and behaviours of the rest of the group.

It is very interesting that he should develop this theory around the time when the government was trying to justify the suppression of demonstrations, and in fact there is very little evidence for this process actually occurring. However, we all know that crowds can behave in a totally different way to individuals.

Let us say that you are thirsty and want something to drink, so you decide to go into a pub. Although you have gone into the pub, you are actually quite self-conscious, so you go and get your drink and sit down. You will probably choose to sit somewhere where you can view what is going on, rather than having your back to the crowd. In this instance you are behaving according to your own code of behaviour, but there is a certain amount of social influence on how you conduct yourself. You would feel ostentatious if you started laughing out loud to yourself, or if you put your feet on another chair, or even talked to yourself. Now picture the same situation with a friend.

You and your friend go to the pub and sit yourselves in a position where you can either both see the contents of the pub or you are directly opposite each other, because what you want to talk about is very private/interesting/personal. You may find yourself laughing out loud or moving about, and generally feeling much more comfortable.

Now imagine the same situation with a group of friends, say ten in total. You will be more raucous, and will laugh and move about far more, feeling less obvious than you would as an individual. Your friends will give you confidence.

Now take this one stage further. Imagine you are all in the pub and you all have fancy dress on, so, in effect, you cannot be identified. What might your behaviour be like now?

As a result of Le Bon's work the idea of 'submergence' was replaced by Festinger et al. (1952), with the more up-to-date concept of deindividuation. They defined deindividuation as 'a state of affairs in a group where members do not pay attention to other individuals as individuals and, correspondingly, the members do not feel they are being singled out by others'. Groups give us a sense of identity and belonging and they also reduce our sense of individuality, where we become identified as part of a whole rather than the whole itself.

In 1969 Zimbardo brought together the two ideas of deindividuation (loss of personal identity) and identification with the mob, and explained that the result of this process was that people were no longer governed by their individual consciences and would therefore act in a different way to the way they would as autonomous individuals. He claimed that if people believe they can be identified and therefore held responsible for their behaviour, they will control their aggressive impulses: the larger the group, the less likelihood of being recognised, and therefore the more extreme the behaviour. So we have an interaction here between behaviour and anonymity, provided either by numbers of people or outfits.

Consider why certain cultures painted their warriors' faces and bodies before they went into battle. The answer should be apparent. Robert Watson (1973) studied 24 different cultures which decorated their warriors in this way and found that they were significantly more likely to commit acts of brutality against prisoners than non-decorated warriors. If you take this one stage further, do the uniforms that any soldiers wear increase their savagery?

Even children are affected by deindividuation. Diener et al. (1976) observed 1,300 children trick-or-treating on Halloween night. Some of the children wore costumes which hid their identity, while others were identifiable. When they were completely anonymous they were more willing to steal money and sweets than the identifiable children.

Interestingly, however, the story of deindividuation does not simply imply that if we are in a group and lose our sense of identity to the group we will behave in a violent and aggressive manner. Not all groups are violent, and not all roles incite violent behaviour. A study undertaken by Zimbardo in 1970 found that women were more likely to give higher-voltage electric shocks to another woman when they were deindividuated (by wearing bulky lab coats and hoods, and not being referred to by name) than when they were identifiable (wearing normal clothes and being referred to by name). However, another study by Johnson and Downing (1979) showed that the nature of the uniform itself seemed to affect the level of shocks rather than the deindividuation. They suggested that the outfit worn by the women in the Zimbardo study was very like the outfits worn by the Ku Klux Klan and that this may have affected the levels of aggression shown by the participants. They therefore replicated the study but had another group dressed as nurses, and they found that although the 'nurses' were all wearing identical uniforms and therefore lacked individuality, they actually gave fewer and less severe shocks. So this gives us some indication that the role is interacting with the means of deindividuation, and that deindividuation can have positive as well as negative effects on behaviour.

Would outfits like these, worn by the Ku Klux Klan, make you more likely to behave differently to how you would normally behave?

Attribution theory

Before we continue it would be useful to identify another psychological theory we have touched on, but not mentioned specifically, especially as this is going to be mentioned again in Chapter 6. This theory, which is also used to explain behaviours, looks at how we attribute causes to the behaviour of others. Take, for example, the study mentioned above. Did it cross your mind that the women recruited by Zimbardo might actually be evil women who enjoyed giving electric shocks to their colleagues? Can you be sure that it really was the outfits they were asked to wear that influenced their behaviour? On the other hand, could it be that Johnson and Downing's participants were all really nice people?

When someone does something, we often try to work out what their motives were. Did they do it because they are a nasty person or because of the situation they were in? At this point we make a judgement about the behaviour by attributing a cause, although we are often wrong because we may not know about the whole situation and may simply judge the person on the basis of a small amount of evidence. Fritz Heider (1958) proposed what is known as **attribution theory**, which helps to explain *how* people attribute causes to their own and other people's behaviour. In fact, the whole idea of attributing causes to behaviour is so strong that we have been known to attribute intentions to inanimate objects: 'The blasted car knew I had to be early today, and so it gets a flat battery.'

This theory suggests that we are very willing to make **dispositional attributions** about others (saying that it was the nature of the person which made them behave in a certain way) rather than excusing their behaviour by the situation they found themselves in (**situational attribution**). Conversely, we are more likely to excuse our own behaviour, explaining that it was the situation which caused us to behave as we did. Heider said that what we tend to do, when we observe the behaviour of others, is to attribute the cause of that behaviour to *either* the person or the situation. He suggested that we really need to consider that behaviour is best explained by considering *both* the nature of the person *and* the situation in which they find themselves. Perhaps Zimbardo's participants were slightly aggressive anyway, but had managed to keep their aggression in check until they found themselves in a situation where they were given the opportunity to unleash it without consequences!

Social identity theory

Situations can affect us in other ways. We have mentioned how being part of a group can influence our behaviour due to the process of deindividuation. There is another group process which may help to explain some of the behaviours we will cover in this chapter: this is the way in which we need to feel that the group we are a part of is the best group, and so we behave in ways that make this seem true, such as favouring our own group or group members over other groups.

Have you ever thought about your group of friends and compared them to other groups of people you know? The expectation would be that you would rate your friends more highly than other groups. Similarly, if you rated your psychology class in comparison to other classes, it is more than likely that you would believe yours to be the best.

You must have come across people who, no matter what it is, always seem to have one better or bigger than yours. Well, this kind of group thinking is very similar, where the belief is that the group to which we belong is bigger and/or better than everyone else's. We also tend to think that our group is the norm, and therefore everyone else will be judged by our standards, which, of course, are the best. It is almost like being egocentric about your group, and this kind of group self-centredness is known as **ethnocentrism**. Another way of looking at ethnocentrism is to think of it as being centred on our ethnic group (but exchange 'ethnic group' for 'social group').

Ethnocentrism seems to occur the minute people are divided into groups. It does not matter what that group is, or on what basis it was formed, but we perceive the group we belong to as being superior to other groups and we develop an **in-group bias** (we are biased in favour of the group we are in). This bias is demonstrated by consistently rating the abilities and characteristics of the group we belong to as much higher than those of other people, even when this is not the case.

Ethnocentricity is linked to the process of **stereotyping**, which involves grouping people usually on the basis of some superficial physical characteristic, such as colour, and then attributing the same characteristics to all the group members. In this section we are going to focus on ethnocentricity rather than stereotyping, although often the results are the same because they may both lead to a kind of **discrimination**.

According to Tajfel (1982), the process of trying to give ourselves some kind of positive self-identity seems to explain why people demonstrate an in-group bias. If we are assigned to a group – any group – either by birth, colour, gender or design, we immediately seem to feel a kind of innate automatic preference for that group over any other group, and somehow elevate the group to a higher status than any other. This in-group preference is really a tactic to increase our self-esteem, and even if the reasons why the groups have been formed are minimal, if our group wins over another group, it will strengthen our feelings of pride in belonging to the winning group and consequently increase our self-esteem still further.

This process was described by Tajfel and Turner (1986) in what is known as **social identity theory**. This theory states that people actually get their identity from the group to which they perceive they belong. However, to gain an identity, we need to make comparisons between our group and other groups, and in order for our identity to be positive we need to see our group as being superior to other groups. If a group believes it is less worthy than other groups, it will be much more likely to accept any discrimination and disadvantage shown towards it without complaint, because it will believe that the discrimination is probably justified. This will result in the group being very unwilling to fight for its cause.

The Stanford prison experiment

The research examples we have covered so far have suggested that there are a number of different factors we can use to help to predict or explain the behaviour of others.

We have seen that people, no matter what they are like as individuals, are likely to be affected by the following situational factors:

- Taking some kind of role – therefore acting according to the rules dictated by the role rather than personal values.

- Wearing a uniform – therefore individuals cannot be identified so readily (deindividuation).

- Being part of a crowd – therefore being affected by social contagion.

- Being a member of a group.

Let us now imagine a type of community which might be affected by these factors. It would need to be a community where people would have to be in different roles. Perhaps the roles would dictate the type of behaviour that was expected. How would the roles be defined – by uniform, perhaps? Would it make a difference if there were a number of people playing these different roles rather than just one or two? One such community might be a prison. Prisoners would have their individual identity removed by wearing uniforms and would have their hair cut in a similar way. Prison officers would also be deindividuated because they would be wearing uniforms. This would give them anonymity when dealing with prisoners or if they were operating in a group, and they might be perceived as being less human and therefore potential perpetrators of aggression. We have also established that this deindividuation process, together with membership of a crowd, is likely to affect the types of behaviour demonstrated and that this may actually result in an increase in aggression. Finally, the role played by the prison inmates would be very likely to affect the way they too behave. All these factors lead us to considering one of the most famous pieces of social psychological research, undertaken by Haney, Banks and Zimbardo (1973) and known as the Stanford prison experiment.

Aims

This study was funded by the US Navy and the Marine Corps, with the aim of helping to explain the conflicts between guards and prisoners in its prison system, where brutality was not unknown. Previous explanations had focused on the disposition of the people involved, with the belief that the prisoners were likely to be 'typical' criminals who would have little regard for the welfare of others and who would be likely to act in an aggressive and impulsive way. On the other hand, the guards were thought to have been attracted to the job because they were potentially insensitive and controlling. Zimbardo was interested in looking at the situational impact on the behaviour of individuals, because if the situation was the reason for the behaviour, the problems could be addressed more easily.

If you are of the opinion that prison should be punitive, you might think it is desirable for the experience of those incarcerated to be brutal and harsh, teaching them a lesson. However, Zimbardo et al.'s research in prisons, talking to current and ex-inmates and those working as guards, showed that the system went beyond brutal and into the realms of the inhumane, rife with both sexual and physical abuse. This has an impact on prisoners on their release, as Haney et al. (1973: 2) pointed out: 'The experience of prison creates undeniably almost to the point of cliché, an intense hatred and disrespect in most inmates for the authority and the established order of society into which they will eventually return.'

Design

The study was therefore designed to find out whether it was possible to explain what was going on within the prison environment by attributing the causes to either situational or dispositional reasons. It was not possible to research this in a natural, real prison setting because the structure of the prison setting and the nature of those involved were variables already present and would therefore confound each other. Therefore it would be impossible to answer the question of which was leading to any brutality. Consequently a simulated prison was set up in the basement of Stanford University (USA) and student participants were recruited through a local newspaper advert, calling for volunteers to take part in a study of the psychological effects of prison life.

The applicants were given diagnostic interviews and personality tests in order to exclude those with psychological or mental problems, or a history of crime or drug abuse. This left a sample of 24 male college students who were healthy, intelligent and middle-class, from the USA and Canada. They were randomly divided into two groups by the toss of a coin so that, in effect, there were no differences between the two groups. One group was assigned the role of prisoners and one group was assigned the role of guards. Zimbardo set up conditions that would result in the prisoners being disorientated, depersonalised and emasculated. Also, for deindividuation to take place, both the prisoners and the guards were given uniforms.

The entire prison study and additional reading are available on the CD-ROM.

One of the 'guards' with a prisoner in the Stanford Prison Experiment

Results

The prison study was supposed to last for 14 days, but was actually terminated after 6 days due to the extreme behaviours of the guards and the intense responses of the prisoners. Prisoners experienced sadistic and humiliating treatment from the guards, and the high levels of discomfort they felt initially caused them to rebel. The differences between the two groups became obvious within a very short space of time, with the guards tormenting the prisoners and imposing physical punishments and even sexual humiliation. The guards volunteered to work extra hours; the prison became dirty and inhospitable; the right to use the bathroom suddenly became a frequently denied privilege; and some prisoners were forced to clean toilets with their bare hands. Over time, the regime resulted in the prisoners accepting the behaviour of the guards and becoming overly passive. At the end of the study, many prisoners showed severe emotional disturbances.

The results of the study demonstrated how social roles (which are environmental factors) can have a significant influence on behaviour, thus supporting the situational rather than the dispositional hypothesis. The conclusions of the researchers were that the structure of prisons and not the nature of those who inhabit them is the source of brutality. They suggested their work be used to contribute to developing training methods for guards.

Man's inhumanity to man

Zimbardo's work has helped in our understanding of some of the causes of man's inhumanity to man, but it seems that this understanding has not been sufficient to prevent it reoccurring. In his book *The Lucifer Effect*, Zimbardo (2007) indicates that his aim was to continue to develop an understanding of 'the processes of transformation at work when good or ordinary people do bad or evil things' (p.5). He explains that he still strongly believes that the situation is an extremely significant factor in determining the behaviour of individuals and suggests that: 'You are not the same person working alone as you are in a group; in a romantic setting versus an educational one; when you are with close friends or in an anonymous crowd; or when you are traveling abroad as when at home base' (p.8).

Zimbardo highlights recent examples of extremely barbaric behaviours which were influenced by the situation in which people found themselves. For example, the genocide of the Tutsis in Rwanda who were systematically 'exterminated' by their neighbours the Hutus. The United Nations reported that an estimated 800,000 to 1,000,000 Rwandans were murdered in approximately 3 months during the spring of 1994. People who had been friends and neighbours turned against each other and carried out unimaginably barbaric acts of savagery towards men, women and children. Some of the Hutu militia, previously ordinary farmers or churchgoers, were interviewed by Jean Hatzfeld (2005) having been imprisoned following the massacres. Zimbardo (2007: 15) cites some of the comments made by these prisoners, which provide some insight into their loss of personal morality and the mindless ideology which made them act in the unimaginable way that they did.

'We were doing a job to order. We were lining up behind everyone's enthusiasm. We gathered into teams on the soccer field and went out hunting as kindred spirits.'

'Since I was killing often, I began to feel it did not mean anything to me. I want to make clear that from the first gentleman I killed to the last, I was not sorry about a single one.'

'We killed everyone we tracked down [hiding] in the papyrus. We had no reason to choose, to expect or fear anyone in particular. We were cutters of acquaintances, cutters of neighbours, just plain cutters.'

'Anyone who hesitated to kill because of feelings of sadness absolutely had to watch his mouth, to say nothing about the reason for his reticence, for fear of being accused of complicity.'

The last factor indicates that the individual concerned had not really lost his individuality, but that he felt unable to resist due to fear that he would be putting his own welfare in jeopardy. How many times do you think this desire to 'stay safe' could explain people's willingness to engage in horrific acts? If we bring this one step closer to home, how many times have people become involved in gangs within schools and bullied an individual in order to stay in with the gang, even though they believed that this was not really the right thing to do?

You may remember the photographs that were printed in the newspapers in April 2004, showing the abuse of Iraqi prisoners at the Abu Ghraib prison. It would be interesting to understand the motivation which drove the individual soldiers who became involved in those events to act in the way they did. Images of ritual humiliation and psychological

This photo shows the torture of a prisoner at Abu Ghraib who was 'wired up' and told that if he fell off the box he would be electrocuted

torture were kept as 'trophies' by the perpetrators, one of whom was female. This 21-year-old female solider claimed that the events were just 'fun and games'.

According to Zimbardo these events, although more extreme, were in effect no different to the events that took place in the Stanford prison experiment in 1972. Zimbardo was involved in the investigations into the events at Abu Ghraib, acting as an expert witness for one of the Military Police prison guards. He testified to the effects of situational forces on the behaviour of the individual Military Police, but despite his efforts to try to convince the military leaders that there were mitigating circumstances, the prisoners were given harsh sentences and were described by the prosecutor and judge as 'rogue soldiers' and 'a few bad apples' – dispositional explanations for their behaviour.

Zimbardo (2007) makes the point that although the situational and dispositional explanations of behaviours are helpful, things are not always that simple. In order to gain a full understanding of the dynamics of human behaviour, he suggests it is necessary to 'recognise the extent and limits of personal power, situational power, and systemic power' (p.x), and how they interact with each other. He goes on to say that in order to change or prevent unwanted behaviour, the whole situation needs to be considered in great detail. Zimbardo acknowledges that 'deindividuation, obedience to authority, passivity in the face of threats, self-justification and rationalisation' (p.xii) are all effective in inducing an individual to behave in an 'evil' way, but he stresses that dehumanisation is one of the central processes. He also mentions that systems are responsible for creating hierarchies of dominance with information being passed down through the ranks. Some of this information is intended to dehumanise the opposition by the use of propaganda in order to make it acceptable for barbaric acts to take place. An example of this comes from the genocide in Rwanda, where a popular radio station was used to rouse the Hutus against their Tutsi neighbours by giving out messages suggesting the Tutsis were cannibals who would eat their children, and, when they were killing the Tutsis, not to spare the children because 'when you kill rats, you don't spare the babies'.

Before we consider the next core study, the question we ought to ask is: Why didn't all the Military Police guards engage in the barbaric acts at Abu Ghraib? After all, there were a number who did not get involved. What factors influenced their behaviour? Were they just especially strong individuals with an unbending moral code? On the other hand, might there have been another group present within the prison, unhappy with what was going on, which consequently gave certain individuals the confidence to remain apart? This brings us on to the next study, which considers, in part, what other conditions can affect the nature of human behaviour.

THE STUDY

Stephen Reicher and S. Alexander Haslam (2006) 'Rethinking the psychology of tyranny: The BBC prison study'

British Journal of Social Psychology, 45: 1–40

BACKGROUND

Reicher and Haslam introduce their study by covering a number of issues. They begin by pointing out that the events of the Second World War, especially the systematic extermination of 6 million Jews, shattered the generally held belief in society that human beings were becoming more civilised over time. These events not only affected the population as a whole, but also had a huge impact on social psychologists, who began to try to understand how humans can be so driven by discrimination and hatred towards their fellow man, and how 'the seeds of authoritarianism, social dominance and power abuse are sown and cultivated' (Reicher and Haslam 2006: 1). They explain that the question which concerned them most was how we seem 'to condone the tyranny of others or else act tyrannically ourselves' (p.2). They pointed out that research, which initially focused on the nature of the individual who perpetrated acts against humanity, had now shifted and was more interested in the nature of the group processes that managed to change inoffensive individuals into monsters (e.g. Milgram 1974; Sherif 1966; Tajfel 1982).

Taking the argument one stage further, the suggestion was that extreme acts against our fellow man *must* be considered by looking at the group; and that, generally, the actions of groups tend to become antisocial in the extreme. Reicher and Haslam also explain that, in their opinion, the psychology of tyranny occurs when one group is more powerful than another, and that the powerful group uses its power in an 'arbitrary or oppressive' way. However, this is not always the case, and the authors make very clear that they do not automatically accept that once a group is given power, it will turn on another group and subject its members to some kind of tyrannical rule.

Reicher and Haslam accept that research by psychologists such as Le Bon and Zimbardo was necessary, and it was this research which helped to change our understanding of the causes of behaviour. Before this work, people often explained the behaviour of individuals by suggesting they were innately evil. However, following the Stanford prison experiment (SPE), Zimbardo and his colleagues formulated the theory that it is the role a person takes on which leads to them adopting brutal behaviour – a case of 'the uniform made me do it'. They argued that the tyranny of the guards in the SPE was typical of how people respond to a role that offers an individual the opportunity to exert power over

Additional information on Tajfel 1982 and Sherif 1966 is available on the CD-ROM.

others. Reicher and Haslam tell us (p.3) that 'Zimbardo and colleagues explained their findings by commenting that guard aggression "was emitted simply as a 'natural' consequence of being in the uniform of a 'guard' and asserting the behaviour inherent in that role" (Haney et al. 1973, p.12)'.

A strong argument against this theory, however, comes from the evidence in the SPE itself. Not all the guards behaved in the same way, not all were arbitrarily unfair in their dealings with the prisoners, not all behaved brutally and not all of them liked the role they had been assigned. If adopting a powerful and authoritarian role does indeed lead to a person taking on the role without recourse to their own conscience, then surely all the guards would have behaved in a similar way? The fact that they did not contradicts the rather deterministic view that roles dictate behaviour in the way that Zimbardo implies, and perhaps this situational deterministic view was overplayed by Zimbardo et al. in their analysis of their findings.

They also point out that the other enormous impact of Zimbardo's work was to highlight concerns about how ethical the study was and how acceptable it was generally to put participants through such a traumatic experience as the SPE. Consequently, it was not possible to assess the reliability of the study as it had not been ethically permissible (until the present study) to carry out a replication of the SPE: 'the ethical concerns that have placed the SPE "off-limits". . .have led to a situation in which the results of that study have become almost inviolate and social psychological inquiry into tyranny has effectively ground to a halt' (p.3). In other words, for researchers who might challenge Zimbardo et al.'s role theory explanation of their findings, there was no way to repeat the study and see if the findings proved replicable.

Consequently there was a lack of any further 'realistic' research, and future investigations were laboratory-based and therefore often unrelated to important social psychological issues. This resulted in a lack of opportunity to look at 'the role of personal and group history or the development of interactions over time', or to:

> undertake studies that create, manipulate and systematically investigate the effects of social environments on human interaction [which can therefore] be seen to have contributed to the increasing dominance of explanations based upon inherent and essentially unavoidable genetic, biological, or psychological propensities. (p.3)

Moreover, Reicher and Haslam argued that the interventions by Zimbardo himself, rather than the spontaneous response to their roles, might account for the behaviour of the guards in the SPE. To begin with, Zimbardo, who played the role of the Superintendent in the prison, was the guards' 'boss', and he told them:

> You can create in the prisoners feelings of boredom, a sense of fear to some degree, you can create a notion of arbitrariness that their life is totally controlled by us, by the system, you, me and they'll have no privacy. . . They have no freedom of action – they can do nothing, say nothing, that we don't permit. We're going to take away their individuality in various ways. In general what this all leads to is a sense of powerlessness. . .

> (cited in Reicher and Haslam 2006: 4)

Given that this was said to them at the start of the study by their 'leader', one interpretation of the guards' behaviour in the SPE was simply that they were obeying the instruction to create a brutal environment, rather than showing how tyranny might be created.

Bearing in mind the time that had elapsed since the SPE was carried out, and the progress made in social psychological explanations of tyranny, Reicher and Haslam considered that Zimbardo et al.'s explanations of tyranny might not be adequate. They argued that there were two reasons to believe they were not:

1 the data produced for the SPE were selective and not all interactions were either filmed or subsequently revealed in the written reports by the authors;
2 the video film data that were produced showed:

that both prisoners and guards challenged their roles not only at the start, but throughout the entire study. In the case of the guards. . .while some exploited their power, others sided with the prisoners, and yet others were tough but fair. Such diversity sits uneasily with the notion that role acceptance is simply determined by the situation. . . (p.4)

Social identity approach

Developments in our understanding of group psychology have resulted in us no longer believing that simply by adopting some kind of role, our normal behaviour suddenly changes in a negative way, or that being a member of a group can lead us to become antisocial. The social identity approach which incorporates **social identity theory** (Tajfel and Turner 1979) and **self-categorisation theory** (Turner 1985) provides an alternative explanation of group behaviour. The social identity approach proposes that groups can have a positive as well as a negative effect on an individual's behaviour. It suggests that the person does not simply act according to a role given to them by someone else, but that their decision to act with or against the group is dependent on whether they 'internalize such [group] memberships as part of the self concept (Turner, 1982)' (p.5).

In other words, if group membership is an important and integrated part of the person's identity, and the behaviour of the group contributes to their sense of belonging and self-esteem, they will act with the group and/or for the benefit of the group. According to this theory, some groups may use their power to become tyrannical, but others may use the power of the group to resist such tyranny. This second theory is what is known as a pro-social explanation, where the result is positive rather than negative.

Researchers in this area have focused on trying to work out *when* people will act as a group to change inequalities between groups (resistance). This means identifying dominant and subordinate groups and seeing when those in subordinate groups would resist. Social identity explanations predict that the members of dominant and subordinate groups are likely to behave in different ways. Those people:

who are positively valued by virtue of their group membership (i.e. members of dominant groups). . .would identify with and act in terms of the group.

For people who are negatively valued by virtue of their group membership (i.e. members of subordinate groups), collective action depends upon two factors in particular: [permeability and security]. (p.5)

In terms of resistance, it is the behaviour of people in subordinate groups that is important. You need to understand the key terms 'permeability' and 'security' in order to understand the authors' interventions and explanations in this study.

KEY CONCEPTS:

Permeability of group boundaries
This refers to the belief a person has about their ability to advance through the social system despite their group membership. If they believe they can advance (the permeability of group boundaries is possible), this belief encourages them to act in ways that might lead to their individual advancement. However, if they believe that they cannot advance (permeability is impossible), they are more likely to see themselves as group members and act collectively as a group.

Security
A second factor that affects whether a person acts individually or collectively is the perceived security of inter-group relations. This is split into two parts: the perceived fairness of inter-group inequalities (legitimacy) and perceived stability.

According to these concepts, people are more likely to act collectively if permeability is impossible. According to this theory, whether they then challenge inequalities depends on whether the inequalities are perceived to be unstable and illegitimate (unfair): 'people should be most inclined to resist domination when they see inequality as both illegitimate and unstable and can thus envisage cognitive alternatives to it' (p.5). That is, they are able to imagine 'cognitive alternatives to the status quo', in other words, they can imagine how things could be different.

In more simple terms:

- If the situation is: fair + unstable = no challenge to authority.
- If the situation is: fair + stable = no challenge to authority.
- If the situation is: unfair + stable = no challenge to authority.

but:

- If the situation is unfair + unstable = challenge to authority is more likely, as more alternative situations can be imagined.

Reicher and Haslam sought to investigate group behaviour in relation to these concepts.

A further reason for revisiting the SPE is given by Reicher and Haslam. They suggest that the dominance of the SPE, and the use of role theory in describing a range of behaviours beyond the SPE itself, 'from prison behaviour to terrorism' (p.6), should be reconsidered. In their study, Reicher and Haslam aimed to test the validity of the claim that 'people "naturally" assume roles' (p.6), because they believed that the analysis of the SPE:

has profound and troubling implications. . . if people cannot help but act in terms of assigned role, it implies that they have little choice, and hence little responsibility, for their social actions. This makes it more difficult to hold tyrants to account for what they do. Moreover, in communicating the message that resistance is futile, the analysis discourages the oppressed from attempting to challenge tyranny. . . (p.6)

Using the social identification approach, Reicher and Haslam planned to 'revisit some of the issues' (p.5) raised by the SPE:

• What are the psychological consequences of inter-group inequality?
• When do people seek to impose such inequality? And when do they resist it?

This study also aimed to test the validity of Zimbardo et al.'s analysis of the SPE and their role-based explanation of group behaviour and tyranny.

They did this through a study similar but, for both ethical and theoretical purposes, not identical to the SPE, and in association with the BBC. This was called the BBC prison experiment and was carried out in December 2001.

AIMS

The authors point out that they did not aim to replicate the SPE, which would not have been possible for ethical reasons anyway. They also indicate that they did not intend to try to simulate a prison, but to assemble another sort of 'institution' which would create inequalities that were real to the participants. This would then provide a setting in which the issues raised by the SPE could be addressed, with the intention of investigating whether the descriptions of group behaviour, specifically role theory, would be evident in this study, or whether the concepts of the social identity approach would offer a better explanation of the behaviour observed.

This was not to be a direct comparison with the SPE, but, it was hoped, would answer some of the questions raised by the SPE, such as:

Do participants accept their roles uncritically? Do those accorded group power exercise it without constraint, and do those without group power accept their subordination without complaint? After all, if the process of role enactment is indeed 'natural', then it should apply in all cases and any exception is troubling for the overall claim. (p.7)

The overall aims of the study were as follows:

(a) To provide comprehensive and systematic data pertaining to the unfolding interactions between groups of unequal power and privilege.
(b) To analyse the conditions under which people (i) define themselves in terms of their ascribed group memberships and act in terms of group identities, and (ii) accept or else challenge intergroup inequalities.

Specifically, we predict that dominant group members will identify with their group from the start and impose their power. However, subordinate group members will only identify collectively and challenge intergroup inequalities when they see relations between groups as impermeable and insecure.

(c) To examine the relations between social, organisational and clinical factors in group behaviour.

(d) To develop protocols that provide a practical and ethical framework for examining social psychological issues in large-scale studies. (p.7)

METHOD

Method and design

A social psychological field study was carried out. The authors describe their study as an 'experimental case study of the behaviour of members in dominant or subordinate positions and of the developing relations between them'. Although it was conducted with the BBC, and formed the basis of four 1-hour programmes on television, the study was independently designed and run by the authors and was therefore 'an ordinary piece of research' (p.6). The researchers describe the study as 'original science filmed', explaining that it was unlike reality TV-style shows, which are designed by TV companies for entertainment purposes, and where academics might be invited to comment on the goings-on (although they did not mention *Big Brother*, this fits the bill of the type of programme they were disassociating themselves from). The authors downplay the role of the BBC in organising or influencing the study, claiming the organisation had a limited role (creating the environment, in line with the authors' guidelines; filming the study; preparing the material for broadcast).

The study aimed to create a hierarchical society in Elstree Film Studios, to the north of London, where the participants would live for a maximum of 10 days. The aim was:

to create an institution that in many ways resembled a prison (but also other hierarchical institutions such as a school, an office, a barracks; see Morgan, 1979) as a site to investigate the behaviour of groups that were unequal in terms of power, status, and resources. What is critical, then, is not that the study environment replicated a real prison (which no such environment ever could), but that it created inequalities between groups that were real to the participants. (p.8)

There were three-person lockable cells to house the 'prisoners'; these, and showers for the prisoners, led off a central area (the atrium). Guards' quarters were separated by a lockable steel-mesh fence. Guards had a dormitory, a bathroom and a mess room.

Plan of the prison showing the layout and the initials of the participants, who were either prisoners (p) or guards (g)

Participants

The recruitment of participants was done through screening those who responded to adverts for male volunteers in the national press or leaflets. Males only were studied so that comparisons with the SPE could be made, and also to avoid the ethical concerns about mixing men and women in the 'prison'. From a pool of 332 applicants, 27 men were selected by a three-phase screening process. A final sample of 15 was chosen to ensure diversity of age, social class and ethnic background.

In the screening process:

1 Prospective participants completed a battery of psychometric tests that measured both social variables (authoritarianism, social dominance, modern racism) and clinical variables (depression, anxiety, social isolation, paranoia, aggressiveness, demotivation, self-esteem, self-harm, drug dependence).
2 Prospective participants underwent a full weekend assessment by independent clinical psychologists.
3 Medical and character references were obtained, and police checks were conducted.

The selected participants were all people who were well adjusted and pro-social. This was done, first, for ethical reasons, and second, to ensure that the sample was generalisable to a broader population and comparable to the participants in the SPE.

The authors claim that the final 15 were randomly divided into two groups of five guards and ten prisoners. However, this was done only after they had been put into matched groups of three, as closely matched as possible on personality variables 'potentially implicated in tyranny: modern racism, authoritarianism and social dominance' (p.9). From each group of three, a guard and two prisoners were randomly allocated. This process acted as a control to ensure that the personality types were spread out across the guards and prisoners. As a further control, this process was carried out blind, with the experimenters not knowing who was being allocated to which role.

Because of the planned interventions in the study, it began with nine prisoners and five guards, with a tenth prisoner introduced at a later stage in the study.

Procedure

The authors present an overview of the study:

> Over a period of 8 days, the study examined the behaviour of 15 men who were placed in a social hierarchy of guards and prisoners within a purpose-built environment. Their behaviour was video- and audio-recorded over the entire period, and this was complemented by daily psychometric and physiological measures. The video data were edited into four 1-hour long documentaries screened in May 2002. . . (p.7)

Of course, with 8 full days of observations, interventions and daily psychometric measures, there is much more to it than this!

Let us start at the beginning, by considering the set-up of the study.

Set-up of the study: guards

In setting up the study, the guards were invited to a hotel the night before the study was to begin. Here they were briefed as follows:

- Informed they would have the role of guards in the study.
- Shown the prison timetable (e.g. cleaning rota, work duties, prisoner roll calls, exercise and recreation time).
- Told they would be responsible for making sure that the institution ran smoothly and ensuring the prisoners performed all their tasks.
- Asked to draw up a series of prison rules, under headings given by the authors, and to draw up punishments should the prisoners violate the rules. They were given no guidance on how to do this, except that they must respect a set of ethically determined rights for prisoners.

- As in the SPE, the guards were informed that no physical violence would be tolerated, but beyond this it was stressed that they could act as they pleased (p.11).

Day 1 of the study: guards

- In the morning of Day 1, guards were taken in a blacked-out van to the institution. The blacked-out van was used so that the inside of the prison would be the guards' total sensory experience of their environment for the duration of the study.
- They were briefed about the layout of the prison and resources available to them to help enforce their authority, including keys to all doors, the guards' observation post, with full cell surveillance system installed, access to an upper level, a social isolation cell for punishment, and resources such as snacks and cigarettes that they could give or withhold as punishment or reward. They could also put the prisoners on a bread-and-water diet.
- The guards had well-made uniforms, which they put on after the briefing, and prepared for the arrival of the prisoners by practising the procedure for introducing a prisoner to the prison.

Set-up of the study, Day 1: prisoners

Prisoners arrived one at a time. On arrival they had their heads shaved and were given a uniform consisting of a T-shirt printed with a three-digit number, loose trousers and flimsy sandals. The prisoners were given no information other than the prison rules and a list of prisoners' rights, which were posted in their cells. The only other information they received was a short loudspeaker announcement by the researchers, which told them that no violence was permissible and that, since the allocation process might not have been reliable, the guards would be looking for 'guard-like' qualities in the prisoners, with a possibility for 'promotion' on Day 3 (see the permeability intervention below).

Planned interventions – introduction of variables to test the impact of specific concepts from the social identity approach

In contrast to the SPE, which the authors of this study describe as 'exploratory', this study had a theoretical basis and was intended to test the social identification approach as an explanation of group behaviour, so the authors planned to introduce variables through a set of time-series interventions. Three interventions were to be made:

1 Permeability – a possibility for the promotion to the role of guard from the role of prisoner was introduced. Guards were told they had been selected for their reliability and initiative, but that these measures were not always reliable, so they were to check out any prisoners who showed 'guard-like' qualities to

suggest that they might be promoted. Prisoners were also informed of this possibility of advancement to the other group (permeability) on arrival, through a loudspeaker announcement.

The incentive to want to move from prisoner to guard was apparent in the inequalities between the two groups:

- Guards had all the power and authority.
- Guards had superior and well-made uniforms.
- Guards had superior living conditions, including superior food and extra drinks and snacks.

On Day 3 such a promotion was made by the guards, using a selection procedure suggested by the researchers, after which there was an announce- ment that there would be no further promotions or demotions (the prisoners would now believe that permeability was impossible).

2 Legitimacy – 3 days after the promotion (Day 6), all guards and prisoners were to be informed that the allocation to roles had actually been random, and there was no real difference between guards and prisoners, but it was too late to make changes now. This would mean that the division of groups which had previously appeared legitimate now lost its legitimacy.

3 Cognitive alternatives – a day after the legitimacy intervention, a tenth pris- oner was to be introduced. Although he was no better informed about the study than all other participants, he was chosen specifically as he had a background as an experienced trade union official. It was assumed he would raise the possibility of group-based negotiations (given that the set-up would by then be illegitimate and changeable): 'it was envisaged that his introduc- tion would enable the prisoners (and the participants more generally) to envis- age the achievement of a more equal set of social relations' (p.11). In other words, it was expected that he would encourage the participants to imagine cognitive alternatives to the status quo.

Data gathering and recording

1 Observational data: the prison set-up was designed so that all participants could be both audio- and video-recorded at all times. All audio channels and four video channels were recorded at any one time throughout the study.

2 Self-report data: participants completed a daily set of psychometric tests. The key variables reported here were:

(a) social variables: social identification, awareness of cognitive alterna- tives, right-wing authoritarianism;
(b) organisational variables: compliance with rules, organisational citi- zenship; and
(c) clinical variables: self-efficacy, depression (p.10).

To prevent test fatigue, not every test was given every day (see Results, below).

3 Biochemical measures: a daily saliva swab was taken, from which measures of cortisol were taken, as an indication of stress levels. (The data for stress are not reported in this version of the study.)

RESULTS

The authors divide the results into two phases:

1 **Rejecting inequality**
   In the first phase of the study the guards did not identify with their roles, and therefore did not stick together as a group. Initially, the prisoners failed to identify as a group and acted individually in the hope of promotion, but after the promotion on Day 3, they increasingly identified as a group and worked collectively to challenge the guards. 'This led to a shift of power and ultimately to the collapse of the prisoner–guard system' (p.12).

2 **Embracing inequality**
   In this phase, the participants decided to operate the study as a single self-governing 'commune', on an equal footing. However, this was not successful as it did not develop a system for dealing with internal dissent, and was unsustainable in the face of opposition which arose. By the end, participants seemed more predisposed to tolerate a harsher guard–prisoner system which some now proposed.

Phase 1: Rejecting inequality (days 1–6)

Social identification

The pattern of social identification in the prisoners was as predicted. While they believed that permeability was possible, there was less collective action and more individual action towards the goal of promotion. However, after the promotion on Day 3, and once it was apparent that group boundaries were impermeable, the prisoners acted more collectively against the guards.

Reicher and Haslam quote the behaviour of one cell of prisoners before and after the promotion to fully illustrate this. (**Note:** Participants are identified only by initials; 'g' or 'p' after their initials indicates their role, 'p' for prisoner and 'g' for guard.) In this cell the three prisoners were JEp, KMp – both of whom had worked hard to get promotion and failed – and PPp. After the promotion, all three realised that the only way to improve their position was to change the system. From the outset all had been very unhappy with the unequal conditions of guards and prisoners: JEp had said he wanted to be a guard 'because they get all the luxuries' (p.13).

The authors quote this extract to show how the prisoners planned and justified collective resistance:

JEp: Hopefully we'll get [TQg] in. That's the person, he's the target.
KMp: No. I mean obviously I think it's going to be a lot of fun for us to do this but I don't think [TQg]. . .I feel so. . .I just feel. . .
PPp: Listen, listen mate I, you've got to, you've got to start forgetting about other people's feelings and what they're doing because the days when

you're sitting here starving hungry and you've got f**k all and you've got nothing mate and you've got a ratty little bed and a stupid little blanket to sit under and they're under there in their duvets, they've got everything they want and they're not giving two f**ks about you. So – think on and f**k them. KMp: I think they do care about us. But guys I'm going to back you all the way. You should no' doubt me. (p.13)

Before the promotion the prisoners were interested in 'what *I* will do'; after the promotion it changed to 'what *we* will do'. Their behaviour changed from compliance with the authority of the guards to conflict.

For the guards, the results were not as predicted. In contrast to the SPE, and against the authors' predictions, the guards here failed to identify with their high-status, positively valued role in the prison, resulting in a failure to cohere as a group. The authors note that some guards were reluctant to impose their authority, and their failure to internalise their role led to a weak sense of group identity.

The self-report data (psychometric testing giving quantitative data) confirm the observational data, showing that although the guards started out with the higher sense of social identification, this reduced after Day 2 when they had to enforce the system, whereas the social identification of the prisoners increased, as predicted, after the promotion on Day 3.

Social identification as a function of assigned group and time

Security of inter-group relations
The aim had been to create insecurity by use of the legitimacy intervention (on day 6 when the prisoners and guards were told that the allocation to roles had actually been random), but this proved not to be necessary as the way the groups emerged naturally created a sense of illegitimacy. The prisoners became more cohesive and collectively challenging of the guards, whereas the guards failed to act as a group, and their weak and ineffective management of the institution led to beliefs that the original groupings were not legitimate – the guards were just not up to the job.

An illustration of the challenge of the prisoners to the guards' authority was when the three prisoners of Cell 2 set up a challenge to see what would happen. JEp threw his plate to the floor and demanded better food, and as guards tried to deal with this, KMp and PPp chipped in with their own demands – for a cigarette and a plaster for a blister. The guards could not decide whether to take an authoritarian role or make concessions. In the end, TQg decided to give a cigarette to PPp to get all the prisoners back in their cell. The prisoners' response to this was that they were delighted, saying things like 'that was f**king sweet'. The guards, however, bickered among themselves, with TAg saying: 'This is only day 4. They can see what happened today and now they can do whatever they want' (p.15). From this we can see that both the prisoners and the guards clearly understood that the system could be changed (they could imagine cognitive alternatives to the status quo).

The introduction of the tenth prisoner (DMp) had been planned to introduce cognitive alternatives, but since these were already apparent he might not have been necessary. However, since he had been told he would join the study, the authors introduced him as planned on Day 5. What he did do was to offer further alternatives to the status quo, especially questioning the whole idea of the prisoner–guard division, encouraging collective action against the researchers, for example in relation to the level of heat in the institution.

Quantitative measures show how cognitive alternatives to the status quo became more apparent to participants through the study.

Awareness of cognitive alternatives as a function of assigned group and time

Acceptance of the unequal regime: Compliance and organisational citizenship
As the study progressed, the impact of social identification and security became apparent in the reducing compliance of the prisoners to the guards' regime over time.

Compliance with prison rules as a function of assigned group and time

Measurement of a further variable also shows how the prisoners were less willing to support the guards' authority as time progressed. This variable, organisational citizenship, measured the willingness of the participant to act above and beyond what was required to make the system work.

Organisational citizenship as a function of assigned group and time

Observations of the prisoners' behaviour confirmed this decline in compliance and lack of cooperation with the system; for example, being insubordinate at the prisoner roll call, or the complaints about food made collectively by a group of prisoners.

Collective self-efficacy and mental health
The prisoners became more successful in their challenges and undermining of the guards' authority. This can be seen in the quantitative measurement of collective self-efficacy and depression over time.

Collective self-efficacy as a function of assigned group and time

The results show that the prisoners' sense of group success increased over time, whereas this variable decreased for the guards. This matches the data for social identification. The guards' lack of ability to act collectively led to more observed despondency among them than these quantitative data suggest.

In terms of depression, the graph shows clearly that although the prisoners were more depressed at the start of the study, this trend had reversed completely by the end.

Depression as a function of assigned group and time

The combined impact of these variables was that by Day 6 the prisoners were strong enough to plan and execute a plot to destroy the guards' now weak and ineffective regime. This culminated in a breakout of prisoners from Cell 2 and their occupation of the guards' quarters, bringing the guards' regime to an end.

Phase 2: Embracing inequality (days 7–8)

After the collapse of the guards' regime all but two of the participants agreed for the study to continue as a 'commune', with all participants working on an equal basis. Successful at first, the commune failed since those who had challenged the guards' regime felt marginalised in the commune, and they challenged and undermined it, for example by not doing their chores, then by violating communal rules, and then plotting to overturn the commune. The commune had not developed a way to deal with disciplining rule breakers and this made it difficult for it to succeed in the face of subordination.

A chance factor, a poor-quality breakfast on the commune's second day, Day 8, was interpreted as a sign of the researchers' disapproval of the commune, and what was now proposed by some (one ex-guard and three ex-prisoners) was a new regime, more harsh than the first. PBp's comments show what the new regime was to be like: 'We want to be the guards and f**king make them toe the line, I mean *on the f**king line*. No f**king talking while you are eating. Get on with your food and get back to your f**king cell' (p.22).

The supporters of the commune were passive and despondent in the face of this. In debriefing, some said that although prior to the study they would not openly support such a harsh regime as the one now being proposed, they found they were less opposed to it after their experience in the study.

Why would this be the case? The authors considered changes to the attitudes of the participants over the course of the study in terms of a right-wing authoritarian scale. As you can see clearly from the graph comparing the allocated prisoners and guards, both groups increased on this variable through the course of the study. The breakdown of the commune and the willingness to let someone else take responsibility for making the system work might account for the increase in authoritarianism. This increase in authoritarianism occurred in conjunction with the proposal for the new regime.

Right-wing authoritarianism as a function of assigned group and time

Interestingly, analysis of the authoritarianism rating of remaining participants wanting to be guards in any new regime had not declined significantly, whereas the authoritarianism rating of the ones supporting the commune had increased steadily over time.

Right-wing authoritarianism as a function of self-selected group and time

Gridlock: The end of the study

Since the authors considered that the new regime could not be enforced without a level of force not permitted in the study, and because the existing system had failed, the authors report that they considered the study to be gridlocked and to have come to a 'natural point of termination' (p.24). The study was therefore ended at noon on Day 8, with participants remaining for a further day for debriefing.

DISCUSSION

Before giving their explanation of group behaviour based on the social identity approach, the authors try to pre-empt and account for four possible criticisms that might be made of their study. The following table sets out these criticisms and the authors' responses.

Criticism	Authors' response
The role of television • Participants were only play-acting and faking their roles, and looking for 'celebrity status'.	• Play-acting was unlikely over an extended period (8 days), and the psychometric data, which is harder to fake, supported the observational data, suggesting the observed behaviour was valid.

Criticism	Authors' response
• Surveillance explains the behaviour observed.	• Play-acting does not explain the observed behaviour, especially in terms of the willingness to accept the move towards tyranny in the final stages. • Surveillance cannot account for changes in behaviour that occurred: surveillance remained constant, but attitudes and behaviour changed, and, importantly, changed in the ways the study had predicted. • The authors argue that 'surveillance is everywhere (anyway)' and that it is a normal part of our everyday lives, so the study should not be discounted simply because it was broadcast on TV.
The role of personality • The personalities of certain people, especially prisoners JEp, PPp and PBp, and not group processes explain the behaviour that was observed.	• The authors agree that personalities play a part, but point out, for example, that PPp had always personally opposed the guards' regime, but was unable to *actively* oppose it until this became the will of his group (i.e. after the promotion on Day 3), so the impact of an individual's will was dependent on the group will; it did not happen just because he was personally 'rebellious'. This was also true of the environmentalist prisoner, FCp, quiet for 6 days, then becoming prominent in setting up the commune, when the group will allowed his particular skills, knowledge and personality to direct them. Their relationship to the group thus influenced participants' success as individuals, in directing group action according to their personalities. • In addition, changes in personality variables seemed to occur across the study; for example, authoritarianism increased. It could therefore be argued that the study impacted on personalities, and not the other way round.
The authors failed to create real power and inequalities between the groups, so the study tells us little about group processes and tyranny	• The guards' behaviour in the study was not because they had too little power, but because they had too *much* power and were reluctant to use it (e.g. they had the power to reward and punish, were able to make the prisoners perform roll calls, etc., and were

Criticism	Authors' response
• The guards did not have any real power to wield, even if they were inclined to do so.	the given power to promote a prisoner). It seems that they were afraid of being seen as authoritarian. The study appears to have given them a fear of their potential power, not too little power in the first place.
The study's claim to be an 'experimental case study' can be questioned because the manipulation of the independent variables (e.g. the promotion as an example of permeability) may not have had the claimed effects	• As in all studies, there are difficulties operationalising variables, even more so in a complex study such as this one. However, the researchers used manipulation checks to establish the validity of their interventions, specifically checking that the observed behaviour could be explained in terms of the social identity principles on which interventions were based. They also used their multiple sources of data to confirm their findings (e.g. see the data graph on cognitive alternatives on page 68).

In the case of all these criticisms, the authors argue that while each one impacts on the study, none alone can adequately account for the study's results in their entirety. In order to explain fully the observed and recorded behaviour in the study, an explanation based on a social identity approach offers the best explanation.

The authors' social identity account of tyranny

Before giving their explanation of the findings, the authors make a very clear statement that the analysis of their findings is at odds with the analysis of the SPE by Zimbardo et al.:

> 'the simplest and clearest finding of our study is that people do not automatically assume roles that are given to them in the manner suggested by the role account that is typically used to explain events in the SPE.'

An alternative account to role theory is thus offered, where the components of the social identity approach are used to explain the findings. For example, the move from permeability to impermeability (the promotion) had a strong influence on prisoner group identification, as predicted. The increasing insecurity in inter-group relations affected the willingness of prisoners to challenge the guards' authority. The concept of legitimacy explains why the prisoners challenged the guards (when it was clear the guards were not functioning properly as a group and therefore were not up to doing their job). This factor of legitimacy also explains why the participants as a whole did not challenge the researchers, as to do so would be a breach of their agreement to take part. There were two occasions however, when the researchers were considered to be breaking their side of the bargain (it was too hot in the prison, the guards' supplies were not replenished), and in both cases talk of 'mutiny' (p.30) was the result, again showing that loss of legitimacy can lead to challenges to inequalities/unfairness in a system.

The consequences of social identification are also discussed by the researchers, and they suggest that to understand fully the impact of factors on group behaviour from this theoretical approach (e.g. the role of collective self-efficacy and social support) further study is required.

The impact of TV cameras

The researchers suggest that the presence of the TV cameras had an impact on the study in two ways:

1 The response of the guards and their reluctance to be seen as authoritarian shows that because they were able to consider the judgements made of their behaviour beyond the context of the prison, extreme situational explanations of group behaviour (such as role theory) really do not account for their behaviour.
2 It seemed to confirm that

'extreme behaviours can be restrained by making actors visible, and hence, accountable to broader or yet-to-be encountered audiences' (p.30).

The authors' explanation of tyranny

In contrast with the SPE, the authors of this study suggest that instead of tyranny being explicable in terms of the 'psychological dysfunctionality of groups', this study suggests that tyranny can be explained 'in terms of the dysfunctionality of group failure' (p.24). In other words, it is the *failure* of groups that leads to the conditions from which tyranny might arise.

From this study they cite two examples of group failure: the failure of the guards to fulfil their role, which led to the collapse of the guards' regime; and the inability of the commune to use discipline to enforce its rule, which led to the collapse of the commune.

The authors argue that after the failure of a group and the breakdown of a system, people are willing to give up some of their core principles in order to establish a system that works. For example, the guards had been willing to give up their power so that the commune might work. At the collapse of the commune, the participants were willing to accept a new, harsher system, even though they would not have supported such a system openly at the outset. Indeed all the participants opposed the inequalities of the system designed by the researchers, so what would induce them now to create a system that was even more unequal? The authors explain this:

rather than people 'naturally' preferring any given form of social order, it appears that, when group members fail to impose an order based on their own existing norms and values, they are willing to adapt those values (or adopt new ones) in order to create viable order rather than have no order at all. (p.32)

CONCLUSIONS

The authors conclude that their results agree with the SPE in that to understand tyranny it has to be investigated in terms of group processes and not on an individual basis. However, where they disagree with the SPE is in the *explanation* of the group processes that lead to tyranny.

Whereas the SPE concluded that 'the toxic combination of groups and power lead to tyranny' (p.33), the authors of this study argue that strong groups can, depending on their norms and values, behave either antisocially or pro-socially, so tyranny is not an inevitable outcome.

On the other hand, the extensive problems caused by failing groups result in them being more likely to accept extreme situations proposed by others, and this is when tyranny can seem an attractive alternative – a viable system being preferable to an unworkable one: 'in short it is the breakdown of groups and the powerlessness of groups that creates the conditions under which tyranny can triumph' (p.33).

Supporting this argument, the authors argue three points:

1 It is consistent with contemporary thinking in social psychology (social identity approach).
2 It is consistent with the accounts of the rise of tyranny from other disciplines. For example, the historian Hobsbawm wrote in 1995:

the optimal conditions for the triumph of the ultra-right were an old state and its ruling mechanisms which could no longer function; a mass of disenchanted, disoriented and disorganised citizens who no longer knew where their loyalties lay; strong socialist movements threatening or appearing to threaten social revolution, but not actually in a position to achieve it. . . These were the conditions that turned movements of the radical right into powerful, organised and sometimes uniformed and paramilitary force. (p.33)

3 It can be used as an alternative analysis of what happened in the SPE. After their initial rebellion and being led by their ringleader to believe that Zimbardo would not permit them to leave, the failure of the prisoners to act as a group allowed the tyranny of the guards to emerge and prevail, much as the failure of the commune might have allowed a tyranny to emerge in the BBC experiment.

The SPE, it seemed, had closed debate about the nature of tyranny by suggesting that studies could not be carried out ethically in this area. However, the authors say that a major strength of the BBC study is that it shows how such studies can be operated ethically and that the debate on tyranny can be reopened, especially in light of the fact that the findings of this study are in contrast with those of the SPE.

They do admit, however, that their analysis contains 'large and controversial claims', and they invite further research on this topic. They claim that this is essential if their discipline of social psychology is to advance.

COMMENTARY: METHODS AND ISSUES

Research method, design and data gathering

The authors describe this as an 'experimental case study', and it was carried out as role-play simulation (similar to the SPE). The study was audio- and video-recorded, and finally edited into four 1-hour programmes broadcast on BBC TV. The authors themselves attempt to address two problems with these methods: first, the problem that the nature of role play and the TV recording might mean that all the participants were doing was play-acting; and second, the problem of controlling and recording the effect of the variables they attempted to manipulate in the study (see Discussion, above).

Being a case study, along with audio- and video-recording for 8 days, as well as carrying out daily psychometric tests, this study offers a great deal of both qualitative and quantitative data. This is a strength of the study, as is the fact that the researchers used a wide range of data-gathering methods – observation, self-report and biochemical measures – in their study.

Does the study raise any ethical concerns?

For this study to be justified in the first place there had to be good reason for attempting to create a situation similar to the SPE, given the ethical concerns that were raised by the behaviour of the guards in that study. The researchers' justification was to further the understanding of how groups behave and how tyranny might emerge. Their aim also included the introduction of variables such as permeability and legitimacy, to see if this had an impact on challenges to inequality, as was suggested by the social identity approach.

To ensure the study was carried out ethically, the researchers discussed it with colleagues, and proposals were submitted both to the University of Exeter's ethics panel and to the Chair of the British Psychological Society's Ethics Committee. In addition, the following (ethical) safeguards were built into the study:

(a) Potential participants went through 3-phase clinical, medical, and background screening to ensure that they were neither psychologically vulnerable nor liable to put others at risk. . .
(b) Participants signed a comprehensive consent form. Amongst other things, this informed them that they may be subject to a series of factors – including physical and psychological discomfort, confinement, constant surveillance and stress – which may involve risk.

(c) Two independent clinical psychologists monitored the study throughout, and had the right to see any participant at any time or to demand that any participant be removed from the study.

(d) A paramedic was on constant standby in case of illness or injury.

(e) On-site security guards were provided with detailed protocols clarifying when and how to intervene in cases of dangerous behaviours by participants.

(f) An independent 5-person ethics committee – chaired by a British Member of Parliament – monitored the study throughout. This committee had the right to demand changes to the study's set-up or to terminate it at any time. (pp.8–9)

The study might have run for 10 days, but was brought to a stop on Day 8. Although this was not done explicitly for ethical reasons, it was clear that the proposed new regime might have been too harsh to be permitted under the ethical guidelines all the participants had agreed to follow, and it was also clear that the previous system, the commune, had broken down. Otherwise the researchers report that the study raised no ethical concerns and none of the safeguards had to be used: 'After the study, the ethical committee published an independent report and characterized the conduct of the study as "exemplary"' (p.9).

Is the study useful?

By reopening the discussion about the emergence of tyranny by conducting this study, the authors have made a positive contribution to the discipline of social psychology. Also, by suggesting that tyranny is not an inevitable outcome where powerful groups exist, and that powerful groups can also act pro-socially (for example, to resist tyranny), the authors argue that this study might help psychologists to 'reconnect with policy makers'. In other words, there might be positive changes to society that social psychology could advise on and contribute to.

Even Zimbardo, who does not have much that is positive to say about the BBC study, confirms that it has one very important implication:

I want to thank these researchers for demonstrating a point that I have long argued in favour of as a means to reduce prisoner abuses, namely greater surveillance of guard–prisoner interactions. This BBC-TV research shows that such violence can be eliminated if all parties in a prison setting realize that their behaviour is open for scrutiny and evaluation. . . (Zimbardo 2006: 53)

The study itself seemed to confirm that 'extreme behaviours can be restrained by making actors visible, and hence, accountable to broader or yet-to-be encountered audiences' (Reicher and Haslam 2006: 30). The implication here is that if surveillance equipment were introduced in prisons, the brutality and abuses reported to take place could be reduced or eliminated.

Validity and reliability of the study

Throughout their BBC prison study, Reicher and Haslam were at pains to point out and counter possible criticisms against their conclusions. In addition, they used their different data sources to support the reliability, and therefore the validity, of their findings. For example, they used the data from the psychometric testing to confirm their observational data.

Reicher and Haslam have presented a challenge to the validity of the analysis made by Zimbardo et al. of the way that tyranny emerges, based on their SPE. Does this study refute the theory that powerful groups and roles lead to tyranny and adequately replace it with a social identity-based explanation of tyranny? As the researchers modestly point out, this is just one study, and further research is necessary if their theory is to be confirmed.

Of course, given that both the SPE and the BBC study were simulations that required participants to role-play as guards or prisoners, it could be argued that the studies lack sufficient ecological validity to be used as explanations of how tyranny really emerges, or of the impact of groups on behaviour in the real world. The emergence of tyranny occurs in a complex socio-economic, political and psychological context which would be impossible to replicate in any simple, simulated environment, especially ones as controlled and short-lived as these two studies have presented us with.

Zimbardo was invited by the *British Journal of Social Psychology* to write an article in which he responded to the BBC study. He largely dismissed the study as a 'scientifically irresponsible "made-for-TV-study"'.

Postscript

Reicher and Haslam have indicated that the theory of deindividuation cannot always be given as an explanation of antisocial behaviour in groups, although it is a very useful way of understanding such responses. What we need to remember is that there are instances of deindividuation which do not produce antisocial behaviour; in fact, the behaviour that deindividuation can produce could be described as liberating.

Chrissie is having a party and you are there advising her what sort of music to have and what drinks to provide. You have a discussion about how the furniture should be arranged and whether you should make room for dancing. Both of you have had all afternoon to get the place ready, and you are now dressed up and ready for the first guests to arrive. The music is playing and you are really excited. Chrissie says she is very nervous about how the party is going to go. Is it going to be good? Will many people turn up?

Two hours later, the party is going reasonably well, but people are still a little stand-offish and not mixing as well as you had hoped they would. There seem to be small groups of people in different places, and the atmosphere definitely leaves something to be desired. Suddenly all the lights go out. There is a power cut. A couple of lighters light up, but there is lots of giggling and people actually start talking to each other. They are no longer so self-aware and feel much more confident to talk to each other.

The lights are out for about half an hour. Although there is no music, it does not seem to matter because everyone is talking and joking, and they all seem to be enjoying themselves. Suddenly the power comes back on again. Within a very short space of time, the magical atmosphere has diminished. People have become self-aware and identifiable again.

See CD-ROM for activities, websites and further reading.

This process was described in an experiment carried out in 1973 by Gergen et al., known as the black room experiment. Gergen et al. had two groups of subjects who spent an hour together. One group of subjects were in a completely darkened room and the other group were in a normally lit room. In the dark room, the subjects were far more friendly, chatting to total strangers, exploring the room and some even beginning to discuss far more serious matters. Even more amazing was that 90 per cent of the subjects actually became intentionally involved in physical contact with each other, 50 per cent hugging each other and 80 per cent admitting to being sexually aroused. In contrast to this, the control subjects talked politely in the light for the whole hour.

The Social Psychological Approach

Researcher(s)	Focus of study
Milgram	Obedience to a malevolent authority
Piliavin, Rodin and Piliavin	Helping behaviour in the New York subway and factors that influence helping
Reicher and Haslam	To consider whether the principles of social identity theory might explain people's behaviour in an institutional setting (BBC prison experiment)

The social psychological approach aims to investigate our social behaviour: how we behave in (and sometimes because of) the presence of others. In particular, researchers have looked at social interaction or social influence. This involves studying how our actions can be affected by others, for example an authority figure, as in Milgram's study. Some studies of social influence suggest that our behaviour is influenced by the context in which we find ourselves, such as Zimbardo et al.'s Stanford prison experiment. Reicher and Haslam's study suggests that our behaviour is affected by our group identity.

Some social psychological studies focus on social cognition. These aim to explain how our social understanding and the beliefs we hold influence our behaviour. When we are trying to understand why someone has done or said something, do we look to the person or do we look to the situation for the causes of the behaviour? The Piliavin et al. study on the New York subway demonstrates how helping behaviour changes according to the social situation, for example, there was no diffusion of responsibility in the enclosed space of the subway carriage. This study illustrates an aspect of social cognition, in terms of the cost–benefit analysis a potential helper makes in an emergency situation, showing that the way they think influences the way they behave.

STRENGTHS AND WEAKNESSES

The social psychological approach

- The social approach helps us to consider how far we act according to our own free will and how far factors in the social environment may determine our behaviour. Two of the studies we have considered in this chapter show that we are more influenced by others than we might like to think (Milgram; Zimbardo et al.). These challenge our belief that we act autonomously (according to our own free will).

  While we remain responsible for our actions, and the playground wail of 'He made me do it!' is no defence, it is very important for us to understand how we respond to social influence or social behaviour. For example, it is useful to recognise that authority figures have control over us, because armed with this information we should be able to work out that we have to be very careful to whom we give such authority. Milgram's work can be seen as dark and depressing, on the one hand, revealing something negative about humanity. On the other hand, however, Milgram said that although it seems we are 'puppets' of our social environments, we are in fact 'puppets with power'. In a democracy we have power to choose those in authority, and Milgram's work cautions us we should treat that power with respect and use it wisely. Reicher and Haslam, however, looked at social influence from another angle, focusing on those participants who did not follow their role – the guards in Zimbardo's study who were not cruel, but firm and fair – and considered in their own study that if it is not the roles they occupy that might lead people to support a tyranny, what exactly might the factors be that induce people to support a tyrannical regime? Is it their free will or are other social and cognitive factors at work and influencing their behaviour?

- The social approach can offer possible solutions to problems in the real world. Zimbardo et al.'s work shows us that if we had the inclination and resources to do so, we could reform the prison service and perhaps solve the humanitarian issues surrounding how we treat those who have wronged us and those who watch over them. Unfortunately, this remains a fantasy in most cultures, where the emphasis of the penal service is on revenge and punishment, and the outcome is high recidivism by prisoners on release, and consequently more misery.

- On a more positive note, the study by Piliavin et al. showed that, contrary to the case of Kitty Genovese and the depressing levels of help demonstrated in laboratory studies, the people on the New York subway did come forward to help a fellow passenger in need. This demonstrates the problems with laboratory studies of social behaviour, which lack ecological validity and are not good predictors of real-life behaviour.

- There are a number of methodological problems that arise when studying social behaviour. Demand characteristics may be a problem. In laboratory studies especially, findings may not be valid because subjects are simply responding to the demand characteristics present in the study. Orne (1968) suggests that this was what was happening in Milgram's study.

- There are difficulties applying controls to people, so it is hard to establish that the IV is a causal factor. This is especially true in field experiments, such as the one carried out by Piliavin et al. on the New York subway. Also, field experiments and independent groups designs are the most likely experimental method and experimental design to be affected by extraneous variables.

- Validity over time makes us question the value of research carried out a long time ago. Given that Milgram's obedience study and the Piliavin et al. study (subway Samaritan) were both carried out during the 1960s, this means we must be cautious in generalising the findings from those studies to people today.

- Cultural differences in behaviour are often overlooked when generalising results, and this leads to findings being used to describe people in general, when in fact the research carries an ethnocentric bias. For example, can the social psychological studies in the core studies which were carried out in New York and at Yale University in the USA, and at the Elstree Film Studios in Hertfordshire, UK, be used to generalise to a broader population, in particular to non-western cultures?

Cognitive psychology

Almost everything we do causes us to think. We think about what we are going to do, and then we think about what we have done. We plan, we discuss, we imagine, we remember, we try to make sense of both the concrete and the social world around us, and even when we are unable to do this, we continue to try. Sometimes, working out why produces the wrong answer, but the processes involved are all interlinked, and they all involve cognition.

Before the invention of computers, our understanding of how we processed information was limited. Much of the work in psychology involved simply looking at behaviour by observing the types of responses that were produced by different types of stimuli. There was little research on what happened between the stimulus and the response, not only because the techniques to investigate these processes were limited, but also because knowledge in this area was quite basic. However, the computer analogy opened up a whole new way of looking at the way the brain processes information. This information-processing approach works as follows:

1. Input – through one of the senses (e.g. eyes or ears).

2. Processing – this occurs using currently installed software (previous experience and knowledge).

3. Response – which may be action or chosen inaction.

Cognitive psychology is involved in understanding the middle process, that is, how the information is processed and what kinds of choices are made. Many of the choices we make may not be rational. For example, we may know that chocolate is fattening and that we desperately want to lose weight, but we still buy a large bar of chocolate and eat it. Logic suggests that this would not happen if processing were based on logic alone, but we are often totally illogical. However, this information-processing model has opened up study in this area, allowing us to investigate these processes using laboratory-based methods and experiments.

This idea of information processing is somewhat removed from the perspective of reductionism, which suggests that all our responses can be reduced to the most basic explanation. Take, for example, the chocolate analogy. The reductionist explanation might be something like this: chocolate-eating produces a feeling of happiness which the body desires; therefore, the decision to eat chocolate can be reduced to the most basic explanation, that is, we are simply responding to a biological need produced by our bodies – this sounds like a very good explanation if you want to excuse your future chocolate consumption! However, in order to satiate this feeling, we need to have knowledge of where to obtain chocolate, what is required to buy it, how to get to the shop, and so on. Therefore, we might consider the reductionist approach as aiding our understanding of how cognitive processes work and interrelate.

Cognitive psychology covers a number of areas – memory, perception, language, thinking and attention – and all these processes are interconnected. You would find it very difficult to do one without involving another. For example, you cannot identify an object you have seen without thinking what it is called. In fact, you will not even try to identify it unless you happen to be looking in the right place at the right time (paying attention to it); and if you identify it as something frightening, you will have to work out how to escape. There is also a huge debate about the fact that you cannot think without language, and this is mentioned later in this chapter, in the section on language (see page 131).

One of the questions psychologists frequently ask is whether we are born with cognitive skills or acquire them as we mature. Most psychologists believe that we are born with very basic skills, and that most of our skills develop through a process of maturation and experience (see Chapter 4).

This chapter focuses on three areas of cognition:

1. The topic of memory is addressed by looking at the structure and function of our memories and how accurate they really are.

2. We will then consider social cognition, by addressing how we integrate and assimilate social information in order to facilitate relationships, and will consider how people with autism have difficulty with these skills.

3. The last section focuses on whether language is an innate ability in humans or is simply learned, and whether it is beyond the capability of other species to acquire language.

Memory

We will begin this section by looking at one of the most fundamental and complex of human cognitive abilities: the human memory. In fact, when considering cognition, it is hard to start anywhere else, because what we have stored in our memory forms the basis of what makes us who we are and dictates how we behave. It is for this reason that the section on memory is the longest in this book.

What is memory?

It is difficult to find a precise definition of 'memory', but it is often referred to as the ability to retain information and demonstrate retention through behaviour. If we could not retain and use information that we have already discovered, it would mean that for every new experience we would have to process huge amounts of information, which could be very costly in terms of the time it might take.

> Brian was on holiday in Africa. He was sitting by a lake, watching some beautiful creatures flying above the surface of the water. He was not sure what they were, but they looked almost translucent, reflected in the sunlight. Then he noticed a ripple on the water, and suddenly something long started to appear. It was green in colour and looked quite shiny. Whatever it was, it seemed to be getting longer as it approached him. Then he saw what looked like two little beady eyes on the top of what must have been its head, and they were looking at him. Suddenly it came out of the water towards him, its long body propelled by four short, thick legs, and it flicked its long, leathery tail. Its mouth opened, and snap. . .

In this example, if Brian had been able to store information in his memory, he would have been aware that lakes in Africa may well be inhabited by crocodiles, and that their shores are not the safest places to sit and contemplate the day. Because he had to process each piece of information as he received it, the time it would have taken to realise that the creature was not friendly was too long to enable Brian to save himself.

Memory is a fundamental part of each of us and our everyday lives. Our memories serve to tell us who we are, to help us make sense of the situations in which we find ourselves, and to enable us to make plans for the future. In fact, memory is so much a part of what and who we are that it is almost impossible to imagine what it must be like to have no recollection of anything. Think of all the things you do automatically every day which rely on stored knowledge, such as getting dressed, finding your way round, talking, writing and reading, recognising people, remembering past events or information you have been told. Is there anything you can do without referring to something you have stored in your memory?

How does memory work?

People who have lost their memory, for whatever reason, are called amnesics. The classic portrayal of amnesics in the media tends to suggest that they forget everything, but this is not the case. If you think of the things we learn and store in our memories, such as a knowledge of language or how to dress ourselves, you will realise that amnesics rarely lose these abilities. What they seem to lose is the memory of who they are, because they have no information relating to their past. These past memories are not stored as if they were recorded on videotape – although this is a commonly held belief by people who do not understand how memory works. Television dramas tend to support this idea, with dramatic scenes of hypnotherapists gaining access to previously lost information by hypnotising their clients. What actually happens is that we seem to unconsciously select information to store, and overwrite similar experiences until they become merged into one memory. Memory is a dynamic process which is constantly being updated or changed by our experiences.

Although psychologists often consider what happens when memory becomes disrupted, they are also interested in how memory is structured and how it actually works. The structures are the various component parts, like short-term memory and long-term memory, and the processes are how information is taken in and stored and then recalled.

Psychologists have discovered that there are a number of factors which influence whether information is stored or simply forgotten. You do not remember all the information you are told: you may remember the gist of it or a reasonable amount, but only for a limited period, no matter how hard you tried to learn it (think of examination revision). However, it has been found that we do tend to store information on a more long-term basis if it is very different to other information, if it is rich in detail, if it is connected to other things we know, or if it is personally important to us.

The three processes of memory

We are now going to look at how we take in information and store it, and how we can access it when we need to – the three processes of memory. In order to understand what these processes are, imagine looking up a telephone number in your local directory; then you put the directory away; and finally you write down the number.

1. The first process involves **encoding** the information, that is, you took the relevant numbers into your memory system. Therefore, encoding is the acquisition of knowledge and the creation of an internal representation to be stored.

   There are three types of encoding:

   - **Acoustic/phonetic encoding**, or encoding for sound, is when you hear in your head what someone has just said to you, or you keep information in your head (in this case, the telephone number).

   - **Visual encoding** is used to produce an image of what something or someone looks like.

   - **Semantic encoding**, or encoding for meaning, is when you process information by thinking about what it actually means rather than what it looks or sounds like. This seems to produce the best storage. In fact, this method is so good that it is often used to remember lists of things. Take, for example, the colours of the spectrum. You probably know that they are red, orange, yellow, green, blue, indigo and violet. How can you remember what order they come in? The best way is to take the first letter of each word, R, O, Y, G, B, I, V, and then make a sentence which has meaning, using those meaningless initials (e.g. Richard of York gave battle in vain). This method of semantic encoding is called using **mnemonics**, or memory aids.

Terms in bold are included in the Glossary for Chapter 3 on the CD-ROM.

2. The second process is the **storage** of the information. This requires you to retain the information in an understandable form so that you can then go on to the third process. With our phone number, we will probably have to keep saying it to ourselves as a way of storing the information. This is because the numbers have little meaning and are not really of any great importance to us.

3. Finally, you undertake the **retrieval** of the information, that is, you get the information back from where you stored it. This is done either by recognition, which involves matching a stored item with something in your environment, or by recalling it, that is bringing it back into your conscious awareness.

Continuing with the idea of the telephone number, when you went to write it down having put the directory away, you would have had to recall it as you would not be matching it against any other numbers. However, the chances of remembering it for any length of time are fairly remote. On the other hand, you are unlikely to have problems remembering your own phone number. This seems to indicate that there is more than one type of memory: memory which does not last for very long (**short-term memory – STM**) and memory which lasts perhaps for ever (**long-term memory – LTM**).

Types of memory

The first psychologists to notice that there is more than one type of memory also discovered that people who sustained brain damage sometimes lost either their STM or their LTM. This indicated that there must be different types of memory store, and they used this information to help them try to understand the component parts of memory and how they fit together.

Sensory memory

The first type of memory is known as **sensory memory**. This is necessary because if we do not retain an impression of what we have experienced, we will be unable to decide whether we want to begin to process it adequately in order to understand it or to disregard it. Look around the room you are in. There are lots of objects in the room which you are aware of, although perhaps not in any detail. If you were asked to look for a pen you would need to be aware of the potential of all the objects before you could decide whether or not they are pens, or whether they are likely to contain a pen. If the impression is that a pen may be present, you would decide not to disregard the objects and would process them further.

It is called sensory memory because it refers to a fleeting memory which is registered by the sensory receptors of sight (**iconic memory**) and sound (**echoic memory**). This information is stored within these receptors and not at a central location; it lasts for seconds and then it is gone. For example, imagine you are watching TV or reading when someone speaks to you. Just as you are about to say 'What did you say?', you realise that you can 'play back' the words which are still echoing in your head, but only for a few seconds after the event, and then that 'sensation' is gone.

Short-term memory

Psychologists, including Atkinson and Shiffrin (1971), decided that information which stayed in consciousness after encoding entered short-term memory, while information which left conscious awareness but could later be recalled had been put into long-term memory.

Research suggests that both visual and auditory information from sensory memory is successfully passed on to STM, which allows us to store it for long enough to be able to use it (Sperling 1963; Broadbent 1958). An example of how this works is retaining the phone number for long enough to dial it, although it may be forgotten soon after. It is also the memory store that allows us to have a conversation with someone. You may not remember the whole content of a conversation, but if you could not remember any of what the person you are talking to has just said, how would you be able to answer them? Therefore, you need to retain that information for a short period of time.

We know that the capacity of STM is limited. In 1956, George Miller gave the most famous account of the capacity of STM in his article, 'The magic number seven, plus or minus two'. Here he claims that we can retain between five and nine pieces of information in STM. He also explained that we can increase the capacity of STM by joining pieces of information together. If I asked you to remember the digits 0, 2, 0, 7, 9, 4, 6, 1, 4, 3, 2 individually, you would find that your STM memory was full, but if you put those letters together to form chunks, you would not have a problem remembering them – 020 7946 1432.

Another example of how we can increase STM capacity is by putting together information that would otherwise have no meaning. If you were asked to remember the letters T, W, A, I, B, M, B, A, B, B, C, you might be able to do so, but if you were asked to remember TWA (Trans World Airlines), IBM (the computer company), BA (British Airways) and BBC (British Broadcasting Corporation), it is likely that you would have no trouble at all. Such organisation of information increases the storage capacity of STM by imposing units of meaning on otherwise unrelated items, each unit equalling one 'chunk'.

Long-term memory

Some of the things we experience or learn as we grow up stay with us for very long periods – sometimes for the whole of our lives. This information has gone into long-term memory and seems to be fairly stable. No one has ever filled their LTM, although sometimes it feels as if you cannot store any more information. When we say we have forgotten something, this often means that we are unable to retrieve information from our long-term memory. We believe that one cause of forgetting is a result of the memory trace no longer being available (having decayed), which could be through lack of activation of information or through interference from other memories. This interference could be in the form of overwriting the memory or confusing it with other similar memories. Another cause of forgetting may be a result of not being able to get at the stored information, that is, lack of accessibility. This is when you know you know something but cannot actually remember what it is that you know.

Clive Wearing

The case of Clive Wearing illustrates how important our memories are to us and how they make us the people we are today, with our past experiences and our future aspirations.

Clive was the chorus master of the London Sinfonietta, a brilliant musician, with a wonderful career and a delightful young wife. One day he complained of a headache, which was the beginning of a cruel and vicious illness. The cold sore virus (herpes simplex) had attacked part of his brain and caused irreversible damage. This resulted in the loss of both his STM and LTM. According to his wife, 'He lives in a blinkered moment in time with no past to anchor it to and no future to look ahead to.' He recognised his wife when she visited, but forgot having seen her the minute she went out of the door. If she walked back into the room, he could not remember the previous encounter, so he acted as if he had not seen her for years and greeted her with the same enthusiasm as he did only five minutes before. His case is one of the most upsetting, as he had lost all sense of who he was and where he was going. He had no recollection of his past and no idea of any future.

Clive Wearing

Models of memory

Using the information-processing idea, psychologists have constructed a number of models of memory to explain how memory works. (You should think of a model as being no more than a theory.) Psychologists then use various experiments to try to support the model, but if the results show that the model is not quite right, they then have to modify their original design.

The multi-store model (Atkinson and Shiffrin 1968)

Atkinson and Shiffrin proposed the first model of memory, which was very simple and involved information passing into sensory memory, then into short-term memory and finally into long-term memory.

According to this model, incoming information is received by the sensory register and is either selected for further processing or lost. If it is selected, it goes into short-term memory. Here it can be retained for a limited period of time before it is lost, unless we choose to transfer it to long-term memory. The way this happens is that we have to say it over and over again to ourselves, which is called rehearsal. In the diagram, rehearsal is shown by the loop in the STM. According to this model, unrehearsed items are forgotten whereas stored items can be retrieved.

There is a significant amount of evidence to support the multi-store model, and it is worth considering this in order to decide whether the model is acceptable or just too simplistic.

Support for the multi-store model

The first kind of evidence comes from **free recall experiments**, where people are asked to remember lists (of 20 words, for example), and then recall the words in any order they like. Evidence has shown that participants usually recall more items from the end of the list, but they also recall quite a few from the beginning of the list.

It has been suggested that this is because the first words enter STM, where there is probably no other material, so they are likely to be rehearsed and thus transferred to LTM (the **primacy effect**). As more words are presented, the STM capacity fills up and there is no chance to rehearse or transfer later words to LTM. Therefore, the items at the end of the list can only be retained in STM (the **recency effect**, Murdock 1962). It is believed that the reason why the words in the middle are usually lost is because they cannot be rehearsed sufficiently to transfer them into LTM. You may have experienced something similar yourself in a lesson or a lecture. Immediately after the lesson you may recall the beginning and the end, but remember very little of the information you were given in the middle.

There is further support for the multi-store model from people who have sustained brain damage. There are individuals who have lost one part of their memory, but the other is intact (i.e. they have lost either their STM or their LTM).

One piece of evidence comes from a person known by his initials, KF, who was studied by Shallice and Warrington (1970). KF was in his twenties when he had a motorcycle accident, as a result of which he suffered damage to the left parieto-occipital region of his brain, which left him with a damaged STM. If he was given a list of numbers to learn, he found he could sometimes recall two items, but often only one. His LTM was not damaged, however, and he could remember things that he had 'stored' before his accident. The strange thing about him was that he seemed to be able to learn new information even though his STM was impaired.

Although this evidence supports the multi-store model, it also questions its accuracy as it challenges how the model works. The model states that the only way we can store information in LTM is by first taking it into STM, then 'rehearsing' it, and finally passing it into LTM. If KF had a damaged STM, how did the information get into LTM? This is the kind of evidence which led people to question the validity of the model and to undertake further research into alternative explanations for the working of memory.

There are a number of further examples of amnesics which support the model. One is HM, who suffered with severe epilepsy from the age of 16. In fact, his epilepsy was so bad that he had a number of seizures on a daily basis, which seriously impaired his quality of life. In 1953 he went into hospital for surgery to remove part of his temporal lobes, as this was where the seizures originated. The seizures stopped immediately after the surgery, but within hours the medical staff discovered that HM did not recognise them and could not find his bedroom in the hospital. It appeared that he was also unable to store any new information. Although the operation was a success in terms of what it set out to achieve, the cost to HM was the loss of his ability to transfer any new information to his LTM, although his STM was seemingly intact. Interestingly, he can remember his life up until a few years before the operation, but any new information is lost as soon as it is learned. Again, this provides evidence that STM and LTM are separate systems, although perhaps they are not as simple as was first hypothesised.

Weaknesses of the multi-store model

The multi-store model has a number of weaknesses. You may well have experienced instances when something fairly meaningless has happened to you and you probably do not think about it again. Then, out of the blue, whatever it was springs to mind. That incident has been transferred to LTM without you having repeated it over and over to yourself. According to the multi-store model, this cannot happen.

Another problem with the model is the description of STM. Remember that STM is believed to have a limited capacity and is 'fragile', in that the information can be disrupted easily or lost. If it is simply a passive 'holding bay' for information which can be disrupted in this way, it would indicate that the information is not processed at all. But how do you decide what information to store long-term and what information you can discard?

Imagine you are given a tube containing seven sweets. If you try to push another sweet into the end of the tube which is closest to you, a sweet falls out of the far end.

No matter what you do, you cannot fit more than seven sweets in that tube. Now imagine every piece of information around you as a sweet. There are so many sweets that you could put into the tube that there is never a shortage (these sweets could be spoken or read words or numbers, or visual images such as faces or objects), but you cannot 'see' the sweets unless they are in the tube.

How do you decide which ones to eat (i.e. store on a permanent basis)? If they are rushing through the tube (STM) quickly and are simply filling vacant spots, this implies that you are passive in the process. The problem is that you cannot be passive, because if you were, you would not actually analyse the nature of the sweets sufficiently to decide which are worth eating and which ones you should allow to fall out of the tube (i.e. you would not be able to decide which information to send into LTM). Therefore, you must analyse these sweets (information) to a certain extent.

This whole idea contradicts the multi-store model, which states that STM is a passive store where no information processing takes place. As we have seen, you *must* process the information in order to decide whether you want to store it or not.

> Carole was on a diet, but she was given a large box of chocolates for her birthday. When she was given them she decided that she would eat them slowly, a couple every day, in order not to make her diet pointless. For the first couple of days, she looked at each one before deciding whether she wanted to eat it or not. She looked for the soft centres and noticed the shape, and whether it was milk or plain chocolate. She could describe in detail which ones she had eaten and what they were like. On the third day she felt really miserable. When she got in from college she grabbed the box of chocolates, sat down in front of the TV and proceeded to eat her way through the remainder of the box. She paid no attention to the type of chocolate and did not even notice what each one tasted like. She was so fed up that she just kept on eating until they were all gone – and then felt very sick!

If you were to ask Carole what the chocolates were like, do you think she could tell you about all of them, or would she only remember the ones she had deliberated over when she first opened the box? Carole would probably only remember the ones she ate on the first day. The reason is that she processed far more information about these than the others. This would indicate that the information she stored was the information which received more processing. The information which received little processing was forgotten. As we have seen, Atkinson and Shiffrin's model would claim that the only way the information would have been stored in LTM was if it were rehearsed, or said over and over again. Surely Carole did not say 'dark chocolate truffle' over and over again to herself?

It would make sense to conclude that rehearsal is not necessarily the process we use to transfer information from STM to LTM. It seems likely that it is not simply repeating information to ourselves which decides whether or not that information should be put into long-term storage. Perhaps it has something to do with the amount of processing we give to pieces of information?

The levels of processing model

Craik and Lockhart (1972) supported this theory of processing with their model of memory. They argued that it is not rehearsal as such which is important, but rather what is done with the material *during* that rehearsal (i.e. how well it is processed). They suggest that it is this alone which will determine the duration of the memory. The methods we use for this processing are those we looked at when we talked about encoding (see page 86, above), that is, what it looks like, what it sounds like and what it means.

Craik and Lockhart claim that iconic processing (what something looks like) requires shallow processing. If you go on to consider what something sounds like, that requires additional processing. If you then take into account what the thing actually means, you will have to process the information more deeply still.

There is a problem here: the only way we can test what has been stored is to look at what we can remember. If the only way we can test depth is to look at how many words we can remember, and if how many words we can remember is taken as a measure of depth, then what we are really saying is that the only things which will be retrievable will be those that have been stored, and the only things which have been stored will be the things that are retrievable. This gives us no idea of how well we processed the information we have retrieved; so if we accept the levels of processing model, we have to conclude that the processing used to store information must have been semantic processing. However, further research has shown that it is the information and its relevance to the participant which will be more effective in deciding whether information is stored or not.

The working memory model

In another criticism of the multi-store model of memory, Baddeley and Hitch (1974) suggested that the idea of short-term memory being a kind of passive store (and a small one at that) was inadequate. They said that this idea of STM should be replaced with a '**working memory**' store – a kind of conscious work area, which has the ability to hold several facts or thoughts in memory temporarily while solving a problem or performing a task. According to their model, working memory consists of four parts:

1. The **central executive** (responsible for **executive function**), which is like our conscious awareness. The term, which is a business metaphor, suggests that the central executive monitors all the different departments within an organisation so that the company trades in the most efficient and effective way. According to Shallice (1982), this supervisory attentional system has a limited capacity and is used for tasks which involve planning or decision making, helping when automatic processes appear to be running into difficulty (e.g. while driving, you find you are approaching an area with complex roadworks) – in novel, dangerous or technically difficult situations.

2. The **phonological loop**, which is like an inner voice.

3. The **visuospatial sketch pad**, which is like an inner eye.

4. The **episodic buffer**, which is a limited-capacity, temporary storage system capable of integrating information from the phonological loop or the visuospatial sketch pad, with information from LTM, into a single representation of an episode. It is thought to be controlled by the central executive. We might think of it as a 'holding bay' where information is stored temporarily, allowing the central executive to think about the information and manipulate and modify it if necessary. According to Baddeley (2000: 421), the episodic buffer 'provides not only a mechanism for modelling the environment, but also for creating new cognitive representations, which in turn might facilitate problem solving'.

Evidence to support the idea of a working memory model comes from investigations into the activity of the frontal lobes of the brain when participants are required to carry out tasks such as planning, focusing attention on an object, switching between tasks and focusing on two tasks which need to be performed at the same time. The idea behind such tasks is that if the working memory is required to work hard, the central executive has to manage the increased workload. Participants who have completed such tasks have been found to have increased levels of blood flow in specific areas of the frontal lobes (using PET scans and MRI techniques – see Chapter 5, page 249).

The concept of working memory is not really of great concern to us here, although it becomes more relevant in the next study in this chapter where poor executive function is considered to be an explanation of some of the difficulties experienced by people with autism. However, if you are interested in reading more about the workings of our memory, this model is the one which is now more widely accepted as an explanation of how we actively process information in conscious awareness and briefly store the information to be processed. It can help to explain tasks such as verbal reasoning and mental arithmetic, although there is still a lack of evidence to support *all* aspects of the model.

Is memory like a tape recorder?

So far, we have looked at how memory seems to be structured. We now need to return to the notion that information is not stored in our memory in the same way as a video recorder would record information, unchanged throughout the course of our lives. Our memory does not document everything we experience and recall it as necessary. In fact, many of the things we experience are not stored, and other things are stored inaccurately.

It was a cold afternoon in late September and two women were standing talking, outside their adjacent front gates. Both carried bags of shopping and one woman had a young girl standing by her side.

'I can't believe your Emily is going off to university. It only seems like yesterday when she was playing in the front garden with our Paul,' said the other woman to the girl's mother.

The young girl shuffled. God, she was bored, and all she wanted to do was go inside and watch TV.

'Come on, Mum, I'm cold and I want to finish packing.'

'I remember the first day your mum and I took you to school,' said the other woman, totally ignoring her comment. 'You had a cream-coloured coat on, and just as you were going into the school you slipped over on the ice and made your coat all dirty, and you cried and cried. You refused to go in and you were clinging to your mum's hand and begging her to take you home. It only seems like yesterday.'

'No, Elsie, that wasn't her first day at school. That was when we took the children to see Father Christmas, and she had asked me if she could wear her new coat so she would look smart when she went in to tell him what she wanted for Christmas. Don't you remember, it was your Paul who pushed her over on the way into the shop?' said Emily's mother.

'No, it wasn't,' said Emily. 'I remember that coat and falling over, but it was when I was on my way to Sophie's birthday party and I didn't want to go in because I had mud on my knees.'

How do we know which was the true story? Each version was true for the teller, but the actual truth may have been a different version altogether!

The next section helps to explain how we use our memories in order to make sense of our environment, rather than simply having a list of information that we draw on as and when necessary. It will also help you to understand how our memories become distorted – or positively inaccurate.

Schema theory

Schema theory helps to explain many pieces of research, especially the work of Loftus and Palmer, the core study described in this section (page 99) which focuses on memory.

Endel Tulving (1972) suggested that we have two different types of memory: **episodic memory**, which is a memory of episodes (or events in our lives), and **semantic memory**, which is a memory of facts (e.g. trees lose their leaves in winter). Sometimes the experience of an episode leads us to learn new facts. Often (even when we do not have a damaged memory) we remember the facts rather than the actual episode. Why this happens can be explained in part by schema theory.

Constructing schemata

Each fact that we learn as a result of our experiences becomes part of a schema, which is a kind of packet of information about something. It may help you to think of schemata as files in the drawer of a filing cabinet. You have schemata about school, work, holidays, clubs, picnics, parties, and so on. You simply open the drawer of the filing cabinet in your head, take out the relevant file and look up the information in a fraction of a second.

We have schemata for all different types of objects, events and situations and they are put together from the experiences we have had and the information we have gathered. They seem to contain a kind of prototype which develops from this information, and the amount of detail they contain will vary accordingly.

Think back to your fifth birthday. What do you think you did on that day? The majority of you would say that you had a party with a cake, cards and presents. It is very unlikely that you actually remember your fifth birthday, but you will have no problem thinking what it was probably like. You make inferences about the situation, using information about what happens at birthday parties, stored from past experiences and acquired information. In other words, you are describing what your schemata lead you to believe it was like, rather than how it really was. As you will see in the Loftus and Palmer study, the expectations caused by our schemata can lead us to produce inaccurate and distorted versions of events. This is another example of the errors in human processing that make us question the machine analogy proposed by the information-processing model.

Schema theory shows how we make use of our memory to enable us to repeat quickly and efficiently behaviours or experiences that occur regularly in our lives, or to manage experiences similar to those we have lived through before. Our knowledge of a typical (or perhaps stereotypical) trip to the supermarket means we are able to do the weekly shop efficiently, without having to keep learning how to do it. By putting schemata in order, we are able to produce a script or template for what to expect and how to behave.

As we have seen, schema theory emphasises the fact that what we remember is influenced by what we already know. It also helps to explain how the ideas, beliefs and attitudes we hold have an effect on what we will remember about an event.

Other areas of research have demonstrated how our schemata influence our memories. If you were asked to imagine going to a restaurant and told to list 20 things that happened during the course of your time there, you would include many of the same things as other people such as being seated, reading the menu, ordering food, having drinks and paying the bill. Such a study, conducted by Bower, Black and Turner (1979), involving 32 people, found that 73 per cent included the following six events on their list: sitting down, looking at a menu, ordering, eating, paying the bill and leaving the restaurant.

The subjects in this piece of research named the same events as they obviously had experience of restaurants and knew exactly what went on. Now imagine you are a small child and the only 'restaurant' you have been to is McDonald's. What sort of things would you describe if you were asked the same question? Then you visit a Harvester or Beefeater restaurant, and your knowledge of restaurants increases enormously as you realise that restaurants involve sitting down at a table, reading the menu and having food brought to you rather than having to queue for it. Then you visit somewhere like the Savoy in London and things are different again.

With growing experience and knowledge, the packet of information contained in your brain which stores information about a certain event will increase in size as you get older. You will be able to use this stored knowledge to answer questions and interpret conversations without having to have all the details presented to you. You would understand what was meant by, 'We went to the Harvester last night and the service was excellent', without wondering what on earth the person was talking about.

How do schemata affect memories?

1. A schema guides the selection of what is encoded and stored in memory. You are unlikely to remember irrelevant details of events (e.g. what clothes you wore when you sat your GCSEs, assuming that it was not school uniform). A schema also provides a framework to store new information, like a file marked 'restaurant'.

2. You abstract information from events. This means that you take out and store only some of the information from different events if there are a number of them which are all very similar. To return to the example of your fifth birthday, it is likely that all you can remember is general information about birthdays – presents, cakes, parties, and so on. This also happens with conversations – you only remember the gist of them, not all the contents.

3. Because we have integrated lots of information into our schemata, they help us to interpret different situations about which we have very limited knowledge. We may end up having to use inferences in the light of past knowledge and previous experiences.

4. Memories can also be distorted to fit prior expectations, and in order to make them consistent with your existing schemata, they may actually be transformed. This is how eyewitness testimony gets blurred – you see what you expect to see.

5. A schema may also aid retrieval. You can sometimes remember what happened by searching through the information you have already stored in a schema, to see if you recognise what is required.

Schemata and stories

The idea of schema theory was introduced by Frederick Bartlett in 1932 in order to explain why, when people remember stories, they regularly leave out some details and introduce what he called 'rationalisations' which they use to make the stories make sense. He investigated this using a story called 'The war of the ghosts', asking people to recall a story which contained unfamiliar information. He found that they did not remember the story as it was told, but made errors in their recall, because they used their schemata to interpret the story and provide information which they believed was included rather than what was actually there.

Bartlett asked people to recall the story at intervals over time, showing that distortions occurred. The story was made more westernised, for example, with 'fishing' substituted for 'hunting seals'. In addition, the amount recalled decreased over time and there were further distortions.

Bartlett believed that when people remember stories, there is a tendency for them to sacrifice detailed recall in favour of 'making sense' of the information provided. He demonstrated that rather than being like computer memory, where input information is retrieved unaltered, human memory is **reconstructive** in nature. When we process information, we try to make it logical, sensible and coherent. As we have already seen (above), this means that we include what could or should have happened according to our expectations, so our memory is likely to be an imperfect record of events and can be a complete distortion, governed by our biases and prejudices. You may be unaware of ever doing this as it is not a conscious process, but if you want to see it in real life, just ask two squabbling siblings for their version of events and see how much they differ.

THE STUDY

E.F. Loftus and J.J. Palmer (1974) 'Reconstruction of automobile destruction: An example of the interaction between language and memory'

Journal of Verbal Learning and Verbal Behaviour, 13: 585–9

BACKGROUND

Bartlett's ideas are still widely accepted as they explain how the information we take in is affected by already existing schemata representing previous knowledge. His work, however, has its critics. His findings were largely qualitative, as it is very difficult to establish objective measures of memory distortion. Later researchers, however, have undertaken laboratory studies to investigate scientifically the reconstructive nature of human memory and to consider some of the factors which lead to these distortions. An eminent researcher in this field is Elizabeth Loftus, who, along with colleagues, has carried out a series of studies particularly concerning the reliability of eyewitness testimony.

It is interesting that eyewitness testimony was once considered one of the most important factors in court cases. Many suspects were found guilty as a result of their identification by witnesses and witness reports of events. But if human memory is reconstructive, should we rely on this in a court of law?

Loftus was concerned not only with the fragility of memory, but also with the effects of stress on the ability of victims to recall facts. Loftus and Burns (1982) showed their subjects a film of a hold-up and then tested their memory for details. The experimental group saw a violent version of the film where one of the members of a group of young boys is shot and collapses on the floor, clutching his bleeding face. The control group saw the same film, but this scene was omitted. Instead, their film changed to a scene inside the bank where the manager is explaining to staff and customers exactly what has happened.

Loftus and Burns found that subjects who saw the violent version had significantly less memory for details of events before the shooting. Most subjects failed to mention that one of the boys had a large number '17' on his jersey, which was very obvious from the film. There were actually 16 items that subjects could have recalled, but those who had seen the violent version of the film recalled significantly less than the other group on 14 of those items.

The core study that we are concerned with here focuses on the effects of language on memory changes. Loftus suggested that there are two types of information that affect our memory of an event:

- information gained at the time of the event;
- information gained after the event (subsequent information).

Loftus was interested in how you can actually change a witness's recollection of an incident by subtly introducing new information during questioning, that is, *after* the event. This depends on how language is used. For example, one study (Loftus and Zanni, 1975) showed how changing the structure of a question could lead people to reconstruct an event and 'remember' false facts. In the study, film clips were shown and the independent variable was manipulated by asking one of two versions of the critical question:

- In one condition, subjects were asked: 'Did you see **a** broken headlight?' – this question suggests that there may or may not have been a broken headlight.
- In the second condition, subjects were asked: 'Did you see **the** broken headlight?' – the use of the definite article 'the' here suggests that there definitely was a broken headlight, so the subject should have seen it.

The results showed that more of those in the second condition reported seeing a broken headlight, even though there was no broken headlight in the film.

AIMS

Loftus and Palmer carried out two experiments to investigate the effects of language on memory. Their expectation was that information received after the event in the form of leading questions would be integrated into a person's memory. It would form part of the memory and cause the event to be recalled in a way that was consistent with the subsequent information they were given.

KEY CONCEPTS

Leading questions

Loftus and Palmer point out that it was already known that 'some questions are. . .more suggestive than others', and that a legal concept of 'leading questions' existed, along with rules for the use of such questions in the courtroom.

Their definition is as follows: 'A leading question is simply one that, by its form or content, suggests to the witness what answer is desired or leads him to the desired answer.'

We have already considered the example of the broken headlight. Examples from everyday life might include: 'You don't mind babysitting your little brother, do you?', or 'My bum doesn't look too big in these jeans, does it?'

METHOD

Two experiments were carried out to see whether leading questions could change a person's memory of an event. The first experiment also tested the established theory that witnesses are not very good at estimating the speed of vehicles.

Experiment 1

Method and design

This was a laboratory experiment, and the experimental design used was independent groups.

Subjects

Forty-five student subjects were tested in groups of various sizes. For test purposes, it was designed that overall there would be five conditions, with nine subjects providing data for each condition.

Apparatus

Equipment was needed to screen seven film segments from the Evergreen Safety Council of the Seattle Police Department. Each segment lasted between 5 and 30 seconds. The films were safety promotion films, and four of the seven clips contained staged crashes. (There would have been serious ethical concerns about showing real crashes.) The staged crashes had the advantage that the speed at which the vehicles were travelling when they crashed was known: for two of the films it was 40 mph, for one, 20 mph, and for another, 30 mph. This meant the accuracy of speed estimates could be measured.

There were also sets of questionnaires corresponding to the film clips for each subject, to be completed after each clip.

Procedure

All the subjects were shown the seven film clips and were given a questionnaire to complete after each clip. There were two parts to each questionnaire. First, they were asked to 'Give an account of the accident you have just seen', and second, to answer a set of questions relating to the accident. Of the questions asked, the one the researchers were interested in was about the speed of the vehicles at the time of the accident.

In order to counteract order effects, the groups were presented with a different order of films. The entire experiment lasted about an hour and a half.

KEY CONCEPTS

Critical questions

In an experiment, the critical question (or questions) is what is used to measure the dependent variable. It is common for these to be masked in a questionnaire by the use of distracter questions, so that subjects cannot respond to the demand characteristics present when just one question is asked. The fewer questions that are asked, the more likely it is that subjects will work out the purpose of the study and behave so as to support the hypothesis or scupper the study. This needs to be avoided, as it affects the internal validity of the study.

The independent variable was manipulated by changing the wording of the critical question about the speed of vehicles at the time of the accident, using a different verb in the question. The authors theorised that the stronger the verb, the higher the speed estimate would be. The standard format of the critical question was: 'About how fast were the cars going when they _____ each other?' There were five verb conditions: 'contacted', 'hit', 'bumped', 'collided' and 'smashed'.

Each subject received one of the five critical questions in their questionnaires. This means that the independent variable in this experiment was which verb condition the subject was tested in. The dependent variable was the mean speed estimate in miles per hour per condition, thus giving a quantitative measure.

RESULTS

We will look at these in two parts.

1 How accurate are the witnesses' speed estimates?

The accuracy of subjects' speed estimates in miles per hour for the four staged crashes were as follows:

Film	Actual speed (mph)	Mean estimated speed (mph)
1	20	37.7
2	30	36.2
3	40	39.7
4	40	36.1

These results support previous studies in that they indicate that people are not very good at judging how fast a vehicle is actually travelling.

2 Does changing the verb in the critical question affect speed estimates?

The mean speed estimates in miles per hour for each of the five verb conditions were as follows:

Verb	Mean estimated speed (mph)
Smashed	40.8
Collided	39.3
Bumped	38.1
Hit	34
Contacted	31.8

Inferential analysis of these results showed that they were significant, at the $p < 0.05$ level. This shows that the form of the question affected the witnesses' answers.

Why does the wording affect the subject? Loftus and Palmer offer two interpretations. First, it may be due to response bias. This is the tendency to give a response in a certain direction according to the situation. If a subject cannot decide between 30 and 40, the word 'smashed' may cue the response of 40, as it suggests a higher speed. Second, it may be that the language used causes a change in the subject's memory representation of events. Loftus and Palmer say: 'The verb "smashed" may change a subject's memory such that he "sees" that accident as being more severe than it was.'

Loftus and Palmer carried out a second experiment to try to establish which of these interpretations was true. They theorised that if the person's memory had been changed, then they could be expected to 'remember' other details which did not occur, but which would fit in with their belief that the accident took place at a higher speed.

Experiment 2

AIMS

The aim of the second experiment was to see if subjects asked the 'smashed' question would be more likely than two other groups to report seeing broken glass in a filmed accident, when tested one week later. They were compared with a group asked the 'hit' question, and a control group not asked to make a speed estimate. Broken glass would be expected in an accident occurring at high speed, but no broken glass was actually shown in the film. A positive report of broken glass would suggest that the memory of the event was being reconstructed as a result of information (in the form of leading questions) received after the event.

METHOD

Method and design

This was also a laboratory experiment, using independent groups.

Subjects

One hundred and fifty student subjects were divided into three groups, with 50 subjects in each condition.

Apparatus

Equipment was needed to screen a film showing a multiple car crash. The clip lasted less than 1 minute, with the accident itself lasting less than 4 seconds.

Each subject completed two questionnaires. The questionnaires completed immediately after viewing the film clip asked subjects to describe the accident in their own words and to answer a series of questions (Questionnaire 1). The critical question asked subjects to estimate the speed of the vehicles.

There were three conditions:

- 50 subjects were asked: 'About how fast were the cars going when they smashed into each other?'
- 50 subjects were asked: 'About how fast were the cars going when they hit each other?'
- 50 subjects were not asked about the speed of vehicles, and thus acted as a control condition.

A second questionnaire (Questionnaire 2) contained ten questions about the accident. The critical question was: 'Did you see any broken glass?' Subjects responded to this by ticking yes or no.

Procedure

This was a two-part procedure, with subjects seeing the film and filling in one of the three versions of Questionnaire 1 on one day, and returning a week later to complete Questionnaire 2.

RESULTS

Subjects in the 'smashed' condition gave a significantly higher speed estimate than those in the 'hit' condition, 10.46 mph and 8 mph respectively, supporting the finding from the first experiment that the wording of the question can have a considerable effect on the estimate of speed.

Subjects in the 'smashed' condition were also significantly more likely to answer 'yes' to the question 'Did you see any broken glass?' than those in the 'hit' and control conditions. The differences between the control and the 'hit' conditions were negligible.

The distribution of yes and no responses to the question 'Did you see any broken glass?' was as follows:

Response	'Smashed' condition	'Hit' condition	Control
Yes	16	7	6
No	34	43	44

DISCUSSION

The conclusion of the second experiment was that the verb not only affected the estimate of speed, but also the likelihood of subjects thinking they had seen broken glass. Loftus and Palmer explain this by suggesting that subjects took in information from the original scene and then merged this with information given after the event. This produced a memory of the event made up of some of the original information and subsequent information received when they were questioned about it. We are inclined to make our memory make sense, so those subjects who believed the accident had taken place at a higher speed, and was therefore more severe (those in the 'smashed' condition), were more likely to think that broken glass was present.

COMMENTARY: METHODS AND ISSUES

Research method, design and data gathering

The experimental method was used in this study, with both experiments employing an individual groups design. The strengths and weaknesses of this method and design can be applied here.

Quantitative data were gathered and the data-gathering method was self-report by questionnaire.

KEY CONCEPTS

Strengths and weaknesses of self-report data-gathering methods

Self-report data are the data gathered from interviews, questionnaires and psychometric tests, and the detailed notes made in case studies, such as those by Freud (Little Hans) and by Thigpen and Cleckley (The three faces of Eve).

Self-report data can also mean simply asking subjects to answer questions, such as 'Which has more?' in the Samuel and Bryant study on conservation.

The advantages of using self-report data are that we are able to measure cognitive variables such as memory, knowledge and attitudes, which cannot be either observed directly or tested for in any biological test. Without self-report, the study by Loftus and Palmer on memory and language would not be possible, for example.

However, the validity of self-report data can be questioned where subjects are able to deliberately falsify their answers. This may be because they are responding to demand characteristics present in the study, or because of evaluation apprehension: they lie to give a socially desirable answer in order to avoid being judged negatively.

Does the study raise any ethical concerns?

Although the subjects knew that this was a test of memory, the hypothesis about leading questions was not revealed to them, and distracter questions were used to further conceal the exact hypothesis. This was necessary in this study to ensure that demand characteristics did not affect the findings. The researchers chose to show clips of car crashes from safety films which did not contain gruesome images (not even any broken glass!), so they should not have upset the subjects or caused them harm.

Given the findings of the study, we could describe it as ethically worthy, since it contributes to the debate about how witnesses to events should or should not be questioned in order to get a true picture of what happened.

Is the study useful?

Loftus and Palmer's study is one in a series of studies which showed that it is possible to distort the memories of witnesses. This has considerable repercussions for the police. Such studies have led to a great deal of research being carried out into the best way for police officers to question witnesses. However, if the misleading information is blatantly incorrect, people are less likely to take it in and overwrite previous information.

Look again at the responses of subjects in the second experiment. Of 150 subjects questioned, 121 answered correctly, no, including over two-thirds of the subjects in the 'smashed' condition. So perhaps it is not so easy to change a memory for an important event, and we must be careful not to exaggerate the extent to which the recall of witnesses is affected by leading questions.

Validity and reliability of the study

One of the challenges to the internal validity is that the findings of the study are low in generalisability. Where college students are used as subjects in psychological research, generalisability beyond the sample, and to the wider population, is low. For both experiments, Loftus and Palmer drew their sample from a population of university students.

Since most psychologists undertake research while working at a university, the student body provides them with the perfect opportunity sample. The researcher just needs to put up an ad on the noticeboard with the offer of money (or, for psychology students, the possibility of marks towards their course) and stand back to avoid being killed in the rush. Perhaps that is an exaggeration, but the fact is that students are plentiful on campus, and many researchers have benefited from using the time- and cost-effective sample that an undergraduate sample base can provide. The researcher is able to carry out the study from the comfort of their workplace, and students earn some money – so why are student samples a problem?

In order for a sample to be generalisable to the wider population, you need a broader sample than that enticed out of the university library or the student bar.

Sears (1986) reviewed the use of student samples in psychology and considered the problems presented in terms of biasing factors that reduce generalisability, and the consequences of basing our view of human psychology on such a narrow sample base.

Biasing factors include the fact that students tend to represent only a narrow age range, and the upper levels of family income and educational background. This means that they present us with a biased sample, as no other age groups are represented. Moreover, students are not even typical of their own age group, as they are university students because they have displayed the cognitive skills required to gain entry, and in order to do this they tend to be more compliant to authority than their peers in general.

Sears goes on to say that laboratory studies, such as that by Loftus and Palmer, compound the problems, since the students will be more willing to comply with researchers' requests, especially if studies they participate in form part of their course. So we should always be cautious when making generalisations from studies using student samples. (For a well-written and concise review of Sears' work, see Banyard and Grayson 2000.)

In terms of the reliability of the findings, both the experiments carried out provided evidence that memory of an event can be distorted by information introduced afterwards. This supports the reliability of the theory that language – in this case, leading questions – can distort memory.

Since the findings of the two experiments agree, we describe them as being concurrently valid, that is, each supports the validity of the other.

As the study is carried out in the controlled conditions of the laboratory, it is low in ecological validity. In the study, the subjects were asked to watch the film clips and were prepared to recall what they had seen. Accidents happen spontaneously in the real world, and our memories of such events will obviously be different without the luxury of prior warning. We also have to question whether watching film clips of staged accidents leads to memories being laid down or recalled in the same way as they might be under the stressful and distressing circumstances of being a witness to a real car crash involving real people.

Autism and the theory of mind

Although the next section may not seem at first to be linked directly to cognitive psychology, we are going to look at how important cognitions are to another area of our lives – social interactions. Our ability to take in all available information, process it effectively and draw accurate conclusions affects not only our learning ability but also our social skills. If we are unable to use our 'social cognitions' effectively, we can misinterpret or misunderstand different situations, and this can have a dramatic effect on our relationships with others.

You will probably have experienced a time when your social cognitions were not as accurate as they should have been, and this might have resulted in acute embarrassment.

> Julie gazed at Rhys with her wide blue eyes. She snuggled closer and linked her arm in his as they stood outside the door. Rhys was overwhelmed with joy. He had known Julie for a long while and had always adored her, but he thought she had no interest in him. She had been so cool and so distant in the past, but here she was, touching him, looking at him, almost hanging on his every word. Suddenly, after all this time, she seemed so attentive and so affectionate. Perhaps she had realised how devoted he was and how he would always take care of her, how he would make her happy and provide for her all her life. He could feel his heart beating loudly and hoped she wouldn't realise how he could hardly contain himself. He just wanted to hold her in his arms and to kiss her soft pink lips. He turned to face her and started pulling her towards him, his lips aiming at her slightly open mouth. He could feel the world racing beneath his feet and the sound of a million fireworks going off in his brain. 'What on earth are you doing?' shrieked Julie, pushing him away, leaving him in mid pout. 'I was only using you as a decoy while that horrible bloke from up the road went past. He keeps following me and I'm not interested.'

In this section we are going to consider what happens when some children do not develop effective social cognitions and the impact this has on their lives. These children have a condition known as autism, and one thing that seems to be common to children with autism is that they have tremendous difficulty with social relationships.

Autism and autistic spectrum disorders

Autism is often referred to as a communication disorder and is characterised by three main areas of difficulty, all of which relate to social interactions. These three main areas of difficulty are known as the **triad of impairments**, and are used to help identify children who have autistic spectrum disorder. These areas of difficulty are:

1. Difficulties with social interaction – Difficulties in relating to other people, or understanding other people and social situations.

2. Difficulties with communication – At the extreme end of the spectrum, children with autism may have minimal language, or difficulty with both verbal and non-verbal communication (e.g. taking language literally, or not being able to read facial expressions or gestures).

3. Difficulties with imagination – A lack of imaginative ability which will affect the quality of play. These difficulties with imagination are often replaced by obsessive,

repetitive behaviours, such as watching things that spin, tapping and scratching, flicking fingers, rocking, and showing a strong resistance to change.

Looking in more detail at the impact of these difficulties will help you to gain an insight into the challenges faced by people with an autistic diagnosis.

Difficulties with social interaction

Autistic children find it difficult to form meaningful relationships with others, including their parents, and this usually results in a degree of heartbreak for the parents. In normal development, the bond between parent/caregiver and child develops very early on. Babies make eye contact with their parents when being fed; they cry for attention or to be picked up; they smile from about 4 weeks of age – they are active in their communication with parents and quickly learn how a smile, giggle or happy scream can draw attention from others. From about 7 months they develop stranger fear and separation anxiety, showing that they have developed emotional attachments.

Autistic children do not develop in this way. Those on the extreme end of the spectrum do not seek attention as babies, unless they are uncomfortable or wet. They do not make eye contact, even seeming to look through you, rather than at you. They do not smile and they appear to be unaware of others. Not until they are two or three do they form some sort of attachment to their caregivers/parents, and even then this may not be of the same quality as a normal child–parent bond.

Difficulties with communication

Just focusing on language for a moment, it is worth mentioning that children with an autistic spectrum disorder often fail to communicate in any way, either verbally or non-verbally, to the extent that they may not use eye contact. This is because they do not see any reason to communicate with other people. When there is no communication, the child will not explore their ability to vocalise or learn new sounds, so their language acquisition will not develop effectively, leading to a delay. Alongside the delay may come frustration because the child will be unable to make their wishes known. When they do speak, they are unlikely to use eye contact or hand gestures.

Lack of eye contact in children with autism is often the first indication of their poor communication skills. As mentioned, their language development is very slow and in fact 50 per cent of people with autism never learn to speak. The language they do develop may differ from the normal use of language, for instance, they may repeat what others say. The child is not responding to the meaning of what is being said, but simply repeating the words. This is known as echolalia. If all the child does is repeat back, parrot fashion, what you have said, then the conversation is non-existent.

These difficulties with play and communication lead to severe social difficulties for the autistic child. In the most extreme cases, the child can be left in total isolation in an apparently impenetrable world of their own.

Difficulties with imagination

An autistic child will join in and play only if an adult insists. They usually play alone and tend to focus on repetitive actions with an object such as spinning a hoop on their arm, or passing keys from one hand to the other. They do not engage in what is called socio-dramatic play or pretend play as normal children do, such as playing house, pretending to be Superman or dressing up. Normal children also engage in shared games where they take on different roles and act out scenarios together, using their imaginations and social skills to move the plot forwards.

Difficulties with imagination often result in an obsessive insistence on particular routines or interests as a way of coping with a world that appears confusing and unintelligible. If you can imagine not understanding the rules of the social world that you live in, it must seem like a scary place – unpredictable and sometimes hostile. In order to manage it, you would probably like to retreat into your own world where things are predictable, ordered and manageable. In fact, many of the ritualistic and repetitive actions of autistics, such as twiddling objects or tapping, are simply a way to reduce over-arousal and consequent discomfort by focusing on one small and apparently meaningless action. This would help to explain why people with autism get extremely distressed when things are changed or disorganised.

In the film *Rain Man*, Dustin Hoffman gives a very good portrayal of an autistic adult, Raymond. The character is extremely upset by any change in his routine. Any alteration,

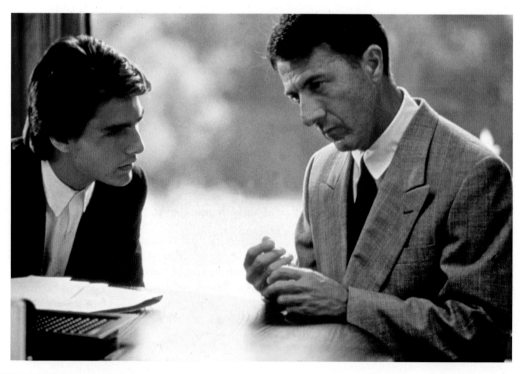

In the film Rain Man, *Dustin Hoffman accurately portrays the fear and discomfort of an autistic person subjected to a change in routine*

however small, can cause a person with autism to demonstrate inexplicable rage, where they will scream wildly and lash out and may be very difficult to calm down. Their resistance to any change, and their extremely negative responses to any changes in routine, can make living and dealing with autistic adults and children very challenging.

In addition to an obsession with routine, autistic children and adults develop obsessions with specific tasks or objects. As children in the playground, we were all familiar with the idea of crazes such as collecting and swapping football stickers, playing marbles, and so on. The obsessions of the autistic person are extreme versions of this type of behaviour. They become focused on one particular activity or interest, and the level of detailed and complex knowledge acquired can be mind-boggling. The focus of these obsessions varies according to the age of the child. Many young children are fixated on dinosaurs or Thomas the Tank Engine, while older children may become obsessed with trains or astronomy or even something as bizarre as different types of burglar alarm system.

It may be through such enthusiasms that one in ten people with autism seem to develop a particular skill or gift. Baron-Cohen calls these **islets of ability**. The autistic person paradoxically develops skills which normal people cannot, such as playing a piece of music immediately after hearing it, being able to draw architecturally detailed drawings of buildings from memory, or specific and unusual mathematical skills such as the card-counting skill that Raymond has in *Rain Man*. A real-life example comes from Oliver Sacks (1985) who described the particular skills of John and Michael, 26-year-old twins with autism. They both had a remarkable memory for digits and could remember up to 300 digits with ease, even though they could not manage simple addition or subtraction. If you gave them a date in the past or the future, they could immediately tell you on what day of the week it fell or would fall.

While the existence of such skills is academically fascinating and attracts a great deal of attention, it is not usually the case that they are of any benefit to the individual who possesses them.

Central coherence and autism

Recent research has indicated that people with autism seem to have difficulty integrating information so that it makes sense, and this may help to explain some of the problems associated with the condition. Frith (1989) suggested that people with autism have a cognitive deficit in what she calls their '**central coherence**'. In order to understand what she means, we will consider some examples.

If you were asked to describe the figure below, you are quite likely to say it is a triangle, whereas it is actually three lines. You have integrated the information so that it makes sense to you.

Is the image below a 'P', or is it lots of S's?

```
SSSSS
S       SS
          S
S       SS
SSSSSS
S
S
S
S
```

What you are probably doing here is seeing the 'bigger picture'. You are integrating the parts so that they have more meaning. This ability was first identified by the **gestalt psychologists**, based in Germany, who put forward the idea that 'the whole is greater than the sum of its parts'. They suggested that we integrate information in order to make sense of it, rather than looking at each individual component.

Frith suggested that people with autism do not tend to be affected by the context of an object but are able to see each part for what it is, rather than perceiving (or misperceiving) it as a whole. This has been investigated by looking at people's ability on an **embedded figures test**, where you have to find a simple shape embedded in a larger figure.

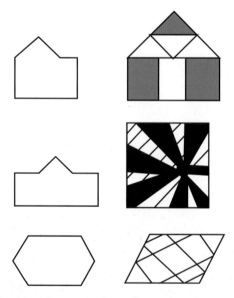

Can you see the embedded figures in these illustrations?

Happé (1997) looked for further evidence of lack of central cohesiveness by investigating a sample of 16 participants with autism. She found that they mispronounced **homophones** (words which are spelt the same but pronounced differently), despite reading them in a context which would have indicated the correct pronunciation. For example, if you read the sentence 'There was a tear in her eye', you are unlikely to pronounce the word 'tear' as you would if you read the sentence 'There was a tear in her dress'. This provided further evidence that the autistic participants were not looking at the 'whole' when reading, but simply reading each word individually.

Campbell et al. (1995) also found that children with autism can identify a famous person just as well being given part of their face or the whole face, presumably because they look at each part of a person's face rather than the face as a whole. Perhaps this lack of executive function – the ability to bring together all the pieces of information – can help to explain the difficulties people with autism have in making sense of social interactions and social situations.

Theory of mind

Social relationships

As children grow up in a social world they need to learn the way in which social relationships, which are a feature of their lives from birth, actually operate. The ability to make friends and to behave appropriately is quite a complex task which we are not taught directly. We might be instructed in social etiquette (table manners, saying please and thank you, and not interrupting when someone is speaking to us), but we are not taught to look at another person when they talk to us, or to retain an appropriate social distance.

We develop an understanding of gestures and facial expressions, we can sense uncomfortable atmospheres, and we do not always have to ask how someone is. We can also understand that language does not need to be interpreted literally, and that people do not always say what they mean. For example, if you were told to pull your socks up when you had failed an assignment, you would not immediately bend over and literally pull up your socks. You would know that the person was telling you that you would have to make more effort in the future. Most of us are also able to put ourselves into another person's shoes – imagining how they must feel or what they might want, without actually experiencing their lives.

All these skills develop as we get older, and as our cognitive ability matures, so does our capacity to process all the information we gather from our experiences. By the time we reach our teenage years we are likely to be proficient 'social interactors'.

It is interesting to note that most children who have no developmental problems seem to share an understanding of unwritten social rules

Egocentricity

In his theory of cognitive development, Jean Piaget argued that children between the ages of 2 and 7 years, who are in what he called the pre-operational stage, are very **egocentric**. To put it simply, they are centred on their own egos to the extent that they are unaware and unconcerned about others because they do not understand that others are not the same as they are, and may have different perspectives and feelings. This is the difference between selfishness and self-centredness. Self-centredness is being centred on the self, where all your thoughts and feelings focus on you, what you want, what you need, what you feel. Selfishness is when you know what effect you are having on others but choose to ignore it and simply gratify yourself, so in some respects it is much worse than self-centredness.

An example of how egocentricity influences the behaviour of small children is often seen in the supermarket. Have you ever noticed, when you are waiting in the checkout queue, the little child whining in front of you? Mother is there trying to unpack a huge pile of food from her trolley, with a tiny baby in her arms crying. She is obviously fraught and wanting to escape and the toddler is pleading, 'I want some sweeties.' The whining gets more and more insistent until he is having a full-blown tantrum, lying on the floor, screaming and kicking. Although you may feel like physically ejecting him from your vicinity, remember that Piaget would argue that he has absolutely no idea how his mother feels and that is why he is behaving in this way.

Piaget claimed that this kind of **egocentrism** (or self-centredness) continues until the child is leaving the pre-operational stage, which he suggested was at approximately 7 years of age. However, later research has indicated that children as young as 4 years have begun to see things from the point of view of others. The problem with much of the early research on children's development was that the children were often tested in unfamiliar or unnatural situations.

KEY CONCEPTS

Studying children in naturalistic environments

Conducting research in an unfamiliar environment is likely to produce results which may be caused by the design, rather than being the result of manipulation of the independent variable.

The best idea would be to look at the child in their normal environment. Bearing in mind that the family environment will have the most influence on a young child, it would make sense to carry out this kind of research in the child's own home. In fact, Hinde (1987) argued that unless we look at relationships in their social and cultural contexts, they will have little meaning, as we will be unaware that some behaviours, which may appear unusual out of context, actually have a great deal of meaning in the relevant environment.

Considerable research has questioned the lack of social awareness suggested by Piaget. If children really are totally egocentric, they are unlikely even to be aware of the moods of other people. However, researchers such as Stern (1977) have suggested that this awareness occurs much earlier than Piaget maintained. Stern noticed that children as young as 1 year can tune in to the moods of others. We have all seen instances where a baby will cry if the mother cries, and laugh if the mother laughs. Stern called this ability 'affective tuning', and claimed that it becomes more highly developed during the second and third years of a child's life. It seems that children are extremely interested in emotional states and are ready and willing to learn about them, and more to the point, that this is a normal developmental process which is generated by biologically hard-wired tendencies. This suggests that children have an innate predisposition to learn about the emotions of others and to develop an awareness of what other people are thinking. When children have mastered this ability, they will have developed what is known as a **theory of mind**.

False beliefs

Researchers have investigated the theory of mind by looking at children's abilities to understand **false beliefs**. There are two types of 'beliefs' that are investigated in the research on false beliefs:

- A **first-order belief task** requires the child to think about another person's thoughts about a real event. For example, the child would have to explain that 'Jack believes that the shop is closed, even if the shop is open'. Children with normal development should pass these tests by the age of 4 years.

- **Second-order beliefs** require the child to think about a second person's thoughts about a third person's thoughts about an event. For example, the child would have to explain that 'Jack believes that John believes that the shop is closed, even if the shop is open'. Children with normal development should pass these tests between the ages of 6 and 7 years.

One of the original studies was undertaken by Heinz Wimmer and Josef Perner (1983), and involved a small boy called Maxi and a bar of chocolate. The story required children of different ages to attribute a false belief (using a first-order belief task) to another person, and it was acted out with dolls. The story went something like this:

> Maxi puts his chocolate in a red cupboard and then goes to play outside. Unknown to Maxi, his mother moves the chocolate to a blue cupboard. Maxi then comes back from playing and wants to get his chocolate. A child who has heard this will be asked, 'Where will Maxi look for the chocolate when he comes back?'

Obviously the correct answer is the red cupboard, because that is where Maxi put it and where he believes it still is. If the child has an understanding of false beliefs, he will realise that Maxi will have a false belief as to where his chocolate will be found. If, on the other hand, the child does not understand that people can see things differently from the way that the child himself sees them, he will answer that Maxi will look for the chocolate in the blue cupboard because that is where it really is.

Wimmer and Perner found that all children younger than 4 years typically said that Maxi would look in the blue cupboard. This indicated that they could not take into account the fact that Maxi did not know that the chocolate had been moved.

Lacking a theory of mind

Having an idea of how children develop a theory of mind, and how important this is to their social functioning, we can imagine how awful it must be for a child who has no concept of how other people think and feel. If they are unaware that other people have thoughts and beliefs which are totally different from their own, they will be unable to 'mind-read', that is, to understand how other people feel and how they will react to different situations. Imagine being unable to assess how someone is responding to you when you meet them. How would you feel if you were not sure whether they liked you or not, or whether they were angry, upset or bored with your company? Under normal circumstances, having a theory of mind would help you in the following interaction.

> 'Do you like my new dress, Miriam?' squeaked Edna, as she wrestled with the buttons at the front of the vivid purple dress. 'I think it is soooo sexy, and I love the way the front shows off my cleavage.' Miriam grimaced. The buttons looked like they were on maximum tension, hanging on to both sides of the dress and trying to hold back the flow of excess flesh between them. One more inhalation of breath would result in the whole row just popping off and projecting across the other side of the room. As for the cleavage, it was more like two giant marshmallows trying to escape from the tight line of the bodice. If she bent over, they would escape, smothering the top of the dress. And why that colour? It would make someone with even the strongest constitution feel nauseous.
>
> 'Yes, it looks lovely!'

Now imagine the same situation, but in this instance Miriam has no theory of mind. Her answer would have been something along the lines of: 'It looks absolutely awful. You are much too fat to wear it and the buttons look like they are about to burst. And the colour makes me feel sick!'

What would Edna's response be to this? She would likely become either extremely upset or incredibly angry, but Miriam would have no concept of what her response would be because she had simply told Edna the truth.

Autistic children rarely seem to develop any sort of theory of mind. Having a theory of someone else's mind is a higher-order skill which requires integrating a considerable amount of information. If a child can only process one piece of information at a time, it is not surprising that children with autism find this extremely difficult. It is a very complex task to try to see things from someone else's point of view and to identify their mistaken beliefs.

Causes of autism

Despite the knowledge we have about the nature of the condition, there is no one identifiable cause for autism.

Parenting

In the mid twentieth century, it was thought that autism might be due to the way a child was brought up. Dr Bruno Bettelheim, a developmental psychologist, theorised that autism was the result of cold and unloving mothers (refrigerator mothers), who did not stimulate their children, but this theory was discarded with the understanding that autism was a biological and not a psychological condition.

Genetics

In the late 1970s, research pointed to the fact that there might be a genetic connection, when it was discovered that the twin of an autistic child had a greater than average chance of also being autistic. More recent research has supported this theory. For example, Bailey et al. (1995) studied 27 pairs of **monozygotic** (also known as MZ or identical) twins and 20 pairs of **dyzygotic** (also known as DZ, non-identical or fraternal) twins, where one of the pair was autistic. They found that 60 per cent of MZ pairs both had autism, whereas autism was not present in the second twin in any of the DZ pairs. The concordance level in MZ twins indicates a strong degree of genetic influence.

Research has also indicated that siblings of autistic children are very slightly more likely to be identified with autism than the general population. However, no single gene or combination of genes has been identified as a cause, and if genes alone cause autism, scientists would find it very difficult to explain the increasing number of autistic cases.

Chromosomal abnormalities

Researchers have found evidence that may link several chromosomal abnormalities to autism. The disorder sometimes occurs along with identified genetic conditions, such as:

- **Fragile X syndrome** – the most common inherited form of mental impairment or learning difficulties. It is the result of a change or mutation in a single gene, which can be passed from one generation to the next.

- Untreated **phenylketonuria** (PKU) – results in the body being unable to process part of a protein called phenylalanine, which is present in almost all foods. If the phenylalanine level gets too high, it can damage the brain and cause severe mental retardation.
- **Neurofibromatosis** – mainly affects the nervous system and is caused by a change in a gene which may be inherited from parents or the result of a spontaneous change for no known reason. The condition causes non-cancerous tumours to grow on nerves throughout the body, which can cause considerable problems.
- **Tuberous sclerosis** – growths form on the brain and look like rounded swellings (tubers). Over time, the growths become hard, due to a build-up of calcium salts.

Environmental catalyst

It has been suggested by some researchers that autism may be caused by a variety of physical factors, all of which affect brain development. The suggestion is that the child may have a predisposition which comes from their genetic make-up; and physical factors such as environmental toxins or vaccinations may either exacerbate the genetic condition or actually cause autism.

Autism and gender

According to the National Autistic Society, the ratio of boys to girls with autism is estimated at 4:1, but apart from this difference, autism is a disorder that is found across all socio-economic classes and across all racial and ethnic groups.

Simon Baron-Cohen (1999) has suggested that autism is no more than an extreme form of the male brain. In his paper he cites studies which provide evidence that men and women from the general population differ in the area of cognition, suggesting that women are better at language tasks, tests of social judgement, measures of empathy, perceptual speed, matching tasks, fluency of ideas and fine motor coordination, mathematical calculation tests and pretend play in childhood. On the other hand, men are better than women at mathematical reasoning, tasks where they are required to find embedded figures in an abstract drawing, tasks where they have to imagine how an object will look when rotated, some (not all) spatial skills and target-directed motor skills such as gliding.

Baron-Cohen also talks about two skills, **systemising** and **empathising**. In 2005, he was interviewed by Randall F. White, MD, FRCPC, for the American clinician's website, Medscape. In the interview he described systemising

> as the drive to analyze or construct a system. It could be any kind of system – a mechanical system such as a computer, or a natural system such as the circulatory system of the body. Or it could be an abstract system like mathematics. The key thing is that when you systemize, you identify the rules or the laws that govern that system in order to predict how it will behave.

Empathizing is completely different. It's about being able to imagine what someone else is thinking or feeling, and having an emotional response to the other person's feelings.

He continues by explaining that:

In the general population, you find that, on average, males have a stronger drive to systemize and females have a stronger drive to empathize. Those are the two cognitive processes we've been focusing on to try to understand autism and why it should be more common among boys than girls. We've found that people on the autistic spectrum show an exaggeration of the male profile.

It also appears that people with autism are even more skilled at the male-superior tasks, and less skilled than 'normal' males at the female-superior tasks.

Diagnosis of autism

Autism used to be a relatively rare condition which, according to Uta Frith, writing in 1993, affected only 1 or 2 children in every 1,000. More recently, Baird et al. (2006). writing in *The Lancet*, suggested that the prevalence of autism and related autistic spectrum disorders is much higher than was previously recognised. They suggest the minimum number of children with some form of autistic spectrum disorder is 1 in 100. This statistic suggests that over half a million people in the UK have autism. However, they do discuss the fact that the increase may also be influenced, in part, by better diagnosis or the broadening of diagnostic criteria.

Although autism was first recognised in 1943 by Kanner, it was not accepted as an official diagnosis until 1980. Until this point it had been considered a type of childhood schizophrenia – the 'aloneness' of the autistic child is very like the behaviour of people with schizophrenia whose disordered thoughts cut them off from others. However, it became clear that this was not the case, as autistic children do not develop schizophrenic symptoms as adults. Nowadays autism is a medical diagnosis which has specific criteria laid down in ICD-10 (International Classification of Diseases from the World Health Organization) and DSM-IV (Diagnostic and Statistical Manual of Mental Disorders, a US publication).

People who are diagnosed with autism will have a tremendous variation in the degree to which they are affected. This means that no two children with the disorder will be totally alike as some have little or no speech, while others may have fluent speech; some may shy away from social contact, while others will tolerate considerable interaction. A child on the more extreme end of the autistic spectrum is likely to suffer from severe disabilities, which will continue into adulthood. Thus autism is not simply a childhood disorder, but rather one which may extend the dependence we associate with childhood across the adult lives of those with the condition, leaving families and authorities to deal with the individuals who need lifelong care.

Oliver Sacks (1995) has written about Temple Grandin, an autistic adult who holds a PhD in animal sciences, teaches at Colorado State University and runs her own business.

Temple has developed ways of coping with the symptoms of her autism and is able to live a full and independent life, although it has to be pointed out that her social skills remain highly impaired – she chooses to live alone, and admits she has a better understanding of the feelings of cattle than she has of the feelings of her fellow humans. The way she deals with human interaction is to refer consciously to a kind of database in her memory, which has stored factual information about how to behave and respond, rather than having the kind of innate skills that most of us have.

The autistic spectrum

One technique which has attempted to address the issue of identifying the variation in the presentation of autistic disorders, is to consider the difficulties that children experience as being somewhere on an autistic spectrum. This relatively new term includes the subgroups within the spectrum of autism, such as children with high-functioning autism and **Asperger's syndrome** (children who show the same characteristics of autism to a greater or lesser extent, but are of average or above-average intelligence, and give the appearance of having good communication skills, although this may not really be the case). If you imagine a line with autism at one end and Asperger's syndrome at the other, which then borders on normality, this may be a helpful way of picturing what is meant by the autistic spectrum.

The variation in severity of each impairment from one child to the next presents problems when it comes to reaching a diagnosis. What makes matters even more confusing is that children may have one or two of the impairments which will affect their ability to interact with others, but will not be sufficiently impaired in all three areas to be labelled 'autistic'. Similarly, how do you quantify an 'impairment'? What is normal, and who decides? Is this not just a little bit subjective?

Work by Baron-Cohen and his colleagues attempted to find what he called a **core deficit** in autism – the idea being to find one difficulty that all people with autism have in common. If a core deficit were found, it might help to explain why people with autism behave as they do. Perhaps more importantly, finding a core deficit would help to eliminate the subjectivity that may occur when trying to diagnose the condition. Baron-Cohen et al. (1985) conducted research investigating whether autistic children had a theory of mind by using a false belief task. The results indicated that some of the autistic children could answer the belief question correctly, and some of the children in the control groups could not. The results were therefore inconclusive, and indicated only that although there was evidence that a theory of mind was underdeveloped in autistic children, they did not show that a lack of theory of mind is a core deficit in autism. However, Baron-Cohen has continued to conduct further research in this area, looking in greater detail at the methodology that has been used in past studies and investigating theory of mind in adults.

THE STUDY

S. Baron-Cohen, T. Jolliffe, C. Mortimore and M. Robertson (1997)
'Another advanced test of theory of mind: Evidence from very high
functioning adults with autism or Asperger syndrome'

Journal of Child Psychology and Psychiatry, 38: 813–22

BACKGROUND

Do very high-functioning adults with autism and Asperger's syndrome (AS) have
difficulty with mind-reading in the same way that children do? If lacking a theory
of mind is a core deficit of autism, then it should be apparent in people of all
ages across the autistic spectrum.

Research by Baron-Cohen (1989) had suggested that adults with autism do
have problems mind-reading. However, a number of researchers dispute the fact
that theory of mind is a general problem in the population of very high-functioning
adults with autism and AS. For example, Ozonoff et al. (1991) and Bowler (1992)
tested adults and found that some of them passed the theory of mind tests.

In this study, Baron-Cohen et al. question the validity of these findings as
evidence that adults with autism or AS have an intact theory of mind on the basis
that the tests given were too easy. Common tests of theory of mind for children fall
into two categories: first-order and second-order tests. Second-order tests are
more difficult, but even these are designed to measure the theory of mind of a
normal child aged 6 years, as Baron-Cohen and his colleagues point out:

> Finding a 30 year old individual with autism, of normal intelligence, who
> can pass a theory of mind test at the level of a normal 6 year old does not
> lead to the conclusion that they are necessarily normal in this domain. All
> we can conclude is that they have intact theory of mind skills at the level
> of a 6 year old. (pp.813–14)

Obviously, if an adult could read a picture book designed for a 6-year-old, we
would not consider them to have the normal reading level of an adult, and
Baron-Cohen et al. are saying that the same goes for very high-functioning
adults with autism and AS when considering theory of mind.

What Baron-Cohen et al. suggest is that previous researchers had failed to
note that neither first- nor second-order tests are complex tests of theory of
mind. The fact that adults can pass these tests does not mean that **mind-
reading** poses no problem for them; it may be that the tests have a ceiling
effect, that is, they are too easy, so everyone tested can achieve full marks.

The authors go on to describe the method used to test theory of mind by
Happé (1994), who tested adults with autism and AS on what they refer to as an

'advanced' test of theory of mind. Happé's method was called the **strange stories task**, which required the subjects to understand the characters' mental states in order to demonstrate theory of mind. Adults with autism and AS had more difficulty with this than the controls, again providing evidence to support Baron-Cohen's earlier work that adults with autism and AS have difficulties with theory of mind. This test, however, measured the level of theory of mind of a normal child aged 8–9 years; although this was advanced in terms of being beyond what typical first- and second-order tasks assess (the 6-year-old level), it is still not really an adult test of theory of mind.

In order to test whether very high-functioning adults with autism or AS have problems with theory of mind, a new adult test of theory of mind was devised for this study. The task extended Happé's ideas and was called the reading the mind in the eyes task, or the **Eyes Task** for short.

The Eyes Task

In the Eyes Task, subjects have to interpret parts of faces, by choosing one from a pair of given mental state terms to describe what the face suggests the person is thinking or experiencing.

The design of the materials and the way they were presented to subjects were standardised as follows:

- The photos were always of the same area of the face.
- The photos were always the same size.
- The photos were always black and white.
- The faces were taken from magazine photos.
- Each picture was shown for 3 seconds, with a forced choice between two mental state terms printed under each picture.
- The experimenter said to the subject: 'Which word best describes what this person is feeling or thinking?'
- The 'foil' (wrong) word was always the semantic opposite of the target (correct) word. (Whether the correct mental state concept was presented on the left or the right was randomised across the subjects.)

The total score possible (all correct) on this test is 25. An example of the photos is on the next page.

Both basic and complex mental state terms were included in the test. Basic terms included 'happy', 'sad', 'angry', 'afraid'. Complex terms included 'reflective', 'scheming', 'arrogant'. The full list is shown below.

Construction of the Eyes Task

Baron-Cohen et al. explain the construction of their eyes task as follows (p.4):

- In discussion, the target word for each pair was generated by four judges, two male and two female.
- A 'foil' word (the semantic opposite of the target word in all cases) was selected.

No.*	Target term	Foil
	Table 2	
	Target Mental State Terms, and Their foil Terms	
1	Concerned	Unconcerned
2	Noticing you	Ignoring you
3	Attraction	Repulsion
4	Relaxed	Worried
5	Serious message	Playful message
6	Interested	Uninterested
7	Friendly	Hostile
8	Sad reflection	Happy reflection
9	Sad thought	Happy thought
10	Certain	Uncertain
11	Far away focus	Near focus
12	Reflective	Unreflective
13	Reflective	Unreflective
14	Cautious about something over there	Relaxed about something over there
15	Noticing someone else	Noticing you
16	Calm	Anxious
17	Dominant	Submissive
18	Fantasising	Noticing
19	Observing	Daydreaming
20	Desire for you	Desire for someone else
21	Ignoring you	Noticing you
22	Nervous about you	Interested in you
23	Flirtatious	Uninterested
24	Sympathetic	Unsympathetic
25	Decisive	Indecisive

*Stimulus number.

- These were tested on a panel of eight judges (four male, four female), all independent raters and blind to the hypothesis of the study.
- All eight independent raters agreed unanimously on the application of the target words to the eye pairs.

Validity of the Eyes Task

The authors stated that 'The Eyes Task is designed to be a "pure" theory of mind test, at an advanced level'. By this, they mean that the test is not affected by executive function (no attention switching, planning, and so on), and there is no central coherence component – by presenting only parts of the faces there is no 'whole context' to interpret.

The authors say that the Eyes Task could equally be called a test of mind-reading (in the sense of working out what someone is thinking or feeling), and the authors use the terms 'theory of mind' and 'mind-reading' interchangeably in this study.

To establish the validity of the Eyes Task as a test of theory of mind, subjects were also tested using Happé's strange stories test (described above, page 122). If both these tests were indeed relatively advanced tests of theory of mind, then if the subject had difficulties with one test, they should also have difficulties with the other.

Because the Eyes Task involves basic aspects of emotion recognition and face perception, it was necessary to make sure that the subjects were able to manage both of these skills. Therefore two control tasks were added to the procedure; a basic emotion recognition task and a gender recognition task. The idea was that if the subjects got the emotion recognition task incorrect (e.g. not identifying happy and sad) or if they were unable to identify whether someone was male or female, this would suggest that their cognitive ability in terms of facial recognition was impaired and therefore they would fail at any more complex task.

The study acknowledged the common belief that females are better than males at mind-reading, so it also aimed to investigate gender differences on the eyes task in the normal population.

AIMS

The study tested the following predictions:

- Adults with autism or AS, despite being of normal or above-average IQ, would nevertheless be impaired on a subtle theory of mind test.
- Within the normal population, females would be significantly better on this test of theory of mind than males.

METHOD

Method and design

This was an experiment using an independent groups design. Each subject was tested individually in a quiet room, either in their own home, in the researcher's clinic, or in a laboratory at Cambridge University.

Subjects

Three groups were tested.

Group 1:

- 16 subjects with high-functioning autism (HFA) or AS (4 had HFA and 12 had AS)
- 13 males, 3 females
- Age range = 18–49 years, mean age = 28.6 years
- Those with HFA had shown the classic signs of autism (autism compared with language delay) and met the criteria for autism on DSM-IV
- Those with AS met the same criteria for autism, but without language delay, and met the criteria for AS defined in ICD-10

These subjects were selected for being of at least normal intelligence (IQ of greater than 85 – average is 100), as assessed on the WAIS-R (Wechsler Adult Intelligence Scale Revised) test. In this, the group was quite rare, described by Baron-Cohen et al. as being cases of 'pure' autism or AS, that is, without the mental handicap that is so commonly associated with autism. They were recruited through clinical sources known to the researchers and from volunteers who responded to an advert in *Communication* (the magazine for the National Autistic Society in the UK).

Group 2:

- 50 normal, age-matched adults
- 25 males, 25 females
- Age range = 18–48 years, mean age = 30 years

These subjects were selected from the general population of Cambridge (although members of the university were excluded from this group). It was established by self-report that none of them had a history of any psychiatric condition. The subjects were selected randomly from a subject panel held in the university department. They were assumed to have IQ in the normal range.

Group 3:

- 10 adult patients with **Tourette's syndrome**
- Age-matched with groups 1 and 2 (age range = 18–47 years, mean age = 27.77 years)
- 8 males, 2 females, all diagnosed by Dr Mary Robertson on the basis of DSM-IV criteria for Tourette's syndrome

All these subjects were attending a referral centre in London. They were selected for being in the normal IQ range, established by the use of the short form of the WAIS-R (the short form was used with these subjects as they were only available for study for a limited time).

Groups 1 and 3 were also tested using first- and second-order false belief tests. If they had failed these tests they would have been excluded from the study, although none failed. This was carried out as a control, so that any difference on the Eyes Task could be attributed to mind reading problems in these two groups beyond the level of which a normal 6-year-old was capable.

Controlling extraneous subject variables

The group with Tourette's syndrome was included as a control in this study to ensure that any difficulties on the eyes task experienced by the HFA and AS subjects were not caused because they had an organic, childhood-onset psychiatric disorder. The authors point out that while autism and AS are different from Tourette's syndrome in many ways, they share enough similarities for the inclusion of these Tourette's subjects to act as a control.

The similarities between the subjects in this study with autism or AS and those with Tourette's syndrome are as follows:

- All had intelligence in the normal range.
- All had suffered from a developmental disorder from childhood.
- All these disorders cause disruption to both normal schooling and normal peer relations.
- It is suggested that all these disorders involve abnormalities in the **frontal cortex** of the brain (although in different areas of the frontal cortex in Tourette's from autism and AS).
- There is a lot of evidence to suggest that these disorders have a genetic cause.
- All these disorders affect males more than females (p.6).

The authors theorised that if the problem with theory of mind in adults with autism and AS was indeed caused by their autism, and not from just 'having any disorder', then the subjects with Tourette's should have no difficulties on the Eyes Task. They predicted that the Tourette's syndrome group would not differ from the normal group on the Eyes Task.

Procedure

Each subject was tested on four tasks, and the presentation of tasks was randomised to control for order effects. The four tasks were:

1 The Eyes Task
2 The Strange Stories task
3 Two control tasks:
    - The gender recognition task
    - The basic emotion recognition task

On the gender recognition task, the subjects were shown the same sets of eyes used in the Eyes Task, but on this test they were asked to identify the gender of the person in the photograph. This had a maximum score of 25, the same as the eyes task.

The basic emotion recognition task (the emotion task) involved judging photographs of whole faces displaying the basic emotions (based on Ekman's

1992 categories). Six faces were used, showing: 'happy', 'sad', 'angry', 'afraid', 'disgust', 'surprise'. Two examples are shown below:

RESULTS

Performance on the Eyes Task

As predicted, the findings showed that the adults with autism and AS did have more difficulties on the Eyes Task than both the control groups, and there was no difference between the normal subjects and those with Tourette's syndrome on the Eyes Task.

Condition	Mean score (total = 25)
Adults with high-functioning autism or AS	16.3
Normal adults	20.3
Adults with Tourette's syndrome	20.4

The eyes task: results by condition

The analysis of gender difference in performance on the Eyes Task also gave results in the predicted direction: males had more difficulties than females.

Condition	Mean score (total = 25)
Normal males	18.8
Normal females	21.8

The eyes task: gender difference in the normal subjects

Even when the adults with autism or AS were compared just with the normal *males* (who found it harder to correctly score than the normal females) there was still a significant difference in the performance of the Ss with autism in correctly identifying what a person is thinking from their eyes.

Performance on the Strange Stories Task

When completing the Strange Stories Task, the subjects with Autism or Asperger's Syndrome made errors on this task and were significantly impaired relative to the controls. Interestingly, no subjects with Tourette's Syndrome made any errors. However, the details of these results were not included in the study, although it was mentioned that full details of the task, including coding and results, were reported separately by T. Jolliffe (1997) in an unpublished PhD Thesis (University of Cambridge).

DISCUSSION

Do adults with autism or AS have problems with theory of mind?

The conclusions the authors drew from their findings were that despite having normal or above-average IQ, adults with autism or AS had difficulties on a subtle theory of mind test, the Eyes Task, suggesting that not only children but also adults with autism have problems with theory of mind and attributing mental states to others. This shows that individuals with autism or AS have difficulties with mind-reading at stages of development and at higher IQ levels than previous studies had suggested.

The authors give four reasons to support the validity of the Eyes Task as a measure of theory of mind:

1 The target terms are mental state terms.
2 The target words are not just emotion terms, so it is more than just an emotion test.
3 The same results are found on Happé's strange stories test as on the Eyes Task, making the results from the eyes task concurrently valid with an 'existing advanced test of theory of mind'.
4 There was no difference between the adults with autism or AS on the two control tasks (gender and emotion), suggesting that their poor performance in the Eyes Task was not due to other perceptual or social cognitive skills.

The authors found no correlation between the IQ and eyes task scores of the adults with autism or AS, and the fact that some of these subjects had university degrees suggests that the ability to mind-read, as required by the Eyes Task, is an ability independent of general intelligence.

The fact that the subjects with Tourette's syndrome did not differ from the controls on their performance in the Eyes Task suggests that the difficulties demonstrated by those with autism or AS were not due to having any developmental neuropsychiatric disorder.

How do the findings from the Eyes Task relate to studies on gaze direction in children with autism?

The difficulties that the autistic and AS subjects had with the eyes task mirrors difficulties that young children with autism have in understanding the importance in the eyes in signalling mental states:

- Toddlers with autism often fail to understand that gaze direction is a signal of attention.
- Young children with autism fail to understand that gaze direction might indicate what a person is focusing their intention on or referring to, or may act as an expression of their goals or desires.
- Preschool children with autism, unlike children without autism of the same age, also fail to recognise gaze direction as a cue to indicate when someone is thinking.

Are females better at mind-reading than males?

As predicted, within a normal population, this study showed that normal females were better at recognising mental states on the Eyes Task than normal males. The authors point out that while this study indicates that there is a difference, it does not explain why: 'the female advantage on the mindreading task could be taken to reflect genetic or socialization factors. . . This remains to be investigated further.'

Note: Baron-Cohen did investigate these findings further in 1999, when his research indicated that women are better at language tasks, tests of social judgement, measures of empathy, perceptual speed, matching tasks, fluency of ideas and fine motor coordination, mathematical calculation tests and pretend play in childhood.

COMMENTARY: METHODS AND ISSUES

Research method, design and data gathering

The study employs the experimental method, using an independent groups design, comparing very high-functioning adults with autism and AS with normal subjects and subjects with Tourette's syndrome. The normal males were also compared with the normal females.

The data-gathering method was self-report, as all subjects verbally reported their responses to the researcher in each task.

Data gathered was quantitative, and statistical analysis was carried out to establish any differences between conditions.

Does the study raise any ethical concerns?

The study was carried out according to the British Psychological Society (1993) ethical guidelines. The subjects were not deceived; they gave their informed consent; they had the right to withdraw; and they were generally not negatively affected by their experience.

Is the study useful?

This study has intrinsic value as a piece of psychological research. It furthers our understanding of the extent of the problem of theory of mind across the autistic continuum. It demonstrates that the problem extends beyond childhood, showing that not only children but also adults have problems mind-reading – interpreting the mental states of others. It also shows that the problems seem to be unrelated to levels of general intelligence.

In terms of real-world applications, one area where the study may be of use is in helping to understand how best to assist people with autistic spectrum disorders to develop more effective social skills. People with autism may be able to learn how to interpret eyes more effectively by taking account of other visual cues, such as mouth or body language, in order to understand someone else's state of mind. The tasks may also be useful as an aid to the diagnosis of people with autistic disorders who are at the mild end of the spectrum.

Validity and reliability of the study

The authors discuss the validity of the eyes task as a measure of theory of mind (see 'Discussion', above). They employ control tasks to increase the validity of the task by accounting for other perceptual or social cognitive skills that could account for difficulties on the eyes task. In addition, they establish concurrent validity of the Eyes Task with Happé's strange stories test.

KEY CONCEPTS

Concurrent validity

If the outcome of a test of a particular behaviour correlates with scores on an established test of the same behaviour that has previously been agreed as valid, then the second test is described as being concurrently valid with the first.

In this case, the test that was already validated as an 'advanced' test of theory of mind was Happé's strange stories test. By showing that subjects' scores on this test correlated with their scores on the new test of theory of mind, the eyes task, the authors were able to provide evidence for the validity of their new test as a true measure of theory of mind.

There are problems with the ecological validity of the Eyes Task. In their discussion, the authors raise the point that their 'very advanced test' of theory of mind, the eyes task, is still simpler than having to interpret people's mental states in a real-life social situation. To begin with, the test is static, showing only partial faces, and this is not typically how we see people – usually they are whole and animated!

The authors suggest that a better stimulus might be to show films to the subjects, as this might be more like a real-life situation. However, this would involve other perceptual and social cognitive skills which might confound the study. Therefore, they defend their choice to use the Eyes Task in this study, calling it a 'pure' test of theory of mind.

Language

The last area of cognition that we are going to consider is language. A question over which there has been much psychological debate is whether the ability to learn language is pre-programmed or hard-wired into the human brain, or whether it is dependent on the environment in which the child is raised. In other words, language development has been a core topic in the **nature–nurture debate**.

The core study on language at the end of this section will raise questions not only about what we mean by language, but also about whether language is a **species-specific behaviour** which sets humans apart from other animals. Before considering this study, we are going to look at how children's language develops.

Children's language development

We are born with certain abilities, and these improve as we get older as a result of learning. However, some of these abilities not only involve learning experiences, but also require physical maturity in order to reach the level of skill we have as an adult. For example, children cannot walk when they are first born although they are born with a reflex which allows them, if supported, to move their legs as if they are walking. The problem is that they cannot fully support their own weight on their legs, and their necks are not strong enough to support their heads. They are unlikely to be able to walk before ten months of age, and often they may be over a year old before they launch themselves into action without needing to hold on to things. By this stage, their physical body will have developed sufficiently to allow them to master this skill.

The development of language follows a very similar route because a baby is born with the ability to make a noise – it can cry! However, even if it were familiar with language, understood it and knew the words it wanted to say, it could not speak as soon as it was born because its mouth is not the right shape to do so. At birth, our tongue is too big and our

A summary of the stages of language development in human infants between the ages of 0 and 2 years

Age (approx.)	Stage	Description	Nature or nurture?
2 months	Cooing (prelinguistic)	Baby makes 'ooh' and 'aah' sounds, which generally signal pleasure or excitement.	Nature – cooing is a cultural universal, that is, it occurs in all babies in all cultures at approximately the same stage, and this implies that the behaviour is innate.
6 months	Reduplicated babbling (prelinguistic)	Babies babble in all sounds, even those not present in the language spoken around them. The sounds are repeated (e.g. 'mamama'or 'dadada').	Nature – supported by the argument that even profoundly deaf babies babble at this time and in this way. This is also a cultural universal.
11 months	Jargon babbling (prelinguistic)	Babbling changes to use only the sounds present in the language to which the child is exposed. This process is known as phonemic contraction. The child babbles in sentence patterns and rhythms (knows the tune but does not yet know the words).	Nature – emergence of this type of babbling in children at the same age universally suggests that some inborn potential is maturing in the child. Nurture – phonemic contraction and copying sentence rhythm and inflections are only possible if the child has been exposed in the environment to spoken language. The fact that deaf babies do not babble in this way, and, in fact, stop babbling altogether at about 9 months shows the importance of environmental influence at this stage of development.

(Continued)

Age (approx.)	Stage	Description	Nature or nurture?
1 year	One-word	Children produce single words, with names of objects usually being the first words to appear, tending to centre on things that are important to the baby, such as food, animals and toys. Using single words, the baby can convey more than the meaning of the word itself. This use of one word to represent a whole concept is called holophrastic speech. Depending on the context, if a child says 'milk' this could mean, 'That is milk', 'I want some milk', 'The cat is drinking its milk', or even, as the child upturns its glass on the table, 'Oops, I appear to have accidentally spilled my milk, Daddy'.	Nature – emergence of this stage in children at the same age universally suggests that some inborn potential is maturing in the child. Nurture – the words acquired by the child are dependent on the language they are exposed to. For example, a child growing up in a German-speaking environment will not refer to milk as 'lait', as a French child would.
Towards the end of the child's second year	Two-word	Combining words to make two-word utterances enables the child to be clearer about the meaning of what is being said. Combining words to create novel utterances or to extend the meaning of utterances is called **creativity**. These two-word utterances again convey more meaning than you think. For	Nature – the sequence of the development from one- to two-word utterances in children at the same age universally suggests that some inborn potential is maturing in the child. This is also supported by the fact that the development of the type of two-word utterance also occurs universally, again illustrating the

(Continued)

Age (approx.)	Stage	Description	Nature or nurture?
		example, 'That car' may mean, 'That is a car', with 'is' and 'a' left out; this omission of the little words is typical at this stage. The structure of these two-word utterances led to early researchers describing them as 'telegraphic speech'.* **Note:** Children develop the type of two-word utterances in a universal sequence: • Agent + action (Daddy run) • Action + object (eat biscuit) • Location (Mummy chair) • Possession (my ball)	importance of maturation in the development of language.

* Telegrams were communications sent by Morse code, each letter tapped in laboriously by the operator. As a result, the sender paid by the word. In order to save money, telegrams developed their own language, in the same way that text messaging has a language of its own. For example, instead of sending, 'I'll see you on Sunday afternoon', you might send, 'See Sun afternoon'. The most famous example of this (and it may be a myth that it was ever used) is the message 'Stop Press!' sent by newspaper journalists who wanted the printing presses to be halted in order for their hot story to take priority.

palate is too low for speech. As we mature, the relative sizes of these parts change, and soon we are able to make the sounds which are the first steps towards developing language.

The table beginning on page 132 provides a summary of the stages of language development in young children.

Syntax and grammar

From the age of 3 years, children continue to learn new words, increasing their vocabulary further and allowing them to express themselves more effectively. They also continue to develop an understanding of grammatical rules.

One of the studies which actually provides an indication of just how much our vocabulary increases over the first years of our lives, and how much learning we undertake without realising, was carried out by Seashore and Eckerson (1940). They concluded that 19-year-old college students had a vocabulary in the region of 150,000 words (other samples have estimated as many as 250,000). This means that between the ages of 1 and 19 years, we have to learn, on average, 21 words a day! Providing that we master **syntax**, this will equip us to produce complex sentences. Syntax refers to rules of grammar, such as using the pronoun 'he' for a male or adding an 's' to a noun to make it plural. Syntax also dictates the structure of utterances, commonly referred to as word order. Even in the two-word stage it is apparent that children have some understanding of word order; for example, a child will say 'my mummy' rather than 'mummy my'.

From the age of 3 years, children's utterances increase in length and complexity, and up until the age of 6 or 7 years children learn to master the rules of grammar. This involves applying the rules with increasing effectiveness. Interestingly, the rules are ones the child has deduced and inferred rather than rules which have been taught formally. We can see the rules the child is using in the kind of errors they make, which are particularly obvious in English because it is not a completely regular language and has many exceptions to the general rules of grammar. These errors are called 'virtual errors', because if English were regular, the child would be getting it right. For example, the child may have deduced that to talk about something which has already happened, they need to add 'ed' to the verb (obviously they do not analyse it exactly in these terms), so 'I look' would become 'I looked'. However, with an irregular verb like 'to run', the child might say 'I runned', because s/he is **overgeneralising the rule**.

Plural forming also produces some errors, as the rule of adding an 's' to make a plural does not always work. For instance, 'cat' becomes 'cats', but we do not refer to more than one sheep as 'sheeps'. One of the nicest examples of this was given by Hetherington and Parke (1986), when they described a child they knew who 'used the word "clothes" and insisted on calling one piece of clothing a "clo"'. One of the authors of this book can confirm this error from observation of her own son, then aged 3 years, who asked for a 'va' to put the daisies he had picked in!

Parents are not unduly concerned about these errors, as the important thing is to get the meaning of the message across, and 'I runned' achieves this. It is only later that the child will get formal instruction on the irregularities of the language that they have not managed to pick up for themselves along the way.

Is language development a result of nature or nurture?

The easy answer to this question is that language development relies on both nature and nurture. Certainly the universal sequence and timing of the stages of language development indicates the key role of nature in the process. Children with the most diverse levels of cognitive ability still manage to master the complex rules of grammar with little or no difficulty and no formal teaching. This should really reinforce the idea that there must be some sort of pre-programming to allow this level of learning to take place. Perhaps we have a kind of language 'processing box', which, once it starts to work, allows us to extract the rules of grammar of our native language without any conscious effort on our part. This suggests that the physical construction of our brains, which, through maturation seem to be hard-wired to assist language development, are important precursors for the development of human language.

But what about the role of nurture? Does the processing box work simply by being placed within earshot of a television or radio which emits the spoken word? It seems that this is not the case, as evidence has indicated that children only develop language provided they are given the opportunity to interact with other children or adults. We know this from studies of children who have been raised without language.

The importance of interaction

A study by Bard and Sachs (1977) looked at whether children simply pick up language from hearing it spoken around them. They studied a child called Jim who had normal hearing, but whose parents were both deaf. The parents used sign language to each other, but they did not use it with him. He listened to the radio and watched television, so he heard spoken language regularly, but he was unable to pick up the rules of grammar from passively experiencing language. His speech was seriously retarded and was not corrected until he started sessions with a speech therapist at the age of about 32. Fortunately, his speech improved dramatically from that point. This study provides us with evidence that we need to talk with other people in order for normal linguistic skills to develop, and demonstrates the importance of nurture.

The role of parents and caregivers

It seems that adults alter their use of language when talking to young children by simplifying it – using what is known as '**motherese**'. It seems to be unconscious, although we all do it. Obviously, whatever the reason for doing so, it is easier for children to understand. It goes without saying that mothers and caregivers play a particularly important role in a child's language development, and the kind of conversations they have with babies seem to follow a pattern:

- They hold one-way conversations (before the child has started to speak).

- They take turns with the baby, first with sounds, then with words, so that they respond to the baby's noise by making one back, and then the baby will make the next noise (this seemingly simple activity is an important part of the socialisation process).

Adults interacting with very young children frequently interpret and expand what the child says; for example, if the child says, 'My book', the mother might respond by saying, 'Yes, that's your red book over on the table.' They will describe objects surrounding the child, explain things in simple terms and answer questions with simple language. These basic activities are the building blocks of language development, and it seems that without them, children's linguistic skills fail to develop at the usual rate. In fact, children who have delayed language are often found to have parents who have not followed these seemingly natural patterns of response.

The critical period for language development

In 1967, Lenneberg suggested that there was what he called a **critical period** for language development and language learning. By this he meant that learning would take place with ease during a certain period of time, but after this critical period, learning language would become much harder. He pointed out that the stages of linguistic development were both uniform and universal, which could only mean that children are somehow biologically prepared for language. He justified this critical period by suggesting that it was controlled by physical changes in the brain, and maintained that up to puberty it was possible to learn language easily, but that after puberty it would cause problems. It seems that there is no convincing evidence for the physical changes in the brain, and there are many instances of adults who move abroad and learn new languages fluently, with little effort.

One study which gives some support to Lenneberg's ideas was the case of Genie, a child who was found in Los Angeles in 1970. She was discovered when she was 13 years old, although she looked about 8. She had been kept in a small room from the age of 20 months and punished if she made any noise. She was confined to a small, curtained room and strapped to a bed or a 'potty chair', so she could not walk around or interact with other people. In fact, she was beaten if she made any noise, so she grew up in an environment of extreme social and physical deprivation. Her case was reported by Curtiss (1977) as she was an ideal subject for an in-depth case study on late language development.

According to Lenneberg, Genie had passed the critical period and therefore should have had tremendous problems learning language. However, she did learn a kind of primitive language, although her speech was never normal and she spoke in a kind of high-pitched, squeaky voice. She also lacked the ability to speak spontaneously and often had to deliberate about what she wanted to say. She managed to learn some elements of sign language too, but as a case subject Genie was not ideal. It seems that she had some kind of brain damage, but unfortunately it was impossible to work out whether this damage had occurred at birth or was a result of her early years of deprivation – so it was a flawed study from the start.

The major theories of language acquisition

We have now mentioned the two main theories of language acquisition – the nature theory (processing box) and the nurture theory, which involves the child having verbal interactions with adults and other children. It is important to understand a little more about these theories.

Operant conditioning

If you accept that children need to interact with other people in order to learn language, and that the type of linguistic interaction varies according to the age of the child, you must accept that nurture is extremely important in the development of language. However, we have not considered how the child actually learns language. The first major theory of language acquisition suggests that language is simply learned in the same way that we learn other behaviours, that is, we learn by operant conditioning. This theory was proposed by Skinner in 1957.

B.F. Skinner

Skinner was a **behaviourist**, and 'hard' behaviourists believe that all behaviours and abilities are learned. Skinner therefore suggested that if adults praise the child, reinforcing whatever it is doing, this will make it more likely for that behaviour to be repeated. (Think of a child learning to say 'mama' and 'dada' – the excitement that Mummy and Daddy demonstrate would be enough of a reinforcement to make it more likely to happen again.)

The idea behind this kind of learning is that we learn by making an association between what we are doing and a positive result. The result, as we have seen, may be that the parent praises or laughs at the child. This means that the child is more likely to repeat the sound it has made, and gradually it comes to shape the sounds into actual words. It may also be that the child receives something as a result of what it says or does; for example, if the child asks for a sweet and is given one, this will be the reinforcement for that kind of vocalisation. This would continue while the child learns the rules of grammar, because they will receive approval for grammatical correctness, even if this is not directly obvious.

Critics of this theory argue that it is difficult to explain how children learn the sheer number of words, especially words which do not relate to anything physical. How does a child learn abstract words, such as 'thinking', 'wondering', 'explicit' or 'positive', by operant conditioning? This theory also implies that children go through a gradual and lengthy process of trial-and-error learning, but as we know, children learn language extremely quickly and these rules would not be mastered in as short a time as 6 years. The other aspect of language acquisition that is not explained by the theory is how we come to make up our own unique sentences and change the words which have been spoken as a statement into a question. Surely we would only use language that we have heard before? Yet we produce totally novel sentences every day of our lives. Also, parents prefer their children to speak the truth rather than lie, and they have been observed reinforcing ungrammatical truths, rather than grammatical lies (Slobin 1975). Why, then, do children not grow up speaking ungrammatically when it was this kind of language which was reinforced?

Language acquisition device

The other contender for the explanation of language acquisition is Noam Chomsky, who put forward his opposing theory in 1965. Chomsky is a **nativist** who believes that we are biologically programmed to learn language. His argument suggests that parents do not pay close enough attention to children to provide the kind of systematic reinforcement that would be needed for this kind of learning. He agrees that language must be learned – because if you had been born in Italy you would speak Italian, not English – but he believes that we are in some way biologically programmed to learn language, and that this biological programming explains how we manage to do it so successfully and so quickly.

Noam Chomsky

Chomsky proposed that children have an innate processing box which he calls a **language acquisition device** (LAD), and this enables them to collect the information about grammatical rules and vocabulary from the world around them. He believes that the child acquires a 'deep and abstract theory' which lies behind the words of a language, regardless of whether that language is French, English or Chinese. This explains why any child can be brought up in any country and can effortlessly pick up the general grammatical principles of that language (what he termed the deep structure), even though the surface structure or actual words may change.

To back up his theory, Chomsky states that children pick up rules about language too rapidly for it to have come from their experience. An example of this is their ability to reverse pronouns in a sentence, depending on who is speaking:

> Mummy says to little Johnny, 'I am going shopping now. Would you like to come with me?'
>
> Little Johnny replies, 'Yes, I would like to come with you.'

The child refers to himself as 'I' and the person he is talking to as 'you' very easily, yet the language the child hears from the other person has these pronouns the other way round.

Chomsky also argued that of all the noises children are subjected to, speech is the only one they pick up, and they master its complexities even though they may never be taught grammar formally. They cannot acquire language simply by imitating parents either, because parents do not speak to their offspring in two-word sentences, but this is still a recognised stage in language development.

Language – the last bastion of human uniqueness?

Having covered the development of language in children, and considered the two main theories as to how this takes place, we will now consider the question: are humans the only species with the capacity for language?

If you were asked if animals communicate, your initial response would probably be to say, 'Of course they do', and you would be right. But what we need to be aware of here is exactly what we mean by communication. Most other animals communicate with each other by gesture, by smell and even by sound. The bee dances as a way of communicating to the other members of the hive where they can find pollen. If it dances in a sickle shape, this indicates a different direction to dancing in a figure of eight. Monkeys can indicate whether impending danger is in the sky or on the ground according to what kind of shriek they make. Dogs, foxes, cats, and so on, communicate their territory by scent. Most animals and birds communicate threats to others of the same species by patterns of behaviour that are easily understood. The male stickleback, for example, uses the red underside of his belly as a way of demonstrating territorial aggression to other sticklebacks.

However, most commentators are quick to distinguish between communication and language. If you were asked if animals have language, you might not be so quick to say yes. Although you may have heard people say, 'My dog understands every word I say to him', or even believe this yourself, it seems extremely unlikely that this is true. Evidence shows that although dogs can be trained to respond to verbal instructions such as 'sit' or 'stay', they cannot identify these words if they are hidden in a sentence.

Whether or not an animal can learn language has been investigated by attempting to teach language to other species. If we are biologically programmed to learn language (as suggested by Chomsky) and no other species has this ability, perhaps it is an innate ability which only humans have evolved. However, if other species can be taught to use language, it might support Skinner's theory that language is learned. It might also suggest that we are not so different from our close relatives in the animal kingdom, and would question the position taken by some that animals are inferior creatures over whom our dominance is morally justified.

You will no doubt be familiar with Charles Darwin's theory of evolution and know that, in evolutionary terms, our closest relatives are the great apes. There are four great apes: gorillas, orang-utans, **chimpanzees** and **bonobos**. (The last of these might not be familiar, but you will learn more about bonobos in the core study at the end of this section.) In order to find out whether another species was capable of learning a language, it made sense to start with our close relatives.

Thanks to films such as *King Kong* and *Congo*, most of us would think twice about poking a gorilla with a big stick. However, *Tarzan* and his sidekick chimp, Cheetah, and those cute tea adverts on the television have given the common chimpanzee an altogether cuddlier image. Trixi and Allan Gardner, who took on the task of raising a female chimpanzee, Washoe, in a human environment in the first attempt to teach sign language to a chimpanzee, were under no illusions. Specialists in rats and spiders, they were more used to animals that were bred for study and could be kept in a box on the laboratory counter. They were quick to point out that 'affectionate as chimps are, they are still wild animals'. It is important to remember this as we discuss attempts to teach language to animals.

Can an ape learn language?

It seems that the answer to this, like the answer to so many questions is, 'It depends'. First, it depends on what you mean by 'language', and second, it depends on what you mean by 'ape'. In order to consider whether animals have the capacity for language, we first need to consider what we mean by language.

What is language?

According to Banyard and Grayson (1996), language is 'a small number of signals (sounds, letters, gestures) that by themselves are meaningless, but can be put together according to certain rules to make an infinite number of messages'. The key factors here are the rules that we use which are well defined. An example of one of the rules we use is the rule of syntax, the order of the words we use in a sentence (e.g. subject – verb – object).

> He hat the put on.
>
> The lorry green out of the garage rolled.

Although we may think we know very little about English grammar, the sentences above are obviously wrong.

As we know, language is important to humans because it is necessary to help us socialise with others, and we are creatures who need to be social. Deaf people use sign language, which has the same grammatical structure as spoken language and can transmit the same information. For humans, language is vital for the transmission of ideas, to help us understand the world and to organise our thoughts; and language acts as a useful tool for learning about our personalities from how other people react to us. Language also enables us to communicate our intentions and to exert control over our environment.

A number of researchers have described lists of features which seem to be the essence of language. Hockett (1959) listed 13 design features, while Aitchison (1983) proposed that there were only 10 which she considered essential to make the difference between communication and language:

1. Use of the vocal/auditory channel

2. Arbitrariness (use of neutral symbols (words) to denote objects, etc.)

3. **SEMANTICITY (use of symbols to mean or refer to objects/actions)**

4. Cultural transmission (handing down the language from generation to generation)

5. Spontaneous usage (freely initiating speech, etc.)

6. Turn-taking (conversation is a two-way process)

7. Duality (organisation into basic sounds and combinations or sequences of these)

8. **DISPLACEMENT (reference to things not present in time or space)**

9. **STRUCTURE DEPENDENCE (the patterned nature of language and use of 'structured chunks', e.g. word order)**

10. **CREATIVITY (what Brown (1973) calls productivity; the ability to produce and understand an infinite number of novel utterances, including combining words to increase meaning)**

It is obvious that many of these do not seem to be present in the communications of animals. In fact, the four features **in bold** are those which Aitchison considered to be unique to humans. This is a useful definition of language for us to use here, although we should consider whether this description of language is somewhat ethnocentric. It is a bit like the goalkeeper in a game of football selecting a place to put the goalposts after the match has finished. One of the problems with deciding whether an animal has language or not is that definitions of language change. In other words, the goalposts are moved, and this has frustrated some researchers who work in the field of primate language. Still, we have to accept that language needs to be defined, and the above outline will serve our purposes for the time being.

What is an ape?

Having decided on what we mean by language, we now have to consider what we mean by 'ape'. Since the 1930s, attempts have been made to raise common chimpanzees (and, more recently, gorillas) to communicate linguistically. As the great apes are supposedly our closest relatives on the evolutionary scale, you can see why they were seen as the most likely candidates in attempts to teach an animal language. The problem was that early attempts were unsuccessful, which is not surprising, as the vocal equipment of apes is not adequate to deal with the range of sounds used in human language. Although they make lots of different sounds, these are more like shrieks and are very unrefined. They are usually made when the chimps are either excited or frightened, and seem to relate to the situation they are in. The rest of the time they are silent, so we could interpret the sounds they do make as being a very primitive, situation-specific noise rather than anything else. In fact, it is quite hard to imagine why the researchers believed that chimps could speak in the first place.

Teaching chimpanzees sign language and symbols

Kellogg and Kellogg (1933) were the first to attempt this and raised a female chimpanzee with their own child, but she never managed to utter a word! Hayes and Hayes (1951) tried with another female chimpanzee, Viki, who after 6 years only succeeded in saying the words 'up', 'cup', 'mama' and 'papa', and these words were somewhat unclear. This confirmed that the chimpanzee lacked the vocal equipment to enable it to make human vocalisations, even if it were so inclined.

Despite failing to teach Viki to speak, the Hayes' study did spark an idea for a method of teaching language to a chimpanzee that might be more likely to succeed. When she 'spoke' her words, Viki always accompanied the word with the same gesture, such as covering her nose as she said the word.

A further study by Allan and Trixi Gardner (1969) noted that chimps beg and make similar gestures spontaneously, which suggested that they might be able to learn a language if it were based on gesture rather than vocalisation. In other words, could a chimpanzee be taught sign language, the language used by deaf humans? The language the Gardners selected was American Sign Language (**ASL**) and the chimp they chose as their case study was Washoe (named after Washoe County, the location of the University of Nevada which was where the Gardners worked as researchers). Washoe was a wild captured infant female chimp, who was between 8 and 14 months of age at the beginning of the study. In order to use ASL, the Gardners, and those research assistants who would be Washoe's human companions, had to learn to sign. This was the first in a series of studies that attempted to teach apes ASL.

Capitalising on chimpanzees' natural propensity to copy, imitation of gestures and signs was encouraged. The Hayes had trained Viki to produce her 'words' with the prompt, 'Do this'; and a similar game was developed in order to encourage Washoe to imitate signs. She would happily imitate actions, but not always when asked or in the appropriate situation. The trainers would tickle her as a reward (or reinforcement) for that behaviour. However, she was not always cooperative, and even when she was she would sometimes become angry, sometimes aggressive, and would not take part any more. The Gardners remind us that this is one of the drawbacks of working with a wild animal: 'Pressed too hard, Washoe can become completely diverted from her original object; she may ask for something entirely different, run away, go into a tantrum, or even bite her tutor.'

With Washoe, as in the subsequent studies which attempted to train apes to produce language, instrumental conditioning was used. The Gardners used operant conditioning techniques. If she made a sign that was not totally accurate, the trainers would aim to get her to produce a better sign by shaping her fingers. This 'shaping' of the sign was progressive, and eventually she could be expected to produce a clear sign before it was accepted, acknowledged or rewarded. In this respect, Washoe's language learning was not like the acquisition of children's language. Children do not need to be instrumentally conditioned to acquire language; both vocabulary and syntax are acquired spontaneously in children, with no need for training.

Nonetheless, at the end of the study, the Gardners were convinced that Washoe had acquired signs and was using signs to stand for objects, as well as combining signs to create novel utterances, such as 'listen dog' or 'go sweet'. They suggested that work with other species should be carried out extensively before 'theories of language that depend upon the identification of aspects that are exclusively human' are accepted. They also believed that with refinements to their training process, work with other chimpanzees would exceed what they had achieved with Washoe in this first attempt at teaching sign language to a chimpanzee.

In 1972, three years after the Gardners published their results on Project Washoe, Duane Rumbaugh was working with another chimpanzee, Lana, at the Yerkes Regional Primate Research Centre in Atlanta, Georgia (USA). Rumbaugh did not use ASL, but instead employed a system of symbols, or **lexigrams**, to represent words. These symbols were arbitrary, that is, they did not look like the objects they stood for. Unlike Washoe, Lana lived in a laboratory and interacted with a machine. She could ask the machine for food, ask the machine to open a blind, play music, and so on. To do this, she had to press a sequence of signs, in the right order.

Teaching chimpanzees grammar

In 1973, another researcher, Herbert Terrace, began his project with a chimpanzee called Nim Chimpsky (after the famous linguist Noam Chomsky, who was of the opinion that chimpanzees could not be taught language). Terrace had ambitious aims and set his sights high, aiming to achieve what other researchers had only hinted was possible, by reporting the way chimpanzees combined words or symbols, to demonstrate that Nim knew grammar. Sue Savage-Rumbaugh, the lead researcher in our core study (below), pointed out in another study that 'the demonstration of syntax' was the 'holy grail of linguists, and, by default, ape-language researchers' (Savage-Rumbaugh and Lewin 1994: 53).

Working with 60 sign language teachers over 4 years, Nim learned much the same as the other chimps trained in ASL, and eventually had a vocabulary of 125 signs. He made many double word combinations, as other chimps had done (Washoe began spontaneously combining signs once she had learned eight to ten signs).

Terrace and his team were initially convinced that Nim was displaying grammar, and after Nim went back to the Institute of Primate Studies in Oklahoma, Terrace eagerly reviewed his extensive video footage of Nim's interactions. The more he watched, the more his initial belief in Nim's 'grammar' changed to doubt. He noted that by age 4, three-quarters of Nim's signing was in imitation of his teachers, and much of it focused on requests for food or play activities. The language-like utterances of apes were a form of the Clever Hans effect (see below), Terrace concluded. Savage-Rumbaugh points out that Terrace's conclusion was that 'Nim fooled me'. The research paper he and his team presented in 1979 concluded that the 'utterances' of apes were best described as imitations of their teachers, or were unconsciously cued by their researchers, and were not examples of sentences using grammar.

Criticism of ape language studies

The criticism of ape language studies was further compounded in May 1980, when a conference was held by a researcher called Seboek, whose negative opinion was clear six months before the conference, as Savage-Rumbaugh and Lewin (1994: 50) later reported: 'Ape-language is prey to the **Clever Hans effect**, or worse, opined Seboek. The results of research are to be explained as a result of "unconscious bias, self-deception, magic and circus performance".'

At the beginning of the twentieth century, an amazing demonstration of animal intelligence was being taken from town to town by his owner Willhelm Von Osten. A horse, called Clever Hans, appeared to be able to do arithmetic. A maths problem would be written on a blackboard and clever Hans would stomp out the answer using his hoof. He was so rarely wrong that it was assumed that Hans was a very clever Hans indeed.

However, all is not always as it seems. Hans *was* a clever horse, but not for his ability to do mathematical functions. He could read his owner very well, and Hans was able to sense the right answer, as his owner gave involuntary and unconscious cues when Hans had reached it and therefore should stop. This was pointed out to Von Osten, and proved by showing that Hans could not get any answers right if Von Osten was not present, or if Von Osten did not know the answer himself. Von Osten was very disappointed when this was revealed to him, as he had not intentionally defrauded his audiences and believed himself that Hans was getting the answers right on his own.

The Clever Hans effect, then, means that the ape language researchers were misinterpreting the behaviour of the chimps as 'language' because they did not realise, like Von Osten, that they were unconsciously cueing the responses from the chimps, or were priming the chimps, whose responses were mere imitation of the signs made to them by their human companions. Examination of footage of both Washoe and Nim, for example, confirmed that imitation accounted for a large part of the chimps' signs.

This is an example of unconscious experimenter bias.

Seboek's conference was given the title 'The Clever Hans Phenomenon: Communication with Horses, Whales, Apes and People'. Three ape language researchers attended: Duane Rumbaugh, who had worked on the Lana Project; Sue Savage-Rumbaugh, who between 1975 and 1980 worked with two chimpanzees, Sherman and Austin; and Herbert Terrace. The first two attempted to support their findings with what they believed were scientific data which countered the arguments that cueing and priming by researchers accounted for ape language, but this was not what the conference concluded.

Herbert Terrace, on the other hand, reiterated his negative views on ape language after working with Nim. Seboek concurred with his view, ending the conference saying, 'In my opinion, the alleged language experiments with apes can be divided into three groups; one: outright fraud, two: self-deception, and three: those conducted by Terrace'. As a result of Terrace et al.'s research paper in 1979 and this conference in 1980, ape language research was viewed with scepticism by academics. It consequently became difficult to publish research in the field.

In between the Terrace paper and the Clever Hans conference, Sue Savage-Rumbaugh and her fellow researchers had published their work on Sherman and Austin, and believed they had scientific evidence to suggest that apes are capable of some aspects of language. Sue Savage-Rumbaugh had worked with Washoe after she left the Gardners, and had married Duane Rumbaugh, the researcher responsible for the Lana project. She had wide experience with apes who had been claimed to have language, but had doubts about how much imitation, cueing and wishful thinking might account for claims that apes could understand language, especially spoken language. She had witnessed first-hand Washoe's limited ability to respond to spoken instructions, and in her work with Lana had also found that the chimp could not respond accurately to spoken requests.

Although she went to work with Rumbaugh in 1974, two years into the Lana project, Sue Savage-Rumbaugh chose to focus first on studying and comparing the behaviour of the great apes at the research centre. She was gradually drawn into the Lana project, however, and this was the start of her career as an ape language researcher.

In 1975, she began her work with two chimpanzees, Sherman and Austin. Sceptical about the language abilities which had been claimed for other chimps, and aware of the criticism that the researchers might just be cueing the animal's responses, the emphasis with Sherman and Austin was on getting them to communicate with each other. It was also an aim of the study to demonstrate that their 'language' could go beyond using symbols associatively to trigger outcomes such as getting food, and to show that chimpanzees could use symbols referentially, indicating an understanding that a particular symbol *means* a particular thing. This put the emphasis on trying to demonstrate not what symbols the chimps could use, but what their use revealed about what they *understood* by the symbol.

Language comprehension develops before **language production** in children, and comprehension outstrips production throughout our lives. (For example, you are capable of *reading* this book – language comprehension – but would you be capable of *writing* it – language production?) Savage-Rumbaugh theorised that it is not only production which can signal that an ape has language. Surely if the ape understands language, he could be said to have language? This represented a turnaround in studies of ape language, no longer focusing on language production and getting apes to demonstrate as many signs as possible, but turning the focus to language comprehension and trying to work out whether the ape could understand that symbols (or signs or words) stand for something.

Chimpanzee	Study	Method and results
Viki	Hayes and Hayes (1951)	Tried to reinforce Viki for spoken language. After 6 years this was shown to be unsuccessful as she was able to 'say' only four words.
Washoe	Gardner and Gardner (1969)	Used ASL to try to encourage Washoe to use signs. The signs were taught in a naturalistic environment, based at the Gardners' home in Nevada, by imitation, instrumental conditioning and shaping. Washoe acquired signs and appeared to use them semantically.
Lana	Rumbaugh (1977)	Lana was taught to use a symbolic system to produce language. Here, a lexigram, or symbol, was used to represent words. Lana communicated by pushing the symbols on a machine, and had to press the right symbols in the right order for her requests to be granted.
Nim	Terrace (1979)	Terrace focused his study on trying to get Nim to demonstrate grammar. He was initially optimistic and thought that Nim's chaining of signs indicated word order and grammar. On reflection, he noticed that the videotapes of the chimp suggested that the majority of the utterances were simply imitations and did not represent a chimpanzee using sentences.
Sherman and Austin	Savage-Rumbaugh (1979)	Using the lexigram system, the focus of this study was to see if the chimpanzees understood that words mean something (that they stand for something). The emphasis was on communication between the chimps to avoid the problem of researchers priming or cueing the chimps.

Examples of attempts to teach common chimpanzees language (language production studies)

Taking all things into account, in 1980 the general belief among academics – even Herbert Terrace, who had invested a great deal of time and work trying to teach language to a chimpanzee – was that apes were not capable of acquiring language, and that anyone who said they were, was either deluding themselves, succumbing to the Clever Hans effect, or, worse still, deliberately defrauding the public.

Based on her work with Sherman and Austin, Sue Savage-Rumbaugh did not agree. Sherman and Austin showed that chimps could be trained to use symbols as referents, but could not acquire this ability spontaneously, and, like other studies, showed that their language production was highly contingent on being fed as a result. Although they did not seem to understand spoken language, this study suggested to Savage-Rumbaugh that if the focus was on comprehension rather than production of language, then apes did have the capacity to demonstrate some aspects of language. An ape she was to meet in 1980, and with whom she is still working today, was to convince her that not only was she right about this, but that she had underestimated what apes might be capable of in terms of language comprehension.

So can an ape learn language? We said earlier that first it depends on what we mean by language. We have seen that studies which focused on language production and the use of grammar by chimpanzees were unsuccessful, or the claimed successes were subject to the criticism that researchers were cuing or priming the chimps' responses. Savage-Rumbaugh changed the focus to language comprehension, and began, with Sherman and Austin, to tease out the aspects of chimps' understanding that are language-like. So if by language we mean 'language comprehension', then it may be that our answer will be yes, apes can learn language.

Next we said that whether an *ape* can learn language depends on what we mean by ape. Kanzi is the main subject in our core study (below). Kanzi is a male **bonobo**, not a common chimpanzee, whom Sue Savage-Rumbaugh saw born in captivity and has worked with since he was 6 months old.

Sue Savage-Rumbaugh working on teaching a chimp to use lexigrams

THE STUDY

S. Savage-Rumbaugh, K. McDonald, R.A. Sevcik, W.D. Hopkins and E. Rubert (1986) 'Spontaneous symbol acquisition and communicative use by pygmy chimpanzees (*Pan paniscus*)'

Journal of Experimental Psychology, 115(3): 211–35

BACKGROUND

Work with common chimpanzees claimed that their language comprehension skills were better than their production skills. However, data, when closely inspected, was either incomplete or showed that understanding was limited to a few phrases drilled in contextually specific situations. Critics, focusing on what was claimed to be 'language' used in language production studies in common chimpanzees, argued that this too could be put down to the animals responding to the cues and prompts given by their human companions and therefore wasn't really language at all.

The focus of this study, however, was language comprehension, rather than language production. The authors considered that if an ape:

- began to understand spoken English without being trained to do so;
- could do more than just respond on cue;

then this would suggest that the ape would possess language abilities similar to those of humans, and 'even if the ape were unable to speak, an ability to comprehend language would be the cognitive equivalent of having acquired language' (p.214).

Was Kanzi, a bonobo, such an ape?

KEY CONCEPTS

Bonobo

Bonobos were the last of the great apes to be identified. Having been discovered in the Congo (called Zaire from 1971 to 1997) in 1922, they were first called 'pygmy chimpanzees', as they are very like common chimpanzees (*Pan trogladytes*), but smaller. However, they were identified as a separate species in 1922 and called bonobos (*Pan paniscus*).

It is believed that humans and chimpanzees had a common ancestor. Five million years ago, the lineage split into two, with one line leading to man (*Homo sapiens*), and the other leading to both bonobos and chimpanzees.

Bonobos' natural environment is in a remote region of Africa. In the 1970s, an American researcher, Randall Sussman, led a team observing them in the wild:

To reach the region from the USA [you] must first fly to Brussels for a connection to Kinshasa, Zaire's capital city. From there to the Lamako forest requires an eight-day riverboat ride, a two-day trip by Land Rover, and a day's hike through swamp to the research station's base camp. . . The remoteness of the region explains the world's long ignorance of the bonobo, and until recently protected the animals from danger by human exploitation. (Savage-Rumbaugh and Lewin 1994: 114)

In this study, the researchers point out that there are marked differences between the bonobo and the chimpanzee. As early as 1925, a researcher called Robert Yerkes had compared a bonobo (Chim) with a common chimpanzee (Panzee), although at the time he believed they were both chimpanzees, as bonobos had not yet been classified separately. Chim seemed an extraordinary animal, much brighter than Panzee and more humanlike in behaviour.

Further research has confirmed that, in comparison with common chimpanzees:

- bonobos make more frequent eye contact, gestures and vocalisations;
- bonobos' vocalisations are more frequent and elaborate;
- bonobos' male–female ties are very close, whereas in chimpanzees they are weak;
- male bonobos take part in infant care, while male chimpanzees do not;
- in the wild there is a balance of males and females in bonobo groups, whereas there are more females than males in groups of chimpanzees;
- food sharing is common between adult bonobos, whereas food sharing is limited to mother and offspring in common chimpanzees.

The differences in gestures, eye contact and vocalisations suggested to the authors that bonobos might be better prepared to learn language than other apes. Studies of bonobos showed that they were brighter than chimpanzees, and this again suggested they might be better subjects than chimpanzees for an animal language study.

The authors also explain why no bonobos had been used in ape language studies before: 'This is primarily attributable to the difficulty in obtaining these animals. They are rare, both in captivity and in the wild, and it is presently illegal to export them from their severely threatened native habitat' (p.214).

AIMS

The aim of this study was to report on the language acquisition of Kanzi, a bonobo, and his younger sister, Mulika. The report covers a 17-month period, beginning when Kanzi was 2 years and 6 months old.

The language acquisition in the bonobos was compared, where appropriate, with that of two common chimpanzees, Sherman and Austin, studied earlier (1975–80).

METHOD

A case study was carried out, focusing primarily on one bonobo, Kanzi, but also including early data of his younger sister, Mulika's, language acquisition. The data were gathered by observation.

It is important to point out, as the authors did, that the findings of the study were 'serendipitous', a lucky accident. They tell us that the study is 'not an experiment, rather a description of events that lead us to the conclusion that Kanzi. . .was acquiring symbols spontaneously at two and a half years of age. . .followed by a developmental account of this phenomenon across the subsequent 17 months' (p.214).

A longitudinal design was used in this study, reporting over a 17-month period of Kanzi's language acquisition. (Comparisons with the common chimpanzees reflected data gathered over a 10-year span.)

KEY CONCEPTS

Longitudinal versus snapshot designs

In a **snapshot** design, different groups of people are tested at the same point in time and their performances are compared. Examples from the core studies include the subway Samaritan study by Piliavin et al. (Chapter 2), and Samuel and Bryant's study on conservation (Chapter 4).

The advantages of snapshot studies over longitudinal studies are that they are relatively quick and inexpensive to carry out, can easily be replicated to test the reliability of findings, and are relatively easy to modify. This final point means that if design faults become apparent, the study can be repeated with modifications to eliminate them. It also means that variations of the study can be carried out easily to investigate fully the variables which may affect behaviour.

In a **longitudinal** study, one subject or one group of individuals is studied over a long period of time, taking regular samples of behaviour. This design means we can track development and monitor changes over time. In the Savage-Rumbaugh et al. study, for example, it allows us to see the development of Kanzi's language. The longitudinal approach also enabled the researchers to make comparisons between Kanzi and common chimpanzees.

Subjects

Four great apes are reported on in this study: Kanzi, Mulika, Sherman and Austin.

The main focus of this study is a bonobo, Kanzi. He was born in captivity at the Yerkes Regional Primate Centre in Atlanta, Georgia (USA), on 28 October

1980. Kanzi was assigned to the Language Research Centre at 6 months of age, accompanying his mother, Matata, a wild-caught female bonobo, who was the intended subject for the language study. Matata was not Kanzi's biological mother, but had kidnapped him from his mother, Lorel, when he was just a few hours old.

On 22 December 1983, Matata gave birth to Mulika, the second bonobo subject in this study.

Both Kanzi and Mulika had experienced separations from Matata as infants (for Kanzi, this was when Matata was removed for breeding purposes, and for Mulika, there was a 4-month separation due to an eye infection). Both bonobos built up a strong bond with their human carers, and although they spent time with their mother each day during this study, both bonobos chose to spend most of their time with people.

The language acquisition of the two bonobos was compared with the language acquisition of two common chimpanzees, Sherman and Austin, previously studied at the Language Research Centre by Sue Savage-Rumbaugh.

Procedure

Kanzi was different from other apes in ape language studies because he was the first to acquire symbols spontaneously, without training. Kanzi acquired symbols while his mother was being trained, and he was never trained or directly reinforced to acquire symbols. He seemed to have learned to use lexigrams spontaneously.

In a longitudinal study where a great deal of data are gathered, the procedure and reporting of data can be very thorough and complicated, and this study is no exception! The procedure is broken down into sections, which we will consider in turn, as follows:

1 Description of the environment where the apes were living
2 The communication system used with the apes
3 The exposure of Kanzi and Mulika to lexigrams – how the bonobos learned
4 Data recording and criteria for language acquisition in the apes
5 Formal testing carried out with the apes

1 Description of the environment where the apes were living
The apes all lived at the Language Research Centre. There were two sides to this centre: 'chimpside', where the ape language studies were carried out, and 'childside', where work was done with children and teenagers with special educational needs to help them develop language.

In the chimpside, the apes could either be outdoors or indoors, depending on the weather.

The naturalistic outdoor environment had the following characteristics:

- The centre was set in a 55-acre forest.
- Every day, food was put at 17 sites in the woods, with the same foods always in the same place. In warmer weather, the chimps would not be fed indoors, so they would have to go out, with their human companions, and gather food in the woods, therefore creating the most natural behaviours possible. Most of their day was taken up doing this.
- Having foods placed in the same locations each day gave an opportunity for teaching Kanzi, and once he had acquired a few symbols he was shown photos of some of the foods, from which he selected what he wanted to eat and was then taken there. He quickly learned the location of all 17 foods and could guide others to each location, often holding the photo all the way. Later, when he had acquired more symbols, he used lexigrams to indicate his food choices. Mulika learned to do this in the same way as Kanzi as she got older.
- Once at the location selected by Kanzi, if the food selected was not eaten, he would be asked if he wanted to put it in the backpack. If he indicated yes (e.g. by pushing the food towards the backpack), the food would be taken. If he did not indicate in this way, the food would be left at the location. Having food from different locations in the backpack gave the opportunity for further communication. If Kanzi indicated 'juice', he would be asked if he wanted the juice in the backpack or if he wanted to go to the location for juice. If he wanted the backpack juice he would touch the backpack; if he wanted to go to the location he would gesture in that direction. (When Kanzi was 3 years old, a blind test was run with an experimenter who had never been in the woods with Kanzi. A description of this is included in the Results section, page 166.)

The indoor environment had the following characteristics:

- During the day, Kanzi and Mulika were asked to help with activities such as laundry and food preparation. They always wanted to play games (e.g. hide, chase, tickle, playbite). They often helped spontaneously in simple jobs like wiping up spills, washing up, spraying the hose, and so on.
- They were allowed to travel from place to place at the centre (with their human companions), for example to visit their mother, Matata, or to go to the childside.
- They played with toys in their free time (e.g. clay, bubbles, dolls). Kanzi was very fond of balls and often carried more than one at a time. They watched videos of people and animals they knew at the centre. At night, Kanzi asked to watch TV and was shown films with lexigram overlays that were interesting to chimps.

2 The communication system used with the apes

KEY CONCEPTS

Lexigrams

Lexigrams are pictures or symbols that are used to stand for words. They are arbitrary, that is, they do not look like the word or object they are being used to describe.

Visual symbol system	Based on the system developed by Duane Rumbaugh with a common chimpanzee (Lana). It consisted of a keyboard of symbols, which lit up when they were pressed. A lit symbol was the equivalent of uttering a word. Each symbol, or lexigram, was arbitrary, that is, it did not look like the object or word it stood for.
No. of symbols	Initially 8 lexigrams At the end of this study, 256 lexigrams.
Sound	Kanzi's keyboards were connected to an electronic voice synthesiser, so that words were spoken when the symbols were pressed. This was added after it was discovered that Kanzi understood spoken English.
Mobility indoors	Lana used only a stationary keyboard, in one place in the room.

	Sherman and Austin used three keyboards connected to the computer by extension cords, allowing the chimpanzees to move the keyboards from room to room with them. Kanzi used similar keyboards to Sherman and Austin.
Mobility outdoors	Kanzi used a number of battery-powered keyboards, attached to a portable computer and portable voice synthesiser (limited battery life). Kanzi also used 'pointing boards', consisting of laminated cards showing photos of all the lexigrams. Kanzi and Mulika would communicate by pointing to the photo of the lexigram they wanted to use. **NOTE:** The pointing boards had not worked with Sherman, Austin and Lana, as the common chimpanzees tended to make sweeping gestures towards the card and it was not clear which lexigram they were trying to indicate.
Other means of communication	When communicating through lexigrams, the human researchers also used spoken English and gestures, including approximately 100 ASL (sign language) gestures. The aim was to communicate with the chimpanzees in whatever way worked, and any form of response from the chimpanzees was accepted.

3 The exposure of Kanzi and Mulika to lexigrams – how the bonobos learned
The humans working with the bonobos used lexigrams and spoken English to communicate a wide variety of things. Kanzi and Mulika were taught in a similar environment to that in which Sherman and Austin had been taught, and the same humans who had taught Sherman, Austin and Lana were teachers to Kanzi and Mulika. However, there were important differences in the way Kanzi and Mulika learned language:

- Sherman and Austin were *trained* to use lexigrams and did not *acquire* them in an observational setting.
- There was no speech synthesiser on Sherman and Austin's keyboard, as they did not understand spoken language.
- Sherman and Austin did not use a keyboard outside the laboratory, as it was not clear what they were pointing to on the pointing card. It appeared that the common chimpanzees could only use the lexigrams where they pressed the keyboard to light them up.

Similarities between the environment for Sherman and Austin and the environment for Kanzi and Mulika included:

- attachment to caretakers;
- the opportunity to observe and interact with people;

- exposure to human language;
- exposure to gestures, lexigrams and photographs;
- formal testing;
- opportunities to play, watch TV, and so on.

Name	Kanzi	Mulika	Sherman	Austin
Same trainers	X	X	X	X
Trained to use lexigrams (did not acquire them in observational setting)			X	X
Learned by observation	X	X		
Speech synthesiser	X	X		
Pointing card	X	X		
Lexigrams with lit-up symbols	X	X	X	X
Attachment to caretakers	X	X	X	X
Opportunities to observe and interact with people	X	X	X	X
Exposure to human language	X	X	X	X
Exposure to gestures, lexigrams and photographs	X	X	X	X
Formal testing	X	X	X	X
Opportunities to play (e.g. watch TV)	X	X	X	X

How the bonobos learned language

Kanzi and Mulika did not need to be trained to use symbols; they learned by observation. They used symbols spontaneously, understood spoken language, did not mix up symbols once learned (e.g. they did not use the symbol for apple when they meant orange), and could identify symbols regardless of location.

So instead of a training programme, as had been used with Sherman and Austin, the people around Kanzi and Mulika modelled language use, by using the lexigrams and commenting vocally on their daily activities. Sometimes Kanzi and Mulika would observe the usage of the keyboard, and sometimes they would ignore it.

4 Data recording and criteria for language acquisition in the apes
From the age of 2 years and 6 months, Kanzi's utterances were *all* recorded and coded for 17 months. Those utterances on the computerised keyboard were

automatically recorded. Outdoors, codings and recordings were done by hand and were entered into the computer at the end of the day.

In this study, every one of Kanzi's utterances between the ages of 30 and 47 months, and Mulika's between 11 and 21 months, were included. Their utterances were coded as follows:

- either correct or incorrect; and
- either spontaneous (initiated by Kanzi and Mulika, with no prior prompt or query or behaviour by their human companions), or imitated (utterances that included any part of a companion's prior keyboard utterance), or structured (those initiated by questions, requests or object-showing by human companions, to see if Kanzi and Mulika could give a right answer).

Data recording was done on the spot in real time. There can be problems with the accuracy of such recordings, so a test of reliability was carried out to establish the accuracy of the observations. (This is described in the Commentary at the end of the study, page 168.)

In order to decide whether Kanzi or Mulika had acquired a symbol and added it to their vocabulary, it was important to set up criteria, or rules, for deciding if a symbol had been learned. Earlier studies, such as the Gardners' work with Washoe, had set criteria that insisted on the use of signs on consecutive days, and in the correct context. However, the authors of this study considered these criteria to be faulty, as, with prompting and cues, chimps could give a correct sign in the right context without really understanding it. Also, looking for the sign every day often meant setting up a context for it to be used, and again, this might lead to a cued rather than a real use of the sign/symbol.

The criteria established for Kanzi and Mulika were called a **behavioural concordance measure**. Only spontaneous utterances could be scored, and the symbol would be considered as being used properly only if the behaviour of the ape immediately after the symbol was used was consistent (in concordance with) the symbol. For example, 'if Kanzi requested a trip to the treehouse he would be told "Yes, we can go to the treehouse". However, only if he then led the experimenter to this location could a correct behavioural concordance be scored for the word treehouse' (p.216).

In other words, what Kanzi said had to match up with what Kanzi did. If he asked for a banana and was offered an orange, an apple and a banana, the utterance 'banana' could only be accepted if he selected a banana from the offered selection of fruits; or if he was told he could go and get a banana from a particular location, he would have to lead the researcher to the right place in order for 'banana' to be counted as an utterance. Another way for concordance to be established would be if Kanzi asked for a banana from the backpack and then selected a banana from it (although this was not counted if there were only bananas in the backpack!).

The productive vocabulary of Kanzi and Mulika was scored if they used the utterance correctly on nine out of ten occasions (although these did not need to be on consecutive days, as the bonobos did not use the same symbols every day).

5 Formal testing carried out with the apes
The types of tests used and the results from the tests are described in the Results section, below.

RESULTS

Summarising qualitative and quantitative data from a longitudinal study of this kind can be difficult, given the sheer amount of data collected to be reported. In the research paper, the results section makes up the bulk of the report, and the results are presented under the following headings, which we will follow here:

1 Untutored gestures
2 First appearance of lexigram use for communication purposes
3 Kanzi's progress during the 17 months after his initial separation from Matata
4 Receptive language comprehension
5 Combinations
6 Imitation versus spontaneous utterances
7 Formal tests of productive and receptive language capacity
8 The blind test in the forest

1 Untutored gestures
Aged 6–16 months, both Kanzi and Mulika used gestures spontaneously to get what they wanted. Matata had done this too, but not so much as her offspring did. Sherman and Austin had also done this, but in the common chimpanzees it developed later, and gestures were not as specific as the bonobos' gestures. For example, if Kanzi wanted a nut cracked he would give the nut to a human companion and bang his hand to signal what he wanted. If the human did not seem to understand, he would further gesture by getting a small rock and hitting the nut with it, to show clearly what he wanted to happen.

2 First appearance of lexigram use for communication purposes
Immediately after Kanzi's mother, Matata, left for breeding purposes, Kanzi started to be more interested in the lexigram keyboard. He had already pressed the lexigram keyboard before she left, and the researchers assumed he was just pressing any key and running to the fridge, associating the keyboard with food. However, to the surprise of the researchers, it became clear that he had begun searching for specific lexigrams. It was still assumed that this was not an indication of his using the lexigrams to request things, but it was treated as if it were, much as human children's accidental utterances are often interpreted as intentional and responded to.

Unexpectedly, and again, much to the surprise of his human companions, it seemed that Kanzi had learned that particular lexigrams stood for particular things. For example, if he pressed 'apple' and was offered, say, an orange, a banana and an apple, he would take the apple and ignore the others. The same was true if he pressed 'banana'. This suggested that he was using the lexigrams referentially, to stand for the items requested. His referential use of the symbols was demonstrated even more clearly when he was shown three fruits, gave the right lexigrams for them and was not interested in eating any of them.

Similar examples of this use of the symbols was reported in the daily notes made soon after Matata left: 'After eating an apple and drinking some juice, both of which he had requested on the keyboard, Kanzi again touched 'juice', then picked up the juice, poured it out and began stomping the apple and juice together while displaying a play face' (p.219).

Mulika, who had not observed Matata being trained, but had observed Kanzi and humans using the keyboard, began using symbols at 12 months, earlier than Kanzi. Not observed in Kanzi, Mulika went through a stage of using one lexigram, 'milk', as a general request, then pointing to the object she wanted. The use of the lexigram as a request signal is important here, as she could get what she wanted just by pointing, as she had been doing since she was very young.

She generalised 'milk' in this way for two months, then added a second lexigram, 'surprise', which was just what she got: a food she had never had before. She acquired about a dozen more symbols over the next few months, and 'milk' came to refer only to milk itself.

To suggest how the use of symbols might move from associative use to referential use, the authors describe how Kanzi learned the symbol 'strawberries'.

In children and in apes, new words often only reappear in the context in which they were first encountered, only later being generalised and becoming referential in their use. Kanzi was being taken on the mushroom trail when the word 'strawberries' was first introduced, and the group went off to find some. For a while, Kanzi only used 'strawberries' spontaneously while on the mushroom trail. He could only respond accurately to tests of the strawberry symbol once he began to use the symbol beyond the original context. How might this happen? The authors suggest the following:

> As a symbol's usage becomes expanded to an increasing number of contexts it probably becomes more efficient to abstract some common-alities from all these different situations. It is these commonalities that then become the meaning of this symbol. For example, if Kanzi learns to touch the symbol for strawberries when he wants to travel to the place where they can be found, when he is asking for one to eat, and when shown a photograph of strawberries, he will probably extract the one common referent (red sweet berries) from all those circumstances, and assign to that referent the symbol 'strawberries'. (p.220)

3 Kanzi's progress during the 17 months after his initial separation from Matata

Kanzi made rapid progress in his acquisition of symbols in this time. Using the behavioural concordance measure, his single-word utterances aged 30–46 months comprised 44 lexigrams.

Symbol	Age acquired (months)
Orange Peanut Banana Apple Bedroom[a] Chase Austin	30
Sweet potato Raisin Ball Cherry[b] Peaches Coke Bite	31
Melon Jelly Tomato Orange drink	32
Trailer Milk	33
Key Tickle[c]	34
Coffee Juice[d] Bread	35
Groom	37
Egg	40
Hamburger Water M&M Surprise	41
Clover Matata TV Orange juice	42

Symbol	Age acquired (months)
Mulika Carrot	43
Grab Treehouse Blanket Blackberry[e]	44
Mushroom trail	45
Refrigerator Hot dog	46

Note: Words with superscripts dropped below criterion for the month(s) indicated.
a: 33–46; b: 32–34; c: 44–45; d: 43, 45–46; e: 45.
Source: Savage-Rumbaugh 1986: 221

Cumulative list of Kanzi's symbol acquisition

Mulika began to acquire symbols earlier, but more slowly than Kanzi had. It may be that Kanzi learned more than was realised in the time when he was able to observe his mother being trained to use lexigrams, although when Kanzi was first learning he had a keyboard with 8 lexigrams. Mulika always had a harder task, learning from Kanzi's keyboard with 256 lexigrams.

Mulika's language use met the behavioural concordance requirements on 85 out of 86 occasions within the latter two-thirds of the period covered by this study. Using the criterion of nine out of ten correct consecutive uses (see below), her vocabulary was 37 words:

milk, surprise, juice, bubbles, t-room, jelly, toothpaste, key, go, coke, black-berry, grape, staff office, jello, water, strawberry, cherry, sour cream, ice, banana, blueberry, orange drink, melon, coffee, Kool-Aid, M&M, orange juice, orange, peanut, food, can opener, apple, peaches, bite, Matata, balloon and lemonade. (p.221)

4 Receptive language comprehension

Children understand language before they produce it, and so did Kanzi. To examine his receptive language, a criterion was established to test what he understood. He had to give nine out of ten correct responses when a symbol was used by a person. For example, Kanzi might be asked to fetch his ball (with the human being careful not to glance at the ball or indicate it in any way).

Kanzi's receptive symbol use exceeded his productive use. Mulika's formal test scores (described below, page 165) also showed that what she understood outstripped her productive language use (as measured by the behavioural concordance criterion).

5 Combinations

Kanzi started to use multiple symbols, or combinations, early – within one month of his first spontaneous symbol usage on the keyboard. He used them much less frequently than single-word utterances, accounting for about 6 per cent of his utterances.

Kanzi's use of combinations in the 17 months covered by this study can be broken down as follows:

- Kanzi made 2,805 combined symbol utterances.
- Of the 2,805 combined symbol utterances, 2,540 were non-imitated, and of these non-imitated utterances, 764 were unique, used only once.
- Partially imitated or prompted combinations accounted for 265 of the 2,805 total, with all but 10 of these judged to be in the appropriate context.

The authors compared Kanzi's combinations with those of Nim, the common chimpanzee studied by Herbert Terrace. This showed that Kanzi's combinations tended to add symbols to provide more information (e.g. 'ice water go', to get someone to fetch him ice water). Nim's combinations had often just included meaningless repetitions (e.g. 'play me Nim play').

Most of Kanzi's two-word utterances, however, were best described as joint requests (e.g. 'hotdog coke' was a request for both items at once), or sometimes for both items to be mixed together.

In his three-item utterances, however, he often specified individuals other than himself as the actor and the person to be acted on (e.g. he invented games where he suggested 'A chase B', where A and B were human companions). This is interesting in that his human companions never made such suggestions, so he was not imitating them, and they had not engaged in such games with each other until Kanzi showed an interest in them doing so.

Kanzi	Nim
Person (g) chase Kanzi	Grape eat Nim
Person 1 (g) tickle person 2 (g)	Finish hug Nim
Chase bite person (g)	Tickle me tickle
(g) indicates a gesture used rather than a lexigram in Kanzi's utterance.	

Examples of Kanzi and Nim's three-word utterances

6 Imitation versus spontaneous utterances

Spontaneous utterances accounted for about 80 per cent of Kanzi's single-word and combinatorial (two- and three-symbol) utterances; prompted, imitated or partially imitated responses accounted for only 11 per cent.

Comparisons were made between imitative utterances in Kanzi, Mulika, Sherman, Austin, Nim and a comparable human child acquiring language. Only Nim's level of imitation was significantly higher than the child's. (He differed from the other common chimpanzees here as he did not receive extra training in using symbols as referents.)

Nim also showed a lower proportion of spontaneous utterances. However, the spontaneous utterances by Sherman and Austin often occurred after a teacher had carried out some behaviour (e.g. introducing food to a situation), suggesting that their utterances depended more on situational cues than the spontaneous utterances from Kanzi and Mulika: 'a large proportion of Kanzi and Mulika's utterances were truly spontaneous and were not elicited by the teacher creating situations that required an utterance' (p.224).

7 Formal tests of productive and receptive language capacity

In addition to informal testing of lexigrams which Kanzi and Mulika were believed to know already (e.g. when tidying up, Kanzi might be asked to pick up specific items in order), formal testing was also carried out. This was to test for all the items in Kanzi and Mulika's vocabulary. Kanzi was tested in the 17th month of this study, then aged 46–47 months, and Mulika was tested aged 18–21 months.

Earlier ape language studies were open to the criticism that the animal's 'language' was only in response to being cued 'by the contextual setting, inadvertent glances and so forth' (p.217). The formal tests, therefore, were designed to avoid the possibility of cueing or prompting responses. The tests took the following form:

- They were conducted in the afternoon.
- 20–40 test items were used in each session.
- The time the test took depended on the amount of time spent playing between test trials.
- No test item was repeated in a session, and no two trials were ever the same.
- The test required a correct response where three or four alternatives were presented to choose from (e.g. 'Kanzi might be presented with the lexigrams green bean, apple and tomato, and asked in spoken English to "show me the tomato lexigram"' (p.217); Kanzi might also be shown a lexigram and asked to pick the item it referred to from three photographs).
- Different alternatives were presented for each item, and the same target item was never presented more than once in a test.
- Photos were in colour, 3½" × 5", and different versions of each target item were included. Lexigrams used were 1" × 1" replicas of those on the keyboard.

The performances of Kanzi and Mulika were compared with those of Sherman and Austin on the formal tests. However, Sherman and Austin were found not to be able to match photos to spoken English, so the test matching spoken English to lexigrams, a harder task, was not attempted with the common chimpanzees.

The researchers presented the results of the formal tests in detail, indicating every item tested and the performance of each ape on each test used. Here we will simply summarise the number of correct items from each test.

Type of test	How test was conducted
Matching photograph to lexigram	Shown a photo, the task was to select the correct lexigram to match what was shown in the photograph from a choice of three lexigrams. The photo was shown by a first experimenter, and the lexigrams were placed behind a blind by a second experimenter, without the first experimenter seeing them. This stopped inadvertent glances by the first researcher cueing the response. The second experimenter did not observe the response made by the ape, as this was recorded by the first experimenter who lowered the blind, once the ape had made his/her choice, to see if it was correct.
Matching spoken English to photograph	Three photos were shown, behind a blind again to prevent cueing, and Kanzi was asked: 'Kanzi, can you show me X? X' (thus the target word was said twice).
Matching spoken English to lexigram	As above, but using lexigrams, not photographs.
Matching synthesised language to lexigram	As above, but instead of a researcher speaking the target word, this was generated by the voice synthesiser speaking the target word twice, and Kanzi selecting from four given lexigrams. This test was used to show that Kanzi was not just responding to the tone of voice or other cue from human speech, and was in fact recognising and responding to the word spoken. The machine produced machine-like language which was on a flat tone. This test was used only with Kanzi.

The four types of test

	Match symbol to English	Match photo to English	Match photo to symbol	Match symbol to Votrax speech
Correct	65	56	55	51
Incorrect	1	3	4	15
Total number of items	66	59*	59*	66

* Not all words and symbols could be tested on all trials, as a good photograph to represent them could not be sourced.

Results of the vocabulary tests for Kanzi

Items were scored as correct if the ape got them right on three out of three trials, and incorrect if the ape got them wrong on two or three out of three trials.

	Match symbol to English	Match photo to English	Match photo to symbol
Correct	41	36	41
Incorrect	1	5	1
Total number of items	42	41*	42

* Not all symbols could be tested on all trials, as a good photograph to represent a symbol could not be sourced.

Results of the vocabulary tests for Mulika

	Match photograph to English		Match photograph to symbol	
	Sherman	Austin	Sherman	Austin
Correct	2	3	30	30
Incorrect	28	27	0	0
Total number of items	30	30	30	30

Results of the vocabulary tests for Sherman and Austin

These results show that the bonobos could understand spoken English, whereas the common chimpanzees could not. The researchers also describe differences between the two types of ape while being tested. Although not part of their daily routine, Kanzi and Mulika seemed to understand that the tests were not about something that was going to happen: that is, if they pressed the symbol for juice, they seemed to know that this did not mean they would get juice. In comparison, Sherman and Austin did expect to get juice and were confused by the testing procedure.

Kanzi and Mulika could match lexigrams to photos, English words to lexigrams, and English words to photographs. The results showed that they 'associated various referents with lexigrams. . .these associations were bidirectional, and. . .spoken English words were as closely linked to lexigrams as were the items that the lexigrams represented' (p.225).

The tests also revealed that Mulika understood a lot more than the researchers had previously realised. She understood 42 symbols, more than the 37 she had produced herself at that time.

Sherman and Austin did well on the photo to lexigram tests, but did no better than guessing when it came to tests using the spoken English word. Moreover, during the spoken English tests, the common chimpanzees did not seem comfortable; they 'attempted to avoid them by requesting to go elsewhere; and at times they refused to respond' (p.225). Sherman and Austin both showed a sign of frustration typical in common chimpanzees during the English tests, scratching themselves all over.

On the synthesised language to lexigram test, only carried out with Kanzi, he did make some errors, but this may be because the machine-like language of the synthesiser makes it hard to understand what the machine is saying. His human carers had similar difficulties identifying the words he failed to match to lexigrams on this test.

8 The blind test in the forest

Four months after the 17 food sites were set up in the forest, when Kanzi was aged 3 years, a blind test was carried out in the woods, with an experimenter who had never been in the woods with Kanzi. The experimenter did not know her way round the woods, or the way to the locations where the food was placed, or the way back from the woods to the centre.

If Kanzi could communicate his intention to her using lexigrams and photos, and could lead her to the right locations, this would be evidence that Kanzi was using the symbols referentially, that his behaviour in the woods was not simply being cued, and that he was not being inadvertently guided to the right sites by his usual human companions:

To test Kanzi's capacity to state his intentions to travel to various locations, we enlisted the aid of Mary Ann Romski, who works with children at the Language Research Center. Mary Ann and Kanzi had developed a close relationship during Kanzi's frequent visits to the 'childside', but as Mary Ann was somewhat afraid of the snakes and creatures in the forest, she had never accompanied Kanzi into the woods. . . Mary Ann would be completely lost in the woods without Kanzi's help. If Kanzi said he was going to the treehouse, for example, and then led Mary Ann there, his behavior could not be explained on the basis of subtle cues from Mary Ann. . .

Mary Ann recorded Kanzi's utterances and the route he led her along in going from one food site to another. During the test, Kanzi used photographs on five occasions and lexigrams on seven to announce a proposed destination, with 100% accuracy. Moreover, on all but one journey between two sites, Kanzi chose the most direct route possible. On that one occasion, he exploited the opportunity of being accompanied by someone who did not know that where they were to go was a part of the forest where he normally is not allowed to go. Kanzi therefore demonstrated not only what he knew about himself, but also what he knew about Mary Ann. (Savage-Rumbaugh and Lewin 1994: 142).

DISCUSSION

While acknowledging that the sample of each species used in this study is small, and suggesting that further studies raising common chimps and bonobos together might reveal more, the authors suggest that there is no need to consider the subjects in this study as atypical of their species; and as a result they offer four comparisons between the common chimpanzees and pygmy chimpanzees (bonobos) in their discussion:

1 Common chimpanzees like Sherman and Austin needed to be trained to use symbols, using instrumental conditioning, whereas the pygmy chimpanzees acquired their symbol use spontaneously through observation.
2 Pygmy chimpanzees understand spoken English, whereas common chimpanzees do not. No one trained Kanzi and Mulika to do this, and no one said single words to them over and over again. They only ever heard normal language and extracted words from this. This was an unforeseen outcome of this study, and was integrated into the study as it became apparent (e.g. by adding the voice synthesiser to Kanzi's keyboard).
3 The pygmy chimpanzees and the common chimpanzees differed in the way they used general symbols and specific symbols. Common chimpanzees easily generalise symbols but do not easily learn to specify. For example, they may use 'juice' and 'coke' interchangeably. Pygmy chimpanzees, however, do specify, and once the difference between symbols has been acquired, they do not make such mistakes. For example, Kanzi might call coke 'juice' only if coke is a novel item and no symbol for coke has been used before. Once a symbol for coke is assigned, the mistake is not made again.
4 Sherman and Austin never formed requests where they were neither the actor nor the beneficiary of the request. Nim did not do this either. Kanzi, however, was able to request that A act on B, where neither A nor B was Kanzi himself. The authors suggest (tentatively) that this particular use of symbols by Kanzi might suggest he was following rules: 'The ability to conceptualize and then to symbolically initiate complex forms of interaction between others would seem to be a precursor of syntactical structure, if not the basis itself for the occurrence of syntax' (p.230).

COMMENTARY: METHODS AND ISSUES

Research method, design and data gathering

This was a case study using a longitudinal design, with data gathered by observation. The strength of the longitudinal design is that it allows the development of language use by Kanzi and Mulika to be documented over time, and comparisons to be made between the way common chimps and bonobos learn symbol use.

The case study method allows the in-depth study of the subjects, and the fact that every utterance made by Kanzi in the 17-month period of this study was included in the data analysis shows the amount and depth of detailed data that can be gathered when one subject or small group of subjects is studied over time.

Does the study raise any ethical concerns?

Have the ethical implications as to the rights of primates been considered by this study? Is it acceptable to bring them up in an environment which is so totally different from their natural lifestyle? What happens to such animals after the study is finished? Is it acceptable to remove the primate from the humanised environment it has grown up in, and relocate it to a primate organisation or other holding area?

Validity and reliability of the study

The authors themselves were concerned about the accuracy (validity) of their on-the-spot, real-time observations of Kanzi's utterances. They were especially keen to ensure that his utterances should not be misread and that they were not just caused by the experimenter cueing the ape's response. In order to make sure that their observations were valid and accurate, a test of inter-observer reliability was carried out. First, a 4.5-hour video recording was made of one of the researcher's normal sessions with the apes, doing the usual real-time coding. The researcher who was taped was not aware at the time that the recording would be used for a reliability test, so would not have been able to deliberately influence the results of the reliability check. What was found showed that the real-time recording was very good. The real-time recorder recorded 37 utterances, the video observer 46, suggesting that on-the-spot recordings might miss some of the ape's utterances. In the 37 utterances recorded by both observers, there was 100 per cent agreement on which lexigrams Kanzi used and if they were used correctly in context. There was one disagreement about whether a lexigram use was spontaneous or structured. Of the nine utterances recorded by only the video observer, eight were spontaneous and one was structured. Kanzi tended to get attention by repeating himself when an utterance was not seen.

This reliability check provides support for the validity of the interpretations made of Kanzi's symbol use.

In terms of ecological validity, the study tests a species of ape in a humanised environment that it would not encounter in the wild, and therefore the study lacks ecological validity. In comparison with how children acquire language spontaneously, however, this study is more ecologically valid, providing the bonobo with a model of language use to acquire, than the earlier studies with common chimpanzees, where the instrumental conditioning of symbol use, unnecessary in children's language learning, was essential.

The depth of the data recorded and included in the study also supports the validity of this study's findings. Earlier ape language studies had been criticised for selecting utterances that suggested a level of linguistic competence that could not be established as typical for the ape concerned. This is not a criticism that can be made here, as all of Kanzi's utterances over 17 months were recorded and reported in this study.

Is the study useful?

In that it helps us to understand some of our closest evolutionary cousins, this study has great scientific value. This, and subsequent work in the field of ape language should make apparent for everyone the importance of these animals in understanding our own origins. It should also be clear that conservation of such important species should be of concern to us all.

The applications of the studies carried out with apes such as Lana, Sherman, Austin, Kanzi, Mulika and many that followed them have been used to help children with special needs who are unable to speak to develop ways of communicating, based on the lexigram system and on the methods used to help to teach apes symbol use. Because of this application, the work at the Language Research Center is very useful.

CONCLUSION

The authors conclude that the differences between the two types of chimps are significant and have implications for the rearing of different species – should they be treated identically? Research is continuing to address this issue by rearing both species side by side. The authors also note that 'when such closely related ape species differ significantly in their ability to comprehend spoken speech, the many behavioural differences that exist between men and apes seem less of an anomaly. It is of course behavior, not anatomy, that changes most rapidly, and when an ape can, simply by virtue of human rearing, begin to comprehend human speech, the power of culture learning looms very large indeed. It would follow that if the capacity to understand speech is there, waiting to be tapped into, it would only take one animal who developed an innovative way to produce sounds to push the behavior of a feral group of apes toward the path of language' (p231). The animals in this study, who are considered to be representative of their species, unexpectedly seem to possess a greater ability to acquire some aspects of language than other apes. The findings of this study support the need for further comparative studies between species, without which our understanding of the nature/nurture debate surrounding language may never be complete.

The Cognitive Psychological Approach

Researchers	Focus of study
Loftus and Palmer	Can questioning (language) lead people to reconstruct their memory of an accident they witnessed on film?
Baron-Cohen et al.	Does the Eyes Task show that adults with autism have difficulties with theory of mind?
Savage-Rumbaugh et al.	Can apes learn language?

Cognitive psychology is concerned with the study of mental processes (e.g. memory, language production and comprehension, thinking and reasoning, paying attention and perception). Cognitive psychology considers the brain to be an information processor, based on a computer analogy. The brain inputs, stores and outputs information. Of course, it is much more complicated than this, but this mechanistic model of the brain provides a plausible framework for the study of cognitive processes, which is our current best explanation of what is going on in our heads. Cognitive neuroscience is a discipline that aims to study cognitive processes scientifically. This approach favours the scientific method. Two of the three cognitive core studies present laboratory-based investigations of mental processes (Baron-Cohen et al. and Loftus and Palmer).

The Loftus and Palmer study nicely illustrates the key features of this approach. The study is an excellent example of how the scientific method is used in the cognitive approach. The reductionist approach is used here, homing in on one variable, the changing of the form of a question, and how it impacts on memory. This shows us the strength of such an approach in enabling researchers to isolate an IV and identify the relationships between variables.

What this study shows us about memory as a cognitive process is that rather than the 'tape recorder' or 'computer memory' model that the information-processing approach might lead us to expect, human memory is a distortion of observed events. Moreover, memory is a dynamic process, changing over time and affected by the person's subsequent experiences, driven by their need to make sense of their surroundings and experiences.

The Baron-Cohen et al. study illustrates how a social-cognitive explanation of autism can be used to explain the way that people with autism behave. It shows that the adults with autism share a key cognitive deficit already well-documented in children with autism: difficulties in mind-reading the emotions and thoughts of others, and problems with attributing belief states to other people. This study also demonstrates how highly controlled scientific methodology is used in cognitive psychology.

STRENGTHS AND WEAKNESSES

The cognitive psychological approach

- Studies in cognitive psychology can be useful in helping to explain behaviour, and they have some practical applications in everyday life. Understanding the problems of people with autism and Asperger's syndrome can be useful to those who care for them at home or interact with them in the community. Knowing the reasons behind their unusual and perplexing behaviours may make people more understanding.

  Loftus and Palmer's study demonstrates the frailty of human memory and its reconstructive nature. If we are to rely on human memory in a court of law, then it is a strength of cognitive psychology that we are able to present a coherent explanation of the strengths and failings of eyewitness testimony.

  Sue Savage-Rumbaugh is a pioneer in ape language research. Her research in this field has furthered our understanding not only of the capabilities and limitations of primates in their acquisition of language, but also what the findings imply about the nature of language acquisition in humans and the role of biological preparedness in children's linguistic development. Work with chimpanzees and bonobos using lexigram systems has led to the development of strategies to help severely disabled humans to communicate.

- To study the development of cognitive processes you often have to study children. This means that you have the problem of making sure that the child's answers are not contaminated by others. This usually means bringing the child into a laboratory setting and testing them individually, as was done in the Samuel and Bryant study on cognitive development and the conservation tasks (see Chapter 4, page 187). This way of testing children outside their normal social setting lacks ecological validity. There are also ethical concerns with the study of children which relate to informed consent, deception and harm and distress.

- The emphasis on controlled scientific study in cognitive psychology provides objective evidence in which we can have confidence. It is also easier to test such studies for reliability. For example, the Baron-Cohen et al. study could be repeated quite quickly and easily to see if its findings are replicable.

- The 'machine analogy' is reductionist. The human brain is more than just a machine. The cognitive approach often adopts a narrow focus on behaviour, and ignores important social and emotional factors which may impact on behaviour. For example, would the findings of the Loftus and Palmer study be different if subjects had seen a real-life accident, with all the emotional and physiological changes that witnessing such an event might bring with it?

- While rigorous and controlled studies in the laboratory are useful, the predominance of this method in the study of cognitive processes means that ecological validity is low. On the other hand, if you sacrifice rigour and control in the pursuit of higher ecological validity, as Bartlett did in his work on 'The war of the ghosts' study, you end up with qualitative data which are difficult to draw conclusions from.

- Critics of the cognitive approach would see the narrow focus of the scientific method as a weakness, giving a restricted and limited perspective on behaviour. In other words, the approach could be described as illustrating the negative aspects of reductionism.

- At present, cognitive processes can only be studied by inference, that is, we cannot study them directly; we can only gather what is going on in someone's head by recording what they can or cannot tell us, or can or cannot do, or at best by making recordings of the active parts of their brain (see Chapter 5). Thus cognitive psychology relies a great deal on self-report and observational methods to gather data, and the biases present in each type of measurement may mean that the findings are not valid.

Developmental psychology

Most adults go through life without questioning where their abilities and skills come from – whether they are due to the process of maturation or the result of learning. In fact, unless you study psychology, it is quite likely that this question would not be very important to you until you had children of your own. How many times have you heard parents saying something like: 'You are just like your father/mother/grandma', or 'Your father was always good with numbers/drawing'? These comments imply that many of our skills are passed down from our parents or grandparents. However, when we were born we were unable to sit, walk or hold a pencil, and we certainly couldn't count. Therefore, these skills, *if* they were inherited, took time to emerge, which suggests that maturation must have played a part. The developmental approach to psychology focuses on the debate about whether behaviour is either innate or learned, or if there is an interaction between the two.

In Chapter 3, we introduced the idea that many of the things we are able to do as we get older *are* a result of the interaction between nature and nurture – we are born with some abilities, others develop as we grow older and many more are actually learned, either from adults or from experiences we gain while interacting with the world around us. In the study by Baron-Cohen et al. in Chapter 3 (see page 122) we learned about the development of one aspect of children's **cognition** – the concept of **theory of mind**. This is the ability to attribute mental states, such as beliefs, intentions, desires and knowledge, to other people as well as to ourselves. It also involves the understanding that other people have beliefs, desires and intentions which differ from our own.

Terms in bold are included in the Glossary for Chapter 4 on the CD-ROM.

In this chapter we are going to consider the developmental approach to understanding human behaviour by focusing on the three core studies, all of which contribute to the nature–nurture debate. We are also going to explore two major perspectives in psychology: the behaviourist approach (in the study by Bandura et al.) and the psychoanalytical approach (in the study by Freud). At the end of the chapter we will review these two approaches and suggest how they have been used to interpret other psychological research.

Our acknowledgement of how important childhood experiences are has come from the accepted belief that much of what happens to us as children helps shape who we become as adults. Each study takes a very different view of the development of children and provides an excellent introduction to how nature and nurture combine.

Methodologies used by the developmental approach

Investigating children's development can be fraught with ethical considerations and moral dilemmas. First, how does a small child give their informed consent to take part in research when they probably won't even understand what it means? Second, you are unlikely to be able to take a random group of small children into a laboratory to investigate their behaviour without their parents supervising in some way. This may well influence the children's responses or behaviour, which would spoil the research. Neither can you subject one group to a situation which might have a negative impact on their future behaviour while another group has a life-enhancing experience, without breaching moral and ethical guidelines. As with all psychological research, the methods used have to take into account the well-being of the participants.

Research with children uses the same methodologies as other psychological research: observations, controlled experiments, and so on. Later in this chapter we will look at how Piaget liked to use unstructured and non-standardised questions rather than rigidly controlled methods. However, it is important to remember that research with children has to follow the same ethical guidelines of the British Psychological Society (1993) as any other psychological research. These guidelines highlight the need to ensure that children are not harmed in any way and set out the following:

- If possible, the child participant should give their consent to take part in the research. If the child is under the age of 16 years, their parent, guardian or the person who is *in loco parentis* (in the place of a parent) must also give their consent. In cases where it is likely that the children taking part in research would behave differently if they knew what was happening, the researchers have to get approval for their work from an ethics committee whose members understand the nature of psychological research.

- For research with children (or with participants who have impairments which reduce their understanding) who cannot agree to take part themselves, special procedures are required to safeguard their welfare.

- At the beginning of the investigation, any participant – child or adult – must be told that they can withdraw from the research at any time. If children try to avoid the testing situation, this may be interpreted as a failure to consent to taking part and they should be allowed to opt out of the research.

- When undertaking research that involves children, the ethical guidelines suggest that caution should be exercised when discussing results with parents, teachers or others acting *in loco parentis*. This is because things that the investigators say may be misinterpreted and thought to be more important than they really are. The guidelines are in place to try to prevent these misinterpretations or misperceptions, especially as parents are often anxious about their children's welfare and may worry unnecessarily about the research findings.

Cognitive development in children

If you were told that you would have to entertain a child for the afternoon, one of the things you would probably want to know is how old the child is. Without being an authority on children's development, you would still be aware that small children have very different abilities to older children, and this will influence what they enjoy doing. This is because children's cognitive abilities, especially their thinking and reasoning, differ with age, just as they differ from the thinking of an adult. Therefore, the things that would amuse a small child would be very different from the things that would amuse a 16-year-old. This way of thinking has changed dramatically from a few hundred years ago. In the seventeenth century it was believed that children's minds were a **tabula rasa** (blank slate), as they entered the world without any knowledge or skills. This view implies that *everything* we know is learned (which is really the argument of pure behaviourists – that is, that *all* behaviour is learned). At that time, most people believed that children were simply miniature adults, with the same thinking and reasoning skills. This was why many children were punished for behaviours which to us would seem quite normal for a child, and why they were expected to accept the behaviour of the adults in their lives without question or explanation.

Nowadays we consider childhood to be a special time for learning, demonstrated by a strong focus on nursery schools and educational toys. We no longer believe that children think in the same way as adults. Much of this knowledge is thanks to a man called Jean Piaget (1896–1980), who developed a theory of children's development which is not only one of the most comprehensive, but also one of the most influential theories of our time. Piaget's theory focuses on the idea that development is maturational (to do with the increasing maturity of the child), age-related and universal across cultures.

Piaget's theory

Jean Piaget was not actually a psychologist, which is quite surprising when you consider how important he is in the world of developmental psychology. He was born in Switzerland and trained initially as a biologist and zoologist. He became interested in the relationship between biology and psychology in the early 1920s, especially in how animals adapt to their environment.

Piaget went to Paris to work for Alfred Binet, who was responsible for developing the first intelligence tests for the French Education Department, as a way of testing children to identify those who had learning difficulties. The idea behind the intelligence tests was to compare children on what was believed to be a fixed ability – their innate **intelligence**, that is, the level of intelligence they were born with.

Piaget noticed that different children often gave the same wrong answer to certain questions and that these wrong answers depended on their age. It was as if the children went through different stages of reasoning according to their age. This led Piaget to formulate a theory about intelligence which suggested that it was a kind of biological adaptation which allowed children to develop more efficient interactions with the world around them. Even now there are debates and little consensus about what is meant by the concept of intelligence, and whether it really is fixed at birth or if it can change according to learning and experience. For the moment it is enough that you have an idea of what is meant by the term 'intelligence' in order to understand the nature of the debate.

The needs of small children are taken care of by parents or caregivers, so initially they do not need to have complex skills. Once they are able to interact (and operate) in the world by doing things and making things happen, they need to develop greater understanding of how things work. This requires more complicated thought processes, so the child develops these as necessary.

Piaget realised that the development of mental abilities was not simply the result of a child maturing. He believed that children also need to gain experiences by interacting with their environment. He was of the opinion that children are self-motivated to discover the world – almost to the point that if you put a child in a room with lots of stimulating and interesting toys and games, for example, they would find out for themselves about the properties of those objects and the universal rules that apply to them. Teachers are therefore seen as facilitators rather than directors of children's education, providing opportunities in a stimulating environment to allow children to learn for themselves. This fuelled a massive change in education, with children no longer sitting passively in rows of desks, but becoming active learners, working in small groups to seek out information.

Piaget also recognised that the development of a child's knowledge and understanding seemed to involve a number of stages. To begin with their understanding was quite primitive, and often slightly incorrect, but this would transform as they got older into an increasingly sophisticated understanding of the nature of the world, brought about by interaction with their environment. He also noticed that this transformation often occurred almost instantly, as if they suddenly gained insight into what they were doing wrong. Once this insight was achieved, the children were unable to return to a previous stage of more basic understanding.

The following story will probably help to explain this kind of change in thinking, which we will refer to again later.

Little Johnny had his friend Nigel round to play, and Mother offered them both a drink of cola. She got two glasses out of the cupboard and poured the same amount of cola into each glass so that they were both half full. Little Johnny started wailing (as small children do), 'I want it in my special glass.' Mother looked annoyed, anticipating what might happen next. The special glass that Little Johnny referred to was a tall thin glass, rather than the two identical, transparent, unbreakable beakers she had used originally.

She poured the cola into Little Johnny's special glass, which ended up being full to the brim. This produced a huge wail from Nigel, who started bleating, 'It's not fair, he's got more than me now.'

Mother tried to remain calm. 'There is the same amount in both glasses.'

'No there isn't – he's got more.'

'I'll show you. Let me pour this back into the glass I got out in the first place.' She proceeded to pour the cola back into the unbreakable plastic beaker. 'Look, there is the same amount in both glasses now.'

Nigel was silent for a moment.

'I want my special glass, I want my special glass,' shrieked Little Johnny.

'It's not fair if you do,' said Nigel. 'It means you get more.'

At this point mother wanted to give up.

'Do it again,' said Little Johnny.

Both boys looked in wonderment as the liquid seemed to change volume before their very eyes. Suddenly Nigel let out a shriek: 'It's because the glass is thinner that it makes it all squashed up, isn't it, Mrs Brown? There's not really more in there. It's not really magic, is it?'

'That's right, dear.'

Piaget claimed that each step up the developmental ladder was like a building block and was dependent on having reached the previous stage. He held that these stages were age-related and cumulative. In order to test out his ideas, Piaget undertook a longitudinal case study on his own three children. He observed and questioned them as they grew up, noting the differences in the quality of answers and explanations they gave to a range of problems.

KEY CONCEPTS

Open-ended questions

Returning briefly to methodologies used in the developmental approach, it is worth mentioning here that Piaget believed that **unstructured** and **unstandardised questioning**, which was dependent on the responses of the children being questioned, was the best way of finding out what they were thinking. This would allow him to follow up ideas and beliefs that the children expressed, which, in turn, would give him greater insight into their cognitive abilities. The disadvantage of open-ended questions is that they may be misinterpreted and the wrong conclusions drawn. Although this methodology could be considered somewhat unscientific, Piaget did test some of his hypotheses on other children, so his research was not as biased as it might appear at first.

Due to the nature of his research, Piaget was not really interested in gathering quantifiable data. However, other researchers using open-ended questioning may find it difficult to analyse and quantify the answers.

The central features of Piaget's theory

Piaget said that all babies are born with similar biological equipment (he used the term 'structures'). These **biological structures** are the senses, the brain and reflexes (such as sucking and grasping). He proposed that the complex achievements of older children must have developed in some way from these basic reflexes.

He used the term '**schemata**' to refer to all the cognitive structures, or interrelated and organised groups of memories, thoughts, actions and knowledge, which represented everything that the baby or child knew about objects or actions. He said that these schemata develop from the child's own interactions with the environment, and that any new experiences the child had would lead to the development of new schemata. The way the schemata develop and become more complex involves organising their past experiences and adapting them to any new information they encounter.

Piaget claimed that adaptation has two components: **assimilation** and **accommodation**. He saw assimilation as the process of fitting new information and experiences into existing schemata, while accommodation is the process of changing the existing schemata when new information cannot be assimilated.

To return to the restaurant example used on page 97, if the only type of restaurant you had been to before was like McDonald's (with no waiter and no menu to order from while you sit at a table), the first time you went to a restaurant where a waiter took your order, you would be experiencing new information which could be fitted into your current 'restaurant' schema. If, on the other hand, you had only ever eaten at home and had no idea that you could buy food ready-cooked and eat it on someone else's property, you would not be able to assimilate the new experience in light of anything you already knew about, so you would have to set up a new schema in order to accommodate the new information.

Piaget used these concepts to help explain the different kinds of thinking that occur at different stages of a child's development. One way to think of a stage is as a time of relative stability, when a child will think in a similar way across a wide range of situations or problems. Remember Little Johnny and his friend Nigel? Their thinking (and understanding) was challenged by a new experience, which gave them new information that they could not fit into their old schemata. They had to reorganise their schemata in order to make sense of the new information. This process of accommodation resulted in their ability to understand a process at a new, advanced level.

Piaget identified four major stages in the development of a child's thought, and claimed that all children progress through these stages in this fixed order, although not everyone reaches the final stage. He suggested ages for each stage, although he was aware that the ages were averages rather than actual ages. He also said that children move through the stages at slightly different speeds, depending on their experiences.

The stages are listed below and we will look at each one in some detail:

1. the **sensorimotor stage** (0–2 years);

2. the **pre-operational stage** (2–7 years);

3. the **concrete operational stage** (7–11 years);

4. the **formal operational stage** (11+ years).

As we have already mentioned, Piaget's belief was that children are internally driven to find out about their world, which implies that if children are provided with a stimulating and well-equipped environment, they will explore the environment themselves and find out about the properties of the objects within that environment with little or no guidance.

The sensorimotor stage (0–2 years)

When a baby is very young, the only knowledge it has about the world is based on what it can experience and what it can do, both of which are somewhat limited. Babies are born with reflexes such as sucking and grasping, and they can also move their limbs, for example, kicking and waving their arms. This restricted repertoire of movement limits what they can actually do, although each of these actions results in some kind of sensual experience. They can also see, hear, taste, touch and smell the world around them, and they begin to put together very primitive schemata about their environment. This is why the stage is called the sensorimotor stage, because it is to do with the child's sensual experiences and their motor movements.

During this stage we see one of the biggest leaps in development, as babies go from being helpless, incontinent beings, with limited reflex behaviours, to turning their parents' world completely upside down, exerting their will, arguing and forming strong bonds. They will be able to speak; they may well be potty-trained; they will be able to throw things around; and they will understand that when people leave the room they have not vanished off the face of the earth. They will also be able to solve simple problems (like finding the things you do not want them to find!), and they will have developed their own little personalities.

Biological maturation has a huge part to play here. When babies are born they are unable to sit up or make words, but the growth and development of the body gradually makes each achievement possible. As children realise that they are gaining control over what was initially random movement, this increases their understanding about their ability to interact with the world. These skills become internalised and they begin to think when they want to display various movements, rather than the movements simply occurring by chance.

The way that this development takes place is through maturational changes in babies' brains. You will learn much more about the brain in Chapter 5, especially in the study by Maguire et al. (2000), which considers how taxi drivers' brains can adapt in order to meet the demands made on them by their lifestyle. At this stage, it may be useful to have a little information about what occurs in the brain of a newborn, in order to understand some of the processes that affect the way babies learn.

The newborn brain

When babies are born, their brains are flooded with information from the outside world, which enters via the sense organs (ears, eyes, nose, mouth and skin) and is transported along nerve cells to the brain. Gopnick et al. (1999) have described the development of a baby's neurones (brain cells) as being like telephone wires which communicate with each other. Initially, the wires exist along the main thoroughfares, and the messages arriving via the sense organs are genetically programmed to be transmitted to the relevant part of the brain, but there is little flexibility as to what occurs. As the baby begins to grow, the brain develops rapidly and as the neurones mature, they develop increasing numbers of dendrites, which are the short, branching fibres which extend from the cell body, or soma. These dendrites act as signal receivers, carrying information from the sensory neurones. Having lots of them therefore significantly increases the surface area available on the neurones for receiving incoming information.

Continuing the telephone analogy, it is like all the houses in a road getting their own telephone, instead of being dependent on the public phone box which only allows them to make 999 calls. Once each house has its own phone, they can communicate with other houses in the road. Now imagine that each house has at least four phones – the potential for communication between them has increased dramatically.

To give you an idea of how immense these communication possibilities are, consider that at birth each neurone in the cerebral cortex has about 2,500 possible synapses (or junctions) with other neurones. By the time a baby is 2–3 years old, the number of synapses per neurone has increased to about 15,000. According to Gopnick et al., this is about twice the number of the average adult brain. As we get older, the connections that are rarely used are 'deleted', while those that are used regularly or need to gain more capacity are strengthened. This process is known as synaptic pruning, and it is our experiences that determine which connections are pruned and which are strengthened. This is what we mean by brain plasticity – the brain can mould itself to adapt to new situations.

Piaget noted one crucial development that takes place during this stage: the child's sudden understanding of **object permanence** – realising that objects continue to exist even when they cannot be seen. He claimed that this occurs when a baby is about 8 months old. He tested this theory by looking at whether babies search for objects which are hidden from view. Prior to the age of 8 months, babies cease to look for an object which has been covered, but once they get to about this age, they continue to look for the object in the place where they last saw it, but will not look for it in alternative places. Obviously this is quite a significant development in children's understanding, as the phrase 'out of sight, out of mind' becomes more a case of 'out of sight, I'm going to scream and scream until it comes back again'!

The pre-operational stage (2–7 years)

During this stage, Piaget suggested that children become more able to represent the world using mental images and symbols. As we have already noted, words are really just sound symbols for objects, and it is at this stage that a child's linguistic skills develop. We all use mental images, or pictures 'in our mind's eye', and even speak to ourselves 'inside our heads'. It is at this age that this kind of skill develops in a child. If we have access to very few symbols it would follow that our thoughts may also be limited, but the more they increase, the more sophisticated our thoughts become. Children of this age also demonstrate symbolism in their play, for example, using a banana as a telephone.

It is important not to imagine that the pre-operational child's thoughts are anywhere near as sophisticated as the thoughts of an adult. Their world is still very concrete – things are what they seem, so the child is more influenced by appearance than anything else. However, sometimes their thoughts may be intuitive, that is, based on what they feel or sense is true without being able to explain the underlying principles. This may be why children sometimes seem very intelligent, when in fact they have made an intuitive guess without any logical reasoning to back it up.

Piaget's descriptions of children with pre-operational intelligence tended to focus on their limitations, because he believed that they could not yet apply logical mental rules to actual objects in the world. He described these logical mental rules as 'operations'. For example, addition and subtraction are reversible operations because adding three to a number can be reversed by taking three away again. Piaget suggested that children are not able to apply logical operations until they are about 7 years old.

The main limitations of pre-operational thought

1. Egocentrism

According to Piaget, pre-operational children are egocentric. This means that they see the world from their own point of view and are unaware that others see it differently. We talked about egocentricity in Chapter 3 (see page 114), and how it explains the behaviour of small children having tantrums in supermarkets. Remember, too, that egocentrism is not the same as selfishness, because it is an *inability* to see something from someone else's point of view. Actually, Piaget thought this was the most serious deficiency in pre-operational children's thinking.

Piaget and Inhelder (1956) tested egocentrism with their famous study known as the **'three mountains task'**. They asked children to look at a three-dimensional model of a mountain scene, which was based on a large mountain called Le Salève, across the lake from the city of Geneva. The mountains were placed so that one had snow on the top, one had a cross and one had a small house. The child would have a good look at the model and then sit down at one of the chairs placed round a table. The child would then have a doll seated opposite them and would have to choose a picture showing what the doll could see from the other side of the table.

Piaget found that children under 5 years always picked out the view of what they could see from their own position, and seemed to be unaware that the doll would see something different. He also found that between the ages of 5 and 7 years they knew there would be a difference, but they were not sure what it was. When they reached 7 years, they seemed to be able to cope with the 'in front' and 'behind' perspectives, but not the 'left' and 'right' perspectives. By the age of 8 or 9 years, they would be able to choose the right pictures for all the positions round the table. According to Piaget, these findings clearly demonstrated that children are unable to see things from someone else's point of view until they are at least 7 years old.

Piaget's three mountains task

2. Conservation

Returning again to Johnny and Nigel, they did not understand at first that even though Johnny's mother had not put any more cola in the 'special' glass, it looked as if there were more because the glass was taller and thinner. This is a demonstration of lack of conservation. Pre-operational children are unable to 'conserve' because they do not understand that the basic properties of matter are not changed by superficial changes in their appearance. The serving of cola looked more in the tall glass, and this proved to be even more confusing when it was returned to the original beaker.

This example deals with conservation of volume and is probably the best-known example of a conservation experiment (although studies have also been carried out on conservation of number and weight). In fact, Piaget demonstrated this in exactly the same way with three beakers – two short beakers and one tall one. Both short beakers had the same amount of liquid in them and the tall one was empty. He then poured the liquid from one of the short beakers into the tall beaker and discovered that pre-operational children thought that this changed the amount of water.

When investigating number, Piaget used two rows of counters, equally spaced, and asked the child if there was the same number of counters in each row. The child would dutifully say 'Yes'. Piaget would then spread the second row of counters out and ask the child again if there was the same number of counters. At this point the child would say 'No'.

Piaget used a similar method to investigate children's ability to conserve weight with balls of plasticine. A diagram of the tests he used to investigate the conservation of volume, matter, length volume and area is on the next page.

3. Irreversibility

Piaget also demonstrated another limitation in pre-operational children's thought using these experiments. If we use the liquid experiment as an example, when the water from the tall thin beaker was poured back into the short beaker, the child would be

Type of Conservation	Initial Presentation	Manipulation	Preoperational child's answer
Volume	Two identical beakers are filled with equal amounts of liquid. The child agrees that there is the same amount in each beaker.	The content of one beaker are poured into a beaker of a different shape. The child is asked if there is the same amount of liquid in each beaker.	The child says there is more liquid in the taller beaker.
Number	Two rows of objects (e.g. buttons) are shown to the child. The child agrees that there are the same number in each row.	One row is reorganized by spreading the objects out. The child is asked if there are the same amount of buttons in each row.	The child says the 'longer' row has more buttons.
Weight	Two identical balls of plasticine are shown to the child. The child agrees there is the same amount of plasticine in each ball.	One ball is rolled out. The child is asked if there is the same amount of plasticine in each shape.	The child says the longer shape has more placticine.

Piaget's tests on volume, number and length

quite satisfied that there was the same amount of water in both of them once more. The problem was that the child could not understand why this was and was unable to work it out. They were unable to 'reverse' the operation in their heads.

Reversibility is the ability to reverse the logic of a train of thought. According to Piaget, a 3-year-old girl would be unable to do this. For example:

Adult: Do you have an older brother?

Child: Yes.

Adult: Does he have a younger sister?

Child: No.

4. Centration
This refers to the way a child will focus or centre attention on only one aspect of a task and ignore all the other aspects. This is when they rely on their intuition about what they can see rather than what they can reason. An example would be to put three sticks of equal length on the table in front of a child. The child would then be asked if the three sticks are the same length or if one is longer than the others. The centre stick would then be moved slightly so the three sticks are no longer in line. It is very likely that the child would then say that the sticks are not the same length (the centre stick

will possibly be seen as either longer or shorter), because they will tend to focus on only one end of the stick, rather than both ends.

5. Seriation
Piaget maintained that pre-operational children are unable to put things in order of sequence; for example, if given a number of blocks of varying sizes or varying heights, they would be unable to put them in the correct order by size or height.

The concrete operational stage (7–11 years)

At this stage children cease to be egocentric and acquire 'cognitive operations' – much more complex mental schemata which enable the child to come to logical conclusions about the world. This means that they are now able to put items in order, such as height order, which they were unable to do before. They would also be able to put a sequence of pictures telling a story in the right order because they could logically work out which one comes before the next. However, they still have problems with abstract concepts and principles, and tend to see rules as black and white. When playing a game with a concrete operational child, they will insist that the rules are followed and that you cannot change them in any way.

Formal operational stage (11+ years)

The final stage of development involves the ability not only to reason logically, but also to deal with abstract concepts. Piaget referred to these abilities as the 'logic of combinations', where the child may need to deal with the mental manipulation of several factors at the same time. This stage is where children can do mental arithmetic, which involves retaining and manipulating a number of pieces of information.

Children at this stage also understand that rules can be broken if everyone agrees, such as the rules of board games.

Evaluation of Piaget's theory

A number of studies have been conducted in order to evaluate Piaget's theory of cognitive development. The focus has been on evaluating the accuracy of his stages and the methodology he used. Much of the criticism is based on the idea that children are far more competent at certain ages than Piaget stated. It has been suggested that the language and methodology used by Piaget in his questioning was responsible for many of the children's supposed inabilities. There is little dispute, however, that children go through a sequence of developmental stages, and that these stages do seem to be cumulative and age-related, but the ages specified are not as defined by Piaget. For example, a child of 5 years may be able to conserve liquid quantity, while a different child aged 8 may be unable to do so, but their progress through the stages will be similar.

Object permanence

One criticism of Piagetian theory relates to his ideas about object permanence. Later research has indicated that it is not a lack of object permanence which stops a small child from looking for a hidden object in the sensorimotor stage, but is more likely to be a problem of memory. If a child is shown an object and then it is hidden, they may attempt to see where it has gone but forget where they last saw it and then give up looking. Bower (1971) demonstrated this idea of 'fragile memory' by looking at the searching behaviour of babies as young as 20 days when a ball was hidden. By assessing their facial expressions, he discovered that even the youngest babies showed surprise when a ball was hidden from view, but showed no surprise on its return. If they realised that the ball had not vanished off the face of the earth, it would make sense that its return into view would not cause them any surprise, whereas if they thought it had really vanished they would be amazed by its magical reappearance. By refining the methodology used, Bower demonstrated that babies of all ages show object permanence when the period between hiding and reappearance is short.

Ability to conserve

The ability to conserve has also been investigated by a number of studies which have used slightly different methodologies, with results suggesting that young children can think quite logically in situations they understand. In one experiment carried out by McGarrigle and Donaldson (1974), the children were shown the two rows of counters on a table and asked if there was the same amount in each row. Then, instead of the experimenter changing the layout, a 'naughty teddy' appeared and made the change while the experimenter looked in the other direction. This resulted in the children realising that although the counters looked different, there was still the same amount on the table, and they had no difficulty explaining what had happened. This indicates that the nature of the task really did have an impact on the children's ability to perform in the tasks designed by Piaget. When tasks were more familiar, there was evidence from numerous studies indicating that children could conserve earlier than Piaget realised. Ghuman (1982 in Eysenck 2004), for example, demonstrated that farmers' children conserve weight earlier than other children. This is probably because they are familiar with the weighing and selling of produce to earn a living. Similarly, Durkin (1995) indicated that children are able conserve volume earlier for substances they are familiar with.

It appears that Piaget's suggestion that children of a certain age are able to conserve globally was too sweeping a generalisation. Later research has indicated that different types of conservation are mastered by children between the ages of 6 and 12, depending on the nature of the materials (conservation of volume vs conservation of weight). This shows that there are often overlaps *within* stages (known as **horizontal *décalage***), whereby a child can conserve one material but not another, and *between* stages (known as **vertical *décalage***), whereby they may be able to do some tasks within one stage and some within the next stage.

Egocentricity

Another criticism involves Piaget's claims about the extent of egocentricity in young children. One of the biggest critics of Piaget's methodology was Hughes (1975), who suggested that when given a task which was more familiar to them, children are far less egocentric than Piaget suggested. Hughes arranged an experiment designed to test whether children could see something from someone else's perspective, using objects which were more familiar to the children. If you think about it, unless you lived in the Alps, you would not be very familiar with mountain scenery and would therefore find it hard to imagine what the models in front of you were supposed to represent. Hughes set up a scene using dolls, and asked children to put one doll in a position where it could not be seen by the other. Using this familiar game of hide-and-seek, Hughes found that 90 per cent of children between the ages of 3½ and 5 had no trouble placing the doll accurately.

Dasen (1994) looked at cultural influences on both conservation and egocentricity, and found that Aboriginal children's performance on tasks was greatly influenced by their cultural experiences. He looked at conservation of liquid, weight and volume, and also a spatial task similar to the three mountains task. He concluded that cultural experiences affect the age at which children reach Piaget's developmental stages, but that these do seem to be universal and cumulative. These findings have been supported with experiments in a number of diverse geographical regions, and Segall et al. (1999) support Dasen's claim that ecological and cultural factors only affect the rate at which the stages are reached, not the sequence they follow.

Regression

It also appears that when children are faced with a difficult or stressful situation, they can return to an earlier stage of reasoning (which Piaget said would not occur). This has been seen to happen with the birth of a new baby in a family, when the older child, who had been showing a good rate of cognitive progression, suddenly regresses to a more babyish level. However, we can never be sure whether this is simply attention-seeking behaviour or if they actually forget what they knew.

In conclusion, Piaget has to be regarded as perhaps the most important theorist in the field of cognitive development, but he *describes* the stages of children's development rather than explaining *why* they occur. As we mentioned earlier, the methods Piaget used to investigate cognitive development have affected his conclusions regarding age of transition from one stage to the next. The research indicating that cultural differences have an influence on the speed of cognitive development in some groups does not contradict Piaget's claim that stages are universal. On the other hand, Piaget did not acknowledge how factors such as familiarity with language used, the values of a culture and the experiences of its children would impact on how their brains develop differently (remember synaptic pruning) and, consequently, how quickly they achieve different skills.

THE STUDY

J. Samuel and P. Bryant (1984) 'Asking only one question in the conservation experiment'

Journal of Child Psychology and Psychiatry, 25: 315–18

BACKGROUND

Margaret Donaldson suggested that Piaget actually underestimated the cognitive abilities of young children because he did not appreciate that their cognitive and social understanding are very closely related. In other words, young children fail to demonstrate their cognitive capabilities in Piaget's tests because of their social understanding of the situation. For example, if someone asks you the same question twice, you might think it is because you got the answer wrong the first time.

'What are two and two?'

'Five.'

'What are two and two?'

'Sorry – four.'

This is exactly what happens in Piaget's standard conservation tasks. The methodology he used involved asking the children, after presenting them with two rows of counters, if there was the same number of counters in each row. He would then widen the spaces between the counters on one of the rows and ask the children the same question. As we saw, Piaget found that children under 7 years would generally answer the second question incorrectly, and from this he deduced that they had failed to conserve. From his studies, he set the progression from the pre-operational stage to the concrete operational stage at about 7 years.

Rose and Blank (1974), however, suggested that the child's error was actually a result of them demonstrating a very sophisticated social strategy, by interpreting that the reason the second question was being asked was because they had given an incorrect answer to the first question. Rose and Blank devised a study to test this where they dropped the pre-transformation question (the question asked before the change in appearance had been made). Their study showed that if children were shown the two rows evenly spaced, and then shown one row being changed and asked if there was the same number of counters in each row, more 6-year-olds would get the answer right.

Samuel and Bryant were interested in these findings, which seemed to suggest that the younger children made errors in Piaget's traditional two-question task not because they could not conserve (understanding that a change in shape or form does not necessarily mean a change in quantity), but because they were misinterpreting what the experimenter wanted to hear.

The current study by Samuel and Bryant was designed to establish the reliability of Rose and Blank's findings and to extend this study. Rose and Blank had tested only 6-year-olds, so Samuel and Bryant tested children aged 5–8½, to see if older and younger children were affected in the same way by the one-question task. Whereas Rose and Blank had only tested the conservation of number (counters task), Samuel and Bryant extended the study to include the two other versions of Piaget's conservation tasks: mass (using Play-Doh cylinders) and volume (pouring liquid into taller, narrower glasses or into shorter wider ones).

AIMS

The aim of the study was to test whether the methodology used in Piaget's conservation experiments was the reason why children under 8 years made errors, rather than a true lack of understanding of conservation. The study was designed to use Rose and Blank's one-question method.

METHOD

Method and design

This was a laboratory experiment using an independent groups design.

Subjects

The sample was made up of 252 children from schools in and around Crediton, Devon, UK. Their ages ranged from 5 to 8½ years.

The children were divided first according to age. This gave four groups, each consisting of 63 children. The first group had a mean age of 5 years and 3 months, the second, 6 years and 3 months, the third, 7 years and 3 months, and the final group, 8 years and 3 months. Each age group was then further subdivided into three more groups consisting of 21 children, to provide the three experimental conditions.

Mean age in years	Number of children		
	Standard (two-question) condition	One-judgement condition	Fixed-array condition
5¼	21	21	21
6¼	21	21	21
7¼	21	21	21
8¼	21	21	21

Within each age group, 21 children were tested using the traditional two-question method, as used by Piaget; 21 were tested using Rose and Blank's one-question method, asking only the post-transformation question; and a further 21 were tested in a control condition called the fixed-array condition. In the fixed-array condition, children were only shown the materials after they had been changed, and therefore they did not witness the transformation. This condition would show that the other children were using the information about how the materials looked in the first place to inform their answers to the post-transformation question.

Materials

The materials used were the same as those used in the Piagetian experiments: two cylinders of Play-Doh of equal size (for conservation of mass), two rows of counters, with a maximum of six in a row (for conservation of number), and three beakers of liquid, two beakers of the same size and another beaker which was taller and thinner (for conservation of volume).

Variables

A number of independent variables were being tested:

1 The age of the child – would the older children do better than the younger children?
2 The way the task was carried out – would children do better on the one-question task than the traditional two-question task and the fixed-array condition?
3 The materials used: Piaget suggested that children find the numbers task easier than the mass and volume tasks – would this be shown in the study?

The dependent variable was always whether or not the child got the answer to the post-transformation question right.

Procedure

Children were tested individually under laboratory conditions.

1 The *standard group* was tested using the standard Piagetian task, which involved asking a pre- and post-transformation question, and witnessing the transformation process.
2 The *one-judgement group* was tested using only the post-transformation question, after the children had witnessed the transformation process.
3 The *fixed-array group* was tested by being shown the post-transformation array (not having seen the transformation take place).

The procedure for the standard task to demonstrate conservation of number was as follows. Counters were spread out in two identical rows and the child was asked the pre-transformation question: 'Is there the same number of

189

counters in each row?' The counters in one of the rows were then spread out and the child was asked the post-transformation question: 'Is there the same number of counters in each row?'

The procedure was the same for the mass and liquid experiments, with the mass (Play-Doh) involving flattening (into a pancake) or rolling (into a sausage) one cylinder of Play-Doh, and the liquid condition involving tipping the liquid from one beaker into another of different height and width.

Each child was tested four times on number, mass and volume tasks.

Controls

To ensure that the children really understood, there were four trials in each situation. The order in which the children undertook the tasks was varied systematically to prevent order effects.

First child	number	mass	volume
Second child	mass	volume	number
Third child	volume	number	mass
Fourth child	number	mass	volume

RESULTS

The children were each tested 12 times (4 times on each task), so they had 12 opportunities to get the answer right or wrong. Samuel and Bryant presented their data as the mean number of errors per age group and per condition:

The table below shows that the number of errors made in the one-judgement condition was lower than for the other two conditions in every case. It also indicates that the number of errors made by the children as they got older decreased in every condition. The children in the fixed-array condition made the most errors, showing that they did indeed use their witnessing of the transformation to inform their answer to the post-transformation question.

Mean age	Standard (two-question) condition	One-judgement condition	Fixed-array condition
5¼	8.5	7.3	8.6
6¼	5.7	4.3	6.4
7¼	3.2	2.6	4.9
8¼	1.7	1.3	3.3

The table below shows that the mean number of errors in the 'number' test were lower than the mean number of errors in the mass and volume tests in the one-judgement and fixed-array conditions.

Type of task	Standard (two-question) condition	One-judgement condition	Fixed-array condition
Number	1.476	1.024	1.536
Mass	1.512	1.190	1.714
Volume	1.810	1.595	2.500

After being subjected to a number of statistical analyses, the summary of the results was as follows:

- Children were significantly more able to conserve in the one-judgement condition than in the other two conditions, with children in the fixed-array condition making the most errors. These results establish the reliability of findings in the Rose and Blank study.
- The older children were significantly more able to conserve than the younger children, with each age group doing better than all the children younger than themselves.
- The number task produced significantly fewer errors than the mass and volume tasks.

DISCUSSION

It seems that Piaget was right to suggest that changes in a child's understanding take place over time. As children get older, they understand better that simply changing the appearance of something does not mean that the quantity changes. This was shown by the fact that the children who only saw the fixed array were less able to appreciate this because they could not carry over previous information into the new situation. In fact, adults may well have the same problem. If you were to show an adult two glasses of different sizes containing liquid and ask them if there is the same amount of liquid in each, it is very likely they would either say 'Possibly' or 'No', but they could not be certain.

Piaget also suggested that the number task would be the easiest, and Samuel and Bryant's study clearly shows that he was right in this regard.

However, the findings from the earlier study by Rose and Blank, and the present study by Samuel and Bryant, both suggest that Piaget's method of asking the child the same question twice led children to give the wrong answer when in fact they *could* conserve. This was a result of the children believing that because they were being asked the same question again, a different response was required. The fact that children were better able to conserve on the one-judgement task suggests that Piaget's methodology led him to underestimate the cognitive capabilities of younger children.

The study provides some evidence to support Piaget's theory of cognitive development, and also some findings suggesting that his theory needs to be refined, particularly in relation to the age at which children can conserve.

COMMENTARY: METHODS AND ISSUES

Research method, design and data gathering

The study was an experiment under laboratory conditions, and employed an independent groups design, so all the strengths and weaknesses of these methods apply.

When a study uses children as subjects there are some specific methodological and ethical issues that arise. These are explored below.

KEY CONCEPTS

Methods

This study illustrates both practical and ethical issues concerning the testing of children.

1 Practical issues:
   Children are often tested individually, under laboratory conditions, sometimes by an adult they are not familiar with. This set-up is designed to ensure that children do not contaminate each other's results, and that they do not simple copy a friend's answers or respond to peer pressure. However, it is not usual for children to be out of their social environment and in a laboratory with a stranger. Therefore, we have to question the ecological validity of this method of testing children.

2 Ethical issues:
   Can informed consent be obtained from children? Parental consent is usually sought. At what age do you think a child should be asked to give their own consent? If a parent gives consent but a child does not, should the child be tested? Do you think that children have the right to withdraw? What about debriefing? Could the children in this study be debriefed?

Does the study raise any ethical concerns?

Where minors are being studied it is always difficult to get informed consent from the subjects themselves, and where tests are carried out by adults on children in a school setting, it is highly unlikely that a child would feel able to refuse to participate or withdraw from the study. However, in this case, the test itself was not stressful or harmful and only took a few minutes. In such tests, the child would not be told they were wrong, but just 'Well done and thank you' at the end of the procedure.

Is the study useful?

Piaget's work has been very influential in education. His theory helped to describe the child for teachers and to establish a curriculum (especially in maths and science), which encouraged active participation in the early years and allowed children to learn at their own pace, depending on the stage of cognitive development they had reached. (You can thank Piaget for hours of fun at the sand tray and water tray with beakers when you were in infant school!)

This particular study highlighted two factors which are useful when considering the practice of teaching. It supports Piagetian theory of progressive stages of cognitive development (although it identified that Piaget's focus on specific ages needs to be more flexible, especially with different types of conservation tasks). It also highlighted how important it is to use appropriate methodology in order to identify the level of children's understanding; otherwise the results can be quite inaccurate.

The implications of this study for education are that teachers need to take into account where each child is in relation to known stages, rather than teaching groups of children the same topic in the same way. We are now very much aware that if a child continues to fail in school, they will become demotivated and may ultimately drop out of education altogether. On the other hand, if each child's strengths and weaknesses are identified, their individual needs can be met more effectively in a mainstream classroom.

It might be worth considering whether teaching children according to their level of development, rather than having age-focused classes, would be more beneficial. You might also consider the impact on teacher's workloads when they have to identify the strengths and weaknesses of each child when faced with classes of 30 or more.

Studies such as Samuel and Bryant's further our understanding of how children think, and demonstrate that their cognitive development and social understanding are very closely related. Often it is the social situation that influences whether or not a child will show what they know!

Validity and reliability of the study

Are there any problems with the methodology that lead us to question the internal validity of the findings? The study itself was well designed and accounted for many of the extraneous variables that could have interfered with the validity of the results. The possibility that the answers were given by chance was addressed by the children having four attempts at each conservation test, and order effects were accounted for by varying the order in which tasks were given. One criticism of the number test was that the children may simply have counted the number of counters used, which might explain the level of accuracy with the number task. All the children used as subjects would have been capable of counting to six, and it would take a very short space of time to add up the numbers on the table.

Validity could be questioned on the basis that children often get nervous in laboratory settings and they also have a limited attention span, which may have resulted in their answers being instantaneous rather than considered. On the other hand, the number of trials should have prevented these factors from influencing the results. However, as with all research, we can never be absolutely certain that subjects are not simply responding to even the most carefully designed experimental situation, and it is possible that demand characteristics may have affected the validity of the findings.

Testing children individually and under laboratory conditions is low in ecological validity (see Key concepts, above).

1950s classroom with children in rows

2000s classroom with children working together

Is aggression learned?

One of the central debates in psychology focuses on whether behaviour is innate or learned. This next section concentrates primarily on the influence of learning on behaviour, although the core study looks at the way in which children learn aggressive behaviour by observation. The main purpose of choosing this as one of the core studies is that it allows us to focus on the topic of learning, and to consider the different ways that children learn. The study also adds fuel to the nature–nurture debate in so far as most people believe that we have an innate capacity for aggression, but that the way in which it is demonstrated is learned.

In order to be able to judge effectively whether children actually learn aggressive behaviour, it may be useful for us to consider briefly the theories of aggression which suggest that it is an innate capacity. One argument supporting the idea that aggression is innate comes from the fact that few parents actually teach their children to be aggressive, and yet boys and girls both demonstrate aggressive behaviour from an early age. Therefore we will begin with theories of learning, and later in the chapter we will consider briefly the innate theories of aggression.

It would also be useful to note here that most textbooks include the Bandura core study in the area of social psychology and how the media influences aggressive behaviour. Although we will touch on the 'media effects on violence' argument, this study is intended primarily to increase your understanding of how children learn.

Theories of learning

In order to consider any of the theories about learning, we ought to look briefly at what we mean by 'learning'. Often the idea that we have learned something comes from observing a change in behaviour, such as being able to solve complicated maths problems or riding a bike. The problem here is that often we learn something but do not demonstrate that skill to others, and therefore they may assume that we have not actually learned anything. Imagine that you have learned to knit at school by watching the teacher following a complicated knitting pattern and then having a brief attempt yourself. At the end of the afternoon, you have learned how to do it, but you may choose not to because you think knitting does not look particularly cool!

Generally speaking, psychologists suggest that learning is 'a relatively permanent change in behaviour due to past experience'. We could argue that you have not actually learned to knit because it is not changing your behaviour, as you are not now knitting your own jumpers! On the other hand, you have actually acquired the knowledge of how to knit and this is likely to remain with you for some time (and we cannot be sure that it will not affect your behaviour for ever, because you may wish to start knitting at some point in the future). Hopefully you are beginning to get the idea that defining learning is more complicated than being able to provide a simple definition.

One very useful definition of learning comes from Anderson (1995), who explained that learning is the process whereby reasonably permanent changes occur in potential behaviours as a result of past experiences (which would have been learning situations), but what we must remember is that our behaviours may not *actually* change. This seems to be a pretty good explanation of what really happens when we learn. On the other hand, if we are trying to investigate learning, how is it possible to measure 'potential' behaviours? This is the difficulty that has faced psychologists when researching learning, and devising theories as to how it occurs.

Past research into learning has approached the problem by looking at the outcome, because at least that is measurable: has behaviour changed from point A to point B after the teaching has taken place?

FOCUS ON PERSPECTIVES: BEHAVIOURISM

The behaviourist school was originally established by J.B. Watson in 1913. Watson argued that in order for psychology to be scientific, it must focus on the things which could be assessed objectively rather than inferred.

Human beings respond to a specific stimulus. We talk if someone talks to us; we eat if we are hungry; we get angry if someone provokes us. Each behaviour has an antecedent (a stimulus, or something which provokes that behaviour). Although we might think about our response to a stimulus, we may act simply on instinct. Therefore, anyone trying to analyse human behaviour would find it very difficult to work out the 'thought' part because it may vary for each person, or may be absent, and ultimately, unless we develop telepathic powers, we have no way of knowing whether we are correct!

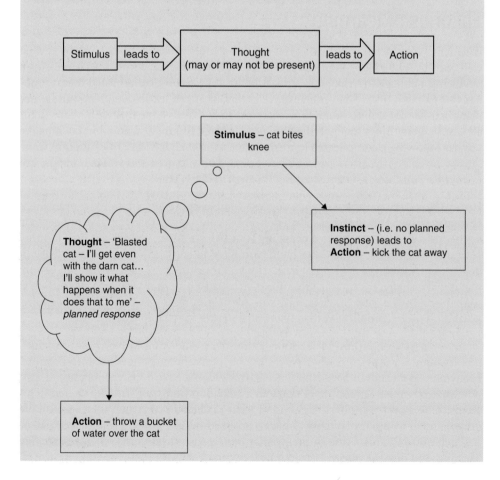

Consider the following example. Your response to a cat biting your knee could be either instinctive (i.e. kick the cat away) or calculated, which entails thought and might involve a bucket of water and a wet cat! How would an observer actually know your thoughts? They may make inferences, but cannot be totally sure. Therefore, the behaviourists suggested that the only answer would be to ignore the thought and simply consider the stimulus and the response, both of which are known (it was the thought part which later interested cognitive psychologists).

Watson also believed that all behaviour consisted of learned responses to different stimuli (which is really a reductionist approach, where all behaviours are broken down to their basic components).

Classical and operant conditioning

We discussed Skinner's theory of how children learn in the section on language acquisition in Chapter 3. Skinner, who was a behaviourist, claimed that all behaviours are learned. He explained that when an adult praises a child for a specific behaviour, this praise will act as a reinforcement, making it more likely that the behaviour will be repeated. The child learns that their action has produced a positive result, so they will repeat the action. The idea behind this kind of learning is that we learn by making an association between what we are doing and a positive result – we are conditioned to make that association. However, there is much more to the theory of conditioning than simply praising the sounds of a small child. Conditioning theory actually helps to explain much of our behaviour, and is also extremely useful when trying to understand the behaviour of animals.

Imagine that you live in a huge house, with four floors. In fact, it is so big that in order for you to hear whether or not dinner is ready, the butler has to sound a huge gong, which vibrates through the whole house. As you grow up, you always associate that sound with food, and it seems that the minute you hear it you can feel your mouth watering in anticipation of the delicious meal that awaits you.

When you leave home, you move into a flat and become responsible for feeding yourself. One day you are walking past some antique shops when you hear the sound of a gong being hit. It instantly makes you think of dinner and you can feel your mouth watering, so you have to go off to the nearest cake shop to get some food.

What you have not realised is that you have become conditioned to associate the sound of a gong with food. Although you know that a gong does not indicate food when you are away from home, you cannot help the reflex response of your mouth watering when you hear the gong being hit.

Pavlov and classical conditioning

This whole process is known as classical conditioning and was described by Ivan Pavlov in 1927, after he discovered that it was possible to teach dogs to salivate at the sound of a bell, rather than at the sight or smell of food. The reason was that the dogs did not consciously salivate to the sound of the bell in the first place, just as you did not consciously make your mouth water to the sound of the gong in the example above. The salivation was a reflex response to an unusual stimulus.

Pavlov discovered that the dogs he was using for experiments started to drool before they were given any food. In fact, they drooled when the keeper approached the cage, or when they saw the bucket the food was carried in, or even the white coats of the keepers. Pavlov was actually interested in the digestion of dogs and was undertaking research which involved collecting dogs' saliva in a tube attached to the outside of their cheeks. He decided to investigate this further, and wondered if he could teach the dogs to salivate at the sound of a bell which, as we have said, was a stimulus that would not produce salivation under normal circumstances.

For a while, Pavlov arranged for a bell to be rung every time the dogs were fed. They learned to associate the sound of the bell with the fact that dinner was on its way, and soon they were slobbering the minute the bell was rung. He had taught them to make the association between a stimulus (the bell) which does not normally suggest food, and a reflex response (slobbering). It is important to remember that classical conditioning involves training someone to produce a reflex response to something other than the original stimulus.

Ivan Pavlov is seen here with one of his dogs during a demonstration: his experiments in 1889 on the mechanism of digestion in dogs established the role of the autonomic nervous system (ANS) and won him a Nobel prize in 1904; he is best remembered for subsequent work on conditioned reflexes, conditioning a dog to salivate in anticipation of food by ringing a bell each mealtime, until eventually the bell alone provoked salivation – these experiments founded behaviourist psychology

The process of classical conditioning is often referred to by a series of simple equations.

Before learning:

Food (unconditioned stimulus) = Slobbering (unconditioned response)

The learning process:

Food (unconditioned stimulus) + Bell (conditioned stimulus) = Slobbering (conditioned response)

After learning has taken place:

Bell (conditioned stimulus) = Slobbering (conditioned response)

The most important part of this concept is to be aware that it is possible to *teach* someone to respond to a stimulus with a reflex response. Aggressive responses are an innate (or reflex) form of defence (we wither, fight or run away when faced with threatening situations). If we meet another situation in the future which we associate with an event we have felt was threatening in the past, we may automatically respond in an aggressive way without thinking (a reflex response again). On the other hand, we may just do our best to escape even if the situation is, in reality, not threatening at all. This second response is the basis of a **phobia** and we are going to consider the way that classical conditioning explains phobias in some detail, as you will encounter the concept of phobias again in the study by Freud later in this chapter.

Phobias

Probably the best-known example of how a phobia can develop is the case of Albert, reported by Watson and Rayner (1920). Poor little Albert was a 'stolid and unemotional' child who was healthy and happy. When he was 9 months old, Watson and Rayner tested his response to a number of different things such as white rats, rabbits and masks, to find out if he was frightened of anything (fear can be considered a reflex response). They discovered that the only thing that frightened him was a hammer hitting a steel bar directly behind his head. Every time they showed him a white rat they struck the steel bar, which was the conditioning process. After they had done this seven times over the next seven weeks, Albert showed fear and extreme distress every time a white rat was shown to him. In fact, this phobia had become so strong that he seemed to generalise the response to any furry creature, hair and even Santa Claus's beard! At this point it would be interesting to know whether his mother chose to remove her son from the study.

Operant conditioning and reinforcement

Of course, there are only so many reflexes to retrain. It is possible to learn other things that have nothing to do with reflexes, such as teaching dogs to beg.

> Mrs Evans had an old English sheepdog called Josephine. When Josephine was little, Mrs Evans decided to teach her to shake hands. She did this by saying 'Shake hands' to her and holding her front paw and

making her shake hands, and every time she did it she gave Josephine a doggie chocolate as a reward. The dog soon learned that by 'shaking hands' she would be rewarded, but the trouble was when she had come in from the muddy garden she would walk up to Mrs Evans and hit her with her front paw, leaving dirty marks all over whatever she was wearing.

What Mrs Evans had done in the example above was to use the process of conditioning to train Josephine to do something which was *not* a reflex response. This process is called operant conditioning, and involves increasing the likelihood that a behaviour will happen again by rewarding that behaviour. Mrs Evans paired Josephine's behaviour of giving a paw with receiving a treat (a reinforcement), until the dog would forget the reinforcement because the behaviour would happen anyway.

The difference between this and Pavlov's theory about how we learn is that Pavlov's learned responses would be triggered automatically by a stimulus, without any sort of conscious awareness. B.F. Skinner pointed out that there was a difference between 'automatic responses' (where the response or action happens without conscious thought) and 'operants', where responses happen initially as a result of voluntary choice. Josephine could have chosen not to shake hands when the process of training started, although after a while the response became almost automatic.

Skinner (1938) described how he taught rats to gain food by pressing a lever using the techniques of operant conditioning. He would allow the release of a food pellet every time a rat approached the lever. Each time, the rat would have to get a little bit closer in order to get the food pellet. This would continue until the rat stepped on the lever, possibly by chance, and this released the food pellet. Finally, the rat would only get the pellet when pressing the lever. The rat learned by having its behaviour reinforced. Skinner shaped the rat's behaviour until the rat learned what was required. Sooner or later, the rat would not have to make the conscious decision, 'Mmmm, I'm hungry. I think I will go and press the lever.' It would simply do it without having to think through the process, having made an automatic association between the behaviour and the result.

Humans also make automatic associations, which we had to learn originally. In fact, you are doing exactly that now: you are reading without thinking about what each letter sounds like or what each word means. You learned to read by a process of operant conditioning, because each time you read a word, either your parents or your teachers would praise you, or you would feel so pleased with yourself that this would be sufficient reinforcement for you to continue. It is often the case that when you teach an animal something, and then take away the reinforcement or reward, they stop doing it. (Unfortunately, Josephine's behaviour was reinforced sufficiently by pats and praise from others who had not experienced the muddy paw treatment!)

This theory can also be used to explain why some small children have screaming fits or behave badly. Their parents are preoccupied with other things, and the child wants attention. The obvious way to get it, they have learned, is to start having a tantrum. That way, parents have to stop what they are doing and pay attention to the small child. In fact, many child guidance clinics specialise in dealing with children with behavioural problems. Frequently, children who seem uncontrollable are referred to such clinics, where the parents' 'parenting skills' are assessed. The reason why the children are so badly behaved is often because they have learned that bad behaviour pays – they get the reward or reinforcement of their mum or dad's attention.

Think about certain types of behaviour that you have learned will get rewards – being nice to granny, working hard for exams, or even washing up. All these have reinforcements that you have learned about which will make it more likely that you will repeat them. Being paid for working is also a reinforcement – the harder you work, the more money you earn and the more likely your chances of promotion. You may even find that you self-reinforce by feeling good about what you are doing!

Social learning theory

Social learning theorists, such as Albert Bandura, are interested specifically in the way humans learn the rules of social behaviour. They agree that all behaviour is learned and that the principles outlined by the behaviourists can also apply to social learning (e.g. the concepts of reinforcement and punishment). They explain that people learn by observing the behaviour of others by an almost unconscious method. The model, or actor, is frequently unaware of being observed, and the observer, or learner, is often unaware that they are actually learning. The behaviour is learned without any reinforcement and may only appear in the future if the reward for that behaviour is worth having.

> Nicholas watched his older brother in action at the local nightclub. His brother was always chatting up one woman or another and was never short of a date. He somehow managed to manoeuvre himself into a position whereby they stood and stared into his eyes and he would say all sorts of flattering things to them. The following week Nicholas approached a particularly attractive young woman who was standing by the bar. Suddenly he found himself standing in the same position as his brother had, repeating almost word for word what his brother had said the previous week. It worked!
>
> The question is, was Nicholas actually aware of what he was doing or was it a pattern of behaviour that he had unconciously learned?

Observation

From the example above, we can see that we learn the norms of our culture and acceptable patterns of social behaviour from the people in our environment. We are sometimes instructed or subtly cajoled by our parents, our teachers and our peers, but more often we simply observe the way that others behave. We learn what is good and what is not acceptable within our culture by seeing who does well and who gets the rewards. Social learning theory suggests that we are more likely to learn these rules (which will vary between cultures) by observing the behaviour of others, and we are therefore more likely to repeat or avoid the behaviours if they are followed by the addition of rewards and reinforcements, or by punishments such as social isolation or exclusion.

Trevor decided to wear his sister's red dress to his fifth birthday party. After all, it was such a pretty dress and he liked the material and the beautiful lace around the neck. Everyone said his sister always looked nice when she wore it and he wanted to look nice too. Just before his guests arrived, he ran upstairs to get changed.

When he came downstairs and walked into the sitting room to greet his school friends, they all stood and stared in horror at his appearance.

Trevor learned that at that point in time, it was not socially acceptable for him to wear a dress. In order to be accepted by his friends, he conformed to the norms of behaviour of his peer group.

Consider the kind of things you might have learned by observation. You could probably list a dozen different ways of killing someone. Now imagine you have been told to disembowel them. In your mind, can you picture what you would have to do and what the person's innards would look like? It is quite likely that you will be able to conjure up a very gruesome picture, which is messy and bloody and probably quite lifelike. But how do you know all these things? Most likely, you will have seen it on TV or at the cinema. You have learned by observing and have stored that information, to be used if and when necessary. However, you have not been rewarded for learning these kinds of behaviours and you are extremely unlikely ever to demonstrate them, which suggests that there is a difference between traditional theories of learning and social learning theory.

Violence and aggression

Bandura's early work indicated that children who have seen another person behaving aggressively will be increasingly likely to demonstrate aggressive behaviour. Later he suggested that aggression is actually something we learn to demonstrate because it seems to pay. An example of this is a child who has become a very aggressive bully at school because he has learned that he will get what he wants – sweets, money or status with the other children. But where has he learned to be aggressive? Bandura claims that children learn by seeing others behaving aggressively during their childhood or adolescence, through their own experience of being bullied, or through observation of the media. The likelihood of them imitating the behaviour will increase if they see someone being rewarded (reinforced) for their aggression, perhaps by getting what they want.

The implications arising from the knowledge that we learn by observation relate to the kinds of images we are exposed to on television. In fact, a number of studies have been conducted to look at whether television and cinema violence result in violent behaviour in real life. The problem with most of this research is that it is not ethical to expose groups of children to violent videos to see how they will act. Can you imagine the responses of parents if you asked them to allow their children to be tested in this way?

Research evidence has shown a link between television violence and later aggression, however. For example, an early study was carried out by Liebert and Baron (1972), where they showed one group of children a violent film and another control group an exciting but non-violent sporting event for the same length of time. The children were then allowed to play with a group of children who had not seen the films, and their behaviour was observed. The children who saw the violent film were far more aggressive than the control group. The problem is that we do not know if there was any measure of aggression in the children before the start of the study. It would have been a huge coincidence, but it is possible that all the children who were aggressive before the study may have been put in one group.

FOCUS ON RESEARCH METHODS: CORRELATIONS

Research into the effects on behaviour of watching violent films involves using a correlational design. This means that the participant is measured on two variables, the first being the amount of time spent viewing (television/cinema) and the second being instances of aggressive behaviour. If there are high levels of one (lots of violent films having been watched) and high levels of the other (manifestations of violent behaviour), this would result in a positive correlation. However, correlations cannot show cause and effect, simply relationships between two variables, and therefore the cause of the behaviour may have been something different, such as a physiological defect in the brain.

Other investigators have tried to measure aggression before a study begins, in order to see how much more aggressive the children become afterwards. An example of this was the study by Williams (1986), who used observations of the children, together with teacher and peer reports, to get an idea of how aggressive they were at the beginning of the study. The idea was to compare the levels of aggression in children who lived in communities where television had only just become available, with levels in children who already had access to television. They found that aggressive behaviour in the children aged 6 to 11 increased during the two years after television had been introduced, but was no different for the children who already had access to television. These results support the idea that being given access to images which will contain some aggressive acts will impact on the subsequent levels of aggressive behaviour of the child observers.

Reinterpreting Freud

It is worth mentioning here that, following the next core study by Bandura et al., we are going to cover the developmental theory of Sigmund Freud. Bandura and other social learning theorists were interested in the work of Freud, but they did not agree with his explanation of why people behave in certain ways and why they often copy the behaviour of a person they are really frightened of, known as the aggressor. Although you will read more about Freud later on in this chapter, it is worth bearing in mind that Bandura et al.'s work was, in part, an attempt to help reinterpret Freud's theory of psychosocial development. Unlike Freud, who claimed that all behaviour came from unconscious motives, they suggested that observational learning occurs spontaneously – children watch and then imitate with no deep, meaningful, underlying motive.

THE STUDY

A. Bandura, D. Ross and S.A. Ross (1961) 'Transmission of aggression through imitation of aggressive models'

Journal of Abnormal and Social Psychology, 63: 575–82

BACKGROUND

In order to demonstrate the power of social learning theory, Bandura designed a study to explore whether children would imitate the actions of different role models when given the opportunity. If they did produce the same aggressive actions, this would show a number of things. It would demonstrate that learning can take place with immediate effect, rather than by the step-by-step process which would involve reinforcement of all the component parts of a behaviour. This was the process advocated by Skinner, and Bandura criticised Skinner's approach as it would take too long for all behaviours to be acquired in this way. It would also show that direct reinforcement is not necessary for a behaviour to be learned, that the original model need not be present, and that the behaviour can be stored up and demonstrated when the appropriate opportunity arises.

AIMS AND HYPOTHESES

The aim of the study was to see whether children would imitate aggressive behaviour when given the opportunity, even if they saw these behaviours in a different environment and the original model they observed performing the aggressive act was no longer present.

Bandura's study aimed to test four hypotheses:

1 Children exposed to an aggressive model would produce more imitative aggressive acts than children exposed to a non-aggressive model and children not exposed to a model at all (the control group).
2 Exposing children to a non-aggressive model would have an inhibiting effect on their aggressive behaviours and they would show significantly less aggression than the control group who saw no model.
3 It was assumed that preschool children would have been reinforced for appropriate sex-role behaviour by their parents: that girls would have been positively reinforced for behaving in certain ways (e.g. cooking, being maternal), while boys would have been negatively reinforced for these behaviours, as they were not deemed appropriate for boys. Therefore, Bandura et al. predicted that the sex of the model would have an effect: children would be

more likely to copy a same-sex model (girls would copy a woman more and boys would copy a man more).

4 Since aggression is stereotypically a male behaviour, boys would have been positively reinforced for this behaviour and girls negatively reinforced. Therefore, Bandura et al. expected boys to imitate more aggressive acts than girls, especially with a same-sex (male) model.

METHOD

Method and design

A laboratory experiment was carried out. The independent variables were:

● whether the model was male or female;
● whether the child was male or female;
● whether the model behaved aggressively or non-aggressively.

This meant that different children were tested in the following conditions:

● observed an aggressive male model;
● observed an aggressive female model;
● observed a non-aggressive male model;
● observed a non-aggressive female model;
● no model (control condition).

This was a matched groups design, where the overall performance of each group was compared with each of the other groups.

The dependent variable was the amount of aggression demonstrated by the child in a later situation (both imitative and non-imitative).

Subjects

In total, 72 children were tested: 36 boys and 36 girls from Stanford University Nursery School (USA), aged between 37 and 69 months (mean age 52 months), that is, between the ages of 3 years and 1 month, and 5 years and 9 months.

The children were allocated to conditions as follows. The control group was made up of 24 children, 12 boys and 12 girls, who would see no role model. The two experimental groups were then subdivided into two groups of 24 subjects each: aggressive model observers (6 female and 6 male children to see a female role model, and 6 female and 6 male children to see a male role model), and non-aggressive model observers (6 female and 6 male children to see a female role model, and 6 female and 6 male children to see a male role model).

Controlling extraneous variables

Matching was carried out in order to prevent subject variables from influencing the results. Since some children are generally more aggressive than others anyway, the children were rated for aggression before being allocated to their groups. This was done by one of the female experimenters and the children's nursery school teacher, both of whom knew the children well prior to the study. The children were rated on a five-point scale for previous displays of physical and verbal aggression, aggression towards objects, and their ability to control their behaviour when they were angry (aggressive inhibition).

The results of the two raters were considered to be reliable because there was significant correlation between them. The groups of six children were then established to ensure that the level of aggression shown previously by the children was matched across the groups, so that no one group was generally more aggressive than another at the outset.

KEY CONCEPTS

Methods: Reliability of inter-observer reliability
This study establishes the reliability of findings and inter-observer reliability between observers/raters.

If a test or measure is reliable, this means that it gives significantly similar results on retesting. For a study or test to be established as reliable, it must be carried out using the same procedure on similar subjects under similar circumstances, to give similar results. The way the results are tested to see if they are similar is to apply correlational statistics. If a significant positive correlation is established, this supports the reliability of the study's findings. This is important because if the findings are not reliable, they will not be valid.

In order to avoid observer bias (i.e. an observer applying ratings or counting categories in a subjective rather than objective fashion) inter-observer reliability needs to be established. This means that two observers rate or observe the same behaviour, and the two sets of ratings are correlated. If a significant positive correlation is seen, inter-observer reliability has been established and the objectivity of the results is confirmed.

In the Bandura study, this stops any conscious or unconscious bias occurring on the part of the teacher or experimenter in their assessment of the children's general aggression.

Models, materials and location

- **Role models:** One male and one female role model were briefed to behave in a standardised way. The same male and female models were used throughout, and therefore played both the aggressive and non-aggressive roles.
- **Location:** The study took place at the Stanford University Nursery School in the USA. There were three rooms used for the study, all being located in the Nursery School. One was in the main nursery school building and two were set away from the main nursery school building although still in the Nursery School Grounds.
1 Room one: The experimental room had a table and chair in one corner, with potato prints and picture stickers (selected because children like playing with them). In the other corner was another table and chair, with a Tinkertoy set (a kind of construction set consisting of dowels and discs with holes in them to

fit them together), a mallet and a five-foot inflatable Bobo doll (which, when you punch it, rocks back up again). This room was located in the main nursery school building and was therefore familiar to the children.

2 Room two: This room, which was away from the main nursery building, contained a number of very attractive toys, including a fire engine, a train, a plane, and a doll with lots of clothes and a cot. The idea here was to try to arouse aggression in all the children by letting them start to play with the toys and then taking them away, saying that these toys were being saved for another group of children.

3 Room three: This room was next door to room two, away from the main nursery building, ensuring that the setting was separate from where the observation of the models took place. Many children thought they were no longer in the nursery school. Room three was also connected to an observation room with a one-way mirror, through which observers could monitor the behaviour of the children. It contained a number of toys, which were always placed in exactly the same position for each child. This standardisation was done to ensure that one toy was not nearer to or more prominent for one child than for another, as this could have influenced their choice of which toys to play with. The toys were considered either aggressive or non-aggressive. *Non-aggressive toys* were dolls, bears, construction toys, crayons, cars and plastic farm animals. *Aggressive toys* were a three-foot Bobo doll, a mallet and peg board, and dart guns.

Procedure

Each child was tested individually in a three-step procedure. The same female experimenter led each child through the three stages.

1 **Stage one** (approximately 10 minutes):
The children in the aggressive and non-aggressive conditions were tested in this step. The experimenter took them into the first room, where they were seated at the child's table and encouraged to play with the potato prints and stickers. The model was then escorted into the opposite corner of the room and told that the Tinkertoy set, mallet and Bobo doll were for him/her to play with. Then the experimenter left the room.

In the aggressive condition the model started by playing with the Tinkertoy set, but after a minute turned to the Bobo doll and started to act aggressively towards it. The aggressive acts were deliberately stylised so that imitation of them would be clear and not just examples of how children would play with the Bobo doll anyway. The physically aggressive acts were repeated about three times in the 10-minute period the child stayed in this room, and they were interpersed with the verbally aggressive responses and non-aggressive phrases.

The physically aggressive acts were:

- laid the Bobo doll on its side, sat on it and punched it on the nose;
- raised the Bobo doll up and hit it on the head with the mallet;
- threw the Bobo doll in the air and kicked it around the room.

The verbally aggressive responses were:

- 'Pow';
- 'Throw him in the air';
- 'Kick him';
- 'Sock him on the nose';
- 'Hit him down'.

The non-aggressive phrases were:

- 'He keeps coming back for more';
- 'He sure is a tough fella'.

In the non-aggressive condition, the procedure was the same except that, once seated at the table, the adult assembled the Tinkertoy set in a quiet, subdued way, and ignored the Bobo doll for the 10 minutes the child was in the room. After 10 minutes, the experimenter came to collect the child, saying they were going to another room now, and said goodbye to the model.

2 **Stage two** (approximately 2 minutes):
Each child, including those from the control group, was then taken into room two, where they were subjected to mild aggression arousal. Having been allowed to play with the very attractive toys for 2 minutes, the experimenter stopped the child and told them that these were her very best toys and she did not let just anyone play with them, but had decided to save them for the other boys and girls to play with. She then told each child that they could play with any of the toys in the next room, and took the child to room three.

- The reason why this mild aggression arousal was induced for all participants was because it was necessary to ensure that all the subjects were 'wound up' and therefore primed to show aggression due to the frustration of being told they could not play with the toys any more. Previous studies had also indicated that observing the aggression of others often inhibits (suppresses) a person's own aggressiveness, and this might mean the children in the aggression condition were less inclined to be aggressive in room three than the other two groups, which would confound the study.
- For the non-aggressive condition, the presence of the non-aggressive model was supposed to inhibit the subject's aggressiveness, and this could be seen most clearly if the children were less aggressive in circumstances where they had good reason to be aggressive, which is why their aggression was aroused in this stage.
- The control group was exposed to this stage to ensure that fair comparisons could be made with the other two groups of children.

3 **Stage three** (approximately 20 minutes):
The experimenter then took each child to room three and stayed with them, as some of the children refused to go into this room on their own or tried to leave before the end of the allotted time (this was presumably because they had been upset by stage two). To avoid affecting the children's behaviour, the experimenter worked discreetly at the other end of the room.

The child was able to play with the toys and their behaviour was observed for 20 minutes through the one-way mirror. Two observers scored the subjects' behaviour at 5-second intervals, which gave 240 observations for each subject. The level of inter-observer reliability was highly significant.

The children were observed for the following categories of behaviour.

- Three measures of direct imitation:
  - imitation of aggressive acts;
  - imitation of aggressive phrases;
  - imitation of non-aggressive phrases.
- Two measures of indirect imitation:
  - the child hit other things with the mallet (remember, the child had only seen the model hitting the Bobo doll with the mallet);
  - the child laid the Bobo doll on its side and sat on it, but was not aggressive towards it.
- Four further types of aggressive behaviour, which were not imitations of the adult role model (this would tell the researchers whether the general aggression of the children was inhibited or increased as a result of seeing one of the two models):
  - striking, slapping or pushing the doll aggressively;
  - behaving aggressively towards any other objects;
  - producing novel hostile remarks aimed at the Bobo doll or other objects (e.g. 'Cut him', 'Shoot the Bobo', 'Knock over people', 'Horses fighting, biting');
  - shooting darts or aiming the gun and pretending to shoot at various objects in the room.

RESULTS

The results have been broken down here to make them easier to digest, but at the end of this section you will find the entire table for the mean aggression scores for all subjects. What do the results tell us in relation to Bandura's four hypotheses?

Hypothesis	What the results showed
Subjects exposed to an aggressive model would produce more imitative aggressive acts than subjects not exposed to any model (the control group) and subjects exposed to a non-aggressive model.	The results showed that this was true for all behaviours.
Exposure to a non-aggressive model would have an inhibiting effect on the subjects' aggressive behaviours and they would show significantly less aggression than the control group who saw no model.	The researchers observed no significant general inhibiting effect, but when the results are looked at by sex of model, the male non-aggressive model can be seen to have a significant inhibiting effect on the children.
The sex of the model would have an effect: children would be more likely to copy a same-sex model (girls would copy a woman more and boys would copy a man more).	Boys showed more aggression if the model was male than if the model was female. Girls showed more *physical* aggression if the model was male, and more *verbal* aggression if the model was female. Subjects who saw the same-sex role model only imitated their behaviour in some categories.
Boys would imitate more aggressive acts than girls, especially with a same-sex (male) model.	Boys did display more *physical* aggression than girls if the model was male, but girls displayed more *verbal* aggression than boys if the model was female.

The table below shows the mean totals of aggressive behaviours and the gender of the role model.

Aggressive behaviours	Female model (mean total)	Male model (mean total)
Imitative physical aggression		
Female subjects	5.5	7.2
Male subjects	12.4	25.8
Imitative verbal aggression		
Female subjects	13.7	4.3
Male subjects	2.0	12.7

Aggressive behaviours	Female model (mean total)	Male model (mean total)
Non-imitative aggression		
Female subjects	21.3	8.4
Male subjects	16.2	36.7
Aggressive gun play		
Female subjects	1.8	7.3
Male subjects	4.5	15.9

The table below shows the mean totals of behaviour for all conditions.

Response category	Experimental groups				Control
	Aggressive		Non-aggressive		
	F model	M model	F model	M model	
Imitative physical aggression					
Female subjects	5.5	7.2	2.5	0.0	1.2
Male subjects	12.4	25.8	0.2	1.5	2.0
Imitative verbal aggression					
Female subjects	13.7	2.0	0.3	0.0	1.7
Male subjects	4.3	12.7	1.1	0.0	1.7
Mallet aggression					
Female subjects	17.2	18.7	0.5	0.5	13.1
Male subjects	15.5	28.8	18.7	6.7	13.5
Punches Bobo doll					
Female subjects	6.3	16.5	5.8	4.3	11.7
Male subjects	18.9	11.9	15.6	14.8	15.7
Non-imitative aggression					
Female subjects	21.3	8.4	7.2	1.4	6.1
Male subjects	16.2	36.7	26.1	22.3	24.6

Response category	Experimental groups				Control
	Aggressive		Non-aggressive		
	F model	M model	F model	M model	
Aggressive gun play					
Female subjects	1.8	4.5	2.6	2.5	3.7
Male subjects	7.3	15.9	8.9	16.7	14.3

DISCUSSION

It appears that although the children who saw the aggressive models were far more aggressive than the other two groups, the gender of the role model had a significant impact on their behaviour.

The female role model seemed to cause confusion in the children, because she was not behaving in a way that they would expect. They made comments like, 'Who is that lady? That's not the way for a lady to behave.' 'You should have seen what that girl did in there. She was just acting like a man. I never saw a girl act like that before. She was punching and fighting but not swearing' (p.581).

The male role model's aggressive behaviour, on the other hand, was more likely to be seen as normal. The children made comments like, 'Al's a good socker, he beat up Bobo', 'I want to sock like Al', and so on. Bandura points out that this may be due, in part, to the children's expectations of behaviour: they already had ideas about what was sex-appropriate behaviour for men and women. For example, one girl said, 'That man is a strong fighter, he punched Bobo right down to the floor and if Bobo got up he said, "Punch your nose." He's a good fighter like Daddy.' The children's comments show that they had clear ideas that fighting is acceptable, even desirable, for males, but unacceptable for females.

Since girls are more likely to have been discouraged from behaving aggressively as this is male-typical behaviour, and boys will have been encouraged to behave in this way, this explains Bandura et al.'s findings that the boys were more aggressive than the girls, and that the male aggressive model elicited the most imitation. Learned appropriate behaviour also explains why the girls were more verbally aggressive and the boys were more physically aggressive in the male aggression condition.

Physical aggression is clearly a masculine-typed behaviour – therefore the boys' domain and not appropriate for the girls – whereas verbal aggression is not so clearly sex-typed and was therefore available as an aggressive outlet for the girls, who may have been suppressing their desire to behave in a physically aggressive way.

The inhibition of aggressive behaviour by the non-aggressive male model can be explained by the fact that male models have a greater effect due to male dominance in society, and also because by playing quietly with the Tinkertoy set, the male model was behaving in a non sex-typed manner.

Do children learn by imitation? This study certainly shows that children can learn as a result of imitation, and without either the child or the model being reinforced. This suggests that modelling is a form of observational learning.

Bandura went on to investigate how modelling leads to learning, developing his social learning theory, which brings together the behaviourist concept of reinforcement and the Freudian concept of identification (which you will learn more about later in this chapter), since behaviour which is positively reinforced is more likely to be imitated, and the person is more likely to imitate a role model with whom they identify.

Bandura et al. showed that learning can occur without the learner receiving reinforcement, but suggested that reinforcement may play an important part in the learner's decision to perform the behaviour at an appropriate point. Therefore, reinforcement, whether direct or vicarious, or self-reinforcement, is one factor which may influence the performance of a learned behaviour.

Remember, just because learning has occurred, it does not mean that the behaviour will be performed. We all know how to stick our heads in the oven, but we do not do it!

COMMENTARY: METHODS AND ISSUES

Research method, design and data gathering

The study was a laboratory experiment and used a matched subjects design. Largely quantitative data was gathered by covert observation. The strengths and weaknesses associated with these methods, type of data and design apply here.

Does the study raise any ethical concerns?

This study raises a number of ethical issues.

1 There is no mention of informed consent being sought from parents, and the young children would not have been in a position to give consent on their own behalf to take part in the study. Perhaps consent was not sought because the researchers thought parents might not consent to their child being involved in a study on learning aggression! Remember, this study preceded Milgram's obedience experiments (explored in Chapter 2) by two years, and researchers were not as concerned about strictly adhering to ethical guidelines prior to the debate on ethics in psychological research that followed Milgram's study.

2 The children were distressed during the study. They were deliberately frustrated in stage two when they were told that the really good toys were to be reserved for other children. We know this was significantly upsetting for some of them because the experimenter had to stay with each child in room three, since some of them were upset and refused to stay on their own or wanted to

leave before the allotted time was up. The children were therefore encouraged (coerced?) to continue with the study when they clearly did not want to. This implies that they did not have the right to withdraw.

3 There is the problem of whether or not the children suffered any long-term consequences as a result of the study. It would have not been possible to debrief the children as they would not have understood what had happened, and it would be very difficult for the researchers to undo any harm that had been caused by the study. Although it is unlikely that taking part in the study made the children significantly more aggressive in the future, we can never be certain. This is one of the major problems with any sort of study which involves looking at the origins of aggressive behaviour.

Is the study useful?

The study is useful to psychology in that it demonstrates observational learning in practice and shows how the different models affected the children.

In terms of applications to real-life settings, Bandura's work has been described as the first in a series of scientific studies into media violence. Later studies used video footage of Bobo-bashing as well as 'live' models. However, Bandura himself warned against interpreting his results as evidence of copycat TV violence, cautioning that learning does not necessarily lead to performance. We must be careful, therefore, not to assume that just because there are violent programmes on TV, these behaviours will be copied in the real world.

The study's results show us that there is a clear difference between the aggressive behaviour of boys and girls; but can this difference be attributed to biology or socialisation? Is it that boys have biological differences, such as higher levels of the male hormone testosterone, which make them more aggressive? Is it that both boys and girls are clearly taught sex-appropriate behaviours by their parents, teachers and the media from an early age, and this accounts for why boys are more aggressive than girls? Bandura et al.'s study fails to shed any light on this.

If we are to make any use of studies that look at aggressive behaviour, it is important to answer a key question – is aggression largely learned or largely innate? If it is innate, this is very difficult to change; whereas if aggression is largely learned, then presumably it could be unlearned, or we could address how we socialise our children in order to reduce their aggression or channel their aggressive behaviour into constructive rather than destructive actions.

Validity and reliability of the study

In terms of its internal validity, the study could be said simply to be looking at how children learn to be aggressive towards an inflatable doll, and not at how they acquire general aggressive behaviours. The fact that the object of aggression was not human may also limit the generalisability of the results to aggressive behaviour towards people in the real world. A Bobo doll is supposed to be punched and hit. What if the adult had been aggressive towards a toy that would not usually elicit aggressive play? What if the adult had torn the arms and legs off a cute teddy bear? Would the results have been the same, do you think?

The study introduces the concept of inter-observer reliability (see p. 206). This is important in establishing objectivity in observational research.

In terms of explaining the acquisition of aggressive behaviour, the study lacks ecological validity. Children are very rarely in a room with a strange adult on their own. If they are, it would be unusual for the adult not to engage the child in conversation, or vice versa. Children tend to learn from adults and peers they know and who can offer their opinions and approval of what is going on; they were isolated from this experience in this study.

Postscript: innate theories of aggression

In order to complete the argument that perhaps we are just innately aggressive and that all this learning theory is just a way of reducing the 'blame', we will have a brief look at the three main theories suggesting that aggression is purely innate. You will probably find these relatively easy to accept – at some point in your life you will probably have felt very angry, but, on reflection, you may have realised that this anger was unreasonable. You may also be familiar with the fight/flight mechanism (which we mentioned earlier and which we will look at in more detail in Chapter 5), which suggests that when trapped, we either come out fighting or run away, without really considering the consequences.

In his hydraulic model of aggression, Lorenz (1950) proposed that aggression is innate. He suggested that aggression builds up within all species – humans and animals – until something happens to trigger its release. He also maintained that this build-up is inevitable. The trigger is usually something specific to each species, such as a dog baring its teeth or a cat arching its back and spitting. With humans, the trigger could be as simple as a stare which is perceived as threatening, or someone driving into a parking space in a car park just as you are about to back into the same space.

Lorenz claimed that these aggressive energies continually build up inside us, just like a tank filling with liquid as a result of a constantly dripping tap – obviously the tank will overflow unless the liquid is allowed to drain off from time to time. Lorenz believed that it was necessary for society to provide opportunities for this level of aggression to be released in a harmless way, such as by playing football or doing national service.

Unfortunately, there is virtually no evidence to back up the idea that allowing a safe method of discharge actually reduces aggression. It may almost appear to work the other way, with people who engage in aggressive sports actually becoming more aggressive. You can probably imagine that if someone is trained to fight, as a boxer for example, and they are better at it than the average person, it will come easy to them to use it as a means of settling any sort of dispute – an automatic response.

Another explanation for aggressive behaviour focuses on biological factors (which may not be innate), such as hormone levels, chromosomes and abnormalities in the physiological structure of the brain (the physiological aspects of our behaviour will be discussed in more detail in Chapter 6). It has often been noted that high levels of the hormone testosterone result in aggressive behaviours (which helps to explain why men are generally more aggressive than women). To back up this argument, Maccoby and Jacklin (1974) concluded that boys are consistently more aggressive than girls after undertaking dozens of laboratory experiments and field studies among different social classes in various cultures. It is also the case that men are charged with violent offences far more frequently than women, with women usually charged with offences against property. It has been found that testosterone levels are actually higher in both male and female prisoners who have been convicted of violent crimes, when compared with prisoners who have been convicted of non-violent offences (Dabbs et al. 1995).

Gender as an explanation of crime provides a link to applied psychology. Statistics confirm that women are convicted of crimes far less than men and this pattern seems to hold true across the world. Studies from a variety of countries show that approximately 80 per cent of crimes are committed by men. The general pattern shows that although men and women commit similar crimes, they do so to a very different extent. For example, women are far less likely to commit robbery, sexual offences or murder. Giddens (1997) found that the highest reported type of crime for women was fraud and forgery, but women still only committed around 20 per cent of all such offences.

These findings are supported by the Crime and Justice Survey (2003), which showed that 13 per cent of men and 7 per cent of women had committed core offences (burglary, thefts from vehicles, shops and people, robbery, assaults and selling drugs), although the difference was not statistically significant for robbery and burglary. The survey also indicated that males were more frequently involved in a wider range of offences and were more likely to be serious or prolific offenders.

Another explanation for aggression, which indicates that it takes more than a sign stimulus to produce an aggressive response, is Dollard et al.'s (1939) frustration–aggression hypothesis. Dollard suggests that if we feel frustrated in our efforts to achieve some kind of goal or to get what we want, we are more likely to become aggressive. Frustration can often lead to the expression of anger, much of which is not directly related to the situation itself.

There is a small problem with this argument, which is that we do not always act in the same way if we are frustrated. Some people simply walk away from a situation if they cannot get what they want, and they seem not to be bothered by it. Seligman (1975) pointed out that continual frustration may lead to us becoming totally passive because we have learned that we are helpless. He calls this a state of **learned helplessness**.

The weird and wonderful world of Sigmund Freud

Phobias and the unconscious

The development of a phobia is not as simple as it might first appear. Freud's explanation for the development of a phobia relates directly to his theory of child development. It also links to his belief that much of our behaviour is the result of the unconscious, which, unbeknown to us, affects the way we behave. In order to make sense of this, we need to look in some detail at the weird and wonderful world of Sigmund Freud.

Freud is often described by his critics – and those who do not really understand much about him – as a complete 'nutcase' and 'sex-mad'. He did have some unusual ideas, which can seem very strange, but he must be commended for being the first person to make the point that things which we are not consciously aware of can have quite a strong influence on our behaviour.

Sigmund Freud

Imagine you are a small boy of 3 years who is regularly beaten with a large cane. It does not matter what you do, you always seem to be in trouble, and every time you are in trouble, your father beats you. He keeps the cane in a cupboard in the dining room, and just before he actually beats you, he whips the air a couple of times with the cane, just to make the point that it is going to hurt. One day, on his way home from work, your father has an accident in his car and dies. Never again are you beaten, and over the course of the next few years the memory fades, until you can hardly remember your father, let alone the caning.

You are now 20, and are at a mate's house, where you have somehow been roped into helping him to sort out his shed. In the corner are some canes which have been used to support plants, although you have not noticed these. Your mate gets one of them and whips the air with it behind your back. Suddenly you feel this horrific feeling of coldness coming over you and all the hairs on the back of your neck stand on end. You are not aware of why the noise provoked such an extreme response because you have no recollection of being beaten when you were small. But the repressed memory has remained in your unconscious and is triggered by the sound.

Repression

The story above is an example of how the memories we have of painful or embarrassing incidents are pushed into our unconscious as our body's way of making it possible for us to cope with them. This can also happen with frightening experiences, or when we are so ashamed of something we have done that in order to prevent ourselves from continual suffering, we push the memory into the deep recesses of our mind. Freud claimed that memories which are painful or damaging are often repressed, rather than forgotten, and therefore they can continue to have an effect on our behaviour without us having any conscious awareness of why. When people repress memories, often the only way to access them is through hypnosis, whereby the person is made to relax so deeply that the memories can be brought to the surface. This perspective is known as the **psychoanalytical approach** and it focuses on the importance of the unconscious mind.

FOCUS ON PERSPECTIVES: THE PSYCHOANALYTICAL APPROACH

The psychoanalytical approach comes from the theories of Freud and focuses on the importance of the unconscious mind. The psychoanalytical perspective holds that behaviour is determined by our past experiences, which have been stored in our unconscious mind.

Freud believed that the mind is made up of three different levels: the conscious, the preconscious and the unconscious.

- The conscious consists of the thoughts that we are attending to which are currently in the mind.
- The preconscious consists of information and ideas which can be retrieved easily from memory and brought into our conscious awareness.
- The unconscious consists of information which is very hard (or even impossible) to bring into conscious awareness.

It is also important to remember that Freud lived in a time of almost Victorian morality, where many aspects of our natural drives were considered base and crude. Consequently, people had far more reason to feel guilty than they would today. Perhaps some of his theories were a way of trying to explain these instincts as natural and normal. On the other hand, he was an unusual man and had many strange aspects to his personality, including the unerring belief that he was right in his ideas (a trait which often accompanies an innate lack of confidence – if you have confidence in yourself, you do not mind being wrong from time to time). He was also obsessive in his interests, very neat, tidy and controlled in his behaviour, and perhaps these traits gave him a sort of security.

Freud's background

Freud was born in Freiberg, Moravia in 1856, but lived for most of his life in Vienna. His father was a Jewish wool merchant who had been trading in Moravia, but on account of a failing business he moved his family, first to Leipzig and then to Vienna. Life was not easy for the family as there was a great deal of anti-Jewish feeling, yet they managed to survive on a meagre income. In 1873, at the age of 17, Freud attended the University of Vienna, where he studied medicine, although he did not graduate until March 1881.

Freud spent three years gaining experience as a clinical neurologist at the Vienna General Hospital and the Salpêtrière Hospital in Paris. It was in Paris that he worked for the neurologist Jean Charcot, who had a keen interest in hysterical illnesses. In April 1886 Freud opened his own medical practice in Vienna and married Martha Bernays later that year. They were extremely poor in the early years, but the marriage lasted for 53 years and Martha bore him six children, the youngest of whom was Anna Freud (1895–1982) who continued to work in the field of psychoanalysis and the treatment of children.

While treating his patients, Freud realised that some of them had what appeared to be real symptoms which had no physical basis (known as **hysteria** or hysterical illnesses). He became interested in what it was that caused these illnesses, which seemed to be more common in women. As part of his search to find an explanation, he was influenced by Charcot's ideas. Charcot taught that in order to understand hysteria he should look at psychology rather than physiology, and he demonstrated the use of hypnosis as a way of gaining access to the underlying psychological causes for these symptoms. It seemed that many of the 'hysterical' patients had something troubling them which they had repressed, such as a painful memory. Once they admitted their concerns, the symptoms seemed to disappear.

Freud also met and became friends with Josef Breuer, who used a different method of treating hysterical illness which simply involved allowing the patient, in a totally safe and non-judgemental situation, to talk freely about his or her thoughts and feelings. Breuer believed that through this process the problems would ultimately surface and, once expressed, would provide a kind of **catharsis** or release, which would ultimately 'cure' the patient of his or her symptoms. Freud started to use Breuer's methods as he thought this was a way for his patients to gain access to the things they did not want to talk about, the things they had buried in the deepest recesses of their minds.

Freud was totally committed to his work, practising as a therapist during the day and writing well into the night. Despite the unpopularity of his theories, his contributions to the world of psychoanalysis comprised 24 volumes. He was obviously an extremely intelligent man although he was obsessive about his work and his private life, and he could be quite obstinate and very self-opinionated. He believed that his ideas were right and he was very intolerant of those who disagreed with him, which resulted in him losing many of his friends. Freud finally fled Austria for London after the Nazi invasion in 1937 and, despite a long battle, died of cancer in 1939.

The structure of the mind

As we have seen, Freud believed that the mind is comprised of three parts: the area we are consciously aware of; the preconscious; and the unconscious mind. He believed that there was no point attempting to gain direct access to the unconscious mind because not only were people unable to do this, but they were probably not even aware of its existence. However, he did believe that when people were not thinking they often gave away information, for example, when they made slips of the tongue. This is what happens when you call your teacher 'Mum', or call a recent boy/girlfriend by the name of the person you were dating previously.

Freud started to use different techniques, such as dream analysis, as a way of gaining access to the unconscious mind with the patients he saw with hysterical symptoms. Remember, many of these were young women. Freud unexpectedly discovered that some of them had suffered from sexual abuse as children. What you must remember was that when Freud was practising, 'sex' as we know it today did not exist. It was not considered proper for women to enjoy sex, for example. Sex was only for making babies as far as women were concerned. Men, on the other hand, had carnal desires and if these were not met by their wife, they would have to take cold showers or seek some kind of solace elsewhere – often with 'ladies of the night'.

Can you imagine the predicament Freud found himself in? He could not blatantly admit that these eminent gentlemen, the fathers or brothers of his female patients, had abused them, and yet this was what he had discovered. He decided to present his findings in 1896, when he gave a lecture on the aetiology of hysteria. He explained that during therapy with patients who had suffered previously unexplained hysteria, it had emerged that they had been sexually abused in childhood, either by an adult or an older sibling, and that until they had had therapy they had been unaware of this. The trouble was that the people Freud was speaking to, who were very influential, responded to his finding with horror and disbelief (or even denial). Freud had to try to rectify the situation he now found himself in and return to a position of favour, so he replaced his theory the following year with what he called the 'Oedipus complex'. What happened, he claimed, was that the abuse was in the mind of the child – a fantasy rather than a reality, and if there was physical evidence of abuse, for example a pregnancy, he explained this away by saying that the fantasy must have become so powerful that the child had initiated the sexual contact themselves.

The id, ego and superego

Returning to Freud's idea that a large part of the mind is unavailable to our conscious awareness, we can see how this links up with his theory of the adult personality which has three basic parts: the **id**, the **ego** and the **superego**. The ego is the only part that we are actually aware of, although the other two try their best to influence our conscious awareness.

Freud tried to explain the workings of the mind in a purely physiological way, although he realised it was not that simple and that the workings of the mind change and evolve over time. He believed that when we are born, we are driven by what he called the **pleasure principle**, which means that we want to have lots of pleasure and avoid anything nasty. This pleasure principle, or id, consists of primitive desires and primeval urges, which are often reflexes, so contain no logical or rational thought. Imagine the small child in the supermarket who we met in Chapter 3. He wants the sweeties and he wants them now, no matter what state his mother is in. He does not care about how she feels because he is totally egocentric and driven by his own desires. We all retain these desires and urges and, ideally, we would all like our desires to be met *now*, not next week or next year. Most of us, however, find ways of dealing with our id.

How do we do this? The next part of the personality to develop is what Freud called the ego. This operates according to what is known as the reality principle. As we start to operate in the real world, we begin to realise that we cannot always have what we want when we want it. So we work out ways of achieving what we want. For example, our experiences and interactions with others will have taught us when to ask for something and when to keep quiet. The ego has no moral basis; it does not consider the moral rights and wrongs of behaving in certain ways, although it does take into account what is and is not acceptable to other people. It realises that if we do follow our desires, we may be excluded by others and this would be pretty awful too (and might make matters worse in the long run). So it tries to satisfy the 'child' within us, in a realistic and acceptable way.

Have you considered where our morals come from? Perhaps Bandura would argue that we learn our moral code of behaviour by observing the behaviour of others, although Freud would disagree. He claimed that the little voice like a parent, which comes to most of us when we are about to do something wrong, is the part of the personality called the superego. It develops as we start to internalise the rules and regulations of our parents and the society in which we live, so it becomes a kind of 'internal parent'. We will look at how this happens in the next section, when we will consider the moral development of the child in slightly more detail. For the moment, it is sufficient to realise that in many ways the superego is as unrealistic as the id. If we always behaved according to a strict set of moral rules, we would become rigid and inflexible.

Freud says that the ego's job is to maintain a state of 'dynamic equilibrium' between these three parts. It has the position of trying to balance them out and satisfy the demands of both the id and the superego. One of the best descriptions of Freud's construct of the personality comes from Nicky Hayes (1994), who claims that the relationship between the three parts is like 'a battle between a sex-crazed monkey and a maiden aunt, being refereed by a rather nervous bank clerk!'.

Freud's developmental theory

Freud's theory is called a psychodynamic theory because he claimed that there are psychological forces (psycho) that move or drive us forwards (dynamic) to do things. These are innate instincts. Freud identified two instinctive driving forces. The first is known as Eros, the life instinct, whose main active component is the sexual drive or libido. The second is Thanatos, the death instinct, and its main active component is aggression towards ourselves and others. Freud initially ignored the aggressive instinct, but found it hard to explain the dreadful loss of life and carnage of the First World War, so he later incorporated Thanatos as a representation of our innate destructiveness and aggression.

Freud believed that the development of a child's personality is based on these biological drives, which evolve through a number of biologically determined stages. He believed that the strongest drive was the libido or sexual instinct, and he maintained that babies and young children are capable of sexual pleasure. (Perhaps the word 'sexual' is too strong here. It might be more appropriate to substitute 'sensual', because Freud was referring to physical pleasure from any area of the body, rather than simply the genitals, which is what adults tend to think of as sexual pleasure.)

Oral stage (0–15 months)

The first stage is the oral stage because the main areas of sensitivity and pleasure are the lips and mouth. The baby gets great pleasure in two ways from putting things in its mouth, even when it is not feeding. One is by sucking and swallowing, and the other is by biting and chewing. According to Freud, if the child's desires are satisfied, they are not left to cry for hours on end without food and they are weaned at the right time, they will be fine. If, however, they are weaned at the wrong time, they will become 'orally fixated', which means that as adults they will have an excessive interest in oral gratification. They will either become compulsive eaters, drinkers or smokers, or constantly chew things like gum, pens and fingernails. If they get excessive amounts of pleasure from sucking and swallowing, they will become too trusting and gullible and easily fooled, whereas if they enjoyed biting and chewing more they would become sarcastic and verbally aggressive. In fact, Freud believed that these people even become incapable of personal love for others, with a tendency to treat people as objects to be used to fulfil their needs.

The evidence to support this stage is somewhat sparse. Kline and Storey (1977) found evidence for two different types of oral characters. The first group showed a cluster of traits which could be called oral optimism: sociability, dependability and a relaxed nature. The other group showed a different cluster called oral pessimism: independence, verbal aggression, envy, hostility, ambition and impatience. What we have to remember here is that we can never be sure whether these were a result of their oral experiences or something completely different!

Anal stage (1–3 years)

In this second stage, the sensitive area shifts from the mouth to the anus. According to Freud, the child now derives great pleasure from either expelling or retaining faeces. Although this seems rather weird, many children do have a fascination with their faeces, and when they first manage to go in a potty, they will often express interest and pleasure in what they have done.

During this stage the child is potty-trained, whereas before they could go when they liked, discreetly protected by the gentle comfort of clean nappies! Now the child learns that in order to get praise from its parents it has to behave in a certain way. No longer can it do as it pleases. This may well be the first type of condition that has been put on the child's behaviour, and it learns that there is a huge significance to defecating. Therefore, if the parents are very strict and overanxious about their child's bowel habits, the child will become excessively worried and frightened about going, and therefore will be an 'anal retentive'. The child will associate the normal functioning with messiness and dirt, and may become preoccupied with orderliness and cleanliness as a reaction to this. Freud claims that this trait will continue as the child gets older, becoming an adult who, instead of holding on to its faeces, will hold on to its possessions instead – in effect, a miser, hoarder or collector of some kind.

On the other hand, if the parents are extremely laid back and even overly lenient about the child's ability to use the potty, the child will go anywhere! This child will become an 'anal expulsive', who will grow up to be overgenerous, untidy and completely indifferent to material possessions. Again, these collections of traits are often found together and provide some support for his analysis, but the explanations he gives as to why they cluster together have received very little support.

Phallic stage (3–5 years)

Freud claimed that the area of sensuality shifts from the anus to the genitals when the child reaches the age of about 3 years. This is the time when children play with their genitals and become inquisitive as to the differences between little boys and little girls. It is also quite normal to see small boys with their hands tucked down the front of their trousers at this age, which you could say lends support to Freud's ideas. The thing is, fascination and comfort (which is the main reason why most little boys hold on to their genitals) are not necessarily the same as sexual interest.

The Oedipus complex

It is during this stage that Freud believed the awareness of sex differences forms the basis of what he calls the Oedipus complex. He claimed that girls feel inferior to or jealous of boys because they have a penis, and that boys believe that because girls do not have a penis, they must have been castrated. During this stage children also have intense emotions, usually directed at the parent of the opposite sex. (How many males actually believe that girls are really castrated boys? Most will say that the thought has never entered their heads although Freud would say that they were repressing their memories, so of course they would not be able to recollect the idea!)

Before we talk about the Oedipus complex, it might be useful to explain who Oedipus was, for those of you who are not familiar with Greek mythology. Oedipus was the son of the King of Thebes, but an oracle prophesied that Oedipus would kill his father. In order to prevent this happening, his father ordered the boy to be put to death. He was rescued by a shepherd and was brought up unaware of his identity. One day, when he was on the road to Thebes, he quarrelled with a man and accidentally killed him, not realising that this man was his father. Later in his life he was made King of Thebes as a result of an act of bravery against a mythical creature called the Sphinx, and subsequently married Jocasta, not realising that she was his mother. When he found out who she was, he gouged out his eyes.

As a result of this relationship between Oedipus and his mother, Freud coined the term 'Oedipus complex' to describe the situation which occurs when boys develop an intense attachment to their mothers.

It is often the case that little boys become quite clingy to their mothers at this age (and often the same is true of girls with their fathers, but we will stick with small boys for the moment). Freud believed that this attachment becomes increasingly intense and causes the boy to regard his father as a rival, especially as the father sleeps with the mother and has the closeness and familiarity with her that the boy would like. However, the boy also sees his father as a powerful and threatening figure who has the ultimate power to deal with this rivalry – namely to castrate him. The small boy is caught at this point between desire for his mother and fear of his father's power.

What we must remember here is that the boy does not have real sexual feelings that we recognise as adults. Most of these feelings are unconscious and cause a kind of internal conflict or anxiety which the small boy has to deal with. Anxiety is an unpleasant state, and we strive for much of our lives to find ways to reduce our feelings of anxiety, no matter how they are caused. Freud claimed that the boy deals with the situation by using a defensive process called sex-role identification. The boy will start to identify with his father and repress any further feelings he has for his mother into his unconscious. He will begin to spend more time with his father, wanting to be like daddy, and this in turn will reduce any further chance of being castrated as his father will no longer see him as a rival. Through this process he will internalise his father's moral standards and this is the core of the child's superego.

KEY CONCEPTS

What does Freud's study show us about identification?
The Freudian concept of identification suggests that we may identify with people whom we perceive as threatening as a way of reducing the threat. This comes from the idea that a boy who suffers from castration anxiety realises that it will be impossible for him to overcome his powerful father, so it would make more sense to 'join' him. This process is known as identification with the aggressor.

This theory helps to explain why schoolchildren often side with bullies, even though they do not agree with their behaviour – it is for fear of being bullied themselves.

The Electra complex

So what about girls? The Electra complex is the supposed female equivalent, occurring in girls between the ages of 3 and 6 years, and manifested by the excessive attachment of little girls to their fathers and corresponding hostility to their mothers. The term 'Electra complex' also comes from Greek mythology. Electra, daughter of the Greek leader Agamemnon, was famous for her devotion and loyalty to her father, who was murdered by her mother and her mother's lover. In order to avenge the death of her beloved father, Electra, with her younger brother's help, murdered the mother she detested, as well as her mother's lover.

The problem was that Freud had not clearly worked out the female side of this developmental process – probably because he found women puzzling throughout his life. The course of the Electra complex goes something like this: the girl will be very close to her mother when she is little, until she discovers that she does not have a penis. This makes her feel inferior and she blames her mother for allowing her to be castrated. She does realise that one way she can feel equal to men is by producing a baby (and this is all from the age of 3 years!), and she sees her father as a potential impregnator, allowing her to have a child of her own as a substitute for the missing penis. She will therefore transfer her affections from the mother to the father.

Why this happens is the main problem with the Electra complex. Boys renounce their feelings for their mother because of the fear of castration by their father, but this cannot be the case with girls, who have already been 'castrated' by their mothers. Freud suggested that males feel that their penis is the thing they value most in the world, but the thing that girls value is loss of love. If the girl continues with her desire to have a relationship with her father she is likely to lose the love of her mother, so she will renounce her feelings for her father and do her best to make her mother love her by being a good girl. The problem is, the fear on the girl's part would be far less (according to Freud) than the boys' fear, and this led him to suggest that girls have a much less developed superego.

Latency stage (around 5 years to puberty)

The sexual drives seem to be removed from consciousness during the latency stage, although they are still there. According to Freud, the child has repressed its memories of the earlier sexual impulses by a phenomenon called infantile amnesia. The child redirects the drives into intellectual development and social activities as it learns about the world beyond the family. The friendships girls make tend to be with children of the same sex, which helps them to deal with any possible sexual thoughts. The problem with this idea is that children from other cultures, where sexual activity is seen as acceptable, show interest in sexual matters throughout the whole of their childhood.

Genital stage (puberty onwards)

With puberty, there is a re-emergence of the earlier drives and the centre of attention is once again the genitals, although this time an adult expression of sexuality is shown through relationships with members of the opposite sex.

Evaluation of Freud's theory of child development

Freud's developmental theory has been challenged and criticised by many researchers, who claim that the theory is untestable. The theory itself was proposed in 1905, when Freud wrote 'Three essays on the theory of sexuality'. This was actually three years before writing about little Hans (see core study below), which suggests that his reporting was biased in order to back up his previously formed theory (that is, it was subject to demand characteristics). Freud only met Little Hans twice and the rest of the information about the boy was reported to him by Little Hans's father, who was a supporter of Freud's ideas. This whole scenario could not be described as objective in any way, and it would be interesting to know how much information Little Hans's father actually missed out when reporting to Freud, as he may only have conveyed what he considered to be important.

If Freud was right, having a father (if you are a boy) is a prerequisite to developing morals, superego, appropriate sex-role behaviour, and so on. What happens to orphans and boys from single-parent families? Is it the case that every young boy without a father fails to develop any morals or an appropriate sex-role? There is considerable evidence from cross-cultural studies that children who are brought up in family groupings which are either extended or different to the two-parent family described by Freud show no problems with either moral or sex-role development.

Freud also claimed that the first five years of life are the most critical, but this almost implies that the rest of your life is irrelevant from a developmental viewpoint. Surely we go on learning from the experiences we have through the rest of our childhood and as adults? As we will see in Chapter 5 (page 243), the plasticity of the brain's cortex means that new learning can take place over time – so is it not possible to rethink and relearn many of the misperceptions we had as children? We would not dispute that early childhood experiences can shape our lives as adults, but unless the experiences are very traumatic, most of us are a product of *all* our experiences, not just those which take place in the first five years of life.

Child development and adult neuroses

The relevance of these different stages of childhood is made clear in Freud's belief that if an adult suffers from any kind of neurosis, it can be traced back to their progression through the stages of development. The poor old adult will either have unresolved problems due to lack of gratification or will have achieved excessive gratification – both as a result of the parental treatment they received. The child will become fixated at one of these stages, either because they have enjoyed it too much, or because they have been deprived of what they really wanted. If they enjoyed it too much, they will not want to leave the stage they are in. If they have been deprived, they will want to stay in the stage for longer in order to achieve the level of gratification or satisfaction they desire. Obviously this put a tremendous amount of pressure on mothers, who were frightened of over- or under-feeding, or who over- or under-stressed the importance of potty-training. The problem was that Freud gave no guidelines as to what the 'right' amount actually was!

The other possibility was that something had happened to them during their lives which they found distressing. They may have had an experience that they found unacceptable or very hurtful (such as rejection by a parent, or even sexual abuse); or they might have done something very wicked or unpleasant (hurt, abused or murdered someone, for example). It may not be something of such significance of course, because even having unpleasant or unacceptable thoughts can be tremendously upsetting to some people, as they feel disgusted that they could even contemplate such horrendous ideas. Whatever the cause, their ego will have stepped in and dealt with the situation, either by projecting the feelings onto something else more acceptable (such as developing a phobia about a related object), or by repressing the memory into the unconscious in order to protect the person. This may then result in the person developing an anxiety or panic attack when they experience a situation which reminds them of what they are trying to forget. The situation may also affect their behaviour; for example, they may become obsessive about certain things but not understand why. Only if that feeling is brought into conscious awareness can the person deal with the situation.

The following true story about Maurice explains how this works. Maurice had been referred to a psychiatrist as he was suffering from obsessive–compulsive behaviour. Obsessive–compulsive behaviour is when you have intrusive thoughts, which are the obsessions, and a compulsion to keep doing certain things. Most people have small compulsions like checking if the door is locked or the gas is turned off, but Maurice's compulsion was getting the better of him.

Maurice explained to the psychiatrist that he was unable to get out of the house in the morning because he had to keep going back into the bathroom to check that the towel was hung straight on the hook behind the door. He told the psychiatrist that he had to make sure that when hung, both sides were of equal length, and then he would close the door very carefully before he left. The trouble occurred when he got halfway down the stairs, because he suddenly imagined that the towel had moved and slipped off the hook, so he would have to go back and check and would end up going through the ritual all over again.

After several hours of therapy, the psychiatrist finally uncovered the cause of this obsessive–compulsive behaviour. Maurice was about 45 years old and lived with his ageing mother, who was a bossy old woman who would not let him do anything. He felt totally trapped living with her and secretly wished she would simply drop dead. One night, while he lay in his bed with his hot-water bottle, teddy bear and cocoa, he had started to daydream. He imagined that his mother had gone towards the bathroom and tried to push the door open, but the towel had fallen off the back of the door and was stopping the door from opening. She pushed and shoved until the door flew open unexpectedly and she fell through the doorway head first, hitting her head on the toilet. She cracked her skull and died. Of course, this was too awful to contemplate and he felt absolutely mortified that he could think of such a dreadful event, so rather than live with the guilt, his ego had pushed the memory out of his conscious awareness and he therefore had no idea why he had begun this bizarre behaviour. Once he had admitted it to the therapist, the obsession and the compulsive behaviour seemed to subside.

This example provides an illustration of how the unconscious can affect our behaviour. Often we repress memories or unpleasant thoughts in order to reduce our discomfort. You may now have some idea of how this might affect our subsequent behaviour.

THE STUDY

S. Freud (1909) 'Analysis of a phobia in a five-year-old boy'

in The Pelican Freud Library, vol. 8, Case Histories 1 (1977) pp.169–306

BACKGROUND

In the introduction which formed the background to the study, Freud talked about Little Hans and the origins of this particular case study. He acknowledged that Hans was not a normal child and had a predisposition to neurosis, so he realised that it might not be valid to generalise from him to all children. He also said that the argument that children are untrustworthy was unfair. Adults are untrustworthy because they are prejudiced and this might influence what they say. Children, on the other hand, may lie, but they lie for a reason, and this reason may well be one of the most important things to consider.

Hans was described as being a cheerful and straightforward child, but when he became 'ill' (by this Freud meant that he developed his phobia), it was obvious that there was a difference between what he said and what he actually thought. Freud suggested that this was because of things that were going on in his unconscious of which he was unaware. In order to put this right, Freud decided that Hans's behaviour had to be interpreted, and the boy had to be told why he was thinking and acting as he was. Freud was emphatic that this was not putting suggestions into the boy's mind, but was only a way of helping him to understand what already existed. This is the process of psychoanalysis, a form of talking cure used by Freud. The idea was for the client to talk freely, and the analyst would then be able to interpret the client's unconscious desires and anxieties, which would reveal themselves to the analyst in symbolic form, for example, in the client's fantasies and dreams.

AIMS

The aim of this case study is to document the case of Little Hans, who developed a phobia of horses. It was used by Freud to support his ideas about the origins of phobias and his belief that they are often influenced by unconscious forces. He also used it to support his ideas on psychosexual development and the Oedipus complex, and the effectiveness of psychoanalytical therapy.

The study reports the analysis of the boy's phobia, a process which was intended to cure him of this 'illness'. It also shows how Freud explained Little Hans's behaviour in terms of an unconscious Oedipal conflict.

METHOD

Method and design

A case study was carried out longitudinally, over a period of months.

KEY CONCEPTS

Case study method

A case study is an in-depth study of one participant or a small group of participants, often carried out over an extended period of time (longitudinally). Within the case study method a number of different data-gathering techniques can be used. For example, recorded interviews, case notes (of therapeutic interviews, for example), observation (as in the Washoe study in Chapter 3) and psychometric tests (which we will see in the study of multiple personality disorder in Chapter 6).

One of the strengths of the case study is its usefulness in describing atypical, abnormal or rare behaviour. In abnormal psychology the case study is seen as a useful way of exploring a participant's past experiences to help them deal with current difficulties. Freud's work derives predominantly from the case studies of his patients.

Another strength is that the data gathered are usually qualitative and rich in detail, so data from case studies can be highly valid. The bond of trust that can be built up between researcher and participant also means that the data are more likely to be valid than if the researcher were a stranger having only one interview with the participant.

However, this close bond between researcher and participant can be a weakness too, as the researcher may lose their objectivity because of their personal relationship with the participant. Their interpretations of data may also be affected by biases formed as a result of their long-term investment in the project.

Another weakness of this method is the fact that replication is not usually possible, particularly where a therapeutic approach has been taken. This makes it difficult to establish the reliability of findings from a case study.

Generalising from the findings of case studies can also be difficult, as the cases selected for study are often unusual or even unique.

Case studies can be costly in terms of both time and money.

Procedure

This case study and the analysis was actually conducted by Little Hans's father, a friend and supporter of Freud. Freud met the boy only twice, on one occasion for a therapeutic session and on another when he paid a social visit to deliver a birthday present to the boy.

The father reported on the boy's behaviour via correspondence (including his own interpretations), and Freud gave directions as to how to deal with the situation, based on his interpretations of the father's written reports and conversations. Freud believed that the reason the analysis could progress using this kind of method was because the father and son had a very special and close relationship.

It is important to note that Hans's father had been making notes on the boy's behaviour and sending these to Freud for a number of years. Freud had asked all his friends with young children to observe and record their behaviour in order to confirm his theory of psychosexual development.

It is also pertinent to point out that Hans's mother had been a patient of Freud's and had met Hans's father through Freud.

Hans's father's early notes and Freud's interpretation of these

The first information that Freud thought was interesting was Hans's interest in his 'widdler' (penis) when he was 3 years old. Hans thought everyone had a widdler, males and females alike, and that the only things that did not have widdlers were inanimate objects. He even thought his baby sister, Hanna, who he was told had been brought by a stork when Hans was 3½, had simply not grown hers yet. Hans liked playing with his widdler, which is quite normal for small boys. However, as this behaviour is often frowned upon, parents tried to discourage their children from masturbating, and Hans's mother was no different.

When he was 3½, Hans's mother found him with his hand on his penis. She threatened him with these words: 'If you do that, I shall send for Dr A. to cut off your widdler. And then what'll you widdle with?' Hans's reply, 'With my bottom', suggests that he was none too perturbed by his mother's threat!

His interest in widdlers was quite extensive; he tried to see other people's widdlers and liked showing his off. He even said to his parents that he wanted to see theirs, and Freud explained that this was probably because he wanted to see how theirs compared to his. Hans thought his mother must have a widdler 'like a horse' and presumably thought that as he got bigger, his would grow too. In fact, much of the focus of his dreams and fantasies during this time concerned widdlers and what they do.

Hans wanted his father 'out of the way' so he could have his mother to himself and sleep with her. This idea had come from spending lots of time with her when his father was away one summer. He had become apprehensive and nervous about things and had been comforted by his mother, who cuddled him in bed. He enjoyed her attention and probably resented having to share her again on his father's return. In fact, Freud believed that he attempted to seduce his mother when he was 4½, by asking her why she would not put her finger on his penis when she was putting talcum powder on him after a bath. She answered that it was not proper, but according to Freud he had 'found an incidental channel of discharge' for his sexual feelings towards her and this resulted in his 'masturbating every evening, and in that way obtaining gratification'.

Freud claimed that Hans feared that another baby might come (more competition?), but suppressed this anxiety, only to have it surface in another form – a fear of the bath. Hans had said he was worried about drowning in the big bath, having previously been bathed in a baby bath. Freud suggested that this fear came from being frightened that if he was naughty his mother would not love him anymore and therefore might let him drown. Hans also expressed jealousy towards his sister and was asked the following question: 'When you were watching Mummy giving Hanna her bath, perhaps you wished she would let go of her so that Hanna should fall in?' Hans answered 'Yes' to this question, which confirmed Freud's idea that this was evidence of his death wish towards Hanna.

Case history: the identification of Hans's phobia and the report on his psychoanalysis

Hans's father wrote to Freud, describing the fact that Hans had developed an irrational fear that a horse would bite him in the street, and that the fear was in some way connected to being frightened by a large penis. His father believed that this was the onset of the illness, and that there was a motive for being ill – he wanted to stay with his mother and never be separated from her, which was the result of a dream where his mother had gone away.

This irrational fear probably developed from two events: overhearing a father say to his child, 'Don't put your finger to the white horse or it will bite you', and seeing a horse which was pulling a carriage, fall down and flail about in the road. It affected Hans sufficiently to make him fear that a horse would come into the room. Freud suggested that there was a connection between putting a finger towards the horse that may actually be bitten and the event when his mother would not touch his penis with her finger after giving him a bath. This connection had something to do with Hans's knowledge that his parents thought masturbation was not a very good behaviour to indulge in. In fact, Hans's father said to him, 'If you don't put your hand to your widdler anymore, this nonsense of yours will soon get better.'

Freud also suggested that Hans's desire to see his mother's widdler was increasing. At this point, his father told him that women did not have widdlers. Hans may have made the association between his mother's threat to castrate him if he did not stop playing with himself and her lack of widdler. Perhaps she was in fact a castrated man who had played with hers too much in the past and had suffered the consequences!

Freud began to make the connection between Hans's father and Hans's fear of horses, and he started to think that this was a symbolic representation of the boy's fear of his father punishing him as a result of his longing for his mother. This connection was made after Freud was informed about a daydream the boy had had: the fantasy of the giraffes.

> **Hans:** In the night there was a big giraffe in the room and a crumpled one, and the big one called out because I took the crumpled one away from it. Then it stopped calling out, and then I sat down on top of the crumpled one. . .

Hans demonstrated what he meant by crumpling up a piece of paper. Hans also explained that he had not dreamed about the giraffe.

Hans: No, I didn't dream. I thought it. I thought it all. I'd woken up earlier.

He then went on to explain that he knew you can't really squash a giraffe with your hands, but explained that he had picked up the crumpled giraffe and held it in his hands until the big one had stopped calling out. Once that had happened, he again explained that he sat down on the small crumpled giraffe.

Father: Why did the big one call out?

Hans: Because I'd taken the little one away from it.

This fantasy was recognised by the father as a re-enactment of what happened in the morning when Hans climbed into bed with his parents. Often his father objected and Freud believed that he was represented by the big giraffe, who was calling out because Hans had taken the little giraffe (mother) away. There was also some discussion about whether the long neck of the giraffe represented a penis, but this was denied by Hans.

Freud's interview with Hans and his explanation for Hans's phobia

It was at this point that Freud himself chose to see Hans and asked him about his fear of horses. Freud suggested to the boy that the horse must represent Hans's father. Hans must be frightened of his father because he was jealous of him and felt hostile towards him (as outlined in Freud's Oedipus complex). The reason why Freud made this analogy between the horse and Hans's father was because Hans mentioned the black on horses' mouths and the things in front of their eyes (blinkers). Hans's father had a black moustache and wore glasses.

Hans explained that he was also frightened of horses biting him, as well as being afraid of loaded carts and buses, which was interpreted as having some kind of analogy with pregnancy, a 'loaded' body which would deliver a competitor for his mother's affections. He then told Freud about seeing the horse fall down and kick about with its feet, which terrified him because he thought the horse was dead and this led him to think that all horses would fall down. Hans's father suggested that when Hans saw the horse fall down he must have wished that his father would fall down and die in the same way. According to Freud, Hans's behaviour towards his father after this 'confession' became much less fearful, and he was much more boisterous and overbearing. He did, however, retain his fear of horses.

Hans then developed a preoccupation with his bowels and *lumf* (German for 'faeces'). He had been in the habit of accompanying his mother or the maid to the toilet until he was forbidden to do so. His father identified another analogy, between a heavily loaded cart and a body loaded with faeces. Then Hans started to talk about Hanna, and his father concluded that the reason for the train of thought was because he thought his sister was *lumf* and was born in the same way as we produce *lumf*. This led to the analogy between loaded carts and pregnancy, horses falling over and giving birth: 'the falling horse was not only his dying father but also his mother in childbirth'. He then described an imaginary friend called Lodi, who was called after *saffalodi*, a German sausage. This time, Hans's father pointed out that the sausage looked like *lumf*.

The final fantasies Hans produced at the end of his conflicts focused on plumbers and being a parent himself.

> The first fantasy involved a plumber who 'took away my behind with a pair of pincers and then gave me another, and then the same with my widdler'. Hans's father's interpretation of this was that the body parts were replaced with bigger ones, like his, which meant that Hans wanted to be like his father.
>
> The second fantasy was that Hans was the father of his own children (his mother was now his wife), and his father was their grandfather, in other words, no longer a threat to the boy as a result of his affection for his mother.
>
> This was the final piece of 'evidence' which showed that the Oedipus conflict was the cause of Hans's problems, and that once he had acknowledged his desires towards his mother (which he did symbolically in his fantasies), his problems would be resolved.

DISCUSSION

The discussion focuses on the fact that this study offers support for Freud's theory of sexuality – the Oedipus complex:

- Hans was sexually aroused by his mother.
- He was jealous of his father's relationship with his mother and frightened of him (castration fear), symbolised by a fear of fingers being bitten by horses.
- He fantasised about taking his mother away from his father (giraffe fantasy).
- He tried to seduce his mother by asking her to touch his widdler.
- He finally admitted he wanted to marry his mother.
- Resolution came with wanting to be like his father (the plumber removing his widdler and behind and giving him bigger ones).

COMMENTARY: METHODS AND ISSUES

Research method, design and data gathering

The case study method was used, with the child being interviewed and a great deal of emphasis being placed on his self-reporting of dreams and fantasies. It was a longitudinal design.

One of the biggest weaknesses of case studies is that contact with the participant over time may well lead to extreme subjectivity. This case study was even more subjective because the child was being 'treated' by his father (emotional involvement), who was a strong Freud supporter (biased), and his mother had been treated by Freud before her marriage (it would be interesting to know why she was treated).

Perhaps some of the interpretations made were because the father was preoccupied with matters sexual or physical. After all, it was Hans's father who suggested that a German sausage looked like *lumf* (faeces). Maybe a sausage is just a sausage if you have never heard of Freud's psychosexual theory of development! Hans's mother and father eventually divorced and both remarried. Between the ages of 6 and 19 years, Hans lived with his father, while his sister went with their mother. Perhaps the relationship between the father and mother was somewhat strained during the time when Hans became phobic, and in fact the father was projecting his own preoccupations onto his son.

Is the study useful?

Little Hans was the only child studied by Freud. When he met Hans, Freud had already formulated his theory of the Oedipus complex, which supports the idea that his report on Hans was extremely biased. Hans was probably quite normal, but became 'phobic' about horses because of a traumatic event which might well have frightened any small boy. It is quite likely that his fear of horses had absolutely nothing to do with his father, but that this idea was introduced and stuck in Hans's memory.

Freud believed that phobias are the result of hidden conflicts in the unconscious mind, and he interpreted everything on that basis. His questioning of Hans can therefore be understood as a way of getting at the unconscious mind and trying to resolve what he saw as a potential cause of trouble for the boy as he got older. Hans's agreement with many of the interpretations offered to him indicated to his father and Freud that they were correct in their beliefs about the origin of his phobia and the Oedipus complex. Hans's final fantasies about wanting to marry and have children with his mother was the final confirmation they needed.

Another way we could interpret the findings of this study would be to suggest that the boy was suffering from what John Bowlby (a famous child psychoanalyst) called '**separation anxiety**'. Bowlby was interested in the effects of early experiences on the emotional development of children. He identified the extreme adverse effects on a child of separation from the mother figure, claiming that 'mother love in infancy and childhood is as important for mental health as are vitamins and proteins for physical health' (Bowlby 1951). He suggested that if a child had been parted from its mother at some time, the child would experience extreme separation anxiety in case the situation happened again, and this intense anxiety would affect their ability to function effectively.

Hans's mother frequently made alarming threats to Hans to make him behave, such as beating him with a carpet beater. His fear of castration was founded on firm ground – after all, his mother had threatened him with castration when he would not stop fiddling with his penis. She also threatened to leave the family, which would have made him quite insecure, and consequently he may have become very possessive and clingy. Hans was actually kept away from his mother when Hanna was born, and this must have made the situation worse: because he was frightened that his mother might leave him, he would have felt very angry and unhappy with regard to his mother. However, knowing that it is not right to be fearful or angry with your mother, he may have projected those feelings onto something else – horses. This idea is illustrated in the following conversation, when Hans talked about a fantasy he had that he had taken a horse out of the stable:

Father: You took it out of the stables?
Hans: I took it out because I wanted to whip it.
Father: Which would you really like to beat – Mummy, Hanna or me?
Hans: Mummy.
Father: Why?
Hans: I should just like to beat her.
Father: When did you ever see someone beating their Mummy?
Hans: I've never seen anyone do it, never in all my life.
Father: And yet you'd just like to do it?
Hans: With a carpet beater.

As there are other explanations for the cause of Hans's phobia, we have to question the validity of Freud's interpretation, and this affects its usefulness. In fact, Freud's theory of psychosexual development is considered to be a nice story, but not an accurate description of personality development.

Despite the fact that Freud's theory of child development is without supporters today, very few people question the major contribution that Freud made to our understanding of behaviour, by describing the influence of unconscious motivation on behaviour and interpreting the purpose and meaning of dreams. In this way, Freud's theories have been highly generative and there is no doubt that he should be numbered among the great minds of the twentieth century. Whether we can count the case of Little Hans among his greatest works, however, is unlikely.

Does the study raise any ethical issues?

Whether you think this case study was good or bad, Hans actually came out of it seemingly unscathed, although we cannot be sure that he would not have been fine anyway (i.e. without any psychoanalysis). When he was 19, Hans met Freud and told him that he was well and that he had no troubles or inhibitions. He also claimed to have no memory of the discussions with his father or Freud which took place during his childhood, and that he got on well with both parents, despite their break-up, but missed his younger sister. However, we can never be sure whether this was really true, or because he was repressing the memory.

We must remember that this case study was intended to support the Oedipus complex which replaced Freud's earlier 'seduction theory'. The change from believing that the parent was responsible for child sexual abuse, to suggesting that it was a fantasy in the mind of the child, however, was responsible for society's reluctance to acknowledge how widespread such abuse really was. Even if there were some overt physical evidence of abuse, such as a pregnancy, the child would be blamed. In this respect, it would have been better if Freud had stuck to his original ideas. This suggests that Freud's work may have done more harm than good.

Validity and reliability of the study

As with all self-report data, there can be problems with validity. On the one hand, Freud suggested that children's memories were in fact quite accurate, but the next minute he was making some fairly stunning leaps by reinterpreting what Hans said to give it a different meaning. Perhaps Hans's memory was originally quite accurate, but the introduction of new interpretations by his father (and Freud) may have affected his subsequent memory of events, or clouded his interpretation of them. In fact, the whole study brings new meaning to the idea of leading questions.

KEY CONCEPTS

Leading questions

We came across leading questions in the Loftus and Palmer study on eyewitness testimony in Chapter 3. Their definition is as follows: 'A leading question is simply one that, by its form or content, suggests to the witness what answer is desired or leads him to the desired answer.'

In Freud's study of Little Hans, Hans's father uses leading questions in his analysis of the boy. (e.g. 'When the horse fell over, did you think of your daddy?' Hans replies, 'Perhaps. Yes. It is possible.')

This is a problem, as it means that the child is being influenced by his father's expectations, which in this instance are very much in tune with Freud's theory of child development, and this means that the findings are not objective.

Psychoanalysts claim that they cannot be judged by anyone except a psychoanalyst, because no one else would understand the procedures and would therefore be biased in some way. In effect, this makes their beliefs and profession unquestionable – perhaps we should simply accept that the case history of Little Hans is true, because until we are psychoanalysts ourselves, we cannot judge it!

The Developmental Psychological Approach

Researcher(s)	Focus of study
Samuel and Bryant	Do younger children than Piaget suggested conserve if only one question is asked in the conservation experiment?
Bandura, Ross and Ross	Can we learn by imitation?
Freud	Is the treatment, through analysis, of Little Hans's phobia evidence of the Oedipus complex?

This approach looks at the development of behaviour, including the development of thinking processes, learning and personality development. While the three core studies focus particularly on child development, it is important to recognise that development is a lifelong process, and psychology in general does not limit its study of development to children's development.

The studies illustrate a number of key concepts in development, including nature versus nurture, maturation, reinforcement and the use of stage theories in describing the process of children's development.

● Samuel and Bryant confirm a maturation process in children's cognitive development, as their evidence supports Piaget's stage theory of cognitive development, which showed that thinking changes as the child ages.

● Bandura et al. show that reinforcement may not be necessary for learning to occur, but may play a large part in affecting whether someone performs a particular learned behaviour or not.

● Freud presents a unique (if largely discredited) view of the development of personality in his theory of psychosexual development, also a stage theory.

As we discussed in the introduction to these studies, two of the developmental studies in this chapter also serve to illustrate two of the major perspectives in psychology: the behaviourist approach (Bandura et al.) and the psychoanalytical approach (Freud). As you will now realise, one focuses very much on the observable and measurable, while the other is open to speculation and interpretation.

STRENGTHS AND WEAKNESSES

The Developmental Psychological Approach

- Developmental research can demonstrate the influence on behaviour of internal and environmental factors. For example, Samuel and Bryant showed the role of maturation, an internal factor in the development of cognitive abilities, as they demonstrated that children's ability to conserve improved with age. Of course, this development can only occur if the child is in an environment that supports it, so both internal and external factors have a part to play in children's cognitive development.

- It is, without doubt, as important to understand the psychological development of children as it is to understand their physical development. This understanding helps us to provide children with what should assist their healthy and happy psychological development, and to avoid things which might have a negative impact on it. For this reason, the value of developmental psychology as a discipline is obvious.

- Studying children raises ethical concerns, including whether or not children can give their informed consent to take part, and the issues of causing harm or upset. For example, Bandura et al. make no reference to obtaining parental consent for a study in which they exposed impressionable youngsters to an adult model behaving in an aggressive way in the aggression condition. All the children were subject to being deliberately upset in stage two, and some children were coerced into staying in room three for the required 20 minutes when they clearly did not want to.

- There are problems with studying children under laboratory conditions, especially where they are tested by strangers in strange environments, and are isolated from their peers. This means that studies which are carried out in this way lack ecological validity. Examples of this are the studies by Bandura et al. and Samuel and Bryant.

- The use of the case history method in the study by Freud provides a great deal of qualitative data. Hans was studied over a period of time to get a full picture of his experiences, thus bringing the advantages associated with longitudinal research.

- Freud's study of Little Hans is affected by researcher bias. Both Freud and Hans's father, who carried out most of the interviews and observations of the boy, believed in Freud's psychosexual theory of development and saw Hans as a 'Little Oedipus'. This affected the way in which they reported and interpreted the boy's experiences. The relationship between the boy and his father might also mean that the boy was susceptible to leading questions, and this reduces the quality of the evidence. For example, when Hans's father asked, 'When the horse fell over, did you think of your daddy?' Hans's response, 'Yes. Perhaps. It is possible', may have been to please his father rather than to express what he truly thought at the time.

Physiological psychology

In many ways it is very easy to forget the physical basis of all human behaviour – our bodies. Our bodies are the most amazing organisms, which are so complicated that it is likely we will never understand absolutely everything there is to know about them. There have also been many heated debates about whether our bodies are all there is to us, or whether we also have a spirit (or soul). If our bodies are all there is, when we die, we must cease to exist. On the other hand, if we also have a spirit, does that die with us or does it go on existing? This is known as the mind–body problem, which questions the basis of consciousness and existence itself. There seems to be no easy answer to this conundrum.

If you are a biologist, you will have already some insight into how our bodies work and you will be familiar with the information in the next section (which is very basic). However, for those of you who have spent your time trying to ignore biology, hopefully this simplistic overview of the physiology of the nervous system will not put you off. You need to have some understanding of the structure of the nervous system because psychology also involves an understanding of physiology. In fact, some psychologists tend to favour biological explanations when trying to understand the nature of behaviour. In order to effectively evaluate *all* approaches to psychology, we are going to consider the physiological approach in psychology and look at the methods used to investigate this area. Once we have done this, we can begin to look at the interaction between what goes on physically and our subsequent behaviour.

The physiology of the nervous system

The way the nervous system is structured is absolutely fascinating. It is so complex and each component is so tiny, yet it seems that our abilities are limitless. With all the technological knowledge in the world, we have not yet been able to mimic much more than the most basic of human abilities. Humans can make assumptions that are correct on the basis of very little information; computers are far more likely to make errors. They cannot use information that is not clear, whereas we process the past, the present and what we know about the future, at the same time. That is not to say that we do not make errors; we just make far fewer than computers.

In Chapter 3 we discussed the information-processing approach, which makes the analogy between humans and computers. This analogy is relevant not only because of the way both humans and computers process information, but also because both use electricity. Obviously we do not have to plug ourselves in to the mains, but we do work by a system of electrochemical changes, caused by external stimuli and by changes in our bodies.

The structure of the nervous system

Terms in bold are included in the Glossary for Chapter 5 on the CD-ROM.

The nervous system includes the **central nervous system** (CNS), which is the brain and spinal cord. This is the central control for all the activities of the body, where information received is processed and there is coordination of actions and reactions, both conscious and unconscious. The nervous system also includes the **peripheral nervous system** (PNS), which consists of a network of neurones which are located around the whole body and are responsible for carrying information from the world to the CNS, and from the CNS back to the different parts of the body. The PNS can also be subdivided into the **somatic nervous system** and the **autonomic nervous system** (ANS).

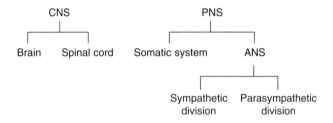

The somatic nervous system is the part that is generally conscious of the responses it is making; for example, the sensory nerves of the somatic system carry information about external stimulation from the different receptors to the CNS. The information is 'decoded', and messages are carried back from the CNS to the muscles of the body, where action is then taken in response. Therefore, the somatic part of the nervous system is responsible for all the muscles we use to make voluntary movements, as well as involuntary adjustments to posture and balance.

The **nerves** of the ANS run to and from the internal organs and are affected generally by information from inside the body (although occasionally they may respond to external information). The messages transmitted by the ANS regulate the function of these internal organs, such as heart rate, speed of respiration and digestion. It is called the autonomic nervous system because many of the activities it controls are automatic and self-regulating, and these continue to take place even if a person is asleep or unconscious.

The ANS can be further subdivided into the sympathetic division and the parasympathetic division.

● The **sympathetic division** is the mechanism that speeds bodily systems up and prepares the organism for activity – it has an excitatory function. It is the fight/flight mechanism which prepares the body for a response, for example by speeding up the heart, dilating the arteries of the essential organs and constricting the arteries of the less essential organs, such as the skin and digestive organs. (We need more blood to the vital organs in order to survive. We do not need to digest things if we are running away – that can be done later.)

- The **parasympathetic division** is responsible for returning the body to normal by slowing it down again and allowing bodily functions to return to their original state – it is inhibitory.

In order for these actions to occur, neuronal fibres from both the sympathetic and parasympathetic divisions supply most organs, and the normal state of the body is maintained by a balance between these two systems.

What are neurones?

Neurones are the cells of the nervous system and are responsible for carrying messages from one part of the body to another. We have three types of neurone:

- **sensory neurones**;

- **motor neurones**;

- **inter-neurones**.

There are between 10 and 12 billion neurones in the nervous system, which will give you an idea of how tiny they are. A nerve is actually a bundle of neurones (like all the coloured wires in a telephone cable), which are held together by **glial cells**. Glial cells are smaller cells than neurones and provide the neurones with nutrients and structural support.

The three different types of neurones all have different functions:

- Sensory neurones transmit impulses received by receptors to the central nervous system.

- Inter-neurones receive the signals from the sensory neurones and send impulses to other inter-neurones or to motor neurones. They are found only in the brain or the spinal cord.

- Motor neurones carry outgoing signals from the brain or spinal cord to the effector organs, such as the muscles or the heart and lungs.

All these neurones form connections with each other in order to carry information around the body by way of impulses, or electric messages. The messages or impulses that travel along our neurones can be thought of as bursts of electrical energy. We talk about these bursts of electricity as bursts of fire. A single neurone 'fires' when the stimulation reaching it from other neurones exceeds a certain threshold. Perhaps one way to describe how this works is to imagine a number of drips falling from various branches of a tree into a large bath underneath – when the bath is full, one final drip will make it overflow. The firing of a neurone is just like this – the sum of lots of stimulation makes it reach a certain level, causing it to fire.

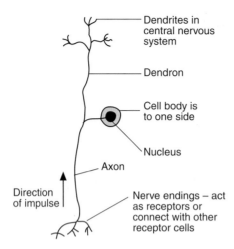

A simple diagram of an unbranched sensory motor neurone, e.g. skin

Some of these impulses are messages to do something (**excitatory messages**), and some are messages to remain inactive (inhibitory messages). The messages are passed from one neurone to another across what is known as a **synaptic gap** (a **synapse** is the junction between two nerve cells) by **neurotransmitters** which are actually chemical messengers. The whole process is extremely complex and it is not necessary for our purposes to go into the way synapses work. Sufficient to say, increases or decreases in the levels of neurotransmitters can affect the speed of message transmission, which, in turn, will affect the way a person thinks, reacts or responds physically to different situations. Many of the drugs that are used to change mood, such as antidepressants, affect the quantity or actions of neurotransmitters in the brain.

What sets these cells apart from other cells is their shape. From the central body of the neurone come lots of small, thin fibres called **dendrites**. Some are very short and others extend over long distances, with lots of branches. Consequently, the shape of a neurone can vary enormously, and it is the shape which dictates both the number of excitatory or inhibitory connections they make with other neurones, and how each one will contribute to the overall functioning of the organism, even though they all work in the same way. There are also different types of nerves: **myelinated** and non-myelinated. Some nerves need to transmit their messages over longer distances very quickly. This is when you would find myelinated nerves, which are nerves surrounded by a myelin sheath. The myelin allows the impulse to 'hop' along the neurone rather than running as a kind of wave, thus speeding up the transmission of the impulse. If the myelin breaks down, the impulse goes very slowly, or is lost altogether, which is what happens in conditions such as multiple sclerosis.

This should begin to give you an idea of the flexibility of the nervous system in terms of the number of connections that can be made between the many different components of the body. In fact, each neurone can make up to 10,000 connections with its neighbours.

A photograph taken by an electron microscope to show the intricate network of neurones and their complex connections

If you imagine a set of roads converging, with roundabouts and junctions and flyovers, giving you unlimited choices as to where you can go, this should give you an idea of the range of connections that can be made with the increasing number of junctions between neurones. No single neurone creates thoughts or behaviours; it is the different patterns of activity that arise from the firing of millions of different neurones which result in different activities. In fact, even when a person thinks they are at rest (and neurones should therefore be relatively quiet), if we were to scan the activity of the brain, we would see that the neurones still seem to be alive, with constantly changing interconnections. If you think how these patterns must increase and interconnect when we are engaged in any sort of task, from complex mental thought to physical activities, it will give you some idea of how active our brains must be. Every time we experience a sensation this will result in new neuronal connections being made, and this pattern will fade away unless the information relating to this experience is stored in our brains for a particular reason.

The brain

The area of the body where most of our neurones are located is the brain. In fact, the brain consists of nothing but millions of neurones. It is the most amazing wiring network, and different areas seem to be responsible for different things. It looks rather like a walnut, with lots of furrows or crevices, which are known as **sulci**. Just like a walnut, it is divided into two halves, called **hemispheres**. The left hemisphere controls most of the right-hand side of the body, and the right hemisphere controls the left-hand side.

Much of the evidence we have about which part of the brain is responsible for particular responses or activities, commonly known as '**localisation of function**', comes from

243

the investigation of individuals who have suffered some form of brain damage. If a certain area is damaged and results in a person being unable to perform a certain action, this would suggest that the damaged area is responsible for the non-function.

Each hemisphere has the equivalent of three layers: the hindbrain at the core, the midbrain and the forebrain (which contains the **cerebral cortex**). Although the cerebral cortex is the area most relevant to us, it is useful to have an overview of how the other structures of the brain assist in our day-to-day activities.

The hindbrain

The **hindbrain** consists of the **cerebellum**, the **pons** and the **medulla**. The cerebellum plays an important part in movement. It is where memories for automatic sequences of actions are stored and any damage to it will cause problems in movement, such as walking or the coordination of fine movements. The pons is a kind of bridge, or connection, between the two halves of the cerebellum. The medulla oblongata is the crossover point between the fibres from the brain and the spinal cord. The medulla also contains lots of vital reflex centres that control and regulate many of our basic bodily functions, such as the cardiovascular system and respiration.

The midbrain

The **midbrain** is smaller in humans and other mammals than in birds and reptiles. It is the top of the brainstem and connects the cerebral cortex (or forebrain) to the spinal cord and hindbrain. At its core is the **reticular activating system** (RAS), which brings sensory information from the spinal cord to the cerebral cortex and takes back motor information. It plays a very important part in maintaining or controlling levels of arousal and may even have an influence on personality. According to Eysenck (1970), people who fit the category of **introverts** have a high level of arousal in their RAS and therefore seek to reduce it, whereas **extroverts** have a low level of arousal and constantly seek to raise it, by choosing external situations which are 'busier' than their introvert counterparts. It is the RAS which influences our ability to pay attention selectively to different stimuli, as well as the way we become used to stimuli which are continuous and therefore not necessarily important. It also has a role in sleeping and waking, because it is when the level of activity in the RAS falls below a certain level that we fall asleep.

How personality influences behaviour provides a link to applied psychology. Research into personality types suggests that extroverts prefer team sports, while introverts prefer solitary sports such as golf. It has been suggested that the reason for this is that extroverts seek the stimulation of playing with others, while introverts perform better when they are less aroused by other people.

Personality has also been linked to other applied areas:

- It has been suggested that extroverts may be more likely to become involved in criminal activities (especially if they also score highly on tests of neuroticism).

- Extroverts prefer working with other people rather than alone.

- Introverts have been shown to be better at vigilance tasks, such as air traffic control.

- Within health psychology, a link has been established between personality type and illness.

The brainstem

The **brainstem**, made up of the midbrain, pons and medulla, is the most primitive part of the brain and is estimated to have evolved more than 500 million years ago. It is often referred to as the reptilian brain because it controls the basic elements of life, with no higher-order thought processes. You cannot form a close, loving relationship with a reptile because it is incapable of thinking and feeling in the same way as even lower-order mammals such as rats and mice. It simply functions from day to day, with a heart that beats, lungs that inflate and deflate, and a maintained blood pressure level; it can move, fight, mate and produce other stereotypical behaviours which give it the ability to survive. Beyond that, none of the characteristics we associate with intelligent life exist, simply instinctive behaviours.

The forebrain

The **forebrain** is the largest and most obvious part of a mammal's brain. The outer layer is called the cerebral cortex and is made up of the cerebral hemispheres. Under the cortex are a number of other structures, including the **thalamus**, the **hypothalamus**, the **pituitary gland**, the **basal ganglia**, **hippocampus** and **amygdala**, some of which form what is known as the **limbic system** (involved in emotional behaviour, motivation and learning). The limbic system is a kind of centre where the more primitive parts of the brain join with the 'newer' cortex and integrate information from the outside world and the internal functioning of the body.

Although these individual structures do not concern us directly, they all have an influence on our behaviour and, for that reason, they are briefly described below.

- The thalamus works as a kind of relay station, linking sensory signals between the cerebral cortex and the sense organs.

- The hypothalamus helps to control the body's internal environment, such as temperature regulation, appetite and thirst. It also influences other motivated behaviours, such as sexual behaviour and emotional arousal levels. Eating disorders can be triggered by a disorder of the hypothalamus; if it is damaged, a person's internal temperature regulation may well be affected, making them overheat or feel extremely cold. The hypothalamus is also involved in the regulation of levels of hormones in the body and controls pituitary gland activity.

- The pituitary gland is actually an endocrine gland (producing hormones). It is attached to the base of the hypothalamus and responds to information from the hypothalamus to release hormones into the bloodstream. The secretions of the pituitary gland control the timing and amount of secretion by other endocrine glands.

- The basal ganglia play a part in voluntary movements.

- The hippocampus plays an important role in the laying down of new memories, so any damage seems to result in a lack of ability to store new information. According to Colin Blakemore (1988), it is the 'printing press' for our stored memories. The hippocampus is also linked to spatial memory, and recent research has indicated that lesions to the hippocampus affect our ability to remember the location of different things.

- The amygdala is important for feeding, drinking, sexual behaviour and aggression. If it is electrically stimulated in non-human animals, such as cats, they will either attack another individual or become very placid. Rabies, which causes animals to become violent, often involves the amygdala. What seems to happen is that it changes how animals interpret information and therefore affects their responses.

A diagram showing the hippocampus can be found in the Glossary for Chapter 5

The main structure of the brain

The cerebral cortex

The **cerebral cortex** itself, as we have seen, consists of two hemispheres, each receiving information from the opposite side of the body. The two sides, which are almost mirror images of each other, communicate via a tract of fibres called the **corpus callosum**. Each hemisphere is divided into four lobes, which are defined by major sulci.

1. The **occipital lobes**, located at the back of the head, are the areas which receive the main input from the visual pathways. The rear of the lobe contains the primary visual cortex; if this is destroyed the person loses their sight.

2. The **parietal lobes** are located between the occipital lobe and the central sulcus (which divides the parietal lobe from the frontal lobe). They are specialised to deal with information from the body such as touch and temperature, and help to interpret body position. They also play a part in vision; it has been found that damage in this area does not result in a failure of vision or touch, but produces disturbances in the integration and analysis of sensory information. A good example of this is the case of a man who had a tumour in his parietal lobe and could recognise a clock as a clock, but could not tell the time from the position of the hands on the clock face.

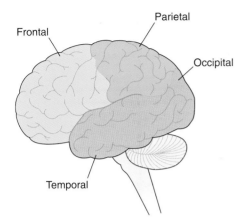

Frontal
Parietal
Occipital
Temporal

Lobes of the cerebral cortex

3. The **temporal lobes,** located on either side of the head near the ears, receive information from the ears about sounds and balance. They also contribute to the more complex aspects of vision, such as face recognition. They play a part in emotion and motivation, and if they are damaged this may lead to extremes of emotional response. **Wernicke's area** is located in the temporal lobe on the left-hand side, and plays a critical role in language comprehension.

4. Finally, the **frontal lobes** seem to be responsible for all the higher-order and more complicated functions, such as thinking, planning and forming ideas. They also play a part in memory formation and retention. Frontal lobes are said to contain our personalities; they contribute to our emotional responses and control our social inhibitions. This area is the last part of the brain to stop growing, and it continues to change even after birth, since the neuronal connections that are located here seem to continue forming. **Broca's area** is found in the left frontal lobe in humans and is critical for the production of language. People who have left-sided strokes (burst blood vessels in the left-hand side of the brain) often lose their ability to speak, and this would indicate that Broca's area has been affected.

The area directly to the rear of the central sulcus is known as the **sensory cortex** and is responsible for receiving any sensory information, such as touch, pressure, pain, smell and temperature. The area at the back of the frontal cortex, directly in front of the central sulcus, is the **primary motor cortex**. This area is responsible for movement, especially fine movement.

Finally, it will be useful for you to be familiar with the term 'grey matter', which you may have heard used when referring to the brain. Grey matter really does exist in the brain. It is a general term given to the regions of the brain and spinal cord that are made up mainly of cell bodies and dendrites of nerve cells, rather than myelinated axons, which look white. Grey matter includes the cerebral cortex, the central part of the spinal cord and the cerebellum and hippocampus.

This coronal section through the brain illustrates the areas of grey matter and white matter (appears as light grey). Coronal sections are sections that are made through the brain from top to bottom, just like looking face on at another person. The white areas in the middle are the ventricles of the brain

Grey matter

Methods of investigating brain function

At the beginning of this chapter, we mentioned that we need to consider the methodologies used to investigate the physiological explanations of behaviour. In this section we are going to look at the techniques which have helped us to develop an understanding of how the brain works. Nowadays it is possible to use a number of **brain-imaging techniques** in order to assess the functioning of our brains.

EEG machines

EEG machines measure brain activity by tracing the electrical impulses under the surface of the skull by sticking electrodes to the scalp. The electrical impulses from each of the electrodes are amplified and traced (or drawn) onto a roll of paper. They are often used in the investigation of sleep, to pick up activity from different areas of the brain, and to detect epilepsy.

CT scans

CT scans, or CAT scans (computerised axial tomography), are used for the diagnosis of pathological conditions such as tumours or degenerative diseases. The patient's head is put in a large, doughnut-shaped ring which contains an X-ray tube on one side and an X-ray detector on the opposite side. The head is scanned from front to back and then the 'doughnut' is moved round a few degrees and another scan is taken. These images are fed into a computer which produces a cross-sectional image of the brain. The 'doughnut' can take images of the head from top to bottom, so that a whole selection of cross-sectional images can be produced to show the size or site of any abnormalities.

A CT/CAT scan machine

MRI scans

MRI (magnetic resonance imaging) is more precise than a CT scan as it shows far more detail in soft tissue. It works using a strong magnetic field and radio pulses. Patients lie in a round tunnel, surrounded by a large magnet which generates a powerful magnetic field. The required part of the anatomy is 'magnetised' and exposed to radio pulses which cause the tissues to give off radio signals that can be measured. Hundreds of measurements are taken which are converted by computer into a two-dimensional picture of the area.

Illustration of an MRI scan

PET scans

PET scans (positron emission tomography) work in a very different way to the other techniques. PET scans actually look at the different levels of metabolic activity in the brain. Every cell in the body needs energy in the form of glucose. In the brain, neurones use glucose from the bloodstream in order to function. Therefore, injecting a person with glucose mixed with a small amount of a radioactive tracer compound makes it possible to see how much glucose each area of the brain is using. The PET scan measures the amount of radioactivity and sends the information to a computer, which will draw cross sections of the brain, showing the areas using different amounts of glucose as different colours. If an area is working really hard, it is going to require more glucose, and this technique makes this easy to identify.

Activity in the brain from a PET scan which shows areas of differing activity

By comparing PET scans of normal people with scans of individuals with some kind of disorder, it is possible to identify the areas that differ. They can also be used to identify the areas that work hardest when we are doing specific tasks, such as listening to music or solving mathematical problems.

The hippocampus

The hippocampus is the part of the brain discussed in the first of the core studies (below), investigating whether brains really do 'change structure' in order to accommodate new information. Before we consider the question of whether our brains really are 'flexible', we need to familiarise ourselves a little more with the hippocampus.

The hippocampus is linked to the conversion of information from short-term to more permanent memory. The impact of a damaged hippocampus is that memories of the past are retained, but new memories are not stored (known as anterograde amnesia), although individuals with a damaged hippocampus can learn new skills. This suggests that there may be different types of memory stores for different types of information (some of which we have covered in Chapter 3).

Another function of the hippocampus is to connect memories with each other, thus giving them meaning. For example, the hippocampus may connect the memory of a

Technique	Strengths	Weaknesses
EEG	Can look at brainwave patterns and detect abnormalities such as epilepsy	Gives no indication as to cause
CT scan	Can identify damaged areas of the brain due to trauma or disease	Only looks at brain structure, not function
MRI scan	Provides more detailed information on brain structure than a CT scan	Only looks at brain structure, not function
PET scan	Identifies which parts of the brain are active during different tasks	Cannot identify precisely which area is active in the brain. Focuses on areas that are active over a 60-second interval, rather than moment by moment (other areas might be active but do not metabolise extra glucose)

visit to a certain location with the information about how you got there and how it looked and sounded. The hippocampus is also associated with the memory of spatial relationships. Evidence of the latter comes mainly from studies of animals. To undertake work on humans is difficult, since it is not ethical to damage a human brain in order to identify the resulting problems!

'Now Professor Neuroblast, I wanted to investigate the effects of removing part of the temporal lobe. I found this patient on the ward earlier today and thought that if we drilled a hole in the right temporal lobe, we might be able to understand what it does.'

'Ah yes, Dr Trefoil, a good idea indeed. Shall we proceed to the ward to find the patient?'

Dr Neuroblast approaches the patient and says gently, 'Now, just lie down on the ground, Caroline. I want to drill a large hole in your head for the benefit of scientific knowledge.'

There are very justifiable concerns about how we can generalise knowledge gained from animal research to humans, but despite reservations, there is no doubt that some of the animal research undertaken has given us much greater insight into cerebral functioning. For example, research by David Oulton in the 1970s using what is known as a radial maze, demonstrated the effects of hippocampal damage on maze learning.

A radial arm maze

In such experiments, rats learn which arm of a maze contains food, which is hidden in a shallow well so it could not be seen simply by looking from the centre. The rats learn very quickly which arm holds the food. Research has demonstrated that rats who have learned the maze but then experience surgical 'damage' to their hippocampus, cannot remember where the food is, and therefore make lots of errors in their efforts to find it. More recent research (e.g. Jarrad 1995) established that rats with lesions to the hippocampus still found it very difficult to remember the location of a submerged platform in a tank of clouded water, despite numerous trials which suggest that the hippocampus does have a role in spatial memory.

An example of one of the patterns used by Chun and Phelps (1999) where participants had to locate the letter 'L'.

Research with humans has also demonstrated the relevance of the hippocampus in spatial memory. One study by Chun and Phelps (1999) involved asking participants to find the letter 'L', which was presented in various orientations among a background of letter 'T's. Some of the patterns were new and unfamiliar, and some were copies of earlier presented patterns. The participants were not told that some of the patterns would be repeated, so they were not expecting to recognise ones they had been shown earlier. The expectation was that the participants with no hippocampal damage would be faster in finding the letter 'L' over repeated trials as they would have learned (although this was unconscious learning) where the 'L' was located. On the other hand, it was thought that the experimental group would show no increase in speed in finding the letter 'L'. This was exactly what happened, suggesting that the hippocampus is needed for learning contextual information.

How flexible are our brains?

Having looked at the role of the hippocampus, let us now consider whether or not brains can actually change size (or rather structure) in order to accommodate new information. It is likely that you have been told at some time that you only have the brain cells you were born with, and as you get older they begin to die off, with alcohol and other damaging substances causing you to lose them more quickly. More recent research indicates that brain cells can actually regenerate. For example, Eriksson et al. (1998) identified the fact that the human hippocampus retains its ability to generate new neuronal cells throughout life, through a process known as **neurogenesis**.

In the 1960s research was undertaken to demonstrate how an enriched (that is, a more stimulating and exciting environment) affected the cortexes of young rats by making their cortexes larger than 'non-enriched' rats. Further studies established that this was due to several factors including increased nerve size, and greater number and length of dendrites (Diamond et al. 1964, Diamond 1988). More studies indicated that it was not simply the young rats who responded to an enriched environment, but that the brains of older rats were also affected. There have also been some further studies using cats and monkeys, as well as the occasional study of human participants.

Jacobs et al. (1993) looked at the portion of the human cerebral cortex responsible for understanding words (Wernicke's area), using deceased individuals who had given their consent prior to death. They compared the effects of enrichment in tissue from individuals who had received a college education with others who had left education after secondary school. The results demonstrated that the nerve cells in the college-educated participants showed more dendrites than those in the secondary school population. Further experiments on human tissue have supported the findings of the animal research and the conclusion that the brain does change in response to enrichment, in both animals and humans.

Having established that brains can change in response to external stimuli, we need to consider *how* they change. One way to do this is to imagine a piece of plasticine. It changes in response to the pressure or moulding that is applied to it. This is what happens with the brain; it changes and responds to the demands placed on it by increasing the cell dendrites and therefore the number of synapses available, in order to meet increased processing demands. These changes can be both functional (e.g. changes in neurotransmitters) and structural (changes in the size and number of synaptic connections between neurones).

Dendrites

In this simple diagram of two neurones, one has only four possible points that can link with other cells. This would prove very limiting and would not allow the transmission of complex messages. The second cell has ten points, which would permit a much wider range of opportunities to link with other cells. If every cell had a higher number of dendrites, the amount of connections they could make would be proportionately higher overall and would allow a great deal more flexibility in responses. It is important to remember that brain cells need to be used regularly in order to maintain their connections with other neurones; otherwise the connections actually disintegrate and disappear, resulting in a change in the rate of neurogenesis.

THE STUDY

E.A. Maguire, D.G. Gadian, I.S. Johnsrude, C.D. Good, J. Ashburner, R.S. Frackowiak and C.D. Frith (2000) 'Navigation-related structural changes in the hippocampi of taxi drivers'

Proceedings of the National Academy of Science, 97: 4398–403

BACKGROUND

The hippocampus helps us to navigate, that is, to find our way round both familiar and new environments. This means that this area of the brain plays an important part in our spatial memory.

If the needs of our spatial memory change or increase, will the hippocampus change to accommodate this? Maguire et al. suggest that it will, and provide evidence to support their theory from animals and birds: 'in some species hippocampal volume [that is, the size of the hippocampus] enlarges. . .during seasons when demand for spatial ability is greatest'. They also point to reported evidence that brain differences exist between humans with different skills, for example musicians and non-musicians, who place different demands on their brains. Maguire et al. claim that studies to date have not provided evidence as to the source of these differences. Is it that people with certain types of brains (predetermined by biology) become musicians? Or is it that the brains of musicians change in response to environmental stimulation and learning? In this study, Maguire et al. aimed to investigate plasticity of the brain (**neuroplasticity** – the ability of the brain to change or adapt as a response to learning) in London taxi drivers.

Someone who wants to be a London taxi driver has to pass examinations set by the police in order to get their taxi driver's licence. This is known as 'being on The Knowledge' and involves approximately two years spent learning how to get around London. This requires them to make increasing demands on their spatial memory. It is for this reason – the increased environmental demands on their spatial memory as they acquired 'The Knowledge' – that they were considered excellent subjects for this study.

AIMS

To investigate the differences in the brain, especially in the hippocampus, in London taxi drivers, and to establish whether, compared with controls, differences in hippocampal volume would be observed. The study also aimed to further investigate the functions of the hippocampus in spatial memory.

METHOD

Method and design

The study was an experiment using an independent groups design, comparing the brains of London taxi drivers with controls who were not taxi drivers.

In addition, correlational analysis was carried out to see if hippocampal changes increased with time as a taxi driver and were therefore likely to be environmentally determined.

Subjects

1 Taxi drivers:
   - 16 right-handed male London taxi drivers, aged 32–62 (mean age = 44).
   - All had been licensed London taxi drivers for at least 1.5 years (mean time as a taxi driver = 14.3 years, range = 1.5–42 years).
   - The average time they had spent 'being on The Knowledge' was 2 years.
   - All had healthy general medical, neurological and physiological profiles.
2 Control group:
   - 50 right-handed males aged 32–62, who had been scanned for the MRI database at the Wellcome Department of Cognitive Neurology.
   - They were selected so that no females, no left-handers, no under-32s or over-62s and no one with health problems were included.

Procedure and measurement

The taxi drivers' brains were scanned using an MRI scanner. These were structural MRI scans designed to investigate the anatomy of the brain (its structure), as opposed to functional MRI scans which investigate the physiognomy of the brain (how it works).

Their scans were analysed and compared with the scans of the control subjects.

The measurement of brain differences used two techniques:

1 **VBM (voxel-based morphometry)** was used to measure the grey matter volume and indicate general brain differences between the two conditions. A voxel is a three-dimensional measurement of volume that allows a computer program to calculate the volume of area, in this case the grey matter in the brain in structural MRI scans.
2 **Pixel counting** was carried out on the scans of the taxi drivers and 16 age-matched controls taken from the 50 control subjects. Pixel counting was carried out by 'one person experienced in the technique and blinded to the subjects' identity as taxi drivers or controls and the outcome of VBM analysis'. A pixel is a two-dimensional measurement of area. It was possible to calculate differences by pixel counting 'slices' of the scan. The scan was

separated into 26 slices and 24 of these focused on the hippocampus, as follows:

- posterior (rear/back) hippocampus – 6 slices;
- hippocampus body – 12 slices;
- anterior (front) hippocampus – 6 slices.

RESULTS

What did the VBM analysis of the scans show?

VBM analysis showed that in the taxi drivers there was an increase in grey matter in only two areas of the brain: the left and right hippocampi. There was an *increase* in grey matter bilaterally (that is, on both the left and right sides) of the posterior hippocampi, but a *decrease* in grey matter bilaterally in the anterior hippocampi.

VBM thus confirmed a structural difference in the hippocampi of taxi drivers compared with controls.

What did the pixel-counting analysis of the results show?

Pixel-counting analysis revealed that there was no difference in the overall volume of the hippocampus between taxi drivers and controls.

However, it did show a regionally significant difference by side (right and left) of the hippocampus (see the table and figure below).

Anterior hippocampus	The non-taxi drivers (controls) had higher hippocampal volume in the right anterior hippocampus than in the left.
Hippocampus body	The taxi drivers showed no difference in overall volume in the hippocampus body compared with controls, but analysis by side showed non-taxi drivers had higher volume in the right side.
Posterior hippocampus	The taxi drivers had a generally higher volume in their posterior hippocampus than the non-taxi drivers.

Results from the pixel-counting analysis of the MRI scans of taxi drivers and controls

Volumetric analysis findings
The orientation of the slices measured in the volumetric analysis in the
hippocampus is shown in the inset picture
(Left) The mean score of the three cross-sectional area measurements from the left
hand side of the brain. Taxi drivers had a significantly greater volume relative to
controls in the posterior hippocampus.
(Right) The mean score of the three cross-sectional area measurements from the
right hand side of the brain. Controls showed greater hippocampal volume in
the anterior area. There was no significant difference between the two groups in the
hippocampus body.

Correlational analysis of changes to the hippocampus with navigational experience in taxi drivers

The authors carried out a correlational analysis to see if there was a correlation between the VBM analysis of hippocampal volume and time spent as a taxi driver ('time spent' included time spent 'being on The Knowledge' and time practising as a taxi driver after qualifying).

The correlational data showed a positive correlation between one brain area only, namely the right posterior hippocampus, with time spent as a taxi driver (see figure below). There was a negative correlation between time spent as a taxi driver and the volume of the right anterior hippocampus. (The authors report that data were removed from this analysis for one taxi driver who had been in the job for 42 years. Given that the next highest length of time in the job was 28 years, the subject was removed from the analysis for statistical reasons as an outlier. The authors report that evidence from this subject was nonetheless consistent with their general findings from the taxi drivers.)

Correlation of volume change with time as a taxi driver: in VBM analysis, the volume of grey matter in the right hippocampus was found to correlate significantly with the amount of time spent learning to be and practising as a licensed London taxi driver, positively in the right posterior hippocampus and negatively in the right anterior hippocampus

DISCUSSION

The authors conclude that 'the data presented in this report provide evidence of regionally specific structural differences between the hippocampi of licensed London taxi drivers and those of control Ss'. Correlational analysis also confirmed that this difference was related to environmental stimulation. Increases/decreases of hippocampal volume in the posterior/anterior hippocampi of taxi drivers with time supports the idea that the brain has changed in response to the demands of being a taxi driver, rather than the idea that people choose to be taxi drivers because they have pre-existing brain differences.

The fact that the hippocampal volume correlated positively with the length of time as a taxi driver suggests that the hippocampal changes occur in line with the demands on spatial memory made by their job. This suggests that the human brain has plasticity, the ability to change (at least locally in the hippocampus) to meet the demands of the environment.

The authors report that their findings are consistent with findings from animal studies of rodents and monkeys, as well as studies of patients with brain damage (lesions). Findings from brain-damaged patients where the posterior hippocampus is not damaged demonstrate that the patients can recall cognitive maps they knew before the lesions were present.

In terms of how the hippocampus contributes generally to our spatial memory, the authors suggest that their findings indicate different roles in spatial memory for the anterior and posterior hippocampi. They suggest that the posterior hippocampus is involved when we are using previously learned information, and the anterior hippocampus (along with the posterior hippocampus) is more involved when we are learning about new environmental layouts.

The fact that the right and not the left hippocampal volume correlated with years of taxi driving experience suggests that the left and right sides of the hippocampus have separate functions. The authors suggest that the right holds 'mental maps' and the left holds memories and events not dependent on using such cognitive maps.

The authors suggest that the increased tissue volume in the posterior hippocampus in the taxi drivers occurs to accommodate their vast knowledge and mental map of the layout of London and how to find their way round the city.

In evolutionary terms, the authors point out that the hippocampus is an 'old' part of the brain which may have evolved to deal with navigation. Although in humans it is also adapted to be involved in other types of memory, such as episodic memory (memory for events), it 'retains an ability to store large-scale spatial information'. While the hippocampus does not operate alone, but works with other areas of the brain to support navigation, the key role of the hippocampus seems to be 'crucial to the storage and use of mental maps of our environments'.

The authors concede that structural MRI does not reveal exactly what is happening in the hippocampus to lead to the changes they observed in taxi drivers. However, they offer the theory that what happens is an 'overall reorganization of hippocampal circuitry'.

The study has implications for the rehabilitation of people who have suffered brain damage. The findings show that, at least in certain areas, the brain is capable of adaptation in response to environmental stimulation. People who have suffered brain damage or disease might be helped in the future if it could be shown that areas of the brain other than the hippocampus could respond and change.

COMMENTARY: METHODS AND ISSUES

Methods and measurement

You need to consider the strengths and weaknesses of the experimental method and of using an independent groups design in relation to this study.

- The laboratory setting for the scans enables the use of highly technical equipment (MRI scanning suite) and allows for precise measurement of data. Both the VBM and pixel-counting analysis provided quantitative data (in mm^3) about the volume of grey matter/volume of the hippocampus.
- The use of technical equipment can be costly, both in terms of equipment and the amount of specialists' time it takes to carry out the tests and analyse the results.
- Physiological methods of measurement, such as brain-imaging techniques, are the only method available for this kind of study of the structure of the brain (you cannot self-report about the size of your hippocampus and it is not directly observable to the naked eye in living participants).

- Without quantitative data, statistical analysis of the differences between the two groups, or analysis of the correlation between VBM measurements and time spent as a taxi driver would have been impossible to establish.

Does the study raise any ethical concerns?

The study was carried out according to the British Psychological Society's (1993) ethical guidelines, so there are no ethical concerns.

- The subjects were not deceived; they gave their informed consent; they had the right to withdraw; and they were not negatively affected by their experience.
- Also, given that the study points towards (albeit probably in the distant future) implications for the rehabilitation of brain-damaged patients, we could describe the study as ethically worthy.

Is the study useful?

The study is useful in that it furthers our understanding of how the brain works, and provides evidence about the plasticity of the brain. As the authors suggest, there are implications for brain-damage sufferers in what this study reveals about neuroplasticity: rehabilitation of individuals who have suffered brain damage might be assisted if it was clear which areas of the brain are capable of adaptation and what environmental cues might stimulate them to change.

The MRI scan is one of a number of brain-imaging techniques that represent relatively new technological advances in science, and are enabling researchers to map the functions and observe the structure of the human brain. As advanced as the technology is, however, it remains limited. As the authors point out, the changes can be observed and quantified, but as yet the underpinning causes of the changes can only be theorised about, and this perhaps limits the usefulness of the study.

Although it may appear that neuroscientists are at present merely scratching the surface of their discipline, studies such as this one are important in leading the way in brain research, and may well be significant stepping stones towards a full understanding of the structure and function of the most complicated phenomena in the universe, the human brain.

Validity and reliability of the findings

The volume differences in the hippocampus were established by two concurrently valid independent measures (VBM and pixel counting), supporting the validity of the findings.

The authors had theorised that the hippocampal changes occurred because of being a taxi driver and not because people who already possessed differences in their hippocampi would choose to become taxi drivers. The validity of this theory is supported by the correlational evidence, which showed that the changes in hippocampal volume correlated with time spent as a taxi driver.

261

Changes in the hippocampus were more marked as time spent as a taxi driver increased.

The validity of the findings is also supported by the fact that evidence from comparative studies with animals and brain-damaged patients are consistent with the findings from the taxi drivers.

A reason to question the validity of this plasticity of the hippocampus being typical of everyone is that the sample is not exactly typical of the general population. It may be that not everyone's brain could or would respond in the same way to the environmental demands of doing 'The Knowledge' and being a taxi driver in London. For a start, there is a clear gender bias in the sample and we cannot assume that female and male brains operate similarly in terms of spatial memory.

In terms of ecological validity, being scanned in an MRI scanner is not something that a person would have to do every day. However, in this case, the variable being measured (hippocampal volume) would not be one that the subjects could actually falsify, so the data are unlikely to be affected by responses to demand characteristics or the artificiality of the laboratory setting, so it does not affect the outcome of the study if the process of being given an MRI scan lacks ecological validity.

Circadian rhythms and sleep

Despite what you may think, sleep is actually a behaviour, although it is more often defined as a state of consciousness. Since we all sleep, it is a topic that often crops up in conversation. Below is a list of phrases you will probably recognise.

- How are you sleeping?
- I'm so tired.
- I'm not tired, Mum!
- I stayed out until four o'clock in the morning and I'm dead today.
- I must get some sleep.
- I can't sleep; I just toss and turn all night.
- I seem to wake up far too early.
- Did the baby sleep all night?
- I wish she would go to sleep.

> - If I don't get eight hours of sleep I can't function.
> - I only need four hours of sleep a night.
> - She is overtired, that's why she is in such a bad mood.

It is not surprising that sleep is so relevant – after all, we spend one-third of our lives asleep. We all know that we cannot do without it, yet it seems such a waste of time. Have you noticed that sometimes, during the week when you have to get up, you can't seem to wake up, and at the weekend when you can lie in bed, you wake up really early when you don't have to? This suggests that our feelings of needing sleep seem to relate to our state of mind. If we are enjoying ourselves at a party we find it easy to stay awake, whereas if we are at home, bored, we feel very sleepy. People suffering from depression feel very tired all the time and sleep more than they would do normally.

We vary in the amount of sleep we need throughout the course of our lives:

- When we are babies, we sleep and wake many times during the course of the day.

- As we get older, many of us sleep only once, at night, although people from very hot countries may well have a siesta during the day when the sun is at its highest in the sky.

- We seem to need less sleep when we are in our teens and twenties, yet with the passing of the years we seem to need more sleep.

- When we are much older, our need for sleep often decreases again.

The reasons for these changes are complex and relate not only to our bodily requirements, but also to the stresses and strains of everyday life. In many ways, the most stressful times appear to require the most sleep, but they seem to be the times when we get the least.

While we are asleep we have periods of relative quiet and periods when we know we dream. One of the most exciting things about sleep can be the dreams we have. You can be anything in dreams, although they are not always about pleasant things. They are sometimes weird, sometimes very enjoyable or erotic, and sometimes they seem to perform the function of providing an insight into our problems. The analysis of dreams was one of Freud's interests, and in some daily newspapers you will occasionally see articles on how to analyse your dreams – although whether this dream analysis actually bears any relationship to reality is another matter!

In order to understand the nature of sleep it would help to have a brief introduction to the rhythms which govern our lives, whether they are 24-hour rhythms or annual rhythms. These cycles of sleeping and waking, and the different levels of sleep, appear to form regular patterns which are known as circadian rhythms, and these form part of the annual rhythms or cycles of life.

Circadian and circannual rhythms

Rhythms in behaviour and physiological processes are found throughout the plant and animal world. These cycles are generally called circadian rhythms (*circa* means 'about', and *dies* means 'day', which explains why circadian rhythms are based on a 24-hour cycle), but they may be circannual (about a year). One of the reasons for these cycles seems to be related to the changing patterns of sunlight and temperature that vary from day to day across the seasons.

Plants and animals respond to these changing patterns by pursuing different behaviours according to the time of year or time of day. Some animals hibernate when the length of day shortens and the temperature falls. Even when the temperature remains mild they become more sleepy, responding to the change in daylight. Other animals collect stores of food, a process triggered by their internal clocks rather than any conscious decision. Birds migrate south and plants begin to lose their leaves. There are similar positive patterns of behaviour in the spring when, triggered by the increasing length of the day and warmer temperatures, animals come out of hibernation and begin to find mates and build nests. Humans, too, follow patterns of behaviour that seem to be stimulated by the length of the day and the amount of light.

Research has attempted to identify what it is that makes us follow these rhythms, and the conclusions drawn are that although light plays a part, this does not provide a complete explanation. Rats and birds which were kept in a constant environment for prolonged periods of time still demonstrated variations in behaviour on a regular basis, which indicates that we must produce endogenous rhythms (generated from within) that are unrelated to light, although they seem to follow a similar pattern to external cues. Research has also demonstrated that light seems to moderate the rhythms and prevents them from going too fast or too slow. Evidence to show the power of light as a *zeitgeber* (timegiver) has been collected from animal studies, where animals which are kept in constant darkness will reset their internal clock, advancing or retarding it when shown no more than a brief flash of light (Aschoff 1979). However, if there is no light available, other environmental stimuli, such as temperature, can serve as a zeitgeber, which is why hibernating animals know when to wake up even if they are hibernating underground.

It seems that humans have a circadian rhythm which follows, approximately, a 25-hour sleep–waking cycle. This natural 25-hour clock can explain why, when we are on holiday, we often stay up later than we would do normally and wake up later too – our biological clock is gaining one hour in 24 so in effect, if we had a 24-day holiday and we got up and went to bed when we wanted to, by the end of the holiday we would be back where we started.

In humans, another cycle which seems to influence our behaviour is our temperature. Under normal circumstances, temperature in the body core (not skin temperature) will rise during the middle of the day and dip slightly by mid afternoon. It will fall again at night reaching its lowest point in the early hours of the morning, whether or not our sleep follows that pattern (this is why we often wake up in the night and feel really cold). It appears, therefore, that temperature must have something to do with how well we sleep. Shift workers, for example, have dreadful problems trying to sleep when their body temperature tells them that they should be up and about.

The function of sleep

Horne (1988) has conducted a considerable amount of research into sleep and has reviewed much of the existing literature. He points out that everything that is alive has some period of rest during a day – even plants, which seem to go into a period of quiescence, or inactivity, at the same time every day. There are three theories which suggest why we need to sleep: for our bodies, for our minds, and as a result of evolution.

Physiological restoration – for our bodies

This theory suggests that the main reason we sleep is to allow our bodies to restore themselves after a hard day. Our bodies do seem to undertake certain processes which relate to restoration when we are asleep, such as digestion, the removal of waste products and protein synthesis, but these processes also happen when we are awake, so that cannot be the only reason. The speed at which cell division takes place is also unaffected by sleep – they divide at the normal rate for time of day, irrespective of whether the person is awake or asleep.

Psychological restoration – for our minds

Sleep may not be essential for our bodies, but it does seem to be essential for our brains. If we do not sleep we may become dizzy and irritable, and find it much harder to concentrate or perform complex tasks. Our memories seem less efficient and we may have problems finding the words to explain what we want to say.

We will consider sleep deprivation studies later in this section. The main finding with all of these is that they illustrate how lack of sleep causes problems with higher-order thinking, and this seems to be related directly to the amount of REM (rapid eye movement) sleep we get (more on this later). There is evidence that people show higher levels of REM sleep following some kind of stressful life event or trauma. Therefore we might assume that the restorative function of sleep is not that accurate for the body, but certainly plays a part in restoring our psychological functioning to maximum efficiency.

Evolutionary theory

Because the length of time we sleep seems to have little or no relationship to what we did the day before, it has been suggested that the function of sleep might be similar to hibernation. We may sleep to conserve energy when the environment is hostile, such as when food is limited, or when we would be inefficient, such as in the dark. It is true that our bodies mimic a kind of mini-hibernation because we have a lower metabolic rate, lower temperature and lower blood pressure when we are asleep.

If we accept this theory, it would make sense to suggest that animals should vary how much sleep they need depending on different aspects of their lifestyles. For example, if it takes them long periods of time to search for food, they should sleep less. If their food is low in nutrients, such as for cattle and horses, they need to eat a great deal in order to survive, so they should sleep less. How safe they are from predators should also enter the equation, with animals such as sheep sleeping less than foxes. Research evidence supporting this idea comes from the average amount of time various animals spend sleeping.

Humans sleep for an average of eight hours per day because the food we consume is much higher in nutritional value and can be eaten at more regularly spaced intervals. Most predators, such as foxes and cats, live in relative safety and will eat only one meal a day, and that meal will contain all their nutritional requirements. Consequently, they can sleep for much longer periods of time in relation to their body size, as foxes sleep for an average of 9.8 hours per day and cats for 14.5 hours per day.

The one problem with this theory, according to Hauri (1979), is that sheep and goats are extremely vulnerable to predators and if sleep was purely an evolutionary activity, why would they sleep at all, bearing in mind that the minute they go to sleep they become even more vulnerable?

How is sleep investigated?

Most of the work undertaken on sleep has been carried out in sleep laboratories. These consist of small bedrooms next to an observation room where the experimenter spends

A participant who has been 'wired up' before sleeping – would this affect your quality of sleep?

the night and monitors the sleeper's behaviour, both by observation and by wiring the sleeper up to a series of recording instruments. The sleeper may also be videoed to record his/her behaviour. Can you imagine how difficult it would be not only to sleep in a strange bed, but also to know you were being watched?

We have discussed some of the techniques for monitoring and measuring the activity of the nervous system earlier in this chapter. However, in sleep laboratories another form of physiological measurement is used to investigate the activity of the nervous system. Here, participants can be wired up to three types of machines, which all work in the same way:

- An EEG (electroencephalogram) measures brain activity: the electrodes are placed over the head to record the electrical activity of the underlying neurones.

- An EMG (electromyogram) measures muscle activity: facial and jaw muscle activity is monitored by electrodes placed on the jaw area.

- An EOG (electro-oculogram) measures eye movements: the electrodes are placed around the eye socket.

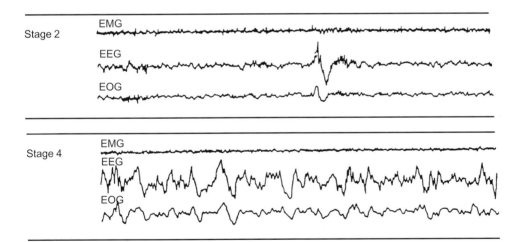

Traces from EEG, EMG and EOG machines

Sleep deprivation

The participants who take part in studies on sleep may have been deprived of sleep or allowed to sleep for limited periods prior to the study commencing. They may even have the type of sleep monitored to see what happens if they are not allowed to enter REM sleep, for example. The types of measurements taken will give a good indication of what is going on. The participants may also be woken at regular intervals or specific times and questioned about dreams or feelings they may be having.

It seems that if we are deprived of sleep or sleep is limited for one night, it has no serious effects: we will simply fall asleep much more quickly and sleep longer the following night. If the amount of time we are allowed to sleep is gradually reduced, then we seem to suffer few effects, but if sleep is suddenly reduced, as in the case of hospital doctors who are on call, our ability to perform certain tasks is also reduced. If the task is simple, no decrease in performance is shown, but if it is a complicated task which needs planning and thought, then performance declines. This supports the idea that the frontal cortex appears to be the area of the brain that requires sleep, as this is the area which is involved in higher-order thinking, planning and problem solving.

In order to test these effects, participants have been given a number of different tasks, including problem solving, reaction time (to see how quickly they respond to a given stimulus) and vigilance (where they have to watch screens and report a change in the display, for example). Participants demonstrated a number of symptoms of sleep deprivation, such as no originality in their responses, staring into space, memory deficits for recent events or information, a decline in their spatial orientation, word fluency and spelling, and speaking in a monotone.

One explanation of the effects of sleep deprivation refers back to work done on the neurogenesis of brain cells. Mirescu et al. (2006) reported that rats which were prevented from sleeping for 72 hours were shown to reduce the production of new brain cells in the hippocampus due to increased levels of a certain hormone (corticosterone). During the following two weeks, when the rats were allowed to sleep normally again, the rate of neurogenesis was elevated to compensate for the reduction of cell reproduction. The problem was that during the period of sleep deprivation, the rats would have been suffering some level of cognitive impairment.

If we accept that it is very difficult to function effectively when we have been deprived of sleep, this helps to explain why sleep deprivation has been used by various regimes as an instrument of torture, with the intention of preventing prisoners from thinking rationally in order to gain confessions or information. Simply typing 'sleep deprivation torture' into an Internet search engine will provide numerous examples of how this technique has been used in the past.

If prolonged lack of sleep can be so debilitating and sleeping in the day is so difficult, this raises rather troubling questions about people who work at night, such as hospital doctors, nurses and airport staff. Without wishing to concern you unduly, it is interesting to note that two of the most frightening environmental disasters happened in the early hours of the morning.

In March 1979 there was an accident in unit two at the Three Mile Island nuclear power station in the USA. As a result of both equipment failure and human error, the core of the reactor was exposed. This generated extremely high temperatures which resulted in damage to the fuel and equipment inside the reactor. It took time to bring it back under control, but by then approximately 400,000 gallons of radioactive water had collected on the floor of the reactor building. Radioactive gases had also been released and remained trapped in the concrete container surrounding the reactor.

The incident at Chernobyl in Russia occurred in 1986 as a result of a well-meaning safety check. It was considered the largest and most hazardous nuclear accident in history and involved an enormous amount of radiation being released into the atmosphere. There was even concern for the contamination of pastureland and sheep kept in the Lake District during that time. It involved a huge number of people and the effects are still being dealt with today.

If these two events were in part the result of sleep deprivation in key personnel, this should reinforce the fact that we should not take the effects of sleep deprivation lightly.

Jim Horne of Loughborough University, who has carried out extensive investigations into the effects of sleep deprivation, reported that five to eight days of sleep deprivation has little effect on the body, although motivation may be impaired and there are sometimes small effects on the immune system (although this is probably caused by the stress of not sleeping rather than the actual lack of sleep).

One effect of sleep deprivation has been identified, however, and this is known as the rebound effect. In order to understand the rebound effect (which is described in more detail in the postscript to the core study below), we need to focus briefly on the stages or levels of sleep which can be identified by changes in electrical activity in the brain.

The sleep cycle

- **Stage one** sleep is the first 'drifting' stage that we go through on our way to deep sleep. It can occur when the natural light fades, as this information is transferred through the eyes to the pineal gland in the brain which starts to produce a hormone called melatonin. Melatonin indirectly makes us feel sleepy and therefore, when it gets dark, we may begin to feel drowsy. If we are in bed, this presents no problem of course, and we start to drift off into stage one sleep. Have you ever noticed that sometimes, just as you are drifting, you jerk violently and it wakes you up? This is when the neurones are discharging randomly before you enter the second stage.

- **Stage two** is deeper than stage one, but we can still be woken easily. The heart rate, breathing and brain activity are slower than at stage one.

- **Stage three** is deeper still, with more long, slow delta waves. We are difficult to wake at this point and the heart rate, blood pressure and temperature are dropping.

- **Stage four** is known as delta or quiet sleep. This is the stage where it is hardest to wake us unless the stimulus is very relevant, such as the alarm clock or a baby crying. This sleep lasts for approximately 30-minute bursts. During this stage we are able to toss and turn and move our limbs as necessary.

A whole sleep cycle lasts for about 90 minutes and involves us moving 'down' through all four stages and moving 'up' again. This 90-minute cycle is present in infants who are fed on demand, and has also been noticed in adult activities. We can be engaged in something for about 90 minutes, but suddenly have the urge to go and get a drink or have a break.

When we return to where stage one would be, we enter a different kind of sleep known as **rapid eye movement sleep** (**REM** sleep), where our eyes dart back and forth beneath closed eyelids. It is different because it is an active sleep – in terms of our brainwaves and eye movements – but, strangely enough, our bodies are actively inhibited from movement. This means that we are, in effect, 'paralysed', so we do not move during this period of sleep. Because the blood pressure rises this is the time when males experience erections in their sleep, even though the rest of the body is immobile. Our pulse, respiration rate and blood pressure increase and our brainwave patterns look like they would when we are awake. It is even harder to wake someone from this sleep than during stage four. It is sometimes known as 'paradoxical sleep', a term coined by Michel Jouvet in the late 1950s. Jouvet was carrying out research into insomnia when he noticed how high brain activity occurred that resembled wakefulness, but at the same time the body was in extreme relaxation and was very difficult to rouse. The term paradoxical literally means apparently self-contradictory, as the activity of the brain and body are in complete contrast to each other.

Most of the research carried out on sleep has considered either types of sleep, sleep deprivation or dreaming, although early studies were beset with numerous difficulties in effectively determining and quantifying levels of sleep. The core study in this area is one that was undertaken by Dement and Kleitman and looked at the relationship between sleep patterns and dreaming using specialised equipment.

THE STUDY

W. Dement and N. Kleitman (1957) 'The relation of eye movements during sleep to dream activity: An objective method for the study of dreaming'

Journal of Experimental Psychology, 53: 339–46

BACKGROUND

One of the problems researchers in the field of sleep and dreaming faced in the 1950s was the problem of measurement. How could you measure objectively if someone was dreaming or not? Prior to this study, researchers had had to rely on the self-report of subjects.

Dement and Kleitman theorised that it might be possible to find an objective way to tell whether someone was dreaming or not by investigating whether physiological phenomena correlated significantly with dreaming. You could then measure these physiological reactions and assume that the person was dreaming. This would reduce the problems of forgetting, falsification and responses to demand characteristics that occur with the self-report method of measurement. A study by Aserinsky and Kleitman (1955) had shown that when subjects were in REM sleep they recorded dream activity more than when they were in NREM (non-rapid eye movement) sleep. Moreover, it was possible to measure REM sleep objectively using an EEG machine. REM sleep is characterised by a low-voltage, relatively fast pattern in the EEG. From this, Dement and Kleitman theorised that it might be possible to find an objective way of measuring whether someone was dreaming or not by investigating whether REM sleep correlated significantly with dreaming.

AIMS AND HYPOTHESES

The aim of the study was to see if the physiological aspects of REM sleep related to the subjects' experience of dreaming. The study aimed to investigate a number of factors:

- First, it was intended to observe and record the length, frequency and patterns of the subjects' REM sleep.
- Second, three hypotheses were to be tested:
  1 There is a significant association between REM and reported dreaming. This would establish that measuring REM sleep would be a valid and objective measure of dream activity for future researchers to employ.

2 There is a significant positive correlation between the estimate of time spent dreaming and the measurement of REM sleep.
3 There is a relationship between the pattern of eye movement and the reported content of the dream.

METHOD

Design

A laboratory experiment was carried out.

- For hypothesis one, the purpose was to compare dream recall in REM and NREM sleep. Dement and Kleitman measured whether the subject was in REM or NREM sleep, as identified by the EEG pattern being recorded, and whether the subjects reported that they had been dreaming or not on being awoken. These data were then analysed to see if there were differences between REM and NREM sleep as regards dream recall.
- For hypothesis two, quantitative data were collected for correlational analysis, to establish whether there was a positive correlation between REM time and estimated time of dreaming.
- For hypothesis three, qualitative data were gathered regarding the content of subjects' dreams and this was compared with observations of the way the subjects' eyes were moving (REM movements can be observed with the naked eye).

Subjects

Seven adult males and two adult females were studied, with five studied intensively and the other four used to confirm the findings.

Apparatus

Subjects were tested in a sleep laboratory, using an EEG machine to measure sleep objectively. Electrodes were attached to subjects' eyes to measure eye movement, and to their scalps to measure brain activity. A doorbell was used to wake subjects and a tape recorder was used to record subjects' recollections of what they had been dreaming.

Procedure

Subjects were tested individually. They were instructed to report to the laboratory a little before their usual bedtime. Subjects were also told to avoid alcohol and caffeine, but to eat normally on the day of the experiment. This was done as a control to prevent the effects of caffeine or alcohol from affecting the findings.

Electrodes were applied to the subjects' heads and faces. To avoid entanglement and to allow the subjects free movement, all wires were gathered at the top of their heads and then led in a single cord to the lead box. Subjects slept on their own, in a quiet, dark laboratory. Their brainwave patterns were recorded constantly throughout their period of sleep.

1 Testing hypothesis one:
At various times during the night, some of which were during REM and some during NREM, subjects were wakened by a doorbell. They had been instructed to record immediately into a tape recorder whether or not they had been dreaming. Return to sleep usually occurred in less than five minutes. To further control extraneous variables, there was no contact with the experimenter before dream reports, in order to avoid experimenter bias. Subjects were not told whether they had been in REM or NREM sleep, and the pattern of awakenings for each subject was varied to avoid bias:
● Two subjects (initials PM and KC) were woken according to a random numbers table, to remove any likely pattern.
● One subject (IR) was woken at the whim of the experimenter.
● One subject (DN) was woken during three REM periods and three NREM periods.
● One subject (WD) was told he would only be woken in REM sleep, but was actually woken in NREM sleep periods too.
2 Testing hypothesis two:
Subjects were woken either 5 or 15 minutes after REM sleep began and were asked to estimate the length of their dream by choosing from either 5 or 15 minutes. These findings were then correlated with the length of time in REM sleep. Subjects were also asked to relate the content of their dream, and the length of the narrative was correlated with the duration of REM sleep before they were woken.
3 Testing hypothesis three:
Subjects were woken one minute after one of four patterns of eye movement had occurred:
● mainly vertical (eyes moving up and down);
● mainly horizontal (eyes moving from side to side);
● both vertical and horizontal;
● little/no eye movement.
They were asked what they had just been dreaming about, and the data were analysed to see if the pattern related to the content of the dream.
The total number of awakenings (for all nine subjects) was 351 times over 61 nights, which averaged at 5.7 awakenings per subject per night. Awakenings were spread out over the night as follows:

● 21 per cent in the first two hours;
● 29 per cent in hours three and four;
● 28 per cent in hours five and six;
● 22 per cent in hours seven and eight.

RESULTS

Dement and Kleitman observed the following about REM sleep:

- All subjects showed periods of REM every night that they slept in the laboratory, as shown by low-voltage, fast EEG patterns.
- The average occurrence of REM was one period every 92 minutes for the whole group, with variations between 70 and 104 minutes.
- The length of REM was between 3 minutes and 50 minutes, and this tended to increase in length as the night progressed.

Hypothesis one: eye movement periods and dream recall

(Note that for all hypotheses, dreaming was deemed to have occurred if the subject could give a relatively coherent and detailed description of the dream.)

- As shown in the following table, more dreams were reported in REM than in NREM sleep.

Subject	REM sleep		NREM sleep	
	Dream recall	No recall	Dream recall	No recall
DN	17	9	3	21
IR	26	8	2	29
KC	36	4	3	31
WD	37	5	1	34
PM	24	6	2	23
KK	4	1	0	5
SM	2	2	0	2
DM	2	1	0	1
MG	4	3	0	3
Total	152	39	11	149

Table showing instances of dream recall after awakenings during periods of REM or NREM (p.341)

- Where no dream recall was recorded, this tended to be in the earlier period of the night (19 of the 39 no-recalls in REM sleep were in hours one and two).

- Subjects were woken 132 times when they had ceased REM by more than 8 minutes, and, of these, only six subjects recalled dreams. However, when woken within 8 minutes of ceasing REM, 5 out of 17 reported dreaming. This indicates that the closer subjects were to REM, the more likely they were to be able to recall their dreams. When subjects were awoken from deep sleep (stage four sleep – a period of NREM sleep characterised by high-voltage, slow waves in the EEG), they were often bewildered and reported that they must have been dreaming, although they could not recall the dream content, or they said that they had not been asleep at all. Sometimes they described experiencing feelings such as pleasantness or anxiety, but could not relate these to dream content.

Hypothesis two: length of rapid eye movement periods and subjective dream duration estimates

- As shown in the table below, there was a significant relationship between subjects' estimate of dream length and the amount of time spent in REM for both the 5- and 15-minute periods. The table also shows that there were significantly more correct estimates of length of REM than incorrect estimates. There were more wrong estimates after 15 minutes, so the longer the subject had been in REM sleep, the less accurate they were at estimating dream length.

Subject	Right	Wrong	Right	Wrong
DN	8	2	5	5
IR	11	1	7	3
KC	7	0	12	1
WD	13	1	15	1
PM	6	2	8	3
Total	45	6	47	13

Results of dream duration estimates after 5 or 15 minutes of rapid eye movements (p.343)

- There was also a significant relationship between length of narrative and REM period.

Hypothesis three: specific eye movement patterns and visual imagery of the dream

The study suggests that the subjects' eye movements related to dream content, indicating that the eyes move as if seeing what the subject was dreaming about.

- There was a strong association between the pattern of REMs and the content of the dream, with horizontal and vertical movements relating to dream reports of looking up and down or left and right. The kinds of situations reported by subjects were such events as looking up at cliff faces or throwing tomatoes at each other.

- Periods where movements were mixed were associated with looking at close objects, and the periods where there was little or no movement were associated with dreams of looking at stationary or distant objects.

DISCUSSION

The results obtained by waking subjects strongly support the connection between REM sleep and dreaming. Dement and Kleitman point out that, on the basis of their findings, 'it cannot be stated with complete certainty that some sort of dream activity did not occur at other times' (p.345), that is, in NREM periods, although they considered this unlikely since their results had shown low recall of dreams in NREM sleep, and because REM sleep occurs in the lightest level of sleep.

Dement and Kleitman recorded that when woken within 8 minutes of ceasing REM, 5 out of 17 subjects in NREM sleep reported dreaming. This may account for some of the recordings of dream recall in NREM, as it may be that those awoken within 8 minutes were still recalling dreams they had been having while in REM sleep.

They suggested that their findings on the correlation between dream recall and length of time in REM sleep indicated that dreams are not instantaneous or happen very rapidly, but rather 'seemed to progress at a rate comparable to a real experience of the same sort' (p.346). In other words, dreams occur in real time.

Dement and Kleitman considered their findings in relation to other studies of REM sleep and of dreaming, and considered that any inconsistencies between findings were due to methodological issues. For example, while Dement and Kleitman recorded periods of REM sleep in their subjects for every night they had been tested, earlier work had not shown this. They put this down to earlier studies recording only samples of behaviour and therefore missing REM periods, or not amplifying the EEG high enough to make accurate recordings of when REM was occurring.

Dement and Kleitman concluded that the measurement of REM during sleep can be used as an objective measure of dreaming. They say that this enables further research to study objectively the effect of other factors on dreaming, such as environmental change, drugs and stress.

COMMENTARY: METHODS AND ISSUES

Research method, design and data gathering

The use of self-report measures for dream recall and dream content presents a problem. As well as general concerns about falsification of data by subjects and responses to demand characteristics, a number of factors suggest that the data collected by self-report from subjects in this study may not be accurate.

- Even though there were far more reports of dreaming during REM and no dreaming during NREM, the reason for the lack of reports of dreaming during NREM may have been something to do with the depth of sleep and the lack of ability of subjects to remember the dream as they awoke from such a deep level of sleep.
- The length of dream narrative was probably influenced by the talkativeness of the subjects, with subjects who were naturally more talkative giving a much longer description of their dreams. This, in turn, might have influenced how quickly they went back to sleep.
- The nature of the method of waking subjects (by doorbell) may have affected their ability to recall the dream.

There are also problems with correlational evidence. We must remember that this study was looking for a relationship between REM and dreaming. Even though a significant relationship was found, we still cannot confirm that one causes the other. Correlation does not mean causation. It may be that their co-occurrence was caused by another variable.

Does the study raise any ethical concerns?

Given the complicated instructions for data recording and the fact that the subject had to agree to sleep wired to an EEG machine in the laboratory, and to be woken in the night, we should assume that their informed consent was obtained for taking part in the study. Neither harm nor significant stress was caused to the subjects in the study, so we can conclude that it was carried out ethically.

Is the study useful?

This study was the first to attempt to study dream activity scientifically. It was highly generative, that is, it led to a great deal of further research in the area of sleep and dreaming. This means it was very useful to psychologists working in this field. On the other hand, issues such as low validity and low generalisability may mean that the findings are not very useful in describing real sleeping behaviour.

Validity and reliability of the study

- Sample biases are present. The disproportionate number of males to females may have influenced the study. We cannot be sure that the results of the study were not simply biased towards the dream patterns of men rather than women.
- The sample size was also extremely small, and this makes it difficult to generalise to all people. Also, since this study used subjects who were able to report to the university laboratory just before bedtime and were people for whom periods of disturbed sleep were not going to cause problems, it may

well be that the individuals who were studied were students, although this is not specified in the study.

- The study was carried out at one university in the USA and therefore has an ethnocentric bias, which means that we have to be careful in making any attempt to generalise the findings to a broader population. This leads us to question the validity of the findings. As discussed above, there is also the possibility that the study might have been affected by individual differences between subjects or by demand characteristics, as well as the use of correlational analysis. These factors all pose a threat to the validity of the findings.
- The situation may have affected the type of sleep shown by subjects; after all, sleeping wired up in a laboratory is not conducive to getting a good night's sleep. Therefore, we could criticise the study for a lack of ecological validity. This again limits its generalisability to real sleeping behaviour, and this means we have to question both the validity and the usefulness of the findings.
- The relationship between patterns of eye movements and dream content has not been supported by later studies. For example, babies in the womb and people blind from birth have periods of REM, yet they must be unable to recall images of objects and events as they have had no experience of these.
- Later studies have also indicated that not everyone follows the pattern of REM sleep being associated with dream recall. For example, some subjects who claim they rarely dream report a low level of dreaming during REM sleep. It seems likely, therefore, that there are individual differences between subjects.

POSTSCRIPT

It was believed that we only dream during REM sleep; however, it has now been shown that we do dream during stage four sleep, though the dreams are not stories like the ones we are used to. If people are awakened from stage four sleep, they are more likely to report a situation or some kind of feeling or awareness, although some of the most terrifying nightmares occur during stage four sleep.

We still do not know the function of dreaming. Some researchers suggest that it is simply a way of putting the events of the day in some kind of order. Some, like Freud, believe that it is our unconscious finally having free rein, and our id running away with itself. Others say it is simply random neuronal firings, which trigger some distant memory or thought that we try to make sense of and therefore turn into part of a story. Whatever the reason, it seems that REM sleep is far more important to us than NREM sleep.

To return to the rebound effect, if we deprive someone of sleep for a night, they will spend more of the next night in REM sleep than normal, but will not necessarily increase the amount of NREM sleep they have missed. This is called the REM rebound, where we seem to compensate for the amount of REM sleep lost. This explains why people are not too bad at having their sleeping hours slowly reduced. What they do is to pack their REM sleep into a shorter period and reduce the amount of NREM sleep. There have been a number of reports as to what happens to humans if they are deprived of REM sleep. Although the findings are contradictory, it seems that people may develop a kind of paranoia where they are very suspicious of other people's motives. They may also have what are often called hallucinations but are really visual illusions or distortions, that is, they are based on some external stimulus, but this is interpreted wrongly (Dement 1960).

Hemisphere de-connection (split brains)

As we have already discussed, the brain is divided into two relatively symmetrical halves. We also know that the left-hand side of the brain controls the right-hand side of the body, and vice versa, but it is not known why this crossover occurs. The two hemispheres are joined by what are known as commissural fibres, and the corpus callosum is by far the largest commissure (cross-hemisphere connection), responsible for carrying the majority of information between the two hemispheres.

It is often misconstrued that the two hemispheres are totally different and have entirely different functions. It is true that they do differ in some ways, but they are nowhere near as different as we are led to believe by some books, which seem to suggest that the function of the left-hand side of the brain is to be clever, rational and reasoning, and that the right-hand side is purely the spiritual, artistic part.

Lateralisation of function

In most people there is some 'lateralisation of function', which means that one side has a different role to the other. In the majority of people the language centres are on the left-hand side – Broca's area is responsible for speech production and Wernicke's area is responsible for speech comprehension. This is the case for the majority of right-handed people, although people who are left-handed may well have their language centres on the right-hand side of their brain. However, it is virtually impossible to give exact percentages, so it is best to accept the fact that the majority of people, left- and right-handed, have their speech centres located in the left hemisphere. This would mean that any damage to the left side of your head would probably leave you unable to speak or understand.

Why this is the case is another matter. One suggestion is that having speech centres in both hemispheres is likely to cause stuttering. It would seem quite likely that both centres would be sending impulses to the muscles responsible for speech, and these impulses may well arrive at slightly different times, so that speech would not be synchronised. Jones (1966) performed a number of operations on patients who had blood clots or tumours near their left hemisphere speech centres and who also stuttered. He knew in advance that they were quite unusual because he had discovered, by anaesthetising one hemisphere at a time with sodium amytal, that they could still carry on a conversation. This showed that they had speech centres in both hemispheres. He also discovered that after the operations their speech was quite normal and that they stopped stuttering!

Much of the evidence that has been gathered about hemisphere function has come from people who have suffered strokes (or cerebrovascular accidents, to give them their correct name). This is the most common source of brain damage in old age and is caused by a blood clot or other obstruction closing off an artery, or by an artery rupturing. This will result in the area around the site being deprived of oxygen or nutrients and the relevant neurones dying. Because the left-hand side of the brain controls the right-hand side of the body, a left-sided stroke will result in right-sided lack of function. This can be quite mild, such as a non-mobile side of the face, or more severe as with hemiplegia, where the whole of the right side of the body ceases to function. What makes it worse is the fact that the person often loses the ability to either comprehend or produce words, so not only are they non-mobile, but they are also isolated in their own little world.

Having made the point that one side of the brain controls the other side of the body, we should note that there are a couple of exceptions to this rule. Some of these are explored below.

Vision

In vision, the input from the left half of each eye goes to the right hemisphere, and the input from the right half of each eye goes to the left hemisphere, as seen below.

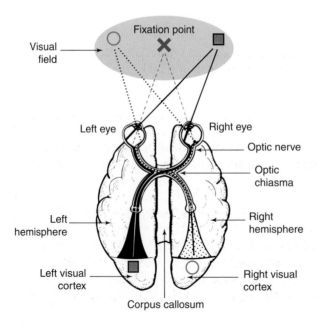

Put simply:

- Light from the world stimulates the receptors at the back of the eye.

- Light from the left half of the world stimulates the receptors on the right half of both eyes (shown by the dotted line), and light from the right half of the world stimulates the receptors on the left half of both eyes (shown by the black line).

- The right half of each retina connects to the right hemisphere and, thus, the right hemisphere sees the left visual field.

The result is simply that things which appear to the right of your nose are 'seen' by your left hemisphere, and things which appear to the left of your nose are 'seen' by your right hemisphere.

Hearing

Each ear receives sound from just one side, but sends 90 per cent of its input to the other side of the brain, retaining 10 per cent on the side it entered. The reason for this is so we can pinpoint where a noise is coming from by comparing the input from both ears – we would not be able to do this if the information went only to one side.

Smell

Information from each nostril remains on the same side as it enters, so odours that are experienced by the left-hand side of the brain are processed on the left.

Touch

Information from the sensory receptors of the hands crosses over, so the information from the right hand goes to the left hemisphere and vice versa.

Activity
There are some fun tasks you can do to explore further the differences between the hemispheres (although they only work for people with intact brains).

- Kimura (1973 a and b) found that right-handed people move their right hand more often than their left when speaking. However, left-handed people show no hand preference. Watch your teachers or friends as they talk and notice whether hand movement and handedness are related.
- Kinsborne (1972) discovered that if one hemisphere becomes more active, the eyes tend to turn towards the visual field of that hemisphere. So if

someone is trying to work out the answer to a verbal problem, they will gaze to the right significantly more often than they will gaze to the left. Similarly, if someone is trying to work out the answer to a spatial question, such as where something is located on a cognitive map (a mental map), the eyes will turn significantly more to the left. However, this is only true for right-handed people, with left-handed people producing inconsistent results. Try this by getting your friends to study puzzle books or puzzles printed in newspapers and watch their gaze direction.

- Hicks (1975) suggested finding a stick that would be quite difficult to balance on your right index finger. Then start talking and see if the task gets harder. Time how long you can balance it for when you are talking and not talking. Again, if you are left-handed the results may be quite variable.

We have established that the main differences between the two hemispheres relate to language. Ornstein (1986) suggested that the right-hand side of the brain is involved in pulling different things together to form a whole picture or concept, while the left-hand side is better for breaking down information into different units for analysis. This is why the right-hand side of the brain is better at spatial tasks and artistic activities, and the left-hand side is better for analytical thought. There is some evidence to support the idea that the left-hand side of the brain is more analytical and logical, and the right side is more holistic and sensory (Rasmussen and Milner 1977). The right brain seems to be related to depression and pessimism. It has also been noted that people who suffer left-brain strokes are often extremely depressed, irrespective of the amount of damage done to the brain, presumably because the right brain is the only normally functioning part, and its whole outlook on life is more pessimistic than optimistic. On the other hand, right-brain damage often leaves the person with an optimistic outlook, even though their prognosis is poor.

Rita Carter (1998: 36) reports the story of a senior American judge who suffered from a right-brain stroke:

> . . .he insisted on continuing at the bench despite having lost his ability to weigh evidence in anything like a sensible way. He maintained an exceptionally jolly courtroom, happily allowing serious criminals to go free while occasionally dispatching minor offenders to lifelong prison sentences. He resisted his colleagues' attempts to persuade him to retire and was finally sacked. Thanks to his right brain damage he seemed perfectly content – if puzzled – by this turn of events, and subsequently enjoyed a long and happy retirement.

Severing the connection

We have now considered that the two symmetrical hemispheres are only slightly different in the tasks they carry out. In order for us to function adequately, these two parts need to communicate with each other, which they do by means of the corpus callosum. This gives the side of the brain without speech centres access to words and descriptions which it would be without if there was no bridge between the two. It is easy to imagine what would happen if that bridge was not there. Such a thought gives new meaning to the phrase, 'the left hand does not know what the right hand is doing'!

There are rare instances of people having the connections between their two hemispheres severed, either as a result of an accident or, more likely, as one of the surgical treatments for epilepsy. Epileptic seizures are a result of abnormal electrical discharges of groups of brain neurones, described by Carlson (1986) as the 'wild sustained firing of cerebral neurons'. The source of the hyperactivity is usually in the temporal lobe and results in the person briefly losing contact with reality, and even experiencing hallucinations. Sometimes the seizures can be more sustained, and these are known as grand mal seizures. During one of these, the person becomes unconscious for a few minutes and experiences muscle spasms which may result in them breaking their bones or damaging themselves; they may also lose bowel and bladder control. When the seizure is over, the muscles relax and the person will wake up, but they are often extremely disoriented and embarrassed. A seizure like this would obviously be quite debilitating and would put the person in some danger, so any attempt to reduce the severity or frequency of such seizures would clearly be of great benefit.

One way of reducing the problem, developed by the late Wilder Penfield, is to remove the 'focal point' or original source of the seizures from the temporal lobe. The focus is identified by EEG recordings before surgery and checked by more recordings during surgery, with such operations carried out on conscious patients. (They need to be conscious in order to make sure that the surgeon does not take away too much brain tissue.) The patient is given a local anaesthetic, and the surgeon removes the skull and layers of dura mater until the brain is exposed. The areas surrounding the identified focal point are stimulated with the tip of a metal electrode to see what sort of response is made. If the area stimulated is part of the speech centre, then that area would be avoided. The benefit of this method is that it prevents excess tissue or essential tissue from being removed. The by-product of such operations has been to give us an excellent map of brain function.

An alternative way of preventing the spread of the wildly excited neuronal firings is to sever the corpus callosum, preventing the other side of the brain from becoming involved and thus reducing the severity of the effects. This method was very successful and it was found that not only did it stop the discharges from spreading, but it also reduced the epileptic seizures to negligible proportions. You would think that an operation of this severity would result in lots of side effects, but, extraordinarily, most of the people who underwent the surgery suffered very few side effects that were noticeable in their everyday lives. In effect, they were living with two brains in a single head, each one functioning adequately. There *were* side effects, however, and it is these effects that form the focus of the core study undertaken by Roger Sperry in 1968.

THE STUDY

R.W. Sperry (1968) 'Hemisphere deconnection and unity in conscious awareness'

American Psychologist, 23: 723–33

BACKGROUND

Before we look at the study itself, you need to know a little about Sperry and his work. Sperry is a neuropsychologist who has conducted a number of studies on split-brain patients while working at the California Institute of Technology. In the early 1950s he undertook research which involved splitting the brains of cats and monkeys. By training the animals he discovered that you could teach one hemisphere a task, while the other hemisphere remained unaware of the information learned. This supported his idea that the brain consisted of two separate modules rather than one unified whole. The importance of his work was recognised when he shared the Nobel prize for physiology and medicine with David Hubel and Torsten Wiesel in 1981. (Hubel and Wiesel pioneered a method of studying the physiology of vision by inserting very thin wire electrodes into the columns of neurones in the optic cortex and recording their response to different stimuli.)

Many of the effects of splitting brains were investigated in the laboratory with relatively simplistic tasks. They involved presenting information to one or other eye so that the information went to the opposite side of the brain. If the information was presented to the far right visual field, it would go to the left-hand side of the brain, which contains the speech centres. Therefore the person would be able to say what they had just seen. If the information was presented to the far left visual field, it would go to the right-hand side of the brain, which has no speech production centre. Therefore the person would know what it was, but would not be able to say what they had just seen. However, if this person was then asked to draw the object with their left hand (with their eyes closed), they could do so. From the diagram on page 280, you can see that each eye has information that goes to the opposite side of the brain, crossing over at a point called the optic chiasma. (If this crossover point were also severed, this would result in information from one eye going to one side of the brain only, and this has actually happened in a few cases.)

The subjects were asked to fixate on a spot in the centre of a screen. The image was projected for one-tenth of a second, which was insufficient time for them to move their eyes enough to send information to the opposite side of the brain. Therefore, for any of the split-brain studies which involve projecting objects for someone to look at, we accept the fact that the information projected on one side of the fixation point (that is, in the far left or far right visual field) is only seen by the corresponding eye and only goes to the opposite side of the brain.

These studies are not really ecologically valid because in the real world the situation would not occur, unless someone had only one eye. However, a later set of studies on split-brain patients, conducted by Gazzaniga et al. (1977), although also lacking ecological validity, showed how important it is for the two hemispheres to connect.

Gazzaniga et al. developed a contact lens which allowed the presentation of sophisticated images to only one side of the retina, and therefore to only one side of the cortex. In one study they presented a female subject, V.P., with a short film showing one person throwing another into a fire. The image was presented to the right hemisphere (with no language), and although the woman was fully alert throughout the course of the film she was only aware of having seen some kind of light. She reported that she felt scared and jumpy but was not sure why, so she explained her feelings by saying that she felt scared of Gazzaniga, although she knew she liked him. It seems she labelled her state of arousal by the situation she was in, namely having contact with her surgeon. She transferred the fear the film had created into a fear of Dr Gazzaniga.

Beneath the corpus callosum is another tract of fibres that connect the more primitive part of the brain – the limbic system. The limbic system is found under the cortex, and forms the junction between the older, more primitive parts of the brain, with their unsophisticated emotional responses, and the more logical, reasoning cortex. Here there is another tract of fibres which connects the two hemispheres – the anterior commissure. Very basic information about emotional responses such as anger or fear are passed from this area to both sides of the cortex, but the more sophisticated responses of the cortex are missing.

The article by Sperry describes the results of a series of experiments undertaken on people who had already had their corpus callosum severed as a treatment for severe epilepsy.

AIMS

The aim was to investigate the effects of this de-connection and show that each hemisphere has different functions; in other words, to map lateralisation of brain function and show that information in one side of the brain is not accessible to the other side.

METHOD

Method and design

The design was a quasi-experiment which compared split-brain subjects with 'normal' subjects in laboratory tests, and compared case studies of all the individual patients.

Subjects

The split-brain subjects were 11 patients who had already experienced a **commissurotomy** prior to the study. The sample type is therefore an opportunity sample. All subjects had a history of severe epilepsy which had not responded to drug therapy. Two of the patients had been operated on successfully to sever their corpus callosum some time before the experiments took place. The remaining 9 had only recently undergone surgery.

Procedure

The equipment used allowed for various types of sensory information to be presented to one or other hemisphere, in different combinations. Visual information was presented by projecting images on a screen in front of the subject. Tactile information would be presented to either the left or the right hand, or to both hands, without the patients being able to see what the object was. A representation of the apparatus is given in the figure below.

Subjects had to remain in silence during the studies unless they were asked questions by the experimenter. This was to prevent them passing information from the left side of the brain to the right side, as sound can be taken in by both ears simultaneously. For example, if the subject identified an object and then said what it was, this information would be available to both hemispheres.

1 Visual investigations:
   Visual investigations involved showing one stimulus at a time to one visual field, or showing two stimuli simultaneously to the two different visual fields.
   • One visual field (targeting only one side of the brain at once):
     These tests required the subject to cover one eye. They were told to look at a fixation point in the centre of the screen. The image was projected for one-tenth of a second on either the left or the right of the fixation point, which would send the image to either the far right or far left visual field respectively. It

was projected for that short space of time to prevent the information going to the wrong half of the visual field if the subject moved their eye, which would send the information to both sides of the brain. This is because there is an overlap in the centre of the visual field (at the fixation point), which means that the right and left brain both get information about objects viewed at that point. For example, the first screen shown below would send the image of a key to the right side of the brain as it is projected in the far left visual field, picked up only by the left eye. The next screen would send the image of the key to the left side of the brain as it is projected in the far right visual field, picked up only by the right eye.

- Both visual fields:
  The subject would look at the fixation point on the screen while two images were flashed simultaneously either side of the fixation point. This screen would send the image of a key to the left side of the brain (because it would be seen by the right eye in the far right visual field) and the image of an apple to the right side of the brain (because it would be seen by the left eye in the far left visual field).

The subjects would then be asked to say what they had seen. Typically, they would say 'key', although they would have no conscious awareness of having seen anything else. They would then be given a pen with the left hand and be asked to draw what they had just seen (although they would have to do this with their eyes closed or with their hand out of sight, because if they could see what they were doing, the dominant hemisphere would interfere with their recall). Typically, they would draw an apple. If they were then shown the picture, they would not know why they had drawn it, as the information about the apple had *not* gone into the dominant left hemisphere, which is the hemisphere containing language (speech).

2 Tactile investigations:
  - One hand:
    - The subject's hands are hidden from their view behind the screen. The subject is then asked to find an object corresponding to what they have seen on the screen.
    - The object is placed in one hand, without the subject being able to see what they are holding, and they are then asked to say what they have been given.
    - The object is placed in one hand, without the subject being able to see what they are holding, and they are then asked to point to what they have been given.
  - Both hands at the same time:
    - The subject works with their hands out of sight. The subject is given two different objects, one in each hand, and then the objects are taken away.
    - The subject is asked to find the objects by touch from a pile of items.
    - The subject is asked to say what they have just held.
  - Both hands at the same time:
    - The subject works with his hands out of sight. He would be told to hold both hands in a symmetrical position without the hands touching. The experimenter then places one hand in a given position e.g. with one or two outstretched fingers.
    - The subject is then instructed verbally or by demonstration to form the same pose with the other hand.
  - Both hands at the same time:
    - The subject works with his hands out of sight. The subject is told to hold out both hands with the palms up and the fingers slightly apart. The experimenter then touches a point on one of the fingers or the base of a finger.
      - The subject is asked to touch the same target point with the tip of the thumb of the same hand.
      - The subject is asked to find the same point on the other hand (using the thumb of the other hand in the same way).

3 Visual and tactile information:
  - Both hands at the same time:
    - The subject is presented with an outline drawing of a hand with a black spot marked, to either the right or left half of the visual field.
    - The subject is asked to touch the same target point with the tip of the thumb (of the same hand) e.g. if shown a picture to their right visual field,

they would be asked to identify the same point on first their left hand (using their left thumb) and then their right hand (using their right thumb).

4 Tests of the right hemisphere:

Because the right hemisphere does not produce language, in order to test if it has any ability to make mental associations, work logically or experience separate emotions from the left hemisphere, the following tests were undertaken:

- The left eye (therefore right hemisphere) is presented with an object on the screen. The subject is asked to pick out similar objects by touch from an array of objects.
- Simple mathematical problems are presented to the left eye. The subject is asked to sort objects by shape, size or texture, using their left hand.
- An array of geometric shapes is projected to both visual fields on the screen. In the middle of this selection is the picture of a nude, which is presented to the left eye only. The subject is later asked if they saw anything other than the geometric shapes. The right hemisphere may respond non-verbally (because the subjects were seen to blush or giggle although they would not know why) and this may reveal what has been seen.

RESULTS

Visual stimuli presented to one visual field

- When subjects were shown an image in one visual field, they would only recognise the image as one they had already seen if it was shown again to the same visual field. The reason for this is that information would have gone only to one side of the brain and not the other.
- If an image was shown in the right visual field (left hemisphere), the subject was able to say what they had seen, could identify what it was from an array of pictures shown to the right eye by pointing to it, and could find it with their right hand from an array of objects.
- If it was shown to the left eye (right hemisphere), the subject was unable to name it, but could draw it (with eyes closed) with their left hand, could identify what it was from an array of pictures shown to the left eye by pointing to it, and could find it with the left hand from an array of objects.

Visual stimuli presented to both visual fields

The subject would be able to say what they had seen presented in the right visual field, but would be unaware that they had seen anything else. If they were given a pen in the left hand and asked to draw with their eyes closed, they would be able to draw what they had seen with the left eye, although they would seemingly have no conscious knowledge of having seen anything else and would be very surprised when they discovered what they had drawn. They would be able to name the object once they had seen the drawing with the right eye.

Tactile investigations

The results of the tactile investigations were the same, irrespective of whether the object was held by one hand at a time or by both hands simultaneously.

- The subject would have no problems identifying an object by name if it was put in the right hand, but if it was put in the left hand they would have no conscious awareness of it. However, they would be able to find it by touch with the left hand in a bag full of objects.
- When the objects were placed in one hand, subjects could point to what the object was with the same hand which had held the object.
- When subjects' hands were placed in a certain shape by the experimenter, they were unable to mirror the shape with their other hand.
- When subjects touched a target point with the tip of the thumb of the same hand, they were unable to find the same point on the other hand (using the thumb of the other hand in the same way).

Visual and tactile investigations

When subjects were presented with an outline of a hand with a black spot marked on it, they were only able to touch the same target point when the hand corresponded to the visual field in which the information was presented e.g. when information was presented to the left visual field, they could do it with their left hand but not their right hand.

Tests of the right hemisphere

- Subjects were able to pick out semantically similar objects; for example, if they saw on the screen a picture of a wall clock with the left eye (therefore right hemisphere) and the only related item in a tactile array was a toy wristwatch, this would be the object chosen.
- Right hemispheres were able to carry out simple mathematical problems.
- Left hands were able to sort objects by shape, size and texture.
- When subjects saw the array of geometric shapes, they would giggle or look embarrassed when the picture of the nude appeared, even though they could not say what they were responding to. This non-verbal response suggests that the right hemisphere has a second conscious entity.

DISCUSSION

The study gave considerable support to the idea that the brain consists of two seemingly independent hemispheres, each with its own consciousness, and that there is no transfer of information between the two sides. For the subjects studied, the dominant hemisphere was the left-hand side, which contains the speech centres. This explained why, when information was presented to the right hemisphere (via the left eye), they were unable to say what they had experienced. The final tests of the right hemisphere give further support to the idea that the two hemispheres have their own consciousness, whereby one responds in a typically human way, by giggling at the nude, while the other has no idea what is going on.

COMMENTARY: METHODS AND ISSUES

Research method, design and data gathering

In order to demonstrate the effects of the surgical severing of the corpus callosum, Sperry tested the subjects under strictly controlled conditions. Using this method he was able to show evidence for brain lateralisation and work out what functions the two hemispheres of the brain perform. The strengths of carrying out research under highly controlled conditions are apparent in this study. For example, without the controls of using the screen to hide their hands from view, flashing the images only briefly and instructing the subjects not to talk unless spoken to, the functions of the two hemispheres would not have been revealed.

The findings of the study would be unlikely to be reproduced in a real-life situation, however, or to have any impact in real life, because a person with a severed corpus callosum who had both eyes open would be able to compensate. This would be possible either because the information would be received by both sides of the brain at the same time, or because the information would be carried to the minor hemisphere by speech. (This indicates that the minor hemisphere – the right hemisphere in right-handed people – must have some speech abilities; otherwise it would not understand.) Therefore, the study lacks ecological validity.

Does the study raise any ethical concerns?

The study is ethical as the subjects consented to be studied, no deception was used and they were neither harmed nor unduly stressed by the experimental tests.

Is the study useful?

Certainly Sperry's work was ground-breaking in beginning to understand the physiognomy of the brain, that is, how the brain works. It revealed the importance of the corpus callosum as a pathway for internal communication between the two sides of the brain.

Validity and reliability of the study

There are two problems with the findings that make us question their validity.

1 The sample was extremely small as the condition is quite rare. We have to question whether studies of the 'abnormal' brain can really be generalised to the 'normal' brain. It may be that the experiences of the subjects prior to the surgery made their brains very different from normal brains anyway. These differences could have been caused by the epilepsy, the life-threatening nature of their disorder or the medication used to try to treat it. Add to this the fact that the subjects have undergone major brain surgery and you can see that there are significant problems with the generalisability of the findings from these subjects.

2 Sperry emphasises in his conclusion to the study that even within this small sample of 11 subjects, there were 'with respect to the deconnection symptoms mentioned, striking modifications and even outright exceptions' among the split-brain patients. If there are individual differences in brain lateralisation in a sample so small, imagine the extent of individual differences we might find in the human brain in the general population.

The Physiological Psychological Approach

Researcher(s)	Focus of study
Maguire et al.	The plasticity of hippocampi in taxi drivers
Dement and Kleitman	Does REM sleep correlate with dream recall?
Sperry	The lateralisation of brain function

The physiological approach considers the impact of our biology on behaviour. Biological influences on how we behave include the brain and nervous system, the endocrine system and genetics. In terms of the nature–nurture debate the physiological approach leans towards the nature side of the argument and has traditionally considered heredity to be important in determining behaviour.

Methods of studying the relative contributions of genetics to behaviour include twin studies, comparing MZ (monozygotic or identical) twins with DZ (dizygotic or non-identical twins). Greater similarity between MZ twins than between DZ twins would suggest that heredity is the cause, since MZ twins share more genes than DZ twins do. Differences in personality, intelligence, likelihood to abuse substances and a whole range of other behaviours have been investigated using twin studies. Twin studies today include genetic analysis studies, which are trying to identify the roles of particular genes, or patterns of genes, in specific behaviours. Results from twin studies are often mixed, not because genetics do not influence our behaviour, but because they interact with other factors such as environmental experiences and the relative contribution of the different factors is difficult to unpick in research. Also, genetic research is a new science. If advances in this field provide evidence of the effects of specific genes on specific behaviours, psychologists will improve our understanding of the influence of biology on behaviour.

The development of technology such as EEG machines, MRI scanning and other brain-imaging techniques has provided a breakthrough in our ability to study the living brain, assisting psychologists and neuroscientists in their understanding of the physiognomy of the human brain, that is, how our brains work. Again, this is helping us to develop an understanding of how and to what extent our behaviour is influenced by our biology.

STRENGTHS AND WEAKNESSES

The Physiological Psychological Approach

- The physiological approach is leading to a greater understanding of the physiognomy of the brain. For example, Maguire et al.'s work on the hippocampi of taxi drivers confirms the role of this structure in the brain in spatial memory and way-finding.
- The approach is very scientific, grounded in biology and uses rigorous scientific methodology in research.
- Even though the approach tries to be scientific, our limited ability to study brain processes directly and objectively means we often have to rely on self-report data, and here demand characteristics may be a problem. For example, in Dement and Kleitman's study, subjects could have falsified reports about whether or not they were dreaming, or about the content of their dreams.
- Brain-imaging techniques rely on relatively new technology. Errors in the images can be caused when the information is made into an image by the machine, or by the interpretation of the person viewing the image. Imaging techniques allow us to see that the brain is active, but active doing what?
- This approach can explain biological influences on behaviour, but researchers must be careful to avoid reductionist explanations of behaviour, that is, seeing the behaviour as being caused solely by biology.
- Studies carried out in the laboratory can be low in ecological validity. For example, Dement and Kleitman had subjects spend the night in their sleep laboratory. We sleep differently when we are not in our own beds, and this certainly must have been the case where each subject was not only in a strange bed, but was wired up to an EEG machine, being observed and being woken by a doorbell at intervals through the night.

The psychology of individual differences

Introduction

In this last section we will look at individual differences, a term often used in psychology. What are individual differences? Put simply, they are the differences between individuals which make it very difficult to group people together as one bunch or 'type'. Of course, we can find things that people have in common, such as their cultural backgrounds, their gender or their age. We may even be able to identify things about their personality or how clever they are, and put them in a group with others who share similar characteristics. What we must always remember is that although we may share characteristics or abilities with others, this is only part of the story. Each of us has also had a unique set of life experiences which has contributed towards making us what we are, and this individuality must be acknowledged, irrespective of our opinions about the differences between us.

You will have realised that our lives are enriched by the huge diversity in the human race – for example, the artistic, literary, scientific, rich, poor, old, young, blonde, brunette, male and female. After all, what a boring life we would lead if we were all the same. The difficulties with considering the wide variations in human beings however, arise when those variations become so extreme that they make certain individuals stand out from the crowd. Take, for example, the physical characteristic of height. What is a 'normal' height? If someone is very short or very tall, are they then abnormal? If that person is 'abnormal', should he or she be treated differently or have allowances made for them like taller doors or longer beds? Once we start to categorise or quantify people, that automatically suggests that there is a normal and an abnormal, and this is fraught with problems. Surely it depends on who is doing the judging? This next section considers how some of these issues relate to the behaviour and characteristics of individuals, rather than their physical appearance.

What is abnormality?

Has it ever worried you how psychiatrists and psychologists determine whether someone is abnormal? After all, most of us at some time or other, go through stages of being

Bao Xishun, one of the world's tallest men

a bit weird, don't we? But where do we draw the line between weird and actually 'abnormal'? And if we are abnormal, does that mean we are mentally ill?

One thing that can change our behaviour quite dramatically is the run-up to impending exams. Have you suddenly discovered how housework takes on new meaning? Bedrooms suddenly get tidied, and even the washing-up seems a better prospect than getting your head down to some really serious work. Isn't this sudden fascination with housework some kind of weird, abnormal behaviour? Then, as the exam gets closer, you feel more and more stressed and unhappy, and instead of being your normal, happy-go-lucky self, you become totally antisocial and very quiet. We could say that your behaviour has showed 'substantial change', but does that mean you have actually become 'abnormal'? Well, maybe it is abnormal for you, but there is a reason for it and surely that makes a difference? It is no more than a kind of temporary abnormality, because as soon as the exams are over, you will revert to your normal self.

> 'Simon's gone loopy. Look at him. What on earth is he doing running up and down the high street at ten o'clock on a Saturday night with only a pair of boxers on?'
>
> 'It's the beer, mate!'

Is Simon abnormal? No, he's probably just happy, and that, plus the alcohol which will have removed some of his inhibitions, has resulted in his decision to run around in his underpants!

You can see that the label 'abnormal' is not quite as clear-cut as it seemed earlier, and cannot simply be assessed by looking at the way someone is behaving at a given moment. We have to take into account how the person has been over a period of time. We need to consider the situation they are in and whether there is a reason for the way they are behaving. Finally, we ought to take into account whether there are any kind of drugs involved, which might have been a cause of their behaviour.

Defining abnormality

There have been a number of attempts to try to find a way of differentiating the normal from the abnormal. The problem is that none of them is really satisfactory.

Statistics

We could begin to look at abnormality by considering some kind of statistical formula, which would help us define who is and who is not abnormal. One way this could be done is by looking at people's 'scores' in relation to the scores of others. This idea comes from Sir Francis Galton, who was the first person to identify the **normal distribution curve**. He set up an anthropometric centre as a tourist attraction in London, and people paid to come and have their physical characteristics measured – height, weight, width of upper arm, lung capacity and strength of grip. He collected reams of data about different physical characteristics from thousands of people. Then he plotted their scores from each characteristic on a graph and found that he had a normal distribution curve. He therefore assumed that if mental characteristics were dependent on physical ones, then mental characteristics would also show a normal distribution curve.

The normal distribution curve (also known as the **Gaussian distribution**) is a bell-shaped curve which has special mathematical properties. The mean or average score falls in the middle because it is the most frequently occurring score – but note that this is only the case in a normal distribution. Using another calculation, which comes directly from the mean (called the **standard deviation**), allows us to find the percentage of people who fall either side of the mean. This can be used mathematically to predict how similar or dissimilar someone is to the population as a whole.

Terms in bold are included in the Glossary for Chapter 8 on the CD-ROM.

If we view statistics to be a suitable way of looking at abnormality, we could consider as abnormal the people who are statistically rare when measured, and fall at either end of the distribution curve. Take, for example, people who have very low IQs or very high IQs, and who could certainly be considered abnormal. People with very low IQs may actually need some support to help them deal with life and look after themselves, but what about the ones with very high IQs? We are far more likely to see them as lucky rather than abnormal in any way. Other measures of personality or mood state could be used in the same way, but being very happy rather than very miserable, again, could be considered lucky rather than abnormal. Therefore, being statistically rare does not actually help when we are trying to work out what we mean by abnormal (in terms of mental illness).

This normal distribution curve shows the bell-shaped curve, with the standard deviations from the mean also shown: 68 per cent of people would fall within one standard deviation from the mean in either direction on the horizontal axis (coloured red on the graph); if we add the red and blue areas together (two standard deviations from the mean), this accounts for 95 per cent of the population; three standard deviations (red, green and blue areas) are equal to 99 per cent of the population

Nonconformity

An alternative way to consider how we define abnormality is to look at whether people's behaviour conforms to what society expects. Have you ever been in the company of someone who has started behaving in a bizarre way (perhaps due to alcohol), or who stands too close to others, or makes personal comments about other people? The chances are you found it quite embarrassing and wanted to remove yourself from the situation. If someone's behaviour makes another person uncomfortable, then perhaps they are abnormal, but it must depend on the audience. After all, not everyone feels uncomfortable about the same things, so it seems the definition here is very much to do with the people watching, rather than the person performing the actions.

Perhaps abnormality does not actually exist, and the concept is no more than a means of social control. When we mentioned Simon's bizarre behaviour on a Saturday night, we realised that he was behaving only in a slightly abnormal way, because it was Saturday and he had been out drinking. What would happen if unusual behaviour was not seen in context? Supposing someone behaved in a way that was seen as a weird or unacceptable and this was enough to have him confined and labelled as being mentally ill? How would he convince people that he was not actually mad?

The following story was written by a patient at a psychiatric hospital. If you read it, it will make you realise that **labelling** someone as abnormal, just because they do not behave in the same way as everyone else, has enormous ethical implications.

Once upon a time, there was a happy man called Joe Odd. He lived in a little hut on the side of a hill with his dog, and from his window he could see right into the distance. Around the hut was a beautiful garden where he grew flowers and vegetables and lots of lupins, because lupins were his favourite flowers.

On weekdays he went to work in the valley where all the people lived in little boxes which all looked just the same, but afterwards he could go home to his little hut and watch the sunset. The people who lived in the boxes thought Joe was very strange because they all watched television. At first they said, 'Why don't you live in a box like us?' So they broke his windows and made up bad stories about him and the police said he was causing a breach of the peace.

'Ain't Joe weird – I bet he's queer. . .or maybe into little boys. . .yeah, a child molester.'

'And he hates everyone. . .he's dangerous. . .let's get him.'

So Joe locked his door and barred his windows and was afraid to go out. The garden became overgrown with weeds. Only his dog stayed by his side. One day a man came to the hut and said, 'Mr Odd, this hut is unhealthy because there is no bathroom, so we are going to pull it down, but we cannot rehouse you because you do not meet the requirements.'

Joe wandered from place to place and stole bottles of milk from doorsteps. One day the police caught him and a social worker came to take his dog to the RSPCA. Joe was so upset that he hit the social worker, so she said he could not be in his right mind and would have to be assessed. They sent Joe to a mental hospital where the doctor examined him and asked him lots of questions about his childhood and his bowel movements, then wrote on some labels and hung them round his neck. Then another social worker wrote a report about how Joe had lived in a hut with the doors and windows barred. So the doctor hung another label round his neck saying 'PERSECUTION COMPLEX', and gave him some pills to make him feel better. Joe did not like the pills because they made him feel strange and he refused to take them, so the doctor hung an 'UNCOOPERATIVE' label round his neck and gave him an injection instead.

Every week the doctor asked him lots of questions to find out what was wrong with him, but Joe refused to answer anymore, so the doctor hung an 'UNCOMMUNICATIVE' label round his neck as well. After a long time they told Joe he was better and they found him a regulation box to live in under the rehabilitation scheme. Joe lived in his little box and from his window he could see lots of other boxes, all looking just the same.

The welfare workers told him he was coping very well, but sometimes Joe still had a feeling he wanted to hit people, only he could not remember why he felt like that, because the pills made his head feel sleepy. The social worker looked at Joe's labels and told him that this was all part of his illness and that it might take a long time before he felt really better. One night he thought he heard a voice in his head saying, 'Come with me. . . I know a beautiful place. . . Come with me.'

'I can't. I am very ill. Can't you see all those labels round my neck?'

'Take them off, Joe,' said the voice again and again and again.

At last Joe lifted the labels from round his neck and threw them away. He was surprised how easy it was, and his head felt so much lighter. He opened the door and followed the voice. He walked for miles and miles and came to a beautiful place with lots of other odd people. He grew some more lupins and played music and painted pictures and flew in balloons, and he bought a cat who followed him everywhere, and everybody there loved Joe. Then one day the people in the boxes found out where he was and said he would have to come back because he was very ill.

A fleet of police cars and ambulances came after him with sirens screaming, and Joe ran along the beach into the waves to escape the noise for ever and ever and ever. . .

Can you see how abnormality is actually quite a frightening concept, because it implies that there is some kind of 'normal' way of behaving, and if we do not fit into that, we can be removed rather than cause our society any sort of discomfort? Although this is a story, the situation can actually become more serious when people who are not willing to conform to the behaviour that society expects, like political objectors, are made to conform by being removed and locked up under the pretext that they are abnormal and therefore mentally ill.

This 'social control hypothesis' has been used to help to explain some of the worst cases of psychiatric abuse. In his book The Gulag Archipelago, Alexander Solzhenitsyn wrote about the chain of prison camps stretching across the Soviet Union, which were full of people who would not conform to rules and regulations which they believed were wrong. The frightening thing is that these situations continue today, for example in areas where non-democratic governments are trying to maintain control. Another example could be seen during Japan's drive for industrial success. 'Bins' (as in loony bins) were used to 'dump' those who were unwilling to conform to the demands of industry. Therefore, in order to instil the appropriate terror, the 'bins' had to be sufficiently unattractive. In fact, the conditions in Japanese mental hospitals were similar to the old Victorian asylums in the UK – overcrowded, dirty and often brutal in their discipline. Between 1955 and 1990, the number of inpatients in Japanese mental hospitals were seen to increase from 100,000 to around 400,000.

Abnormality as coping

Abnormal behaviour could be seen as no more than a way of coping with life. Gary Craven, speaking at an A level revision lecture on Relationships in the 1990s, told the story of a man who found a very bizarre way of coping with a problem he had. Below is a version of the story he told.

> Edward was not unattractive. In fact, he was quite a good-looking man, but there was something rather strange about him. He explained at a self-help group, when all the students were sitting round in a circle, getting to know each other, that his great interest in life was lifts. He proceeded to fascinate everyone with tales of the lifts he had visited all over the world. Initially he thrilled them with stories of the speed of lifts in New York, which rose 60 storeys in a matter of seconds. He filled them with terror when he related stories of the older lifts in Russia, which creaked and groaned and stopped and started as they slowly slid up the shafts. However, half an hour later, they were all semi-comatose.
>
> Then came the time to talk about his experiences with women. When he began to explain that he had never had much luck with members of the opposite sex, suddenly the people became more interested again. He told them how, every time he started talking to a woman, she seemed to move away from him. Suddenly his eyes lit up. 'But I have noticed that when I am in a lift, it is much better. They seem to talk to me there and I get on so well with them, but then the minute the lift doors open, they disappear.'

Edward had no concept of personal distance, and just stood too close to whoever he was talking to. Most of the time, people made their excuses and left, but in a lift, he had a captive audience – there was nowhere to go!

Edward may well have been raised in another culture where people's need for personal space is very different to that in our culture. He therefore had no idea that there was anything unusual about his behaviour, but he *was* aware that people did not seem to like him very much. As a way of coping with this situation, he simply adjusted his behaviour until he found a way to make people talk to him. Not understanding the underlying reasons, but having found himself a reasonable solution, his behaviour had become quite abnormal.

A much simpler example of how abnormal behaviour is simply a coping strategy can be seen in people who are fanatical about tidiness, to the extent that every little thing has to be in its place. This fanaticism can become obsessive and can take over their lives. In order to understand the reasons for this, we need to look at the rest of the person's life. It may be that they have no confidence in themselves and feel inadequate, so they can only just cope with work and their other responsibilities. Extra problems or burdens would just become too much for them, so in order not to make things more stressful, they need to be sure that their home life or office is totally ordered and organised.

The final kind of abnormality I want to mention here is multiple-personality disorder. This mechanism of splitting the personality into a number of sub-personalities is really the ultimate form of coping. Here, part of the personality may then deal with specific situations, thereby protecting other parts from harmful situations, such as abuse. You will read about it later in this chapter (page 327), where multiple-personality disorder is the subject of one of the core studies.

Cultural relativity

By now you will have realised that defining abnormality is going to be extremely difficult, if not impossible. It seems that there is no one thing that allows us to say, without hesitation, this is what we mean by abnormality. If we try to take abnormality as a theoretical concept first and foremost, we should perhaps see if the people who are considered abnormal all share the same features. However, even this does not seem to work, because what is considered abnormal in one culture is seen as perfectly normal in another.

Many practitioners in the western world assume that the behaviours of the white population are normal, and therefore any deviation from this normality by another ethnic group shows some racial or cultural pathology. It should be obvious that what is normal behaviour for that person can only really be judged in relation to the patient's background and culture. The trouble is that this is not always understood. In Britain, West Indian men are more likely to be admitted to psychiatric hospitals, and psychotic black patients are twice as likely as whites or white immigrants to be in hospital involuntarily. Black patients are more often seen by a junior rather than a senior doctor and, even when they are diagnosed with the same disorder as a white person, they are more likely to be given more radical treatments (Littlewood and Lipsedge 1989). It is also well known that in the USA, more black people than white are diagnosed as being schizophrenic every year.

The features of abnormality

Rosenhan and Seligman (1989) tried to get round the problems of identifying what is meant by abnormality. They suggested that if we identify the major features that are more likely to be found in abnormal individuals, we could do a kind of tally – the more you have, the more abnormal you are – and the more abnormal you are, the more likely it is to be related to mental illness! They came up with seven features that are based on statistical rarity and social deviance.

1. **Suffering**
   Suffering is often seen among people who are mentally ill. The problem here is that some people have no concept of suffering, such as people with **psychopathic personality disorders**; and many normal people suffer when they lose someone they love, for example.

2. **Maladaptiveness**
   If someone suffers from maladaptive behaviour, it means that their behaviours are not the sort of behaviours which will allow them to have a fulfilling life because they will probably prevent them from achieving success or happiness. An example of a

maladaptive behaviour is when someone has an irrational fear or phobia about something, for example flying, and cannot go anywhere or do anything which might make such behaviour necessary.

3. **Vividness and unconventionality**
    This refers to behaviour that is very obviously unusual or unconventional. The trouble is there are always unconventional people who are just eccentric rather than mentally ill.

4. **Unpredictability and loss of control**
    Think back to Simon and his escapade in his boxer shorts. His behaviour was certainly unpredictable. However, most of us are relatively predictable and our behaviour is reasonably well controlled most of the time. Therefore, is this a good measure of abnormality and mental illness?

5. **Irrationality and incomprehensibility**
    Premenstrual tension sometimes causes women to behave in an abnormal and incomprehensible way – at least, it probably seems like that to the male members of society. Once the reason for the behaviour is explained, however, it no longer seems quite so irrational and incomprehensible. Therefore we have to be careful when judging someone's behaviour as being irrational, because we can never be sure that their behaviour does not have a good cause.

6. **Observer discomfort**
    Think of Edward and his lack of understanding of acceptable interpersonal distance. Our social behaviour is governed by a set of rules that we seem to learn but are never actually taught. We learn them as we grow up by monitoring other people's responses to our behaviours. When the rules are broken by another person, we generally become very uncomfortable. This will affect how we feel about that person and whether or not we want to go on associating with them – we find it hard to deal with someone whose behaviour is abnormal, compared with the normal rules of our society.

7. **Violation of moral and ideal standards**
    If a woman works as a prostitute, this is likely to be considered a transgression of the accepted moral standards of our society. The reasons for her decision are not taken into account, and she is likely to be judged purely on the basis that earning money in this way is not considered morally acceptable or ideal although it may be, in her opinion, her only option.

These seven features do not actually help us a great deal because most of them can be explained in a number of different ways. Although they could be adapted to fit into different cultures, they also involve an element of subjectivity because it would depend very much on the perception of the person doing the judging. One of us may see behaviour as vivid and unconventional, whereas another person may see it as perfectly normal!

Abnormality as a useful concept

There are times when labelling someone as 'abnormal' can be positive. If we have a person who is extremely distressed and unhappy, and their pattern of behaviour is similar to that of others who are also distressed and unhappy, we can put them in some kind of category which means that we might have a better idea of how to support them. To take an example, this sometimes happens with children who present with difficulties with social interactions and social communication, who become distressed by changes in routine and who may find themselves isolated and anxious. If we look at the nature of the difficulty they are experiencing, we might find it helpful to consider whether they have an autistic spectrum disorder. If this is the case, they will receive specific support both within school and at home, which will make life much more acceptable for them.

Taking a less extreme example, someone who has learning difficulties with literacy, who is diagnosed as dyslexic, may feel a tremendous sense of relief, because that 'label' will have explained their difficulty, without suggesting that it is just because they are not very clever.

It has been recognised that there are lots of different types of abnormality and each one seems to have a number of common features. Although there is a danger in trying to put people into categories and labelling them accordingly, if they are categorised as carefully and accurately as possible, it means that medical professionals do not have to spend ages trying to work out what is going on for each individual person and can perhaps help them that much more quickly. After all, we know that someone with depression for example, will have a whole list of symptoms which are likely to follow on, such as problems with sleeping. These problems could be addressed without having to wait to see how the disorder progresses.

What happens when the categorisation is wrong though, especially when the person may well have been labelled and treated accordingly by medical professionals? Unfortunately, many of the labels of mental disorders automatically mean that an individual will be stereotyped, and this will impact on the way they are treated. Take the case of **schizophrenia**. Many people would describe a schizophrenic as someone who has a split personality, and they would come up with all sorts of behaviours that they might expect to be associated with that categorisation. Well, they would be wrong because schizophrenia is a kind of *disorganised* personality, not a split personality. Split personality is known as **multiple-personality disorder (MPD)** and is also referred to as **dissociative identity disorder (DID)**, which you will read about in the next section. Many diagnosed schizophrenics who are receiving treatment have no symptoms at all. So what is the answer?

Classificatory systems

There are two classificatory systems which are used to identify mental disorders, but they both owe much to the work of Emil Kraepelin (1856–1926). He suggested that groups of symptoms seem to occur together on a regular basis. This meant that these groups of symptoms (syndromes) could perhaps be classed as diseases. He also believed that they had a biological basis and should be treated in the same way as any other illness. Kraepelin suggested (1896) that there were two groups of serious mental illness: 'dementia praecox' (later called schizophrenia) and 'manic-depressive psychosis'. If nothing else, he must be acknowledged for recognising that many mental disorders had a biological basis rather than being caused by external factors such as evil spirits or possession by demons.

The International List of Causes of Death was originally compiled by the World Health Organization as a way of monitoring causes of death throughout the world. In 1939, they added mental disorders to the list, and in 1948 the list expanded further and became known as the **International Classification of Diseases (ICD)**. However, the mental disorders section was not widely accepted and was superseded by the DSM (see below). The current version is the **ICD-10**, which focuses on descriptions which are grouped according to similarities and differences in signs and symptoms, rather than looking at the other aspects of people's functioning in their everyday lives. As some of the signs and symptoms appear in a number of disorders, this makes its use inadequate for psychiatrists.

The Diagnostic and Statistical Manual of Mental Disorders (DSM) was first published in 1952 by the American Psychiatric Association, in response to the ICD. The current version is the **DSM-IV** (1994), and it differs from the ICD because it has a greater number of discrete categories. It also looks at the influence of outside factors on a person as part of the diagnosis. This is obviously much more valid, because the life experiences of a person are very likely to contribute to any kind of disorder.

The DSM consists of five axes or dimensions, which are not only used as a diagnostic tool, but also help with the planning of treatment and prediction of outcomes. Each person is assessed on every axis to give a much broader picture of what is going on in their lives, which is extremely important if we are to give a fair diagnosis.

Clearly, the whole topic of abnormality is fraught with problems. There are so many issues that need to be considered before we risk planting some kind of label on a person, which may well be with them for the rest of their lives. Schizophrenia, for example, is an incurable illness. If someone is diagnosed, they will only ever become a schizophrenic in remission. Therefore, we cannot risk making a mistake.

The key study in this area emphasises just how easy it is to make mistakes when diagnosing mental illness, and how, once someone has been labelled, all their behaviours are seen in a different perspective. If we cannot tell the sane from the insane, it does not leave us with much hope. At least the diagnostic criteria used today are far more sophisticated than they were at the time of the core study, which was carried out in 1973. The DSM-II was in use at the time, and this second version did not have the five axes, but much more simplistic diagnostic labels. The system we now use for categorisation, we hope, is much less likely to be abused than it was in the past.

THE STUDY

D.L. Rosenhan (1973) 'On being sane in insane places'

Science, 179: 250–8

BACKGROUND

David Rosenhan was one of a number of academics in the 1970s who were concerned about the validity and reliability of psychiatric diagnoses. The system being used by psychiatrists at the time of this study was DSM-II. Rosenhan was concerned that the diagnosis was not objective: 'it is commonplace. . . to read about murder trials where eminent psychiatrists for the defense are contradicted by equally eminent psychiatrists for the prosecution on the matter of the defendant's sanity' (p.250). In other words, the same symptoms reported by a patient could be interpreted in different ways by different psychiatrists. This, of course, brings the reliability of the diagnostic system into question.

Rosenhan also points out that 'what is viewed as normal in one culture may be seen as quite aberrant in another' (p.250), and again, this challenges the idea that there is an objective and universal notion of what normality and abnormality actually are.

Rosenhan was not suggesting that odd and deviant behaviour, and the distress it brings to those experiencing it or to those around them, does not exist. He did, however, take issue with the way such behaviour was described and categorised by the system. He wanted to investigate whether the diagnoses given to patients came from symptoms being displayed by the patient themselves, or whether their behaviours were being described as abnormal because they were in a psychiatric setting.

Haney, Banks and Zimbardo's Stanford prison experiment (1973) (see Chapter 2, page 49) aimed to test the dispositional hypothesis, in other words, to test whether it was the dispositions or character traits of the individuals who were in prison, or who worked in prisons, which made prisons brutal places, or whether the brutality was created by the way prisons were organised. The researchers came to the conclusion in their study that the best explanation of prison brutality was a situational one, that the brutality was caused by the way prison life was structured, including social roles, and the consequent psychological effects on those working in and being held in prisons.

Rosenhan's study considers a similar question. Is all the behaviour of patients on psychiatric wards described as abnormal because it is seen as a symptom of the individual's illness? Do the hospital staff identify behaviour which is a normal response to being in a psychiatric unit as 'abnormal' and evidence of the person's illness? He asks, 'do the salient characteristics that lead to diagnoses reside in patients themselves or in the environments in which observers find them?' (p.251).

In other words, is the diagnosis of mental illness flawed because, once on the ward, the person is seen as abnormal and all their behaviours are judged in this context? Rosenhan's study suggests that the descriptions of patients' behaviour were individual when they should be situational.

AIMS

The aim of Rosenhan's study was twofold. First, he aimed to test the diagnostic system to see if it was valid and reliable. He decided to do this by getting himself and seven others admitted to psychiatric hospitals to see if and how they would be discovered to be 'sane'.

Once on the ward, would the behaviour of these '**pseudopatients**' (Rosenhan and his confederates) be considered normal, and not lead to a psychiatric diagnosis, or would their behaviour be considered 'abnormal' because of the context they were in? If the former were true, there would be evidence that the diagnostic system was valid and reliable. If, however, the latter were true, and the pseudopatients were not detected, then, given that:

- the hospital staff were not incompetent;
- the pseudopatient behaved as normally in the hospital as outside it;
- it had never been suggested previously that the pseudopatient belonged in a psychiatric hospital;

the fact that the pseudopatients were not detected would 'support the view that psychiatric diagnosis betrays little about the patient but much about the environment in which an observer finds him' (p.251).

The second aim of the study was to observe and report on the experience of being a patient in a psychiatric hospital. There was little objective evidence on this as doctors did not follow up patients who were discharged, and even if they did, such data might be too subjective (and Rosenhan suggests it might be considered unreliable, as the person was previously considered insane). Researchers had acted as patients in previous studies, but the findings of these may not be valid, since the hospital staff were aware of their presence and may not have treated them like real patients. What would the pseudopatients experience and observe on the psychiatric ward?

Investigating the first aim: could hospital staff identify the pseudopatients as being 'normal'?

METHOD

Design

The admission of the pseudopatients to the hospitals was studied as a field experiment, and data regarding the experience of being a patient in a mental institution were gathered by covert participant observation.

Subjects

The subjects were the hospital staff and patients in 12 hospitals in the USA.

To get a representative sample, the hospitals were in five different states, from the east and west coasts; some were old and shabby, some were quite new; some had good staff–patient ratios, some did not; one was private, the others were federal or state-funded, with one university-funded; some carried out research, some did not.

Procedure

The pseudopatients were eight 'normal' people (five men and three women), and Rosenhan himself was one of them, and the first to gain admission to a hospital. Apart from a psychology graduate in his twenties, all were older and 'established' in their jobs/roles: three psychologists, a paediatrician, a psychiatrist, a painter and a housewife. All used fake names to protect their health records in the future, and the subjects who were working in the health service pretended they were in other occupations, to avoid the 'special attentions' that might be given to people from the health professions.

To gain admission, the pseudopatients were to self-present, or self-refer. They phoned the hospitals for an appointment, and on arrival complained that they had been hearing voices which were unfamiliar, of the same sex and said 'empty', 'hollow', and 'thud'. Any other information given by the subjects was completely honest, including details of their family and personal background and recent life experiences. (**Note:** There had originally been nine pseudopatients, but data from one were omitted from the results because he falsified his personal history.)

These symptoms were chosen because they simulated existential symptoms which come from the realisation that life is really meaningless and so, as moral free agents, we have to create our own values through our actions and accept the responsibility for those actions – we cannot blame our lives on anyone else. This 'What's it all for?' experience is often distressing. Also, there are no reports of existential psychosis in any literature on mental illness, and therefore, it was thought that, although auditory hallucinations are a classic feature of schizophrenia, this would make the diagnosis harder to recognise.

(Schizophrenia = a psychiatric disorder which results in the patient suffering from a disorganised personality. They are likely to experience hallucinations, usually auditory, and delusions of grandeur or delusions of persecution.)

As soon as they were admitted to the ward, the pseudopatients ceased simulating any symptoms and aimed to behave as normally as possible, which they were able to do after the 'short-lived nervousness' they had experienced on admission faded away. This nervousness was caused either by the fact that they were admitted so easily and were fearful of being spotted as frauds straightaway and embarrassed, or, for those who had never been on a psychiatric ward, the novelty of the setting.

RESULTS

All the pseudopatients were admitted to the hospitals, where they remained for between 7 and 52 days (mean length of stay 19 days). Of the 12 admissions (some pseudopatients sought admission to more than one hospital), 11 were diagnosed with schizophrenia and one, with identical symptoms, of course, with manic-depressive psychosis. This has a more favourable prognosis (more likely to get better), and it is interesting that this was the diagnosis from the only private hospital in the sample! When those diagnosed as schizophrenic were finally discharged, it was with the diagnosis of schizophrenia in remission. Therefore, none of the pseudopatients was detected as a fake. This was a clear failure in the diagnostic system and it was observed in all 12 hospitals in the sample.

To say they were not detected means that they were not detected by the *staff* in the hospitals. The patients, however, had their suspicions. In the first three hospitalisations, clear records of patient responses were made, with 35 of a total of 118 patients voicing their suspicions. They said things such as, 'You're not crazy. You're a journalist, or a professor [referring to the continual note-taking]. You're checking up on the hospital'. Most patients, however, were reassured by the pseudopatients' claims to have been sick before admission and fine now, but some held the view throughout that the pseudopatients were not 'real' patients. Why did the psychiatrists misdiagnose the pseudopatients? In general medicine, Rosenhan points out, it is better to err on the side of caution and risk diagnosing a healthy person as sick rather than to 'miss' an illness. These two possible misdiagnoses are called **type 1** and **type 2 errors**.

In inferential statistics, a type 1 error is where you reject the null hypothesis (which states that there is no statistical significance between conditions, or any difference is due to chance), when you should have accepted it. Here we are saying the IV has affected the DV when really it has not done so. A type 2 error is when the null hypothesis is accepted when it should have been rejected: we are saying the IV did not have an effect on the DV when really it did.

When we transpose these two errors onto a medical diagnosis it looks like this:

- Type 1 error = diagnosing someone as ill when really they are not.
- Type 2 error = diagnosing someone as not having an illness, when in fact they do.

Let us take this study as an example. Imagine you are a psychiatrist and you are attempting to diagnose one of the pseudopatients. You decide that they do have a mental illness and you diagnose them accordingly. Of course, we know they are lying about the symptoms they said they had experienced, so we know this is a type 1 error. The psychiatrist, however, does not know what we know. The alternative for them is to decide that the pseudopatient really does not have a mental illness, and risk making a type 2 error. The trouble with this state of affairs is that you could be making a *big* mistake with this error, which could mean that people fail to get the care and treatment they need, or, worse still, you could be putting people's lives at risk.

This may have been why the pseudopatients were given the misdiagnosis in the study – the doctors were being cautious. In this case, they may have decided that it was better to assume the pseudopatients were ill (a type 1 error, since the pseudopatients were not really ill) than to make a type 2 error and risk the possibility of failing to diagnose someone who was in fact ill.

In cases where the diagnosis is not clear, being cautious and risking a type 2 error makes sense in general medicine. However, in psychiatry this is altogether a different issue. If a healthy person is diagnosed as having a psychiatric disorder, this leaves them permanently stigmatised.

If staff mistook fake patients for real ones, would it also be possible that the opposite would occur, and that they would identify real patients as fake ones? A follow-up study was carried out to test this.

FOLLOW-UP STUDY

Rosenhan told the staff at a large hospital, who had heard about the first part of the study and doubted that they would not be able to spot pseudopatients, that some time during the next three months, one or more pseudopatients would attempt to gain admittance to the hospital.

Each member of staff was asked to rate on a ten-point scale the likelihood of the patients who appeared being pseudopatients. Out of 193 patients who attended for psychiatric treatment, 41 were confidently judged to be pseudopatients by at least one member of staff; 23 patients were suspected by at least one psychiatrist; and 19 were thought to be acting by one psychiatrist and one other member of staff. In fact, the 193 patients were all genuine patients, as Rosenhan had sent along no pseudopatients. The hospital staff had been judging regular patients.

ROSENHAN'S CONCLUSIONS

The fact that the pseudopatients were not detected and were each given a psychiatric diagnosis indicates that psychiatric diagnosis is not always valid. Rosenhan's claim that 'we cannot distinguish the sane from the insane in psychiatric hospitals' is actually given considerable support.

In the follow-up study, the finding that approximately 10 per cent of their normal clients were judged as pseudopatients by two staff members, including a psychiatrist, led Rosenhan to conclude that 'any diagnostic process that lends itself so readily to massive errors of this sort cannot be a very reliable one' (p.252).

Rosenhan describes what he calls 'the **stickiness of psychodiagnostic labels**'. He says, 'Having once been labelled schizophrenic, there is nothing the pseudopatient can do to overcome the tag. The tag profoundly colours others' perceptions of him and his behaviour' (p.253).

In the next section, we shall see how the behaviours demonstrated by and information given by the pseudopatients was interpreted according to their diagnoses.

Investigating the second aim: the experience of psychiatric hospitalisation

METHOD

Design

Participant observation was used to observe the behaviour of real patients and the hospital staff, and to record the experiences of psychiatric patients. Pseudopatients also kept a diary and made notes to record their experiences and observations. This was a field study.

Subjects

The subjects were the hospital staff, the real patients and the pseudopatients themselves.

Procedure

Once admitted, the task of the pseudopatients was to behave as normally as they did outside the hospital (where no one had ever suggested that they needed to be in a psychiatric hospital!).

The pseudopatients observed and made notes about their experiences, quite openly in front of staff and other patients.

RESULTS

What was the pseudopatients' reaction to their experience?

The pseudopatients found the whole experience extremely unpleasant, not from associating with the patients, but because of their experiences with staff. It was found that there were instances of serious physical abuse to patients. Rosenhan reports having watched a patient being beaten by an attendant for going up to him and saying, 'I like you'.

Acts of violence tended to go unchallenged. Verbal abuse was also recorded. Morning attendants would often wake patients with, 'Come on, you m–f–s, out of bed!' (p.256). Patients' privacy was minimal and the patients suffered loss of power and **depersonalisation**. They felt as if they were invisible, or unworthy of account, and this threatened their sense of identity.

311

The pseudopatients' note-taking behaviour

Although they had been concerned that their constant note-taking would be challenged or prevented, and had made elaborate arrangements to remove their notes from the wards each day for fear of confiscation, these precautions proved needless.

None of the staff asked them what the notes were, but simply assumed the behaviour was part of their illness. For example, in one case, the comment, 'Patient engages in writing behaviour' was inserted in the daily case notes, as if this were some bizarre and inexplicable symptom of the patient's 'illness'. On another occasion, a patient making notes was told gently by the doctor, 'You needn't write it. . . If you have trouble remembering, just ask me again.' This shows us how the label given to the patient – their diagnosis – affected the way the doctors and staff perceived their behaviour.

That the note-taking was observably 'normal' for someone studying the hospital was expressed by the real patients, many of whom suspected that the pseudopatients were checking up on the hospital. This did not seem to have occurred to any of the members of staff.

Further examples of how labelling affected the staff's description of the patients and pseudopatients

Anyone who has been in hospital will know that it can be very boring. You soon adapt yourself to getting through the day by moving from one routine activity to another, and mealtimes provide a way to structure the day. You find yourself looking forward to the three o'clock tea trolley for your cup of tea and custard cream. On one occasion, patients waiting outside the cafeteria for lunch were observed by a doctor in the case notes to be displaying the 'oral-acquisitive nature of the syndrome'. Rosenhan comments, 'It seemed not to occur to him [the doctor] that there are very few things to anticipate in a psychiatric hospital besides eating' (p.253).

Another example of the staff failing to recognise the situational impact on behaviour was noted when one of the pseudopatients was pacing the long hospital corridors. A kindly nurse approached him and asked, 'Nervous, Mr X?' 'No, bored,' he said. The nurse assumed that his pacing was a symptom of his disorder rather than his response to the unstimulating and monotonous environment in which she was observing him.

One pseudopatient talked about his upbringing and family, which seemed a typical example of how we experience changes in relationships with our parents as we get older. Sometimes we are closer to one parent at a young age, but when we reach adolescence, we find that we have become closer to the other. This may be due to one of our parents finding it harder to relate to small children, but enjoying a new-found closeness as the child matures. It is similar with marital relationships, which do not always run smoothly. Occasionally, minor rows had developed in the marriage of this pseudopatient, which were relatively meaningless. He also reported that his children had rarely been spanked. There seems nothing unusual about this history. However, the case notes talked about him having 'a long history of considerable ambivalence in close relationships, which begins in early childhood'. The notes continue by saying that his relationship with his father changes from being distant to 'becoming very intense. Affective stability is absent'. This last sentence means that his feelings have no stability – implying that he has emotional swings. The report goes on to describe the fact that his efforts to 'control emotionality with his wife and children are punctuated by angry outbursts and, in the case of the children, spankings'. The report has clearly been distorted by the diagnosis to fit in 'with a popular theory of a schizophrenic reaction' (p.253).

If a patient went 'berserk' because he had been intentionally or unintentionally mistreated by an attendant, a nurse coming along would not inquire as to what had happened to lead to the outburst. It seemed not to be an option that the behaviour was a result of immediate environmental factors impacting on the patient, or anything to do with the staff or the hospital. Instead, his behaviour was seen as being due to his illness or perhaps his having been upset by a family visit (especially if they had visited recently).

Medication

Rosenhan reports that 2,100 pills were handed out to the pseudopatients during their stays in the hospitals, although all but two were pocketed or flushed down the toilet. The pseudopatients often found the medication of other patients down the toilet before flushing their own. As long as the behaviour of the patients was acceptable while on the wards, such actions were not noticed.

Staff contact

The staff tended to keep themselves away from the patients except for administrative or practical duties. The doctors were even more remote than the nurses, and seemed to maintain the greatest distance, only seen by patients when they came onto the ward to start their shift and again when they departed, with the time they were on duty being spent in the 'staff cage' or in their offices. Patients spent, on average, less than 7 minutes a day with senior members of staff over the course of their stay. Surely it should have been the other way round, with these senior members of staff who wield the most power being the most familiar with the patients' case histories and behaviours?

The physicians acted as models for those lower down the staff hierarchy. The attendants were the staff on the ward who had least power and were the ones likely to spend most time with the patients. However, they tended to take their lead from the physicians, and avoided contact with patients by spending most of their time in the staff cage.

Two key psychological factors were observed to be affecting the patients (and the pseudopatients): powerlessness and depersonalisation

The pseudopatients reported on the patients' complete lack of power in the psychiatric wards. Their movements were watched and restricted, they had virtually no contact with staff, and their medical files were available to all members of staff, even volunteers.

Acts of violence against patients were observed by other patients, some of whom were pseudopatients writing it all down. The abusive behaviour immediately stopped when another member of staff appeared. The fact that staff were considered credible witnesses and patients were not is an indication of the patients' lack of power.

We have already noted that those with the most power (the physicians) spent least time with the patients, and that attendants spent most of their time in the cage, where the power within the ward was based. The fact that staff went about their business as if the patients were not there, and that the ward staff spent as little time on the ward with the patients as possible, added to the invisibility felt by the pseudopatients.

The patients also suffered from a minimum of personal privacy. For example, physical examinations carried out prior to admission were conducted in semi-public rooms where 'staff went about their own business as if we were not there' (p.256). Once on the ward it was not unusual for toilet cubicles to have no doors and for the 'personal hygiene and waste evacuation' of the patient to be 'monitored' (p.256).

Evidence from the study shows that patients could not initiate contact with staff, that they were expected to be passive and to respond only to any overtures initiated by staff members. Rosenhan illustrates this point clearly with the findings of a study on responses to patient-initiated contact carried out at four of the hospitals. The nature of this study involved recording responses by

Contact	Psychiatrists in Rosenhan's study	Nurses and attendants in Rosenhan's study
Moves on, head averted	71%	88%
Makes eye contact	23%	10%
Pauses and chats	2%	2%
Stops and talks	4%	0.5%
Number of respondents	13	47
Number of attempts	185	1,283

Source: Adapted from Rosenhan, p. 255

The responses to patient-initiated contact

staff to a courteous and relevant request made by the pseudopatient. This was adapted to fit the target person and the setting, but followed along the lines of, 'Pardon, me, Mr [or Dr or Mrs] X, could you tell me when I will be eligible for grounds privileges?' (or 'when will I be presented at the staff meeting?'). The request was never asked of the same staff member on any one day, to avoid irritating them or raising their suspicions, and it was neither bizarre nor disruptive. It was the initiation of a perfectly reasonable conversation.

As you can see from the table, the patients were pretty ineffective when it came to initiating a conversation with a staff member with a polite and relevant question. The response rate for psychiatrists was only about 7 per cent, with the other staff being even worse, responding only about 4 per cent of the time.

As Rosenhan points out, the time a person spends with you can be a measure of your importance to them. Lack of eye contact and lack of verbal contact indicate avoidance and depersonalisation. Given this fact, it is not surprising that the pseudopatients felt deindividuated and unworthy of account. The fact that the majority of reactions were in the 'Moves on, head averted' category shows how they may have come to believe that they were 'invisible' to staff.

Rosenhan compared these findings with a similar study carried out at Stanford University. A female student asked six similar questions (for directions, about college admission and if there was financial aid) of tutors in the university faculty and the university medical centre. In the university medical centre she added a comment after her first question. To some respondents she said, 'I'm looking for an internist', and to others she said, 'I'm looking for a psychiatrist', and to yet a third group she made no additional comment; otherwise the questioning was the same. The results were as follows:

Contact	'Looking for a psychiatrist'	'Looking for an internist'	No additional comment
Moves on, head averted	0%	0%	0%
Makes eye contact	11%	0%	0%
Pauses and chats	11%	0%	0%
Stops and talks	78%	100%	90%
Mean number of questions answered (out of six)	3.8	4.8	4.5
Number of respondents	18	15	10
Number of attempts	18	15	10

Source: Adapted from Rosenhan, p. 255

Responses to questions asked by a female student in the university medical centre

The response rate was generally much higher in the university medical centre than it was for the pseudopatients on the ward. It is interesting that when the female student indicated she was 'looking for a psychiatrist', the percentage response decreased to 78 per cent. This may indicate that people find mental illness quite hard to deal with, and were reluctant to help someone 'looking for a psychiatrist' because of the social stigma associated with mental illness.

What were the consequences of depersonalisation for the pseudopatients?

Rosenhan reports that the pseudopatients were sufficiently distressed by their experience of depersonalisation to instigate a number of attempts to re-establish and assert their identity. The graduate student in psychology asked his wife to bring in his books so he could catch up on his studies, even though this was likely to give away his true profession. Another pseudopatient tried to initiate a romantic involvement with a nurse. He then told staff he was applying to be a psychology graduate and then engaged in psychotherapy with other patients. It is clear from these examples that the pseudopatients were greatly affected by their experience, and these could be seen as attempts to reassert their individuality.

What were the sources of depersonalisation?

Rosenhan considers two sources of depersonalisation in psychiatric hospitals. First, he sees depersonalisation as a product of generally held prejudices towards the mentally ill. 'The mentally ill,' he tells us, 'are society's lepers.' We avoid contact with them at all costs. This is ingrained in the history of institutionalised care for the mentally ill, who were often locked up indefinitely and subjected to brutal treatment. Society's response was not only out of sight, out of mind, but 'if you are out of your mind it is best if you are out of our sight'. Rosenhan points out that the staff in psychiatric wards are not immune from this prejudice, and that it influences them in the hospital setting, just as it does outside the hospital on people in society at large.

The second source of depersonalisation, according to Rosenhan, was a result of the hierarchical structure where, as we have seen, doctors have all the power, patients have none, and those staff in between follow the doctors' model of avoidance of contact with patients. Rosenhan says that this does not mean that the staff were uncaring, in fact, he states, 'our overwhelming impression of them was of people who really cared, who were committed and who were uncommonly intelligent'. However, 'where they failed, as they sometimes did painfully, it would be more accurate to attribute those failures to the environment in which they, too, found themselves than to personal callousness'. In other words, the behaviour of both the staff and the patients can be attributed to situational rather than individual factors.

Other sources of depersonalisation may also be at work; where money is tight, patient contact may be first to suffer. This is facilitated by the extensive use of psychotropic drugs, which control the patients and keep them passive.

ROSENHAN'S CONCLUSIONS

Rosenhan describes how psychiatric hospitals create environments where behaviour gets easily distorted to fit in with diagnostic labels and social prejudices. Consequently, patients are treated in such a way as to perpetuate any problems they may have. Rosenhan suggests the need for further research into social psychology of institutions, both to facilitate treatment and to deepen understanding. After all, would it not be better to work at changing the way we think about people in distress and try to provide the kind of social environment which would help and support them?

> If patients were powerful rather than powerless, if they were viewed as interesting individuals rather than diagnostic entities, if they were socially significant rather than social lepers, if their anguish truly and wholly compelled our sympathies and concerns, would we not *seek* contact with them, despite the availability of medications? (p.257)

COMMENTARY: METHODS AND ISSUES

IS THE STUDY ECOLOGICALLY VALID?

To the extent that the real behaviour of real patients and real staff was observed, the study is high in ecological validity. However, can we consider the reports of the pseudopatients' own feelings and responses as being the same as those of real patients? For example, the experience of the pseudopatients was different from the real patients' experience in that the pseudopatients knew that their diagnosis was false and that they were not really mentally ill. Their experience was comparable to real patients' experiences in that staff were unaware of the false diagnosis of the pseudopatients and treated them the same way as they treated the other patients, and in this way their experience is a valid one.

As to whether the conclusion that there were problems with diagnosis is genuine, there are some concerns that need to be addressed. Although, once they had been admitted, the pseudopatients believed they had stopped showing any signs of abnormality, we cannot be sure that this was the case. If they were anxious and nervous, this might well have influenced their behaviour, both prior to diagnosis and after they had been admitted to the wards. This, and the novel experience of being institutionalised, or being separated from loved ones, may have meant that their behaviour appeared more unusual than they might have thought.

317

The study highlights the ease with which the pseudopatients were misdiagnosed. However, the doctors were not completely wrong in their diagnoses, because after a period of observation they did diagnose the pseudopatients as having schizophrenia in remission, in other words, their absence of symptoms was noted and they were discharged. Nonetheless, this does not account for their misdiagnosis in the first place.

Does the study raise any ethical considerations?

The ethical considerations of the study involve deception, whereby the medical practitioners were deceived by the pseudopatients in the symptoms they claimed to be experiencing. The follow-up study also raises some ethical concerns. It involved real patients being treated with undue suspicion and perhaps not receiving the care they felt they needed. This could have added to the anguish they were already experiencing, as they would not, presumably, have self-referred for psychiatric care if they were not experiencing a considerable amount of distress.

The covert observation of staff and patients on the wards raises the issue that informed consent was not obtained from the subjects. They were not given the right to withdraw and they could not be debriefed. Rosenhan justifies this by pointing out that without concealment of the identities of the pseudopatients, the findings would not be valid. He says that to counteract any effects of this concealment, he ensured that the anonymity of particular hospitals and their staff would be maintained.

What about the ethics surrounding the safety of the pseudopatients? At the outset, Rosenhan says he did not realise how difficult it was to get discharged at short notice from a psychiatric ward. However, with legal advice, a writ of habeus corpus was prepared for each of the pseudopatients on entry and an attorney was kept on call. (Although usually used to compel the police to justify the continued detention of a suspect, a writ of habeus corpus, issued by a judge, would require that a person who is detaining another present the detainee in court.)

The pseudopatients reported that they did not like the experience and wanted to be discharged straight after admission. However, they did as they had been instructed and Rosenhan was able to report their findings.

At least the pseudopatients had the advantage of knowing that they were not mentally ill, and, unlike the real patients, would leave behind them the **powerlessness** and depersonalisation of the institution when they left the hospital. For the real patients who needed care, however, powerlessness and depersonalisation were part of the package. Even if they did get well enough to be discharged, the stigma of mental illness would be with them for ever.

Studies that are highly useful and which lead to change for the better can be described as ethically worthy. It is important to point out that although this study raises some ethical issues, the findings it generated and its purpose in testing and establishing the reliability of psychiatric diagnosis mean that it had a worthy purpose. In this case we can conclude that the end justified the means.

Is the study useful?

At the time it was reported, the study highlighted problems with the diagnosis of mental illness that needed to be addressed. The current diagnostic criteria, DSM-IV, is a great deal more reliable and valid than DSM-II, although there is probably still room for improvement.

To gain admission to an institution now in the USA is much more difficult than at the time of this study. Now the patient must:

1 be diagnosed as having a mental disorder (and diagnosis now takes longer to confirm, e.g. continuous symptoms for 1–6 months for schizophrenia);
2 be suffering from a disorder which could not be treated in a less restrictive environment;
3 be a danger either to themselves or to others.

Because of this, Rosenhan's study would not be possible to replicate. This, of course, is a strength and not a weakness, and demonstrates the impact of studies such as this one on the diagnostic system.

The study also provided evidence of the powerlessness and depersonalisation that was experienced by the patients, the lack of contact with staff, the abusive behaviour that went unchecked and the reliance on medication rather than contact with caring and supportive staff in the treatment of psychiatric patients. Nowadays, the 'total institution' approach to the care of psychiatric patients is considered the exception rather than the norm. Where possible, people are cared for in the community. However, this does not mean that there are not problems associated with such provision. Financial pressures mean that the care that is needed may not be provided. Staff may be overstretched and serve large geographical areas.

Most depressing is that the social stigma associated with psychiatric illness is no less in evidence now than it was in 1973, and integrating people with mental illness into a community that both fears and shuns them can be difficult. Education is a key factor in successful integration.

Multiple personality

What is personality?

Like intelligence, personality is a concept which varies according to the theorist, although we all have a pretty good idea of what the concept means to us. Consequently, it is virtually impossible to give the ultimate definition of personality – suffice to say, we know that each one of us has something unique about us which separates us from others, and we tend to refer to that as our personality.

Personality can be defined as 'the distinctive and characteristic patterns of thought, emotion and behaviour that define an individual's personal style and influence his or her interactions with the environment' (Atkinson et al. 1993: 525). This definition really captures the fact that each of us has distinctive patterns of thought, emotion and behaviour, and it is how these patterns interact that makes us what we are. It also suggests that if each one of us has these patterns, the component parts of each can be compared to those of other people.

The personality traits with which people are most familiar are the traits of introversion and extroversion. Eysenck (1947) describes an extrovert as very outgoing, liking lots of company, someone who seeks excitement and does not mind taking chances. On the other hand, the introvert is quiet and reserved, tends to keep his feelings to himself, prefers his own company or the company of small groups of other people, and is often believed to be shy. We all fall somewhere on a continuum between the two extremes, and we could therefore use a measure of extroversion as a means to compare ourselves with others. However, even if we found two people with very similar measures on a number of different traits, it does not mean that they will be alike. Some of us achieve great things, while others achieve a very modest amount in our lives, and these differences seem to be as much to do with our genetic inheritance, our socio-economic class, our family experiences, our life chances and our culture as they are to do with the type of person we might be. The whole package is too closely linked to be able to extract one aspect and leave all the others behind.

Lawrence Pervin (1984: 3) made the point that:

> Personality research is not the study of perception but rather of how individuals differ in their perceptions and how these differences relate to their total functioning. The study of personality focuses not only on a particular psychological process, but also on the relationships of different processes. Understanding how these processes act together to form an integrated whole often involves more than understanding each of them separately. People function as organised wholes, and it is in the light of such organisation that we must understand them.

The point that Pervin is making is that we really need to look at all the processes that comprise personality and how these fit together to make an individual. We all have a childlike part of us that makes us react in an egocentric or irrational way. We all have a logical and analytical part which allows us to assess situations and make decisions. We have parts which make us sociable or insular, parts which make us jealous, parts which make us frightened, parts which make us resentful, inquisitive, compassionate, and so on. Many of these parts fit in with Freud's theory of personality, whereby the id, the ego and the superego all have a role to play. Other parts do not fit so well with his theory, but they still exist. Each one of us, therefore, is made up of lots of different characteristics in lesser or greater amounts, which, when combined, make us the individuals we are. But what happens when these parts do not fit together to make a unified whole?

Multiple-personality disorder

One of the most fascinating mental disorders is multiple-personality disorder (MPD), or dissociative identity disorder (DID), as it is now known. It is fascinating, partly because it is so rare and causes such seemingly bizarre behaviour, and partly because it is a disorder which has a purely psychological basis. It is not the same as schizophrenia, although the terms tend to be used interchangeably by people who do not know the difference.

People who suffer from DID appear to have all the different aspects of their personality, but rather than forming a unified whole, certain clusters of traits are contained in separate units. Each unit then takes on aspects of an individual personality, so it is as if one body contains lots of different people.

Someone who suffers from DID can therefore have any number of different personalities and each split is locked into its own personal role. Each personality has its own characteristics, likes and dislikes. Each may even live its own life alongside the others, while being contained within one body: the childlike part, the sensible part, the jealous part, the fun-loving part, and so on, which all exist as individual units and often have different names.

In order to be diagnosed as having dissociative identity disorder, the DSM-IV says the person must have at least two separate 'personalities', which are called ego states or alters, and each one must have its own way of feeling and acting that is totally independent from any of the other alters. Each of these alters has to come forward and take control at different times. Their existence cannot be temporary; they must exist for some time and should cause the person quite a lot of disruption, rather than for example simply being the result of taking drugs or drinking too much.

People who suffer with DID are extremely likely to have gaps in their memories. If they are aware of one alter but there are actually three, for example, they will not know what is going on when the other two take turns at being in control. It will be as if they keep having blackouts or lapses in memory, which must be really frightening. What must be even worse is if one unrecognised alter does something that the person is unaware of. When the second alter arrives, it will have to deal with the consequences. In fact, it could be quite embarrassing.

'Hi Jude. How do you feel after your exploits last night?'

'My exploits – what do you mean?' said Jude, looking puzzled.

'You know – after we left the pub last night.' Kathy chuckled.

'I don't know what you are talking about,' said Jude, feeling angry.

'Yeah, right. So how do you explain the garden gnomes that are sitting in your front garden?'

Jude felt a sort of icy shiver. When she went out to get into her car this morning, she wondered why there were hundreds of garden gnomes sitting on her lawn. Her mum was out, and she did not remember seeing them the night before.

'And what about Kevin?'

'Who's Kevin?' asked Jude, still trying to work out where the gnomes had come from.

'Who's Kevin? You're joking. He's the one that ran off with your bra and put it on the statue in the high street – you must have been well gone.'

'I er, I um, I don't know what you mean. No, I mean I really don't know what you are talking about.'

'So I suppose you don't remember moving that bench from outside Boots into the middle of the high street and dancing on it with three balloons and not a lot else to cover your modesty! We were thinking of putting out a hat and collecting money from passers-by.'

At this point Jude removed herself from the conversation.

If each alter has its own memories and patterns of behaviour and relationships, then each one will act in the way it feels is appropriate. Some alters may know about some of the others, but not all of them, and some may be unaware of the existence of any other personality. There are often primary alters and subordinate alters. The primary alters are the main personalities, which manifest most often. The subordinate alters have less relevance and are rarely present, or may even be undetected for some time after the disorder is recognised. Often the subordinate alters may hear the voices of the others but not be aware of who they belong to; in other instances, some of the alters may even talk to each other. Each alter will usually be very different, possibly even of the opposite sex. Some may be older than others, some may be extrovert and some introvert. Each one will have its own patterns of behaviour, its own experiences, its own memories and its own relationships with other people. It is literally like having a number of different people living in the same body, each one making their own decisions and acting out their own roles. They may even have different physical characteristics, for example, one may be left-handed, another right-handed. One may even like one type of food while the next finds it disgusting.

Symptoms and causes of DID

There are four kinds of dissociative disorders which affect a person's sense of identity, and each one may well have a very similar cause. They all result in the person becoming dissociated (or disconnected) from who they were before they developed the condition. This may be caused by simple amnesia (**dissociative amnesia**), or the amnesia may be so dense that the person takes on a new life without realising that they cannot remember the past (**dissociative fugue**). It may be that they lose their sense of self and take on an almost robotic role (**depersonalisation disorder**), or it may be due to the fragmenting of the personality (**dissociative identity disorder**). However, DID is considered more chronic and serious than other dissociative disorders, and the chances of a full recovery are considerably lower.

DID usually starts in early childhood, but may well be unrecognised as it is quite rare and is not likely to be the first diagnosis a practitioner arrives at. In fact, there are a number of theories to explain the cause of DID, but it is recognised today that it is often associated with some kind of traumatic childhood event, such as sexual abuse, although the event is not always sexual in nature. Putnam et al. (1983) surveyed therapists working with DID clients and found that 80 per cent of their clients had suffered physical abuse in their childhood and 70 per cent had been victims of incest. Other research has indicated an even higher incidence.

One explanation of DID is that it acts as a coping mechanism to deal with particularly stressful experiences. In order to understand this explanation, it might be helpful to think about Zimbardo's study of prisoners and guards (Chapter 2, page 51). It appeared that the role the participants believed they were playing in the study had a tremendous influence on their behaviour. If we consider ourselves, we know that our lives are made up of a number of roles and each one is played out according to the situation we find ourselves in. Supposing one of those situations is really horrific; if we can keep that role separated from the rest of our lives, it is a way of protecting us from damage. In effect, it is an abnormality which has been produced as a coping mechanism.

Although DID was recognised in the nineteenth century, it seems that there was a fall in reported cases between 1920 and 1970, but then it increased again. This may well have been due to the popularity of schizophrenia as a diagnosis in the intervening years. One thing that was quite interesting was that there was a rise in the number of alters of diagnosed patients that seemed to coincide with the publication of a book called *Sybil* (Schreiber 1973), which told the story of a woman with 16 personalities. Before Sybil, the number of alters was two or three, but after the book the average rose to ten.

The psychodynamic explanation of DID is that it develops as a result of the **repression** of wishes or desires. Freud claims that children have sensual desires which focus on their opposite-sex parent when they pass through the Oedipal stage. They manage to curb the desires, but if they re-emerge in adulthood, the person may do something rash and impulsive of a sexual nature. If this happens, a way of dealing with it would be to repress the memory into the unconscious (motivated forgetting). If this does not work, another way of dealing with the problem would be to actually split that part of the personality from conscious awareness (Buss 1966), or, alternatively, to cope with the memory by giving the 'part of them' that carried out the act a new, independent identity.

Another theory to try to explain DID is to consider whether it is no more than a manifestation of temporal lobe epilepsy. Epilepsy is a condition where the brain of the person is suddenly affected by a burst of excess electrical activity, which then causes a temporary disruption in the normal transmission of messages between brain cells. The disruption either halts the messages or mixes them up. These disruptions may appear to an observer as a seizure or 'fit', which could be relatively mild, lasting for just seconds and possibly going unnoticed by others, or it could involve the whole brain, which results in the person becoming totally incapacitated and experiencing jerking and shaking. However epilepsy manifests itself, it must result in the person experiencing very disrupted thoughts which they may try to make sense of.

Mesulam (1981) investigated 12 patients with clinical and EEG manifestations which suggested that they had temporal lobe epilepsy. These 12 patients had also reported symptoms of dissociative states. In seven of the patients, the clinical picture was consistent with DID, whereas the other five believed they were experiencing supernatural possession. These cases suggest that in some instances, people who appear to have dissociative states may actually be demonstrating complex behavioural manifestations of chronic **limbic epilepsy**, which can occur in the temporal (and frontal) lobes.

Another study, by Sheehan et al. (2005), reported on a 37-year-old female patient who was diagnosed with DID by psychotherapists who had worked with her over a 6-year period. The woman, who worked as a primary school teacher, experienced a lot of scepticism by mental health professionals and asked if she could have her diagnosis validated by the use of another form of brain measurement, using a **SPECT (single photon emission computed tomography)** scan. She presented both as her 'adult self' and, on another occasion, as 'Emma', an abused girl. SPECT images were obtained from a number of different areas in the brain. The adult had significant asymmetry (with increased activity in *one* of the temporal lobes), while the activity in both of Emma's temporal lobes were indistinguishable from each other, suggesting that they were 'different' entities.

For an explanation of SPECT see Glossary on the CD-ROM.

These results were consistent with an earlier SPECT study which indicated that the temporal lobes (especially the left temporal lobe) might be responsible for the phenomenon of dissociative identity disorder. Sheehan et al. concluded that one possible interpretation of these observations would be that DID is in fact a form of temporal lobe seizure. This is especially interesting because the temporal lobe is more prone to seizure activity than any other lobe of the cortex (Engle 1996).

As we mentioned earlier, possibly the most accepted theory to explain DID is that it occurs in early childhood as a way of coping with traumatic or disturbing events. Learning theorists suggest that the child learns how to deal with the stressful memories by adopting an avoidance technique. The child 'hypnotises' or fools itself into believing that the events have not happened to them, but to someone else, and this someone else becomes another alter. Bliss (1983) discovered that people suffering from DID are easier to hypnotise than controls, and suggested that this might support the idea.

Not surprisingly, women are more likely to develop DID than men. This may well be affected by the fact that the number of girls who become victims of sexual abuse is higher than for boys. A study of 796 college students found that 19 per cent of the women and 8.6 per cent of the men had been sexually abused as children (Finkelhor 1979). Women often present with other symptoms, such as depression or headaches, before the DID is acknowledged. It seems that DID is frequently accompanied by substance abuse, self-abuse or suicide attempts – all of which go along with low self-esteem or guilt arising from abuse.

It is not surprising, then, that children who have been through such traumatic relationships find it hard to deal with what has happened. Of course, they would need to protect themselves from any further hurt, and perhaps this fragmentation is a way of doing so. If this is the case, the treatment must involve trying to convince the person that it is not necessary to split their personality in order to deal with their earlier traumas, and helping them to reintegrate. However, before this can happen, they have to acknow-ledge the actual split. It seems that hypnosis is a good technique to use as it gives the person access to hidden portions of the personality. However, as you will see, it may actually result in the belief that there are other alters – even when these do not exist.

Diagnosis of DID

It is essential that there are very stringent criteria for the diagnosis of DID, because it has been used as a legal defence in a number of court cases. An example is the case of the serial killer known as the Hillside Strangler, who was brought to trial in California in the 1980s. Ken Bianchi pleaded not guilty by reason of insanity, because he claimed he was suffering from DID. A number of researchers were very sceptical about his defence, and, as a result, they decided to conduct some research to find out if it was possible to fake the disorder by using the same method as Bianchi's interviewer.

Spanos, Weekes and Bertrand (1985) conducted research on a group of undergraduate students, which showed that they were able to give an account of a second personality within them, simply by receiving a session of hypnosis which suggested that they either had a second personality or that they had simply blocked off parts of themselves. This evidence casts quite a lot of doubt on the existence of DID, but there are still a large number of professionals who accept DID as a real disorder, even if it is extremely rare.

The final criterion which can be used in diagnosis is to investigate the brain function of DID patients, which was the criteria used for the primary school teacher earlier. This involves looking at whether the brain actually functions differently for each alter. If it does, this suggests that there really are different 'personalities' inhabiting the same brain. There are a number of different ways this can be done, many of which we covered in Chapter 5. For example, using an electroencephalogram (EEG), the activity from two or more areas of the brain can be recorded at the same time. Using a computer, it is possible to look at how these recordings are functionally (or structurally) connected, or if they are actually operating independently from each other. The measure that is under investigation is known as the measure of EEG coherence.

Hopper et al. (2002) undertook the first research to apply EEG coherence analysis to the study of DID. They compared five DID patients to five controls, who were professional actors. This meant they could compare 15 'real' alter states and 15 alters which were simulated by the actor control participants. The results indicated that there were significant differences in the EEG coherence between the person with diagnosed DID and their alter personalities. However, when comparing the EEGs of the actors and their 'alters', no significant differences were found. These results suggest that the real DID patients did have very different personalities 'inhabiting' their bodies, supporting the idea that EEG coherence may be an objective and effective measure of DID.

One of the implications of DID is to do with the status of different alters and the law. Elyn Saks (1992), from the University of Southern California Law Centre, argued that the body should only be considered a container for the person. It is therefore the person who should be to blame and not the body. Obviously in a 'normal' person they are the same thing, but not in a situation where the body contains a number of different 'people'. The problem arises when one alter knows what the other one is doing – does that make them both to blame? Alternatively, if one alter knows what the other one has done, but cannot actually stop it, by law, the alter who has not actually committed the act is not guilty. Surely the one who did not commit the act *is* guilty, though, because they should have reported the act of the other? It is easy to see what a confusing area this is.

One case where DID was accepted was that of Eve White. This was the most carefully documented report of dissociative identity disorder at the time and, as such, deserves a place within the core studies. It is interesting to note that the whole idea behind the therapy was to try to reintegrate the alters into a whole person. This method of treatment recognises the significance of each part of our personality as components of a whole, and acknowledges that we really are complex beings with many different facets.

THE STUDY

Corbett H. Thigpen and Hervey Cleckley (1954) 'A case of multiple personality'

Journal of Abnormal and Social Psychology, 49: 135–51

BACKGROUND

Is the diagnosis of dual-personality or multiple-personality disorder (the precursors of the diagnosis DID) a valid one? Is it really possible for more than one 'personality' to reside in one body, each with experiences, memories and wills separate and distinct from each other?

Thigpen and Cleckley described the scepticism with which psychiatry regarded such a diagnosis; that the MPD sufferer was to psychiatry what the unicorn or centaur was to natural history – simply a myth. Although cases had been reported in the past, notably that of Mrs Beauchamp, reported by Morton Prince in 1909, modern psychiatry in the 1950s tended to gloss over or ignore MPD. The authors suggest that this is probably because of a lack of contemporary and objective evidence. The diagnosis relies heavily on the patient's subjective reporting of experience, and may therefore be the product of the patient's deceit or the observer's wishful thinking, and was (and still is) treated with a great deal of scepticism.

Thigpen and Cleckley, however, believed they might have discovered such a case, and this study is a report of their findings. They too had viewed MPD with scepticism, but now reported that 'our direct experience with a patient has forced us to review the subject of multiple personality. It has also provoked in us the reaction of wonder, sometimes of awe' (p.136).

Had the psychiatrists really encountered the psychiatric equivalent in myth and rarity to the unicorn? Was this a true case of MPD?

AIMS

The aim of this case study was to document the **psychotherapeutic treatment** of a 25-year-old woman, who had a history of severe headaches and blackouts, and whom therapy had revealed appeared to have multiple-personality disorder. The purpose was to review the evidence and consider the validity of the diagnosis.

METHOD

The case study method was used, with the subject (patient) attending for regular therapeutic sessions over a 14-month period. Using notes from over 100 hours of therapy, the researchers documented the evidence for the diagnosis of MPD.

The data, therefore, were heavily reliant on the patient's self-report of her subjective experiences. The therapists also interviewed the patient's husband and family.

As well as the evidence from interviews, tests were carried out in an attempt to distinguish the personalities from each other. Psychometric measures were taken of memory function and IQ, the **Rorschach ink-blot test** was used, and EEG patterns were recorded and compared. A handwriting expert also compared the handwriting of the personalities.

The subject and the beginnings of the evidence of MPD

The patient in the study, given the name Eve White by the researchers to protect her identity, was, on referral, a fairly run-of-the-mill case. She had been referred because of 'severe and blinding headaches'. At the first interview she told of 'blackouts' following the headaches, where she suffered memory loss.

Eve White's marriage was disintegrating and this caused her a great deal of concern and distress. She had a 4-year-old daughter, to whom she was devoted, and this compounded her distress about her failing marriage. At first she was only able to attend for consultation irregularly, as she was travelling quite a distance. After some months of therapy, the authors noted that 'encouraging symptomatic improvement occurred, but it was plain that this girl's major problem had not been settled'.

Her case seemed ordinary, with Eve White being described at that time as a client presenting with 'commonplace symptoms and a relatively complex but familiar constellation of marital conflicts and personal frustrations'.

The loss of memory for a recent trip puzzled the psychiatrists, but they hypnotised her and this seemed to be cleared up. However, it was at this point in her treatment that an event occurred which was to be a key factor in the emergence of 'another' personality in the therapy room. They received a letter from Eve White which appeared to have been finished off by someone else, the writing described as a 'child-like hand'.

Questioned on her next visit, Eve White denied sending the letter, but did remember starting one. She was then agitated and distressed and asked whether it meant she was insane if she was hearing an imaginary voice. This question surprised the therapists, because Eve White had shown no other symptoms of 'schizoid' behaviour, and also because she was able to report the voice with a concern about the experience which was atypical of those patients experiencing auditory hallucinations.

Before the therapists could reply, however:

> as if seized by a sudden pain she put both hands to her head. After a tense moment of silence, her hands dropped. There was a quick restless smile, and in a bright voice that sparkled she said 'Hi there, Doc. . .' (p.137)

She then crossed her legs and the therapists noticed for the first time that they were attractive. It seemed as if someone else, someone other than Eve White, was now present in Eve White's body:

> Instead of that retiring and gently conventional figure, there was in the new-comer a childishly daredevil air, an erotically mischievous glance, a face mar-vellously free from the habitual signs of care, seriousness and underlying distress, so long familiar in her predecessor. This new and apparently carefree girl spoke casually of Eve White and her problems, always using *she* or *her* in every sentence, always respecting the strict bounds of a separate identity. When asked her own name she immediately replied 'Oh, I'm Eve Black'. (p.137)

The therapists were so convinced that this was a 'newcomer', different from Eve White in every respect, that they believed this might be a case of MPD, a major 'find' in the world of psychiatry. From this point on, their interest in and therapy with this client increased.

Differences between and experiences of Eve White and Eve Black

Over the 14 months of therapy, the therapists found out a lot about the personality they called Eve Black (EB):

- EB had 'enjoyed an independent life since Mrs White's early childhood', so had appeared long ago in Mrs White's life.
- Eve White (EW) was not consciously aware of EB, and although told of the existence of EB in therapy, she remained unable to access EB or her memories or experiences. EW was 'in abeyance' or 'unconscious' when EB was 'out' (one 'personality' at a time is supposedly dominant in such cases, and the dominance of the other personality was described as her coming 'out').
- EB, on the other hand, was aware of EW and was able to follow the thoughts and actions of EW as a 'spectator'. Although an onlooker in EW's home life and aware of EW's feelings, EB did not participate in or share them. She dismissed as 'silly' EW's concerns about her failing marriage, and spoke of the devotion of EW to her 4-year-old daughter as 'something pretty corny'.
- EB could at first only be 'brought out' by the therapists while EW was under hypnosis. However, she could 'pop out' at any time in EW's life. The therapists did not know how she did this, but she would not come out at their request without hypnotising EW. However, after a few sessions using hypnosis it was possible to study the two personalities simply by asking one to allow the

other to come out to speak to the therapists. This helped the therapists, but it made life difficult for EW, as now EB found she could get out more and take over. EB being in control often made for unpleasant consequences for EW.

- EB was neither compassionate nor cruel to EW; she seemed unaffected by human emotions. EB was 'shallowly hedonistic', intent only on pleasure-seeking and fun in the present moment. Unfortunately for EW, 'fun' for EB had often meant 'mischief' as a child, and she reported having got EW into trouble with her parents at 6 years old. They had forbidden her from walking through the woods to play with children who lived on the other side, as they felt it was not safe. EB had done this, however, and had only let EW 'come out' to receive the 'whipping' for disobeying her parents.

- It soon became clear that EB was prone to lying. Her 'evidence' in therapy was therefore considered by the authors to be less reliable than that given by EW, who seemed honest and open. EW could substantiate some of EB's stories, however, agreeing that there were times as a child when she had received punishments from her parents without knowing the reason why. Some of EB's claims about her adult behaviour were substantiated by EW's husband and family.

- Until she agreed to be 'introduced' to them by the therapists, EB had managed to conceal herself from EW's family when she was out. She had done this by pretending to be Eve White (imitating her voice and mannerisms and behaviours). When EB's true character had been shown, EW's family considered the 'wayward behaviour, ill will, harshness and occasional acts of violence' as being 'unaccountable fits of temper in a woman [EW] habitually gentle and considerate' (p.139).

- On one occasion, EB 'recklessly bought several expensive and unneeded new dresses and two luxurious coats'. This caused EW's husband to go into a rage for 'wantonly plunging him into debt'. EW tried to protest her innocence, but of course, her husband did not accept this. He did calm down, however, when she agreed it would be a disaster for them to be in such debt and took the clothes back to the shop. EW told the therapists she thought her husband had planted the clothes to make her look as if she had gone mad. This fitted in with the problems they were having in their marriage. EB had not only been extravagant in her shopping, but also 'revels in cheap night clubs, flirting with men on the make.' She also told the therapists, 'When I go out and get drunk. . .*she* wakes up with the hangover. She wonders what in the hell's made her so sick.' Although EB had not been the cause of the marital problems between EW and her husband, it was clear that her behaviours when she was out did little to help overcome them, if indeed any sort of reconciliation were possible.

- Although usually indifferent to EW's 4-year-old daughter, EB did once hurt her, although she denied this (even though there was evidence to the contrary from EW's husband). She did confess to it later, saying flippantly, 'The little brat got on my nerves.'

With all this evidence, the therapists came to believe that EW and EB were indeed two separate personalities, taking turns in the same body. However, they recognised that it was difficult for them to explain to anyone else exactly *what* it was that made them believe that EB was different from EW, drawing the parallel that a man could pick out his wife from 100 other women looking and dressing similarly, but could not give the instructions to a stranger to do the same. They did, however, draw up a comparison between the two to try to catalogue the qualitative differences between them that, for Thigpen and Cleckley, marked out EW and EB as distinctly separate from each other.

FEATURE	EVE WHITE	EVE BLACK
SUMMARY OF CHARACTER	Demure, 'almost saintly'	Party girl, childishly vain, egocentric
FACE	Sweet and sad	Pixie-like eyes dance with mischief
DRESS AND BEHAVIOUR	Dresses sensibly (conservatively); has a stooped posture, is dignified; reads poetry; is well-liked, industrious and capable	Dresses provocatively, is witty, coarse and rowdy; likes to play pranks: her intent is fun, but the consequences are often cruel for others
ATTITUDE	Serious, and distressed by her current problems; did not blame her husband, loved her daughter deeply	Never serious, unaffected by human emotions, grief and tragedy
ALLERGY TO NYLON	Reported no such allergy	Claimed to be allergic to nylon and did not wear stockings when she was out for long periods

Source: **Adapted from pp.141–2**

Summary of differences between Eve White and Eve Black

Of course, this evidence is subjective, and in an attempt to satisfy scientific readers, Thigpen and Cleckley arranged for tests to be carried out to try to establish the two personalities as distinct from each another. Two types of tests were used: psychometric tests, where IQ and memory function were tested, and two projective tests, the Rorschach ink-blot test and a test drawing human figures.

KEY CONCEPTS

Projective tests

In a projective test, the subject is asked to draw something or look at something. The way they draw the figure, or what they 'see' in the ink blot, is supposed to reveal their personality; in other words, they 'project' themselves onto the test and this can supposedly be summarised by a person trained in administering the tests.

Whether such tests provide a valid description of the person is affected by the fact that the respondent may lie, manipulating their responses to try to give a good (or perhaps, bad) account of themselves. The test interpretation will also be affected by the prevailing beliefs of the psychiatric profession at the time of testing, or indeed the personal beliefs held by the tester.

The tests were carried out by a well-qualified expert. The findings are summarised in the table below.

Test	Eve White	Eve Black
Wechsler intelligence test (IQ)	110	104
Wechsler memory test	Superior	Inferior
Projective tests (human figure drawing and Rorschach test)	Indication of: • repression • conflict and anxiety in her role as mother • hostility to her mother	Indication of: • **regression** (the name she used was in fact the patient's maiden name), indicating a desire to return to an earlier period of life, before marriage

The findings from the tests are not conclusive and do not provide evidence that the two are separate from each other.

Attempts at therapy and the emergence of a third personality, Jane

Although a fascinating case for both the therapists and the reader, the purpose for the patient of being in consultation with the therapists was to get relief from her difficulties and distress. The therapists noted that in previously reported cases, the secondary personality 'helped' the other. There appeared to be no evidence of EB helping EW; in fact, all the evidence appeared to the contrary – EB's behaviour when she was out simply made matters worse for EW.

As a therapeutic intervention, Thigpen and Cleckley tried to encourage EB to help. She would, however, only help if it interested her to do so. She would lie and pretend to be helping when she was not, when in fact she was doing the opposite, and 'her behaviour was particularly detrimental to Eve White's progress' (p.142). They did, however, manage to encourage her to cooperate by bargaining with her. It became clear that now she was aware of her existence, EW could block EB out and prevent her from taking over (although EW was still not wholly successful at this). The therapists bargained with EB for good behaviour in return for more time out.

Further revelations came from EB at this point. She could influence EW even when she was not out. It was she, she claimed, who had been the voice EW had heard, and she who was responsible for giving EW headaches. She also claimed to be able to wipe out memories from Eve White, and she used this as an explanation for EW having no memory of beatings she was made to receive at the hands of a man with whom EB had cohabited prior to EW's own marriage. While there were no records of the 'marriage' a distant relative had described to the therapists, there was good evidence that she had lived with a man at this time, although EW denied this ever happened.

After about 8 months, it appeared that EW was indeed getting better. She was no longer with her husband, and her daughter was living with her parents. This latter point caused her great distress, but she was comforted by the fact that she was able to hold down a job and provide for her daughter. She was doing well in her job and was hopeful of a reunion with her husband. EB had been causing less trouble, and rarely 'came out' at work, which she found boring, because she did not want to interfere with the 'breadwinner' when she was earning her keep. However, in leisure hours she often 'got in bad company, picked up dates, and indulged in cheap and idle flirtations', but EW, unaware of this, was spared the embarrassment of this conduct.

However, at this point, when things seemed to be going so well, EW took a turn for the worse. The headaches and blackouts returned, and this time a room-mate found her unconscious twice as a result of the blackouts. What was different was that EB claimed not to be causing the headaches, and, although she did not get headaches, she claimed she was also experiencing the blackouts this time. She told the therapists, 'I don't know where we go, but go we do.'

EW found it hard to work and her new-found confidence waned. It looked as if she would have to be hospitalised, as the therapists thought 'a psychosis was impending'. Although they kept this from EW, they told EB about it by way of warning her off mischief: if EW was put in an institution, so would she be, and this would greatly curtail her activities!

Thigpen and Cleckley also attempted to fuse the two personalities together, on the assumption that they had somehow started off as integrated and later fractured. They did this by trying to call both personalities out at the same time, but this caused the patient more distress and they stopped attempting it.

They then approached this aim by trying to work back into childhood with the two personalities, presumably to take them back to the point where EB emerged. They were able to do this with EW through hypnosis, but never managed to hypnotise EB.

Soon after the headaches and blackouts had returned, EW was in such a session, recalling a painful experience when she had been scalded by hot water as a child, when:

> As she spoke her eyes shut sleepily. Her head dropped back on the chair. After remaining in this sleep or trance perhaps two minutes her eyes opened. Blankly she stared about the room, looking at the furniture and the pictures as if trying to orient herself. Continuing their apparently bewildered survey, her eyes finally met those of the therapist, and stopped. Slowly, with an unknown husky voice, and with immeasurable poise, she spoke. 'Who are you?' (p.144)

Thigpen and Cleckley say it was apparent that this was neither EB nor EW. A third personality had 'come out', and the therapists called her Jane. They studied this 'other woman' and described her as follows:

> she apparently lacks EB's obvious faults and inadequacies. She also impresses us as far more mature, more vivid, more boldly capable and more interesting than EW. . . in her [Jane] are indications of initiative and powerful resources never shown by the other [EW]. (p.145)

The differences between Eve White, Eve Black and Jane

By their descriptions, it is clear that Thigpen and Cleckley could identify EW, EB and Jane by their demeanour and behaviour. But again, this is subjective evidence.

Two more experts were brought in to study the now three personalities, for evidence of observable distinctions between them that would support the diagnosis of multiple-personality disorder. The handwriting of each was analysed by an expert who concluded that 'beyond any doubt they have been written by one and the same individual'. An EEG was used to record and compare their brainwave activity. The results were as follows:

Eve White	Jane	Eve Black
11 cycles per second (normal)	11 cycles per second (normal)	12.5 cycles per second, a slightly fast EEG reading that is sometimes associated with psychopathic personality

Jane and EW could not be distinguished from each other; they were both described as 'normal'. EB, however, was borderline-normal and was distinguishable from Jane and EW.

The way forward for the patient?

Having studied the three personalities for some time, the therapists came to see Jane taking over as a possible answer to EW's problems:

> As time passes, Jane stays 'out' more and more. She emerges only through EW, never yet having found a way to displace EB or to communicate through her. (p.146)

They describe Jane as compassionate for EW's distress and able to come out and help EW at work. They say:

> Could Jane remain in full possession of that integrated human functioning we call personality our patient would probably, we believe, regain full health, eventually adjust satisfactorily, perhaps at a distinctly superior level and find her way to a happy life. (p.146)

However, they claim that it was neither their intent, nor was it in their power, to bring about such an outcome. They ask: 'Would any physician order euthanasia of the heedlessly merry and **amoral** but nevertheless unique EB?'

Although Jane would be a good mother to EW's daughter, and probably would not return to EW's husband and the problems of the marriage, would 'killing off' EW, or allowing her to 'leave forever' for her child's sake be the right answer? Jane thought not. She wrote to the therapists, having 'seen' EW apparently saving a child from being knocked down in the street: 'She [EW] must not die yet. There is so much I must know, and so very much I must learn from her. . .'; and on the saving of the child: 'I have never been thus affected by anything in my four months of life'.

Jane had shared knowledge of both Eves' behaviours after her own emergence, but had no access to experiences or memories of either Eve before she had first emerged, knowing only what she had been told. EW was conscious of neither Jane nor EB, although she was aware of their existence through the reports of the therapists. EB was aware of EW but not of Jane.

DISCUSSION

Thigpen and Cleckley considered that they may not have observed a true case of MPD, but may have been 'thoroughly hoodwinked by a skilful actress' (p.147). However, given that the therapy went on for an extended period of time, during which they noted nothing that would suggest the patient was faking, they state: 'We do not think that any person could over months avoid even one tell-tale error or imperfection.'

Was Eve White's disintegration of personality due to schizophrenia? Thigpen and Cleckley considered this to be unlikely, since none of the personalities showed any symptoms of that disorder.

In moving towards the diagnosis of MPD, Thigpen and Cleckley concede that they may have lost their objectivity because of their involvement with the patient, and therefore their judgement was affected by their relationship with her. They point out that while the three personalities appeared distinct and separate to the therapists, the evidence from objective testing was 'not particularly impressive', and could not provide clear evidence of distinctions between EW, EB and Jane.

The therapists were careful not to make the claim that the case was indeed one of MPD, but suggest that the experiences of their client raised a number of important questions for both psychology and psychiatry. What do we mean by 'personality'? How are we to describe it?

They discuss the case of Mrs Beauchamp, presented by Morton Prince in 1909, and suggest that a review of his work and further study of patients with MPD in the future might give psychiatrists the necessary insight to explain that which could not be explained scientifically at the time of writing up the case of Eve White.

COMMENTARY: METHODS AND ISSUES

What are the strengths and weaknesses of the case study method illustrated in this study?

The strengths include the large amount of detailed and qualitative data gathered about the patient in over 100 hours of therapy. The longitudinal nature of the study made it harder for the patient, if she was faking, to keep up any pretence.

The weaknesses include the possibility that the researchers' relationship with the patient may have affected their judgement of the case and led to them being unwittingly 'fooled' by the patient, or indeed overlooking any evidence that might have suggested she was 'play-acting', or evidence of any other explanation for the behaviour they observed.

Does the study raise any ethical concerns?

The study was governed by medical ethics at the time, rather than the ethical guidelines for research with human participants in use today. The use of a pseudonym was an ethical consideration to protect the patient and her family on publication of the case. The researchers also raise the point of whether it is ethical to 'kill off' one of the personalities (if the disappearance of one of them was akin to their 'death') in therapy.

Is the study useful?

As it presented an intriguing case and asks thought-provoking questions about our use of the term 'personality', the study is useful in encouraging us to further our understanding of human behaviour and experience. However, whether the findings in this unique case can be useful, even to a particular client group, is questionable. The number of people with such a disorder is very small, and it is possible that their differences would so greatly outweigh their similarities as to make the experience of one such case bear little resemblance to any other.

Is the study valid/reliable?

If Eve White was just a 'skilful actress' then the study is not valid. The dependence of the diagnosis on self-report of the patient's experiences contributes still to the debate surrounding DID. The study is quite low in ecological validity, since the data were gathered by self-report in therapy sessions, and therefore may not be a true representation of Eve's everyday behaviour.

It is very difficult, if not impossible, to establish the reliability of abnormal cases such as that of Eve White, which are very rare, if not unique. Replication of case studies in general is difficult because of the extent and detail of the investigations carried out, and in any case we would be unlikely to find someone equivalent to Eve White to investigate.

Postscript

The real name of the subject for this key study was Chris Sizemore. She wrote a book called *I'm Eve* (Sizemore and Pittillo 1977), where she maintained that Thigpen and Cleckley's case study was just the tip of the iceberg. She reported that her personality continued to fragment after the end of the therapy, until 21 separate alters inhabited her body. She stated that there were nine before the time of her therapy and that Thigpen and Cleckley never managed to make contact with them all. There were a number of traumatic events in her childhood which may have caused this fragmentation, although none of them was sexual in nature. She had seen a man drown when she was about 2 years of age, and had witnessed another cut into pieces by a saw at a timber yard. One event which left her traumatised, and may well have been at the root of the fragmentation, was when she was held high off the floor by her mother and made to touch the face of her dead grandmother. She was 5 years old at the time, but even as an adult she could remember the clammy cold cheek. Sizemore believes that the reason she developed these separate personalities was as a way of coping with the harshness of her life.

In 2006, Chris Sizemore and her son Bobby, who is a school guidance counsellor, spoke to students at Stetson University in the USA. They had decided to speak to the university because some of the students at the university had been counselled by Bobby when they were still at school. The university provided a report of the event and the information here is taken and adapted slightly from the Stetson University website.

The focus of the discussion enabled Chris to talk of her struggles with DID. She explained that she had now been 'healed' for 30 years. Her son also talked about what it was like growing up with a mother who had the condition, and said that he could tell, by looking at her eyes, whenever a role-change had taken place.

During the discussion, Bobby explained that his favourite alter was known as the Retrace Lady: She was 'the one I considered my truest mother as I was growing up. She went away during the integration (of the personalities into a whole)'. He also talked about his least favourite, known as Strawberry Girl. He explained that he was shopping on one occasion with the Retrace Lady when he briefly left the store to go to a nearby drugstore. When he returned, he found the Retrace Lady had disappeared and Strawberry Girl had taken her place. 'She had filled more than three shopping carts with every strawberry-flavoured food item she could find in the store.'

Bobby also explained that the only sacrifice he made growing up was the inability to invite friends to his house. He felt safe among all the personalities he met, although he favoured some more than others. He said his older sister Taffy and his father provided family stability. 'I give my sister and father all the credit in dealing with the situation,' he said. 'My sister raised me many times and deserves the majority of the credit for the way the family dealt with (the situation).' His father as breadwinner assumed a burden of expensive medical treatment. Together, they coped as a family in an era when people facing mental challenges were routinely placed in asylums.

Chris explained that she had received more than 40 years of psychotherapy under the care of Dr Tony Tsitos. One questioner asked her why the personality changes stopped. She explained that 'I think of it as a healing'. Tsitos helped her to heal herself by letting 'each personality solve her own problems and let the others know'. In the past, severe headaches accompanied the personality changes. Chris said that when she gets a headache now, the doctor tells her to take an aspirin.

One student asked how Chris deals with people who challenge that MPD is not a real disorder. 'That's their problem,' she joked, before saying that

Duke University researchers analysed the brushstrokes of paintings created by her seven artist personalities. Each had a distinct brushstroke.

Chris said her many personalities arose in response to 'hurtful events' during childhood. Today, 'I don't need them,' she said of the personalities. 'As a whole person, I can face my realities and deal with them.'

See the CD-ROM for further reading with a link to the Stetson University website.

Risk–taking behaviours

Introduction

Some people like nothing better than to sit down and watch a really good film in the warm, while others may prefer to surf in an icy-cold sea in November, or leap out of an aeroplane with only a piece of silk to stop them from crashing to the earth. Some people are interested in art, history or ballet, while others could imagine nothing more boring than walking round an art gallery and would rather climb into underground caverns, often full of water, with only a torch to light their way. Some people like to go on holiday to hot countries and laze about by the pool all day reading a book, while others would rather hike across the countryside, camp on the side of a mountain and battle against the elements. Some people are willing to gamble large sums of money when the outcome is uncertain, while others would rather save their money and ensure it is safe.

What is it that makes some people more adventurous or more willing to take risks than others? Is it something fundamental about their physical make-up or personality that makes them behave as they do, or is it simply that some people think very differently to others due to their past experiences?

Risks exist when things that we consider valuable, such as our money or our life, are placed in a precarious situation. Some risks are the result of choice – for example, parachuting, when we are putting our lives at risk – while others are not within our control. On the other hand, when we think about risks, we also think about gains – for example a large win at the bookie's or the adrenaline high from flying in the air – and this makes us realise that risky situations may also provide opportunities and experiences that would be unavailable to us if we did not to put ourselves in that situation.

'Anyone want to buy a raffle ticket? It's for a good cause. Only £1 a strip.'

Frank heard the request from across the room and felt his pulse begin to race. 'Yeah, mate, give me 10 strips,' he said, before he could stop himself.

> 'Oh, Frank, that's such a lot of money,' said his wife quietly, while tugging at his sleeve, but by this time Frank was on a roll. 'Give me another five,' he said, 'just in case.'
>
> Edward Jones was watching with his wife Enid. 'Shall I buy some?' he asked her quietly.
>
> 'You never win anyway,' said Enid, walking off to look at the cake stall.
>
> 'I will have some,' said Cheryl Brown, 'but I only want pink ones and they must be numbers under 100. Do you want any, Ralph? You always seem to get the winning ticket.'

Raffles are a kind of risk taking behaviour, albeit a less 'dangerous' form than others we have mentioned, and we all know about raffles. We gamble money when we buy tickets, hoping that when the tickets are randomly drawn out of a hat, we will have a winning number. Every person has exactly the same chance of winning, yet the characters in the example above all have very different perceptions about their chances of winning. Some people are very cautious (Enid); some enter the challenge but need to follow certain simple rules, known as **heuristics** (Cheryl); and others have no restraints on their behaviour, finding pleasure in the uncertainty (Frank).

Some types of gambling do have an element of obvious skill, such as playing certain card games, or betting on horses if their form is known prior to the race (form might take into account the horse's breeding and past performance, as well as the breeding and past performance of their rivals). Many other forms of gambling involve nothing more than chance when it comes to winning, such as **fruit machines**, dice games, roulette, raffles and, of course, the National Lottery. The frightening thing is that although everyone really does *know* that most methods of gambling are a game of chance rather than something that can be predicted, individuals have still lost fortunes on the roll of a dice.

In an attempt to answer our earlier question about what it is that makes some people more adventurous or more willing to take risks than others, we are now going to look at gambling. Although gambling is not typical of all risk-taking behaviours, it is a subject with which we are all familiar and when you consider the levels of losses and gains, it can involve enormous risk. It can also be studied more easily in controlled laboratory situations in order to help us understand the cognitive processes that gamblers (and therefore other risk takers) may use.

Gambling and psychoanalytical theory

Psychoanalytical theorists such as Freud would suggest that risk-taking behaviour was not 'normal' and may indicate a disturbed mind or someone with a death wish (remember Thanatos, the death instinct from Chapter 4). However, there is no evidence to support the idea that risk takers are disturbed or wish to take their own lives. In fact, psychological research into the mental health of people who take risks has been inconclusive, or even contradictory and in some cases undertaking risky behaviours, such as sailing round the world, has led to increased pride and self-esteem. More evidence to indicate that risk-taking behaviours are not intended to be self-destructive can be seen by considering risk takers in the workplace, many of whom reach the highest levels of success.

Gambling and evolutionary theories

If you were a parent and your offspring were hungry, and the only way they would eat was for you to take the risk of getting hurt while you hunted wild animals, do you think you would be prepared to take that risk? It would seem that people often think about needs rather than safety, and therefore risk taking could be considered a survival mechanism. Perhaps it is a throwback to the times when only the fittest survived because although the danger from hunting food is past in most modern societies (after all, the supermarket is hardly a dangerous place) the desire may be hard-wired in the brain somehow.

Another theory is that animals take risks for social reasons. Under normal circumstances, when it comes to finding a mate, the beta male (the less superior male) would not stand a chance over an alpha male. By taking risks, the beta male would not have to demonstrate superiority. Instead, if he achieved something by taking a risk which he would not have achieved otherwise, it would make him more attractive as a mate. Interestingly, some studies have also found this phenomenon in humans (Zuckerman 1994), demonstrating that people who engage in risky sports (e.g. parachuting) are viewed as more sexually attractive.

Gambling and personality

There is considerable evidence to suggest that risk takers have a certain personality type. Zuckerman (1950) identified what he called a 'sensation seeking' trait, after carrying out a number of sensory deprivation experiments, which involved individuals being kept in darkness or extreme quiet, in order to look at the effect on human behaviour. He began to suspect that the volunteers for these experiments might share similar personality characteristics, and identified that they were especially adventurous and eager to have new exciting experiences, even if they did involve a degree of risk.

According to Llewellyn (2003), further studies have indicated that people who engage in various high-risk behaviours tend to share the same characteristics, and many of these traits seem to be genetically determined (approximately 60 per cent). Llewellyn also explains that on average men score higher in the sensation-seeking trait than women, although the trait tends to decline as people age. This helps to explain why young men are more likely to die of risky behaviour than women.

Gambling as a genetic predisposition

Black et al. (2006) discovered that pathological gambling does seem to run in families. Their study consisted of interviews with 31 pathological gamblers and 31 controls, and their first-degree relatives (parents, siblings and children). The study chose to look at first-degree relatives because they shared 50 per cent of their genes with the gambler or the control subject. The belief was that if the disorder actually does run in families, it is more likely to become apparent in close relatives, and their findings supported this claim. Donald Black explains:

> Something is being passed along in these families that increases the person's likelihood of engaging in impulsive and ultimately self-destructive behaviour. In some people, it manifests as substance abuse, in others as antisocial behaviour, and in others, gambling. Often the three are combined.

Another study looked at a genetic cause for gambling, by investigating gambling behaviour among 3,359 twin pairs from the Vietnam Era Twin Registry. The findings suggested that there is a genetic vulnerability that underlies gambling problems of varying severities (Eisen et al. 2001). The study also concluded that the co-occurrence of pathological gambling with conduct disorder, antisocial personality disorder, and alcohol abuse/dependence could be partially explained by genes which influence all these behaviours.

Perhaps the day will come when we can accurately correlate all pathological gambling with brain neurochemicals (e.g. watching how risk-taking behaviours rise as the level of a particular neurotransmitter rises). We could then attempt to establish how different genes affect the neurotransmitter systems in our bodies. This would give us the opportunity to identify those who are most likely to become serious risk takers in the gambling stakes.

Gambling as a result of physiological factors

In February 2006, Max Wells, a retired physician from Texas, filed a lawsuit in the USA against GlaxoSmithKline and seven Las Vegas casinos, claiming that side effects of a drug he was taking for **Parkinson's disease** had caused him to lose $14 million. He cited as evidence a study by Leann Dodd et al. (2005), which found that 11 patients with Parkinson's disease who were being treated using a **dopamine agonist** (a chemical that mimics dopamine levels, which are low in Parkinson's patients), all developed pathological gambling behaviours. **Dopamine** works on the limbic system – a set of brain structures, including the hippocampus and amygdala, which supports a variety of functions, including our emotions (see Chapter 5). It plays a central role in the behavioural reward system of both humans and animals, reinforcing all sorts of productive and counterproductive behaviours by making the person feel a sense of enjoyment, which in turn, reinforces the motivation to continue doing the same activity.

If we accept that changed levels of dopamine might affect risk-taking behaviour, then perhaps gamblers' behaviour is somehow affected by their biochemical make-up. There are a number of reasons why dopamine levels in the body may vary – genetic disorders, for example. What we do know is that stress certainly causes an increase. Perhaps risk takers experience high levels of stress? Certainly, some gamblers say that gambling is a way of forgetting their problems.

Gambling as a learned behaviour

Perhaps gambling is a learned behaviour which could be explained both by operant conditioning and social learning theory. If we begin with operant conditioning, we could see how someone might gamble and win initially, and this would act as a **positive reinforcement** to do it again (see Chapter 4). In fact, theories of reinforcement indicate that the most effective form of **reinforcement** is **variable ratio reinforcement**. This is when you know that rewards (reinforcement) will eventually be given, but cannot anticipate when they will occur, so you continue to gamble. **Fruit machines** work on this principle, which is why we keep playing.

See Additional Reading on the CD-ROM.

The other learning theory that might explain gambling is social learning theory, which suggests that we learn how to behave from others (see Chapter 2). We are more likely to learn and maintain behaviours that are seen as appealing and have been reinforced – possibly by seeing someone winning. It would therefore make sense that children who see close family members, who are significant role models, engage in gambling, are more likely to copy them.

Gupta and Derevensky (1997) questioned 477 American children between the ages of 9 and 14 about their gambling activities. They found that 86 per cent of children who gambled regularly did so with family members. They also found that over the previous 12 months:

- 53 per cent had gambled with their siblings;

- 40 per cent had gambled with their parents;

- 46 per cent had gambled with other relatives;

- 75 per cent had gambled in their own homes.

The children's responses also indicated that 81 per cent of the sample had gambled at one point in their life, and 52 per cent reported gambling once a week or more. Eleven per cent said that gambling made them feel important; 27 per cent felt they gambled more than they should; and only 10 per cent of those aged 13–14 were worried about being caught gambling, which suggests that gambling was seen by the vast majority as socially acceptable.

However, not all children who witness gambling go on to copy this behaviour, so there may be other factors at work here.

343

Gambling as a social phenomenon

There has always been a link between social class and gambling, with the assertion that those on lower incomes run the greatest risks from gambling. However, results from the British Gambling Prevalence Survey (1999) supported the idea that different forms of gambling were preferred by different social classes (as defined by occupation). For example, gambling in casinos was preferred by the more affluent, while those in the lower socio-economic groups preferred bingo. Casino gambling, private bets and some aspects of horse racing were *positively* linked to income (that is, the more money available, the more upmarket the venue and greater the level of bets), whereas bingo was *negatively* related to income (the less money available, the more people would bet). On the other hand, horse racing and gambling on fruit machines were more or less classless.

Generally, the findings were that gambling activities bore little relationship to income group, although it appeared that people on lower incomes spent more on gambling as an overall percentage of their income. Problem gambling was more prevalent in the unemployed, in households where the main income came from manual labour, and where the total household income was very low. The survey also indicated that younger people and individuals on small incomes (e.g. students) were the least likely to gamble.

The Family Expenditure Survey (2000–2001) collected data on household expenditure on the National Lottery in the UK. The results indicated that households headed by someone in the skilled manual social class was the most likely to buy lottery tickets, while professional households were the least likely. Perhaps the reason for these trends was the belief that the only way the 'working-class' families with low incomes would ever manage to accrue any amount of money would be to have a large win.

Gambling as an addiction

Perhaps the reason why some people want to gamble is because it has become a kind of **addiction** – this would mean that rational decision making is not possible. If we accept the Canadian Mental Health Education Resource Centre's definition, which describes an addiction as 'a behavioural pattern characterized by compulsion, loss of control, and continued repetition of a behaviour or activity in spite of adverse consequences', we can see that this might be the case.

When we consider what we mean by an addiction, we usually assume that the addiction is to something like drugs or alcohol which, when withdrawn, will produce unpleasant physical and psychological symptoms. Mark Griffiths is leading the way in broadening the definition of addiction to include other activities such as gambling, overeating, exercise, computer games and using mobile phones to name just a few, and he believes that we need to view addiction in its broadest sense. He has studied what he calls 'pathological gamblers' for more than 20 years and in 1996 he argued that there is a set of features which is common to all addictions:

- Salience: the activity becomes the most important thing in their lives and dominates their thinking, making them crave the activity and effectively taking over their social lives.

- Mood modification: they become highly aroused when engaging in the behaviour.

- **Tolerance:** they need to keep increasing the activity in order to achieve the same level of enjoyment.

- Withdrawal symptoms: if they stop the behaviour they feel physical and psychological discomfort.

- Conflict: the activity conflicts with the rest of the person's life and may put them in a state of conflict and discomfort.

- Relapse: even if the person gives up the activity, it is very likely that they will relapse.

On the other hand, Walker (1989: 179) is concerned about whether theories of addiction can be generalised to include excessive gambling:

> A new category of psychological addictions is defined as 'a persistent behavioral pattern characterized by: a desire or need to continue the activity which places it outside voluntary control; a tendency to increase the frequency or amount of the activity over time; psychological dependence on the pleasurable effects of the activity; and, a detrimental effect on the individual and society.'

Walker compares drug addictions with the 'repeated ingestion of nonessential substances which are not drugs', and 'activities which are engaged in excessively', and he concludes that 'in neither case can the category of drug addiction be extended to include these other activities without losing the essential meaning of *drug addiction*' (ibid.).

The decision as to whether gambling can be considered a 'true' addiction is left to you to decide, but for the purpose of this discussion we will accept that there are such people as 'gambling addicts'. If this is the case, perhaps their addiction can explain the risky behaviours they become involved in. They may become totally obsessed with the activity so that it dominates their thoughts. They become excited and elated when they do gamble and as time goes on they have to take more and more risks in order to achieve the same level of enjoyment. As we know, high levels of arousal do not go hand in hand with clarity of thought so their thinking may become distorted, which explains why their behaviour might be irrational.

Gambling and cognitive bias

When trying to understand the reasons for the huge differences in human behaviour, ranging from one extreme to the other, we can only hypothesise. So far we have considered a range of possible explanations as to why some people gamble and others do not, yet we have no definite cause. (We might draw a parallel here with the research into autism: if a definite cause were to be found, the management of 'problem behaviours' would become much easier – see Chapter 3, page 108.) It may be we have to conclude that there is no single, definite cause, and instead try to identify what people who engage in gambling have in common. The answer to that seems to be their cognitive style.

If we consider how we would make decisions in an ideal world, these would be based on gathering all the information in front of us and being able to look at every possible answer until the correct answer was found – very similar to the solving of **algorithms** in mathematics. This way of processing information is very time-consuming and laborious, and often we do not have all the information available, so we may need to refer to past experiences that have led to a 'correct' conclusion, or look at what is available and use our intuition to help us make the appropriate choice. The second strategy, known as heuristics is described by Kahney (1993) as 'rule of thumb, problem solving methods which often succeed but do not guarantee a solution to a problem'. Both these strategies have been studied by psychologists investigating problem solving and decision making in humans.

The rules of thumb used by gamblers are frequently based on stereotypical or preconceived ideas. Gamblers may intuitively compare the situation with their preconceived ideas or limited knowledge, believing that their knowledge represents how things really are. Gross (2005: 446) described the gambler's fallacy very effectively in the following example:

Consider the following possible outcomes of tossing a coin 6 times:

First go: H   H   H   H   H   H

Second go: T   T   T   H   H   H

Third go: H   T   T   H   T   H

Which of these three is the least and which is the most likely?

Most people believe the first outcome is the least likely of the three and the third the most likely. In fact, the probability of the three sequences is identical. Our assumption that coin tossing produces a random sequence of heads and tails leads us to decide that the third is the most likely (because it looks the most random). Such a belief will affect the way that gamblers behave. If they had tried to solve the puzzle using an algorithm, they would have found the correct answer, but may well have spent all day trying to figure it out.

Attributional bias

There are other cognitive biases that are used by gamblers which affect the way they make decisions. One such bias relates to a social psychological concept known as the **fundamental attribution error**. When we attribute causes to someone's behaviour, we are biased towards the view that they are doing something 'because they are like that'.

We believe that what we are seeing them do is what they would always do in a similar situation. We are actually making two mistakes here: we are ignoring the situational factors which influence their behaviour, and we are assuming that people are consistent in their behaviour, which often they are not. Now imagine this in terms of gambling. We sometimes attribute causes to the behaviour of inanimate objects, for example suggesting that the roulette wheel never gives a certain number, or that the row of pears never appears on a fruit machine.

Another related attributional bias is the **actor–observer effect**. This suggests that the fundamental attribution error occurs when we are describing the behaviour of someone else (when we are the observer), but when we are describing our own behaviour (when we are the actor), we tend to describe it in terms of the situation we were in at the time, rather than in terms of our persistent characteristics. This leads to a further bias, called the **self-serving bias**. Here we tend to attribute the cause which presents us in the best light and allows us to preserve our self-esteem. For example, if you got an A in your AS psychology, you might say: 'I am a hard-working, fantastic student and my success is evidence of my brilliance' (an internal attribution); but if you got a U, you might say: 'The textbook was rubbish, so how could I have been expected to pass?' (a situational attribution). Again, in terms of gambling, when the gambler wins it is because they are skilful, whereas when they lose it is because the fruit machine has been tampered with or rigged.

Irrationality

These false beliefs can often explain the irrationality of gamblers. Walker (1992) investigated the false beliefs held by regular gamblers in Australia, and considered whether these were the reason why they persisted in trying to win money. He recruited 27 university students who played either **fruit machines**, **video poker** (like playing against a computer rather than another player) or video amusement games at least twice a week.

The participants played their preferred machines on site (e.g. in clubs, hotels and amusement arcades), playing two games for at least 30 minutes, and then two further games for a minimum of 20 minutes each. The participants had to describe into a microphone what they were doing or what they were thinking about the game (the **thinking aloud method**).

Walker found that:

- 38 per cent of the statements made by fruit machine players when playing were categorised as irrational;

- 80 per cent of the strategic statements (what they were actually doing) made by fruit machine players while playing were categorised as irrational.

The results indicated that fruit machine players verbalised more irrational thoughts than the video poker or video amusement players. They also exhibited greater amounts of irrational thinking when playing their preferred game.

Why do we gamble?

By now it should be clear that the rationale by which some people become involved in risk-taking behaviours such as gambling are numerous. We may understand many of the possible reasons why people gamble – including social class, family experiences, genetic predispositions, neurobiological causes, personality type or cognitive style. However, it is impossible to give one overriding reason why some people gamble excessively and recklessly, why some enjoy the thrill of gambling but do not let it get out of control, and why some have no interest in gambling at all. Perhaps the reason why this occurs is that people with certain predispositions will only *continue* to gamble if they have a particular cognitive style, rather than cognitive style being a cause in itself.

Whatever the causes of our behaviour – whether this is related to social or physiological factors, cognitive style or personality – it certainly appears that no two people think in exactly the same way, and even when they do use the same types of cognitive bias, these biases are slightly different, having been based on their individual experiences.

THE STUDY

M.D. Griffiths (1994) 'The role of cognitive bias and skill in fruit machine gambling'

British Journal of Psychology, 85: 351–69

BACKGROUND

Griffiths begins by explaining that Corney and Cummings (1985) have identified the fact that humans show a number of consistent cognitive biases when processing information. Previous studies of gambling have focused mainly on the illusion of control, which was described by Langer (1975), and explained by Griffiths as 'an expectancy of success higher than the objective probability would warrant' (p.352).

Consider the following situations:

- When you are selecting your own lottery numbers and choice is a factor.
- When you are playing your favourite fruit machine.

Do you think the outcome is under your control in some way? In reality, you have no control, even though you may falsely assume that you do. The outcome is actually a matter of chance.

Wagenaar (1988: 30) considered current and past research into gambling and compared '**normative decision theory**' and 'heuristics and biases' (see below). He concluded that gambling is influenced by cognitive thought processes, and it is these processes which serve to motivate gamblers, rather than 'defects of personality, education or social environment'.

Wagenaar suggests that gamblers actually use a range of **cognitive distortions**, and that although they do not use heuristics more than non-gamblers, they do 'select heuristics at the wrong occasion'. He indicates that when gamblers use heuristics, they feel they have reduced the overall uncertainty of their bet (although this is not really the case).

KEY CONCEPTS

Normative decision theory/descriptive decision theory
In an ideal world, when we make a decision we would like that decision to be the best decision. If the person making the decision is rational, able to think clearly and aware of all the facts, it is likely that the decision will be the correct one. The theory of how this would work is called normative decision theory. The trouble is, how often does this actually happen?

Normative decision theory is a theory about how decisions should be made in a rational world (like using algorithms). **Descriptive decision theory**, on the other hand, deals with how people actually make decisions.

Normative decision theory would make it possible to predict what sort of choices a gambler would make. The problem is that because gambling is an irrational activity, the theory would predict that people would not gamble in the first place (Wagenaar 1988).

KEY CONCEPTS

Heuristics

Heuristics are simple, efficient rules which have been proposed to explain how people make decisions, come to judgements and solve problems. On the whole, these work well in practice, but they can contain cognitive biases or distortions, such as the fundamental attribution error.

Griffiths indicates that the most significant distortions used by gamblers are as follows:

- *Illusion of control* – when gamblers have a higher expectation of winning than is probable because there is an illusion of being able to control what is going on.
- *Hindsight bias* – when retrospectively people are not surprised about what has happened and even believe they predicted the outcome (of a chance event); for example, 'I knew I'd land on Mayfair!' in a game of Monopoly, when of course this depends on a roll of the dice – pure chance (mentioned by Griffiths but not described in the study).
- *Flexible attributions* – when gamblers see their successes as being due to their own level of skill and their failures as due to external forces.
- *Representative bias* – when people mistakenly believe that a sample of results are representative of all results. For example, if they win the first few bets, they believe that these wins are going to represent the level of success for the rest of the night.
- *Availability bias* – when someone uses available information or experience to evaluate the probability of the same thing happening again; for example, if you hear others winning on slot machines, you think this is the norm.
- *Illusory correlations* – the superstitious belief that events go together even when they do not. For example, Henslin (1967) identified that craps players roll dice slowly if they wanted to get a low number and hard if they want a high number.
- *Fixation on absolute frequency* – gamblers measure their success by looking at the number of times they win in a session, rather than considering the relative frequency of wins overall.

These cognitive distortions may explain why some gamblers do not learn by their previous mistakes, and might help to explain their supposedly irrational behaviours. Griffiths does point out, however, that they are not very useful as

Table 1
Summary of heuristics and biases used by gamblers (adapted from Wagenaar 1988)

Heuristic	Brief definition
Availability	The case with which specific instances can be recalled from memory thus affecting probability judgements
Problem framing	When the context in which the problem is framed determines the choice of strategy
Confirmation bias	Seeking information that is consistent with one's own views and discounting disconfirming information
Fixation on absolute frequency	Using absolute rather than relative frequency is used as a measure of success
Concrete information bias	When concrete information such as that based on vivid memories or conspicuous incidents dominates abstract information such as computations or statistical data
Illusory correlation	Variables that seem to covary when in fact they do not
Inconsistency of processing	The inability to apply a consistent judgemental strategy over a series of cases
Non-linear extrapolation	The difficulty in estimating joint probabilities of simple events
Reliance on habits	The choosing of alternatives because it is customary to do so
Representativeness	The judgement of the likelihood of an event made by estimating its similarity to the class of which the event is supposed to be an exemplar
Justifiability	When the justifiable rule is preferred over a rule for which no justification can be given
Reduction of complexity	When complex decision problems are reduced to simple ones before a decision can be made
Illusion of control	When uncertain outcome of an activity can by itself induce in a person feelings of control over the uncertain outcome
Biased learning structures	When observed outcomes yield incomplete information concerning predictive relationships
Flexible attribution	The tendency to attribute successes to one's own skill and failures to other influences
Hindsight bias	When retrospectively people are not surprised about what has happened and even believe they predicted the outcome

predictors of behaviour, as the same heuristic may not be used in all situations, not even by the same individual.

In this study, Griffiths describes the cognitive psychology of fruit machine players, considering the cognitive variables that are involved in gambling with fruit machines:

- Regular fruit machine gamblers consider their actions to be due in some part to skill. Griffiths tested whether this skill was real or simply a mistaken perception on the part of the gamblers.
- Some addicted fruit machine gamblers understand fully that in the long run they will lose every penny that they gamble. However, there is a still a chance to 'win', in terms of how long they can stay on the machine for their money, with

the goal being to stay on the machine for as long as possible using the least money, 'playing with money rather than for it' (p.354). Gamblers implied that skill would be required in order to be able to do this. Skill is being defined here as 'the ability of the individual to affect the outcome of gambling positively (e.g. more gambles with initial money staked and/or more winnings with initial money staked (p.354). Griffiths investigated the level of skill that regular and non-regular gamblers assign to themselves and to playing fruit machines in general.

- Cognitive biases are used by fruit machine gamblers (e.g. specialist features such as 'nudge', 'hold' and 'gamble' buttons give the gambler the illusion of control). Griffiths investigated whether the cognitive biases would be used more by regular than non-regular fruit machine gamblers. Would regular gamblers be more irrational? By 'irrational' Griffiths means 'incompatible or contrary to reason, e.g. **personification of the machine**' (p.354). Personification means treating the machine or talking to it as if it were a person, with its own thoughts, intentions and emotions (e.g. 'it wants me to win'; 'this machine hates me today').

AIMS AND HYPOTHESES

- Hypothesis 1: the level of skill that regular gamblers report is perceived, and when objectively observed there would be no differences between regular and non-regular fruit machine gamblers on level of skill.
- Hypothesis 2: regular fruit machine gamblers would produce more irrational verbalisations when asked to use the talking aloud method than non-regular fruit machine gamblers.

- Hypothesis 3: regular fruit machine gamblers would describe themselves as more highly skilled at fruit machine gambling, and would be of the opinion that fruit machine gambling requires a higher level of skill than that reported by non-regular fruit machine gamblers.
- Hypothesis 4: gamblers in the thinking aloud condition would take longer to complete the task than those tested in the non-thinking aloud condition (see Procedure, below).

METHOD

Subjects

A total of 60 subjects were tested: 44 male, 16 female, with a mean age of 23.4 years. All had played fruit machines at least once in their lives. Beyond this, they fell into two groups – see the table below.

The sample was made up mostly of volunteers, who responded to a small poster put up at the university and local college campuses in Plymouth. In addition, some of the regular gamblers were recruited by a regular gambler who Griffiths knew.

30 regular fruit machine gamblers who played fruit machines at least once a week	30 non-regular fruit machine gamblers who played fruit machines once a month or less
29 male 1 female* mean age 21.6 years	15 male 15 female* mean age 25.3 years

*Griffiths acknowledges the gender imbalance, but notes that fruit machine gambling is male-dominated, so regular female gamblers would be relatively rare.

Design

This was a field experiment, carried out in a local amusement arcade, with the owner's full support, using an independent groups design.

A field experiment was used to avoid the possibility that a laboratory setting for a test of fruit machine gambling might be low in ecological validity.

Procedure

- All subjects were tested individually.
- Each subject was given a £3 stake to gamble on a fruit machine (= 30 'free' gambles).
- All were asked to try to stay on the machine for a minimum of 60 gambles (break even and win back £3 with their stake).

- At 60 gambles, each subject was given the option to stop and keep any winnings or to carry on gambling.
- Griffiths notes that gambling with your own money has been shown in some studies to be a determining factor in the excitement and risk taking associated with gambling. He also noted that gambling with someone else's money has been shown to have a disinhibiting effect (makes you stop, holds you back). However, he quotes evidence from Ladouceur et al. (1991) to justify his choice of giving a £3 stake. Ladouceur had shown that the disinhibiting effect could be counteracted by allowing the subject to keep any winnings that might be made, so this is what Griffiths did.
- All subjects were asked to gamble on a Fruitskill fruit machine unless they objected. Three regular gamblers did object, either because they were not familiar with the Fruitskill machine or because they preferred a different machine. Seven further regular gamblers began on the Fruitskill machine, then changed machines, each changing at least three times.
- Regular and non-regular gamblers were randomly allocated to the thinking aloud (TA) and non-thinking aloud (NTA) conditions. The thinking aloud method was used because 'it is considered probably the best method for a precise evaluation of concurrent cognitive abilities of an individual during a specified activity' (p.356). Also, evidence shows that although the thinking aloud method slows down performance, there is no other negative effect. To test this, Griffiths included his fourth hypothesis, that those in the thinking aloud condition would take longer to complete the task.

KEY CONCEPTS

Thinking aloud method
This is a method for getting subjects to reveal their cognitive processes by literally thinking aloud, saying what they are thinking while they are doing something, such as playing a fruit machine, as in this case.

- All subjects in the TA condition were given the following additional standardised instructions:

The Thinking Aloud method consists of verbalizing every thought that passes through your mind while you are playing. It is important to remember the following points:

1 Say everything that goes through your mind. Do not censor any of your thoughts even if they seem irrelevant to you.
2 Keep talking as continuously as possible, even if your ideas are not clearly structured.
3 Speak clearly.
4 Do not hesitate to use fragmented sentences if necessary. Do not worry about speaking in complete sentences.
5 Do not try to justify your thoughts. (p.356)

- For each subject, and at all stages of the experiment, Griffiths was nearby. While they played the fruit machine he recorded (by observation):

  1 Total time in minutes subject was on the fruit machine.
  2 Total number of gambles.
  3 Amount of winnings.
  4 The result of every gamble.

To gather data to answer the question of whether there is a skill difference between regular and non-regular gamblers, seven objective behaviours were observed and recorded for each subject:

- To record the verbalisations of subjects in the TA condition they spoke into a lapel microphone which was attached to a portable tape recorder. All tapes were transcribed within 24 hours to ensure that Griffiths was able to remember the context of the comments.
- After playing the fruit machine the subjects were interviewed using a semi-structured interview, to gauge their opinions about the level of skill involved in fruit machine playing and their judgement of their own skill level.

RESULTS

These need to be considered in three parts:

1 The differences between the regular and non-regular gamblers on the seven objective behavioural variables. Would there be no differences between the regular and non-regular gamblers on the task?
2 The measure of rational/irrational comments from the content analysis of the verbalisations of those in the TA condition. Would the regular fruit machine gamblers make more irrational comments and show more evidence of cognitive biases?
3 A comparison of the regular fruit machine gamblers and non-regular fruit machine gamblers' opinions of the level of skill involved, and their own level of skill, in playing fruit machines (evidence from the interview stage).

1 Hypothesis 1 was generally true, as shown by the fact that there were only two differences between the regular and the non-regular fruit machine gamblers on the seven objective behavioural measures:

- regular gamblers had a higher playing rate, approximately eight per minute compared to the non-regular gamblers' approximate six plays per minute;
- regular TA gamblers had a significantly lower win rate in gambles, but not in time (i.e. the number of gambles, but not the amount of time elapsed between each win, was lower than for the other groups).

2 Hypothesis 2 was that the regular fruit machine gamblers would be more irrational than the non-regular fruit machine gamblers. In order to operationalise this, Griffiths established (by listening to the tapes) a set of 30 categories of utterance. He then performed a content analysis of all the TA recordings, observing for the 30 categories.

The first four of these categories would show irrational behaviour. The regular gamblers were more irrational, giving approximately 14 per cent irrational comments in total, compared to approximately 2.5 per cent for the non-regular gamblers (see table below).

Griffiths noted that some heuristics were used by the regular gamblers, but they 'did not seem to be abundant' (p. 360).

He cites examples of hindsight bias:

I had a feeling it was going to chew up those tokens fairly rapidly

and flexible attributions:

I'm losing heavily here. . . [the machine's] not giving me the numbers I want. I've just taken a quid off it so it wants its money back

and some completely erroneous perceptions:

I'm only gonna put one quid in to start with because psychologically I think it's very important. . . it bluffs the machine – it's my own psychology

Griffiths points out that the regular gamblers' comments often have examples of personification: 'the machine that chews tokens; the machine that can be bluffed' (p.360). He also says that the regular gamblers were often far more direct, and frequently swore at the machine:

It probably thinks I'm a f**kwit – it's not wrong!
. . .so harsh, it's really f**king me over. . .
I had a feature held and then it stopped them. . . f**king conned. . . bastard machine

For a discussion of the inter-observer reliability of the coding system, see Commentary, below, under Validity and reliability of the study.

3 Hypothesis 3 was measured by various questions on skill in the semi-structured interview phase of the study.

356

Irrational verbalisations categories	Regular gamblers	Non-regular gamblers
1 Personification of the fruit machine e.g. *The machine likes me*	7.54	1.14
2 Explaining away losses e.g. *I lost there because I wasn't concentrating*	3.12	0.14
3 Talking to the fruit machine e.g. *Come on, aren't you going to pay out for me?*	2.64	0.90
4 Swearing at the fruit machine e.g. *You bastard*	0.60	0.08
Total % of irrational verbalisations = highly significant ($p < 0.001$)	14%	2.5%

Results for the four irrational categories of verbalisations from the TA condition

Example question on skill	Responses of regular gamblers	Responses of non-regular gamblers
Is there any skill involved in playing a fruit machine? Is it: • all chance? • mostly chance? • equal chance/skill? • mostly skill? • all skill?	Most regular gamblers said 'equal chance/skill' = 18/30 responses	Most non-regular gamblers said 'mostly chance' = 19/30 responses
How skilful do you think you are compared with the average person? Are you: • totally unskilled? • below average skill? • average skill? • above average skill? • totally skilled?	All regular gamblers reported their skill level as 'average skill' or higher, with 23/30 saying 'above average skill' or higher ('above average' = 18/30, 'totally skilled' = 5/30)	29/30 of the non-regular gamblers reported their skill level as 'average skill' or lower, with 7/30 saying they had 'below average skill', and 12/30 saying they were 'totally unskilled'

Example questions on skill and the responses of the regular and non-regular fruit machine gamblers

The answers to these questions showed that hypothesis 3 was correct. Regular fruit machine gamblers did see fruit machine gambling as relying more on skill than non-regular gamblers, and they also assessed their own skill more highly than non-regular gamblers did.

When asked, 'What skill (if any) is involved in playing fruit machines?', the regular and non-regular gamblers came up with similar ideas. However, four skills were suggested significantly more often by the regular gamblers:

- knowledge of the 'gamble' button;
- knowledge of 'feature skills' (skill chances, etc.);
- knowledge of when the machine will pay out;
- not playing if the machine has just paid out.

These suggest that regular and non-regular gamblers have different ideas about the skills involved in playing fruit machines.

In terms of hypothesis 4, the TA condition did take longer than the NTA condition, but not significantly longer.

Of the 14 regular gamblers who managed to stay on for 60 gambles, 10 of them stayed on until they had lost everything. Interestingly, of the 7 non-regular gamblers who reached 60 gambles, only 2 stayed on until they had lost everything.

DISCUSSION

The results showed that there was no difference between the regular and non-regular fruit machine gamblers (supporting hypothesis 1). However, regular gamblers did stay on the machines for longer, so perhaps they were more skilful, although their skill was shown in the way they were able to make their money last longer. Overall there was no difference in total winnings, although the skill seemed to be that the regular gambler's wins involved higher payouts. The fact is that regular gamblers play faster and more often, and so have more wins than non-regular gamblers (so probably think they are more skilful), but consequently they will lose more money using this technique.

Gamblers who thought aloud took longer to gamble, although the results were not significant.

Some gamblers objected to being told which machines to use, which suggests that they do have an illusion of control over familiar machines.

Regular fruit machine gamblers seem to know in advance that they will play until they have lost all their money, but seem to enjoy staying on the machine for as long as possible, using the least amount of money. This suggests that just playing (rather than winning) is a reward in itself, and supports the idea that the player may be playing for reasons of social involvement, leisure, relaxation or escapism (p.363).

Although regular gamblers made more irrational verbalisations than non-regular gamblers, the number of irrational verbalisations was considerably less than had been found in previous research. Ladouceur et al. (1988) had found in their study that 80 per cent of their regular gamblers' verbalisations were irrational, whereas the total was 14 per cent in the current study (compared to 2.5 per cent of non-regular gamblers).

As expected, non-regular gamblers were found to ask more questions and produce more statements of confusion and non-understanding than regular gamblers. Griffiths said that this was a good way to validate the criteria used to differentiate between the two groups.

When being asked to verbalise what they were doing, the regular gamblers often went quiet for periods of up to 30 seconds, possibly because their actions were automatic and they were not thinking about what they were doing.

The study raised questions about the thinking aloud method. The behaviour of the gamblers who thought aloud did not differ from those in the NTA condition, so it seems that by verbalising what they were doing, the gamblers' cognitive processes were not affected. On the other hand, the data did not appear to explain *why* the regular gamblers persisted in their 'losing' behaviour. Griffiths acknowledges that there was a descriptive difference between the two groups, and suggests that the things they said may have been 'symptoms' of a deeper underlying reason, to do 'with the gamblers psychological and/or physiological constitution' (p.354), although this required further research. On the other hand, Wagenaar (1988) argued that the difference between the two groups of gamblers was just due to the heuristics they used, rather than some deep-seated personality defect.

Griffiths suggests further research into the use of heuristics by employing the thinking aloud method and getting gamblers to use a rigged slot machine to manipulate wins and losses. He is still unsure whether heuristics are affected by the mood of the person gambling or their gambling history, and cites the time when he had a number of wins and how this distorted the reality of the situation.

The hypothesis that regular gamblers would be more skilful than non-regular gamblers was supported by self-comparison ratings and questions about skill factors during play. Griffiths wonders whether the different skills involved such techniques as using the 'nudge' and 'hold' buttons to boost individual wins, thus allowing the gamblers to extend their time playing.

Fisher (1993) said that playing skills are linked with motivations to gamble. She identified three major skills:

Skill	Description
Choosing which machine to play	Taking into account how much money has been put in and how much the machine has paid out.
Knowing the exact sequence of symbols on the fruit machine's reel	The reels differ on each machine, so this may be why players have favourite machines. This would also explain how players use the nudge facility successfully to move on to the next fruit in order to win.
Gambling	Using the gamble button. This button (according to members of the gaming industry) does not increase the winnings and operates purely by chance. Gamblers believe it involves skill to use it effectively. This is therefore a 'pseudo-skill' feature.

See additional reading on the CD-ROM.

In this study, 20 skills were identified by gamblers, and Griffiths suggests that there are a few skills which could be considered more important than others, although he does question whether they are *genuinely* skilful.

Griffiths does acknowledge that probably the most technically skilful element in fruit machine gambling is basic familiarity with the machine, and this will be obvious between regular and non-regular gamblers. He suggests that the real difference is probably cognitive, whereby the regular gamblers process information about skill differently and think there is more skill involved in playing the machines than there actually is. They are also more likely to think the machine is like a person, going so far as treating it like an 'electronic friend'. He points out that this is not uncommon for people who spend a lot of time with particular machines (e.g. cars and boats, games consoles and computers).

Finally, Griffiths suggests that gamblers who are undergoing 'rehabilitation' may benefit from knowing about irrational gambling bias. He suggests that **cognitive behaviour modification** (also known as cognitive behaviour therapy) can help to modify the thought processes of individuals who are habitual gamblers. He suggests using tape recordings of the irrational biases of hardened gamblers to show how irrational they really are (called playback therapy by Griffiths). He cites the case of four of the gamblers in the study who volunteered to hear their verbalisations played back to them. They all commented on how they were surprised at what they had said. One of the gamblers (diagnosed as a pathological gambler according to the DSM-III-R) was re-interviewed at a later date and reported that his gambling had declined as a direct result of hearing himself.

Skill	Description
The hold button	If the player wins, they can 'hold' the symbols for another win. Griffiths describes this as an 'idiot skill', saying it would be stupid not to hold the winning symbols.
Knowing the reels	A genuine skill, according to Griffiths.
Light oscillation	Involves the simultaneous pressing of a button when a light shines through particular symbols.
Lighting up	Sometimes the fruit will have another symbol on it which will light up part of a further array. The player plays again (probably a number of times), in order to find other fruits to light up the next part of the array. The problem is that the machines will not keep the other parts lit for more than a few plays, so it is unlikely the player will get to light up a whole array. This can suggest the machine controls the win rate and the gambler is pitching him/herself against the machine.
Knowing the machine	Players suggest intuitive feelings of knowing when the machine will pay out.

Although there are no actual case studies using this method to promote cognitive restructuring (Walker 1992), Griffiths suggests that knowing in detail about their thoughts and experiences can help to moderate or remove the hardened gambler's motivation to gamble.

Griffiths emphasises that the talking aloud method only allows us to describe the cognitions self-reported by the regular gamblers, and the irrational utterances they make; it does not allow us to predict which cognitive biases lead to or stimulate persistent gambling. However, he suggests that further research might show which heuristics would be used in a given situation, and the talking aloud method might be a helpful method for investigating this. This might also help to explain whether the selection of particular heuristics depends on intrinsic factors (e.g. psychological factors such as mood or desire for escapism) or extrinsic factors (e.g. Griffiths' own experience of fruit machine gambling leads him to believe that big wins while gambling 'stimulate' irrationality). For Griffiths, this is an area that warrants further research.

COMMENTARY: METHODS AND ISSUES

Research method, design and data gathering

The study uses the experimental method. It is a field experiment, using an independent groups design, comparing regular and non-regular fruit machine gamblers. As a field study using an independent measures design, control of extraneous environmental and personal factors may be a problem, so we cannot rule out the possibility that this study failed to adequately control extraneous variables, which is a threat to the validity of the findings.

Data-gathering methods used while the subjects were playing the fruit machines were overt observation of seven behavioural variables, and self-report of thought processes in the TA condition. All subjects self-reported their responses in the interview stage of the study. Overt observation and self-report methods are subject to falsification by participants, and responses could have been manipulated in order to respond to demand characteristics if the participants could have worked out the purpose of the study.

Data gathered were largely quantitative, and statistical analysis was carried out to establish any differences between conditions. Qualitative data were also presented in terms of examples of how cognitive biases might show themselves; for example, personification of the machine can be seen in the comment: 'Can I win more than 10p this time?. . . No!!. . . Obviously the machine's being a bit of a bastard at the moment' (p.361).

The use of quantitative data offers a number of advantages, including the fact that comparisons could be made easily between participants and conditions, showing that there were differences in the way the regular and non-regular gamblers were thinking while they were gambling. Qualitative data, however, gave examples of the specific differences in the ways that the regular gamblers were thinking in comparison with the non-regular gamblers, and specifically highlighted the irrational elements of their thought processes, showing not only that they did think differently, but also giving detailed examples.

Does the study raise any ethical concerns?

The study was carried out according to the British Psychological Society (1993) ethical guidelines.

The subjects were not deceived; they gave their fully informed consent; they had the right to withdraw; and generally they were not negatively affected by their experience.

There is a possibility that some of those four regular gamblers who heard their verbalisations played back to them and were surprised by their behaviour and the things they said while gambling might have gained self-knowledge they found embarrassing or even disturbing. However, since this would not have damaged their self-esteem unduly, and in one instance seems to have acted as a wake-up call to a persistent gambler to change his ways, it could be argued that the end justified the means in this case.

Griffiths tries hard to suggest that there might be a way to rehabilitate problem gamblers based on his evidence in this study that regular gamblers have cognitive biases. His intention of trying to help problem gamblers means that this study is ethically worthy.

Is the study useful?

In the discussion of his study, Griffiths considers whether there are implications in his findings that could assist the rehabilitation of problem gamblers. He says his findings suggest that the difference between regular and non-regular gamblers seems to be a cognitive one (although he cautiously proposes that further research might be needed to fully confirm this!). He suggests that this cognitive difference represents an 'irrational gambling bias' (p.367) in regular gamblers, and that this might be helped by using cognitive behaviour modification.

KEY CONCEPTS

Cognitive behaviour modification
Cognitive behaviour therapy is a form of talking therapy that attempts to help the client change or modify their behaviour by changing their cognitions, their thoughts about themselves and the situations they are in.

Griffiths suggests that this might include using the thinking aloud method while the gambler plays, then allowing the gambler to listen to the tape of their verbalisations while they were gambling. Griffiths gives this the name '**audio**

playback therapy'. He bases his suggestion on anecdotal evidence from the four gamblers who took up the offer to listen to themselves afterwards, and who said they could not believe they had said the things they had said or how they were thinking when they were gambling.

Moreover, Griffiths talks about one subject who was diagnosed according to DSM-III-R criteria as a pathological gambler. On meeting Griffiths at a later date, this subject told him that his gambling behaviour declined and then stopped altogether after the experiment, and that hearing the playback of his tape had played a large part in stopping him gambling, as he had listened in disbelief to his irrational behaviour and comments while gambling. Griffiths says: 'Through this self-introspective process he claimed he realized the futility of his gambling and eventually stopped playing'.

Although Griffiths himself admits there is no evidence that cognitive behaviour therapy has helped pathological gamblers, it might be that it would if the specific behaviours and thought processes, such as those cognitive biases which stimulate the particular persistent gambler, could be addressed, perhaps using his suggested audio playback therapy method.

Validity and reliability of the study

Griffiths refers to validity and reliability a number of times in his study. For example, he justifies his choice of a field setting in the amusement arcade to avoid the problems of low ecological validity which might occur if the fruit machine gambling were observed in a laboratory setting.

Griffiths also considers the inter-observer reliability of the coding system of 30 categories which he designed to perform his content analysis of the verbalisations of subjects in the TA condition.

KEY CONCEPTS

Inter-observer reliability

To establish inter-observer reliability, the observation needs to be repeated by a second observer (either at the same time with the same sample, or at a similar time with a similar sample), using the same categories or coding system.

The two sets of data from the two observers are then correlated, and there must be a significant positive correlation between them in order to establish inter-observer reliability.

Inter-observer reliability needs to be established to ensure that observations and categories are objective and not affected by subjective observer bias.

If the observation proves not to be reliable, this leads us to question the validity of the findings, and reduces the scientific value of the study.

Unfortunately, Griffiths has to admit that his attempts to establish inter-observer reliability were not very successful and showed only low reliability. However, he explains why this might be, saying that both the other observers who tried to apply his coding system were disadvantaged. The first observer could not apply the coding system accurately because of their lack of experience of fruit machine gambling. The second observer, a regular fruit machine gambler, had difficulties using the coding system because of poor understanding of the context in which the comments were made. In other words, the coding system could only be applied by someone who had been present at the time of the recording, understood the context, and had a good understanding of fruit machine gambling. Since only Griffiths was in this position, he was the only one who could apply the categories, which means that the reliability of the coding system could not be established.

Griffiths suggests that the study as a whole leads us to question the validity of the thinking aloud method as a way of observing cognitive processes in gamblers. For example, he notes that at times the regular gamblers would go blank, or silent, for up to 30 seconds at a time, suggesting they had moved from conscious cognitive processing to a form of 'automatic pilot', where they could play without being conscious of what they were thinking. This was not apparent in the non-regular gamblers, and leads us to question whether we get a valid measure of the cognitive processes of regular gamblers.

Other challenges to the validity of the study include problems with demand characteristics. Subjects may have responded, when verbalising their thoughts, when playing the machine or in the interview stage, in ways which they thought the researcher expected or wanted them to behave. This subject bias might lead us to question the validity of the findings and the conclusions drawn from them.

Generalisability issues may also be a challenge to validity. It may be that gamblers in other areas, or those who gamble in different ways (e.g. bingo, scratch cards or poker), might not behave in similar ways to the gamblers in this study. Also, it may be that *volunteer* gamblers affect the generalisability of the findings to a broader population, as volunteers are always an atypical sample and do not represent their target population fully.

We can also question the validity of Griffith's suggested application for his findings (see above: Is the study useful?). Griffiths himself admits there is no empirical evidence of the effectiveness of cognitive behaviour modification in helping problem gamblers stop gambling, and Griffiths' own suggestion is based only on anecdotal evidence, so we cannot be sure if it would work in practice. More research would need to be undertaken before the validity of this application could be proven.

Postscript

Perhaps this is a fitting final study because it emphasises that despite what we know about people, on many occasions their behaviour continues to confuse us. Hopefully, this book has given you some insight into human behaviour and thought, and has made you realise how amazing and complex we humans really are. Each year we achieve a greater understanding of ourselves, but with each possible answer comes a series of new questions.

You will probably have found already that when you tell people you are studying psychology, they will instantly assume that you are psychoanalysing them, and that you are now in a position to put them straight. If only they knew that it is not that easy! Even when you know as much as you do now, all you can do is to pick up patterns and trends in behaviour when you first meet someone. It takes a long time to really get to know people and fully understand what makes them tick, because we are all individuals and what motivates one person may have no influence on the next. But part of the fun is getting to know them, and then trying to work it all out. Even then, you may well get some of it wrong, but if it makes you more tolerant of human weaknesses, then we have done our job.

We are all different and yet we all have so much in common. At least the majority of us only have ourselves to deal with. Imagine having numerous versions of yourself inside your body and having to cope with all of them. . . the mind boggles!

The Psychology of Individual Differences Approach

Researcher(s)	Focus of study
Rosenhan	To investigate the reliability of psychiatric diagnosis by seeing if 'sane' people would be diagnosed as mentally ill; and to observe and report the experience of being a patient in a psychiatric hospital
Thigpen and Cleckley	To report on a possible case of multiple-personality disorder and consider the validity of this rare diagnosis
Griffiths	To investigate cognitive bias in regular fruit machine gamblers

In psychology, the common focus of scientific research is to study representative samples and establish general rules about human behaviour. This is known as the **nomothetic approach**. An alternative to this is to study the differences between people, often focusing on those people who do not 'fit the mould', those who are atypical or even unique. This is known as the **idiographic approach**, and is often used in the psychology of individual differences. In the individual differences approach, researchers study the differences between individuals on certain variables.

The study of atypical behaviours can benefit the individual(s) being studied and can also provide us with insight into the complexity of human experience and behaviour. Two of the core studies in this approach focus on abnormal psychology, considering the diagnosis of mental illness. Both these studies question our classification of abnormality and illustrate the difficulties of describing people as having mental disorders.

In earlier chapters we looked at other examples of atypical behaviour, for example the case of Little Hans and Freud's explanation of the boy's phobia; and the problems that people with autism have with 'mind-reading' the thoughts and emotions of others.

Griffiths' study shows that regular gamblers think differently from non-regular gamblers, and this may explain why some people engage in addictive gambling while others do not.

STRENGTHS AND WEAKNESSES

The individual differences approach

- Studies of abnormal behaviour can be useful in explaining the behaviour and improving the experience of both those suffering from mental illness and those who work with and care for them. For example, Rosenhan's work contributed to the debate over the validity and reliability of the diagnosis of mental illness. This study, and others investigating the diagnostic process, led to revisions in the diagnostic system. The use of biochemical treatments and revisions leading to the development of DSM-IV means that the kinds of diagnostic errors made in Rosenhan's study should not be made today.

  Griffiths' work offers some explanation for why certain people gamble regularly, and the thought processes that enable or compel them to do so. He offers a possible suggestion for a cognitive behavioural treatment to help problem gamblers.

- The use of psychometric measures in the Thigpen and Cleckley study makes for ease of comparison between the two Eves. The fact that they scored very similarly on the IQ test, however, is inconclusive; since they both obtained 'average' scores, this neither confirms nor refutes their separate identities.

- Focusing on an individual, such as Eve White, may improve our understanding of her experience and help to suggest treatments which may help her, and anyone else presenting similar symptoms in the future.

- The other side of this coin, however, is that the rarity of such cases may lead to intrusive investigations and excessive study and testing, which may not help the individual and could cause them distress. There is also the question of whether generalisations from case studies are possible, and it may be that the findings of the Thigpen and Cleckley study would not help other people who might be experiencing the same symptoms.

- Rosenhan's work demonstrates the strength of using covert observation to gather data in a natural setting. The reported experiences of the pseudopatients, and their observations of the staff and real patients, must have made for difficult reading for health professionals working in psychiatric hospitals.

- There are problems with the research methods used in the study of individual differences. Thigpen and Cleckley's work shows how difficult it is to provide qualitative data that are objective or convincing, especially in the controversial case of MPD. Griffiths devised and applied a complicated quantification system for the analysis of the transcripts from the talking aloud method, but failed to establish the reliability of this coding system, again showing the difficulties of providing convincing scientific evidence from qualitative data. Rosenhan's work relies on reports by participant observers, and it may be that they lacked objectivity in reporting what was for them a negative personal experience.

Preparing for the core studies exam

Exams? Nothing to it! All you have to do is know what you need to know, learn it, then reproduce it under examination conditions. As long as you know everything, you will be all right. Easy!

Well, no, it is not easy, but performing well in exams is something that any student can do once they learn the relevant material and the required exam techniques.

The purpose of this chapter is to tell you what you need to learn, give you some insight into methods you can use to learn, and provide you with some ways to test your learning. This should prepare you to put what you have learned to good use when you are doing your core studies exam.

Being aware of what you need to know about the core studies

> Remember one very important factor: the examiners are your friends in this game – they are on your side!

By now you have probably realised that there are 15 core studies to learn. The core studies exam will require you to know these inside out and backwards. The specification tells you what you need to know. Below is a list of the specific aspects of the core studies you need to learn.

- Background to the studies (the context)

- Theories and/or studies on which studies are based

- Psychological perspectives applicable to the studies

- Other research pertinent to the studies

- Information in the studies

- Methods used in the studies

- How the results are analysed and presented; and the conclusions that can be drawn from the studies

- Strengths and limitations of the studies

- General psychological issues illustrated by the studies

- Evaluation of all the points set out above

You also need to study **methods**, **issues**, **approaches** and **perspectives** and relate these to the 15 core studies.

The **methods** are:

- experimental method (laboratory and field);

- case study;

- self-report;

- observation;

- methodological issues such as reliability and validity.

The **issues** are:

- ethics;

- ecological validity;

- longitudinal and snapshot studies;

- qualitative and quantitative data.

The **approaches** are:

- physiological;

- cognitive;

- individual differences;

- developmental;

- social.

For each **approach** you need to be able to:

- describe and evaluate the assumptions of the approach in psychology;

- describe and evaluate various methodologies used by the approach;

- consider pertinent issues, perspectives and debates, context and theory, strengths and limitations, and the implications of core studies of the approach.

The perspectives are:

- the behaviourist perspective;

- the psychoanalytical perspective.

For each perspective you will need to know its assumptions, and its strengths and limitations, illustrated by examples from the core studies.

Learning what you need to know – revising the core studies

Getting ready means being **organised**!

Some things we need to remember; some things we don't. If we are going to remember something, we will probably need to write it down and keep a record of it. Organisation is the key word here. You need a system.

1. You will need to organise your folder(s), to make sure you have notes on all the things you need to know. These are best sorted according to the approaches:

   - cognitive;

   - social;

   - individual differences;

   - developmental;

   - physiological;

   as in the specification, with each approach separated by file dividers. It will probably make most sense if you store them in the order in which your teacher taught them to you. You may also have a section on research methods and issues raised by the studies. The work you have done for the psychological investigations exam can be useful in the core studies too.

2. The next step is to read your folder and look for gaps. Are there any studies – or bits of studies – missing from your folder? Are there any concepts that you do not understand or do not have an explanation for? If so, you can use this book or the CD-ROM to look them up, or talk to your teacher. It is important to work out what is missing and fill in the gaps – you cannot begin your revision if you do not have the complete picture.

3. You are now ready to begin your revision. **Remember**, you are not revising if you are not writing things down. Learning/revising is an active process! You will need to equip yourself with notepaper and pens, and you might like to use coloured pens and index cards too.

Having organised your folder(s) and prepared the necessary materials, you have everything you need. Now you are ready to start learning the studies.

Revision activities

You need to know the stories of the studies. How research papers are presented can help you here, as this provides a structure for your story:

● background and context;

● aims and hypotheses;

● method (design, subjects/participants, procedure, materials, variables);

● results (are findings qualitative or quantitative? are they gathered by self-report, observation or biomedical measures?);

● discussion and conclusion.

You also need to consider the implications of the studies.

There is a blank 'Core studies summary sheet template' on the CD-ROM.

Making summary sheets

You can make summary sheets for each of the 15 core studies. Keep these sheets at the front of your file to read through and work from later. You may have made summary sheets after you covered the study in class, when it was fresh in your mind, but it is also a useful activity for refreshing your memory of the studies towards the end of the course.

Your summary sheets should include the following:

1. The story of the study:

    ● researcher(s) and date study was published;

    ● title of the study;

    ● background, including any real-world events, studies or theories on which the study is based;

    ● aims/hypotheses;

    ● method (design, sample, location, procedure);

    ● results (include how any variables were measured);

    ● discussion points/conclusions.

2. Evaluation points:

    You can use the questions we have used in our commentaries on the studies to help with your evaluation:

    ● What are the strengths and weaknesses of the research methods and data-gathering methods that have been used in the study?

- Is the study ecologically valid? Does the study raise any issues about validity/ reliability?

- What are the implications of the study? Is the study useful?

- Does the study raise any ethical concerns?

3. Key questions about approaches and perspectives:

   - Which approach(es) does the study illustrate?

   - What are the assumptions of this approach?

   - How are the assumptions of this approach made evident in the study?

   - In what way is this study similar to another study from this approach?

   - In what way is this study different to another study from this approach?

   - What are the assumptions of the behaviourist perspective?

   - What are the assumptions of the psychoanalytical perspective?

   - What (if anything) does this study illustrate about the behaviourist perspective and/or the psychoanalytical perspective?

4. What changes could be made to the study, and what might be the effect of these changes?

   You need to be prepared to make suggestions about changes that could be made to the study and explain what you think the likely effect of these changes might be. Changes could be to the:

   - location of the study;

   - type of measurement and data-gathering method used;

   - procedure of the study, including the research method or experimental design used;

   - sample used in the study;

   - ethical considerations of the study (what if the ethical guidelines were strictly adhered to – would this affect the study?).

Throughout this chapter (with links to the CD-ROM) you will find revision activities to help you prepare to answer questions on all these areas.

Condensing your notes

To begin with, your summary sheets may be fairly dense and you might have difficulty squeezing in all the points from the study. This is normal, so don't worry. The next stage in the revision process is to work with your notes and condense them. The reason you will be able to write less and still remember the details of the study is because you will be learning the details as you go along. Once you can write the study on one side of A4, it is time to turn to index cards.

Index cards are very useful for revision. Once you have condensed your notes, the cards act as 'cues' for your memory and are therefore a good revision aid. Using cards gives you a portable set of revision notes, which you can put in your pocket and take with you anywhere. They are also useful for visual learning, as you can include mind maps, pictures, cartoons, diagrams, and so on, to help you remember.

We have a lot of 'dead time' in our daily lives, such as when we are waiting for or travelling on a bus or train. If you have your index cards with you, you can use that time effectively, leaving you with more 'real time' for relaxing and enjoying yourself!

Testing your learning

Use specimen and past exam papers to test your learning. These will give you an idea of the kinds of questions that can be asked about the studies.

You can use index cards to test your memory too. For example, you might make up a set of cards of samples in a study, as follows:

Side one:

> The sample in Milgram's study on obedience to authority

Side two:

> - A volunteer sample drawn from those answering an advert in a local newspaper to take part in a study on learning and punishment
> - The sample size was 40
> - All subjects were male, aged 20–50
> - Subjects were drawn from a range of professions

You can make sets on the aims of the studies, the findings of the studies, the IV and DV in the studies, controls used in the studies, and so on. They are particularly helpful if you are trying to learn definitions or key concepts for a study, as in the example below.

Side one:

> Study: Piliavin et al. (subway Samaritan)
> Key concept = DIFFUSION OF RESPONSIBILITY

The sample in Milgram's study on obedience
to authority

- A volunteer sample drawn from those answering an
  advert in a local newspaper to take part in a
  study on learning and punishment
- the sample size was 40
- all subjects were male, aged 20-50
- subjects were drawn from a range of professions.

Study: Piliavin et al. (subway Samaritan)
Key concept = DIFFUSION OF RESPONSIBILITY

Diffusion of responsibility means that the more
people present, the less responsible each individual
feels (because the responsibility is 'shared out') so
the less likely someone is to receive help. This was
what happened in laboratory studies of helping, but
not in the Piliavin et al. study in the field.

Side two:

Diffusion of responsibility means that the more people who are present, the less responsible each individual feels (because the responsibility is 'shared out'), so the less likely someone is to receive help.

This was what happened in laboratory studies of helping, but not in the Piliavin et al. study in the field.

375

You don't want to spend all your time making the cards, though. Why not join up with a study buddy, share out the card-making tasks and then swap? If you can cajole your mum or dad into helping you revise, they can use the cards to test your knowledge, or study buddies can test each other.

Revision activities are included on the CD-ROM

To help you revise there are lots of activities on the core studies included on the CD-ROM. These include matching activities on the aims, samples, variables, key terms, equipment, concepts and number activities for each of the five approaches.

Methods, issues, perspectives and approaches in the core studies exam

In order to answer the exam questions, you must know about research methods, issues, approaches and perspectives, and how these relate to the 15 core studies. First, we will look at some methodological points, and then at the issues and perspectives. There will be revision activities along the way, so be prepared to join in!

Methods in the core studies

> **From the specification – Methods**
> 1 Experimental method (laboratory and field)
> 2 Case study
> 3 Self-report
> 4 Observation
> 5 Methodological issues such as reliability and validity

Methods 1: The experimental method (laboratory and field)

Experiments can be carried out in the laboratory or in a natural setting. The latter is described as being 'in the field'.

In a true experiment:

- the experimenter manipulates one variable – the independent variable (IV) – to see if it causes a change in another variable – the dependent variable (DV);

- all other variables (extraneous variables) are controlled or kept constant to prevent them from confounding the study; we can therefore demonstrate cause and effect – the IV causes the DV to change;

- participants are randomly allocated to conditions;

- a control or comparison group is used.

Experiments where these criteria are not met are known as natural experiments or quasi-experiments. We have come across examples of these where the IV occurs naturally and cannot be manipulated by the experimenter, as in Baron-Cohen et al.'s study of autism (Chapter 3) and Sperry's study of split-brain patients (Chapter 5).

KEY CONCEPTS

Controlling extraneous variables

Extraneous variables are variables other than the IV that need to be controlled or kept constant in a study, to ensure that the IV alone is the cause of any change in the DV. If an extraneous variable is not controlled or kept constant, it may operate alongside the IV and confound the study, which means we will not be able to work out whether any change in the DV is caused by the extraneous variable or by the IV.

There are a number of strategies for controlling extraneous environmental variables. These include standardisation, randomisation and counterbalancing. One way to control extraneous personal variables is through experimental design – a repeated measures design is best for controlling individual differences across conditions, followed by matched participants and then independent groups.

In particular studies, certain variables need to be measured and taken account of to stop them confounding the study. For example, in the study by Baron-Cohen et al. on autism (Chapter 3), two control tasks – a basic emotion recognition task and a gender recognition task – were used to discount the fact that problems with other cognitive processes, such as difficulties with face perception or emotion recognition, might account for any difficulties subjects had on the eyes task.

Revision activity

You need to know about the strengths and weaknesses of the experimental method and apply these to the core studies. Using your knowledge of the core studies and the evaluative issues set out in the table below, copy and complete the two tables which follow ('Laboratory experiments in the core studies' and 'Field experiments in the core studies').

Copies of these tables are provided on the CD-ROM.

Evaluation of laboratory experiments	
Strengths	**Weaknesses**
• High level of control over extraneous variables	• May lack ecological validity – laboratory behaviour is artificial
• IV can be manipulated and isolated as a causal factor, establishing cause and effect between the IV and the DV	• Internal validity may be low because of possible biasing factors, such as participant reactivity (responding to demand characteristics) or experimenter bias

Evaluation of laboratory experiments	
Strengths	**Weaknesses**
• Allows the use of sensitive technical equipment (EEG, MRI scan) or complicated apparatus	• Deception may be necessary as to the true purpose of the study in order to avoid participants responding to demand characteristics – this raises ethical issues • Restricted samples used mean it is difficult to generalise the findings to people in general • If the study is quasi-experimental in design, this means the researcher does not have full control over the IV

Evaluation of field experiments	
Strengths	**Weaknesses**
• May have high ecological validity – 'real' behaviour can be studied • IV can be manipulated and isolated as a causal factor, establishing cause and effect between the IV and the DV	• Not all field experiments are high in ecological validity. The introduction of stooges can reduce the realism of the study, especially if the stooge behaves unusually • Low control over extraneous variables, so we cannot be entirely sure that there is a causal relationship between the IV and the DV • Covert observation is often used to gather data and this raises ethical issues (deception, invasion of privacy, lack of informed consent, etc.) • If the study is quasi-experimental in design, this means the researcher does not have full control over the IV

Study	IV/DV	Sample	Strengths of lab experiment	Weaknesses of lab experiment
Loftus and Palmer (eyewitness testimony)	Study 1: Study 2:			
Baron-Cohen et al. (autism)				
Samuel and Bryant (conservation)				
Bandura et al. (aggression)				

Laboratory experiments in the core studies

Study	IV/DV	Sample	Strengths of field experiment	Weaknesses of field experiment
Piliavin et al. (subway Samaritan)				
Rosenhan (sane in insane places)				
Griffiths (gambling)				

Field experiments in the core studies

Copies of these tables are provided on the CD-ROM.

Methods 2: The case study method

You need to know about the strengths and weaknesses of the non-experimental methods, as used in the core studies. A case study is an in-depth study of one individual or a small group. Often a case study is carried out longitudinally, allowing development or changes to be observed over time. This method allows a great deal of qualitative data, rich in detail and high in validity, to be gathered. Techniques used in case studies include interviews and psychometric tests, and these methods bring their related strengths and weaknesses to the case. For instance, if the researchers have developed a long-standing and close relationship with the participant, their objectivity may be reduced, and therefore they may be biased in their reporting of the interview. Psychometric tests are usually self-report pen-and-paper tests and are open to falsification or manipulation by a clever participant.

Replication of case studies is very difficult, especially as they are often of atypical or unusual cases (e.g. Little Hans, Eve White), and this means that we have to be cautious in generalising the findings to other people. This, in turn, reduces the usefulness of the findings.

A copy of the table is provided on the CD-ROM.

Revision activity
Copy and complete the following table.

Study	Strengths of the case study method	Weaknesses of the case study method
Freud's case study of Little Hans		
Thigpen and Cleckley's case study of Eve White		

Use of the case study method in the core studies

Methods 3: Data-gathering methods – self-report

You need to know about measurement issues, such as the strengths and weaknesses of self-report methods and observational methods of data gathering.

Self-report measures include asking people questions, getting participants to fill in questionnaires, and interviewing participants. You will learn all about these in your preparation for the psychological investigations examination.

Strengths	Weaknesses
• Cost- and time-effective – can gather large amounts of data in a short time	• May be falsifiable: participants lie (e.g. responding to demand characteristics, or due to evaluation apprehension, they give socially desirable answers); if data is falsifiable, we have to question its validity
• Can measure attitudes/ beliefs/cognitive abilities that cannot otherwise be measured	• Closed questions (forced-response questions) may frustrate the participant, who may then lose interest and not answer carefully, again reducing the validity of the study
• Closed questions/rating scales on questions can provide quantitative data for analysis	• Questions can be leading – suggesting the answer that ought to be given; thus the researcher is influencing the participant's responses (children may be particularly susceptible to leading questions)

The strengths and weaknesses of using self-report methods to gather data: questions, questionnaires, interviews

Revision activity

Using your knowledge of the core studies and the information provided above about self-report data-gathering methods, copy and complete the following table.

A copy of the table is provided on the CD-ROM.

Study	How was self-report used?	Strengths of self-report measures	Weaknesses of self-report measures
Freud (Little Hans)			
Samuel and Bryant (conservation)			
Baron-Cohen et al. (autism)			
Loftus and Palmer (eyewitness testimony)			

OCR Psychology for AS

Study	How was self-report used?	Strengths of self-report measures	Weaknesses of self-report measures
Dement and Kleitman (dreaming)			
Sperry (split-brains)			
Thigpen and Cleckley (multiple personality disorder)			
Griffiths (gambling)			

Use of self-report methods in the core studies

Methods 4: Data-gathering methods – observation

Observations can be carried out in a *natural setting*, as Piliavin et al. did in their subway Samaritan study, or in the *laboratory*, as Bandura et al. did in the third stage of their study on learning aggression. Observation can be carried out *covertly*, without the knowledge or consent of participants, or *overtly*, where consent is obtained and people are aware of the observer's presence. The observer may be a part of the setting or group being observed – this is called *participant* observation, as in the study by Rosenhan, where the pseudopatients observed the psychiatric hospitals from the point of view of a patient. Alternatively, the observer may be outside the setting or group being studied – this is known as *non-participant* observation, as in the observations of the nursery school children through the one-way mirror in Bandura et al.'s study.

Observations often generate quantitative data by establishing codings or categories of behaviour to be observed. For example, one of the behavioural categories established by Bandura et al. was 'Partial imitation: sits on Bobo, mallet aggression'; this was one of nine behaviours being observed for in the 20-minute period in stage three. In the study by Griffiths, the verbal comments made by participants in the thinking aloud condition were categorised so that he ended up with 30 different categories of utterance. He was then able to measure and compare the thinking patterns of regular and non-regular gamblers, by carrying out a content analysis of all the thinking aloud recordings, observing for the 30 categories.

The strengths and weaknesses of using observational methods to gather data are set out in the table below.

Strengths	Weaknesses
• Where covert observation is used, studies can be high in ecological validity, as 'real' behaviour is being observed (NB ecological validity is reduced if a laboratory is the setting for the study) • In participant observations, the observer can get a real insight into the situation being observed, as they experience it first-hand	• Ethical concerns are raised in covert observations • Reductionism where quantitative methods and codings/ratings are used • Observer bias – consciously or unconsciously affecting the results so that they fit in with the hypothesis • Reliability – if only one observer is used, we have to question the reliability/objectivity of the results • In overt (or participant) observations, the presence of the researcher may influence the behaviour of participants and this will mean results are not valid • In participant observations, the observer may lose their objectivity, as they are influenced by their experience of the situation

Revision activity

Using your knowledge of the core studies and the information provided above about observational data-gathering methods, copy and complete the following table.

Study	What was observed and how?	Strengths of observational measures	Weaknesses of observational measures
Milgram (obedience)			
Reicher and Haslam (BBC prison experiment)			
Piliavin et al. (subway Samaritan)			

A copy of the table is provided on the CD-ROM.

Study	What was observed and how?	Strengths of observational measures	Weaknesses of observational measures
Bandura et al. (aggression)			
Rosenhan (sane in insane places)			
Griffiths (gambling)			

Using observational methods in the core studies

Methods 5: Validity and reliability

Validity

A test or measure is valid if it tests what it is supposed to test. In other words, are the findings trustworthy and can we believe they are *true*?

Internal validity is determined by the extent to which a study is free of design faults which might affect the result – meaning that the test is not a true test of what it intended to measure.

Factors which reduce the validity (internal validity) of findings include the following:

- Low generalisability of findings (e.g. sample biases, ethnocentric bias, difficulty extrapolating to other groups of people/settings) – if the findings are not generalisable, they are not valid.

- Demand characteristics – participants taking part in a study will try to work out what the study is about. Demand characteristics are the cues/clues present (given away by the procedure/questions/tasks, or conveyed unconsciously by those carrying out the test), which suggest to the participant what the hypothesis is. There are two responses participants may make, having worked out what they think the study is about:

  – to try to please the experimenter and get the experiment to 'work' – out of a desire to be 'right', they modify their behaviour/answers to fit in with how they think the experimenter expects them to behave;

  – the 'screw you' effect – here the aim is to spoil the experiment by not acting in the way they think is expected of them (this may be just for the sake of it, or because they want to make the statement, 'I am not typical').

Of course, both these responses to demand characteristics mean participants are falsifying their responses, and this means that the validity of the findings comes into question where participants responding to demand characteristics is a possibility in a study.

● If it is possible that a confounding variable has operated systematically alongside the IV, this may affect the validity of the findings. For instance, in independent groups designs and matched subjects designs, it is difficult to control subject variables. In other words, there may be differences between the two groups other than the fact that one has the IV introduced. This means it is possible that subject variables have confounded the study, and therefore we have to question the validity of the findings.

In the Baron-Cohen et al. study on autism (Chapter 3) we came across the concept of **concurrent validity**. This means that two studies measuring the same variable have come up with similar findings. By showing that participants' scores on one advanced test of theory of mind (Happé's strange stories test) correlated with their scores on the new advanced test of theory of mind (the Eyes Task), the authors were able to provide evidence for the validity of their new test as a true advanced measure of theory of mind. The Eyes Task and Happé's strange stories test, therefore, were concurrently valid – each supporting the validity of the other.

Ecological validity is a form of external validity. We will discuss this later in this chapter (page 388) as an issue in the core studies.

Reliability

Reliability refers to the consistency of a measurement. A test or measure is reliable if it gives similar results when repeated in similar circumstances. In other words, if the findings prove to be replicable, which is a key feature of scientific study, then the test or measure is said to be reliable. There are two types of reliability that you need to know about: test-retest reliability and inter-observer reliability.

Test-retest reliability is where the study (or test) is repeated, under similar circumstances to the original study or test. The results from the first test are correlated with the results from the second test, and if a high positive correlation is found between the two tests, this means that the results are consistent, and therefore reliable.

Inter-observer reliability (also called inter-rater reliability) is a form of reliability designed to control for observer bias. One observer's use of a coding or rating system may be inaccurate if they have applied the system according to their own subjective interpretation or bias. To make sure that the rating or coding system (or categories of observation) is objective, another observer uses the same system to code either the same or a similar sample of behaviour. The scores from the two observers are then correlated, and if a high positive correlation is found, inter-observer reliability has been established. An example of this can be found in the study on learning aggression by Bandura et al. The normal aggression level ratings by the children's nursery school teacher were correlated with ratings by one of the female researchers, and the high positive correlation recorded showed that this was a reliable measure of the children's aggression.

Correlational analysis is used to test for both reliability and validity, and this is a common use of correlations in psychological investigations. Of course, this can only be carried out where quantitative data have been gathered and where the study can be replicated easily, as is the case with most laboratory studies. Researchers are least able to establish the reliability of studies that gather qualitative data, as many case studies do. This is a problem, as low reliability brings the validity of findings into question, and if a study is low in validity, this reduces its usefulness.

There is a diagram of the factors affecting validity on the CD-ROM.

Revision activity
- Which core studies use self-report data-gathering methods that can be falsified, leading us to question the validity of the findings?
- Which studies have sample biases that restrict the generalisability of the studies and mean they are not valid measures of people in general?
- Why might brain-imaging techniques, such as the MRI scan used by Maguire et al., not give valid results?
- Why can the validity of the thinking aloud method be questioned?
- Identify two studies from the core studies where it would be relatively easy to establish the reliability of the findings, and two studies where it would be difficult to establish the reliability of the findings.
- Explain the term 'inter-observer reliability'. Use an example from the core studies to illustrate how inter-rater reliability is established.

Issues in the core studies

From the specification – Issues

1 Ethics

2 Ecological validity

3 Longitudinal and snapshot studies

4 Qualitative and quantitative data

Issues 1: Ethics

The participants in psychological studies are people, and we should treat them with care and respect, protecting them from both psychological and physical harm. Psychologists have membership of professional organisations, such as the American Psychological Association (APA) in the USA, and the British Psychological Society (BPS) in the UK. These professional bodies oversee the work of psychologists and provide ethical guidelines to be followed when carrying out research on human participants. These guidelines include the following:

- Participants should be informed of the nature and procedures of the study prior to taking part, so that they can make an informed choice about their involvement, and give their informed consent to participate in the investigation.

There is a spider diagram of ethical guidelines for investigations using human participants on the CD-ROM.

- Deception should be used only if necessary, and as little as necessary. For example, to avoid demand characteristics, it may be necessary to use a cover story to conceal the true purpose of a study. Where deception has been used, debriefing is required.

- Thorough debriefing should be provided, explaining the nature and findings of the study and providing further support, such as counselling, if required or requested.

- Participants should be protected from both physical and psychological harm, including undue stress, while taking part in the study. They should be protected from self-knowledge or experiences that have a negative impact on their self-esteem and dignity.

- Confidentiality/anonymity should be assured and maintained for all those taking part in the study.

- The participants' privacy should not be invaded.

- Participants should be informed of their right to withdraw at any time, or to withdraw their data at the end of the study.

- Participants should not be coerced into taking part or continuing with a study, whether by directly refusing to allow them to stop when they want to, or by implicitly engaging their commitment to continue by payment.

The guidelines represent what psychologists should aim for in their studies, but in reality it is difficult to carry out work that does not at least bend, if not blatantly flout, one or more of these 'rules'.

In deciding whether or not a study which breaches ethical guidelines should be (or should have been) carried out, we need to ask the following questions:

1. Does the aim of the study justify it being carried out? Is it a worthwhile study? Will it explore areas which have not been explored before? Will the results help us to understand behaviour better?

2. If the ethical code was broken, are the findings important enough to justify this?

The salient question when considering the ethics of a study involving human participants is: does the end justify the means?

It has been argued that there is an ethical imperative in psychological research. In other words, there are some areas of our experience and behaviour that psychologists have a moral obligation to investigate. Some studies have shown us a great deal about how or why we behave in certain ways, or have offered effective solutions to real-life problems. Such studies can be described as ethically worthy, which means that they have made positive contributions to the development of our understanding of human behaviour, or have benefited people by suggesting ways to improve their lives. Studies that are ethically worthy can also be described as highly useful (see the section on The implications of the core studies, page 395).

An important point to note here is that some of the core studies were carried out a long time ago. The ethical guidelines that relate to current psychological practice have been amended and refined since some of these studies took place, and, in some cases, as a result of these studies. Some of the studies would probably not be allowed to be carried out in the same way if we wanted to replicate them today.

You also need to note that there are separate guidelines for animal studies, so the comparative study in the core studies (the Savage-Rumbaugh et al. study on Kanzi and other apes in Chapter 3) is not governed by the same ethical guidelines. For ethical concerns raised in this study, see the commentary at the end of the core study (page 168).

Issues 2: Ecological validity

Ecological validity is a type of external validity, which means the extent to which generalisations can be made from the test environment to other situations.

A study is high in ecological validity if the behaviour which participants are asked to perform resembles a behaviour they, or people similar to them, perform in real life. Laboratory studies tend to be low in ecological validity, since the setting is artificial and therefore unlikely to represent 'real-life' behaviour. However, it is not the case that all laboratory studies lack ecological validity, or that a study is either ecologically valid or not. For example, if you wanted to test a person's driving behaviour, you might think that there is no ecologically valid way of doing this in a laboratory. However, testing participants on a driving simulator, or using a computer program based on driving a car, may be *sufficiently* high in ecological validity for your research purposes. It would certainly be higher in ecological validity than seating a participant on a chair, with a Frisbee for a steering wheel, and asking them to mime their driving behaviour!

There can be problems studying social behaviour in the laboratory, or studying the effects of environmental variables such as ambient noise, weather conditions, crowd behaviour, and so on, so there can be problems with the ecological validity of laboratory studies which investigate these areas.

There are also problems with the ecological validity of studies of where children are tested individually in the laboratory, isolated from their usual social environment and tested by people they do not know.

Some researchers argue that the only method which has high ecological validity is covert observation in a natural setting, as this studies people's freely chosen and normal behaviour, without the biasing factor of their knowledge that they are being observed.

A table of examples of ethical issues raised by the core studies is available on the CD-ROM.

Study	Low	High
Milgram	Laboratory study, untypical task	
Reicher and Haslam	Simulated institution/prison is unlike a real prison	
Piliavin et al.		Covert observation of behaviour in natural setting
Loftus and Palmer	Laboratory experiment	
Savage-Rumbaugh et al.	The chimps were kept in captivity in a highly humanised environment, and encouraged to perform behaviours chimps do not naturally perform, including language training through instrumental conditioning in the case of the common chimpanzees, Sherman and Austin	The acquisition of symbol use through modelling is similar to how children acquire language in a natural setting
Samuel and Bryant	Laboratory experiment, children tested alone	
Bandura et al.	Laboratory experiment, children tested alone	
Freud		Covert observation of behaviour in natural setting (the question is: how was this behaviour interpreted?)
Dement and Kleitman	Laboratory study – we do not sleep in a laboratory or wired up to an EEG machine!	
Sperry	Laboratory experiment – subjects restricted (e.g. cannot see hands, no talking)	
Rosenhan	'Normal people' do not usually seek diagnosis of mental illness, or hospitalisation	Covert observation of behaviour in a natural setting

Examples of high or low ecological validity in the core studies

Issues 3: Longitudinal studies and snapshot studies

Longitudinal studies

Longitudinal studies investigate the same subject(s) or participant(s) over an extended period of time: weeks, months or even years. They may be continuous, or researchers may return periodically to sample behaviour (e.g. every few months or years). This design allows us to see how behaviour changes or develops over time. Where the same researcher oversees the study, trusting relationships can be built up with the participants so that it is possible to gather valid data on sensitive issues, since participants are more inclined to disclose information to someone they know and trust. Studying participants over time means a great deal of data can be gathered which is usually qualitative in nature, and this also increases the validity of the findings.

For example, in the study on the pygmy chimpanzee (bonobo) Kanzi, Savage-Rumbaugh et al. studied the animal intensively, recording every utterance he made using the lexigrams and/or gestures to communicate. They did this over a period of 17 months.

The studies by Freud (Little Hans) and Thigpen and Cleckley (multiple personality disorder) were also longitudinal designs. The longitudinal design is commonly used in case studies, and therefore often features in developmental studies or studies of abnormal psychology in the individual differences approach.

The strengths of longitudinal studies include the following:

- A relationship can be built up with the participant(s), so that they have confidence in the researcher and feel secure in providing sensitive information. The relationship of trust established over time can increase the level of detail provided by participants and therefore improve the validity of a study's findings.

- Researchers can build up a detailed picture of the participant(s) over the course of the study. For example, Thigpen and Cleckley interviewed Eve White, Eve Black and Jane in over 100 hours of therapy, building up detailed knowledge of the three 'personalities'. The longitudinal nature of the study made it less likely for Eve White to be faking her symptoms (if she was acting, she made no errors), and this increases the credibility of multiple personality disorder as a diagnosis in this case.

The weaknesses of longitudinal studies include the following:

- Since the researcher has invested a lot of time and effort in the study, they may lose their objectivity or become too involved with the participant(s). This may affect the findings, reducing their validity. For example, Thigpen and Cleckley were aware of their close involvement with, and professional investment in, the case of Eve, and suggested that they might have been fooled by a very good actress.

- They can be expensive in terms of both time and money, and may require a great deal of commitment from the researcher(s).

- Subject attrition can cause problems. Over time, a sample size may reduce as people drop out or lose contact with the researcher. This means that the researchers are left with what is, in effect, a volunteer sample, and this may not truly represent the original sample. Therefore the validity of the findings may be questioned.

- It may be difficult to establish their reliability, as societal or cultural changes that have taken place may make the study impossible to replicate. Reliability may also be difficult to establish because it is hard to find equivalent participants, especially in abnormal cases (e.g. Eve White or Little Hans).

- Once started, they cannot be modified or changed easily.

Snapshot studies

Snapshot studies compare different groups at the same point in time to see a 'snapshot' of behaviour. They allow us to compare groups of different ages or under different circumstances, for example, to see the effects of variables on behaviour, or to see how behaviour changes over time.

For example, in Samuel and Bryant's (conservation) study, Piaget's theory that children get better at conservation over time was tested by studying children in four age groups (5-, 6-, 7- and 8-year-olds) and comparing their performance. They were further split into groups by condition, to see if the one- or two-judgement tasks affected their ability to get the conservation tasks right.

The strengths of snapshot studies include the following:

- They are less time-consuming than a longitudinal study. They allow us to sample changes over time (e.g. in children of different ages), without having to wait for a child to grow and develop.

- Since an independent groups design is used, the likelihood of demand characteristics affecting the study is reduced, as participants are tested in only one condition of the experiment.

- They can be more time- and cost-effective than longitudinal studies.

- As they are quicker and cheaper to replicate, it may be possible to establish the reliability of the findings easily.

- They can be easily modified or changed for further study.

The weaknesses of snapshot studies include the following:

- Since they employ independent groups designs, they can be affected by extraneous participant variables. Individual differences between participants may affect the DV and confound the study.

- The limited sampling of participants' behaviour may give a false impression of their typical behaviour. A longitudinal study may not be affected by this, as more detailed data are collected.

Issues 4: Qualitative and quantitative data

A table showing the relative strengths of quantitative and qualitative data is available on the CD-ROM

Quantitative data are numerical data, such as categories and frequencies, percentages, and so on. It is attractive to gather quantitative data because of the ease with which people's performances on a test or task can be compared. The data are easy to summarise and present, and statistical analysis is possible. It is also easier to establish the reliability of numerical findings, as this can be done by retesting and correlating the results of the first and second tests to see if there is a significant positive correlation. The disadvantage is that quantitative data provide a narrow view of the person, one that is both reductionist and lacking in validity.

The alternative is to gather **qualitative data**, which usually take the form of verbal descriptions, such as reports of what has been observed or written reports of interviews. While it is more difficult to compare, analyse and draw conclusions from qualitative data, or to replicate this data to test for reliability, what you gain is an increase in the depth and detail of the findings, and therefore higher validity.

Scientific study usually implies the gathering and analysis of quantitative data, using inferential statistics to establish cause and effect or correlation between variables. Historically, therefore, psychological investigations have tended to focus on quantitative methods of analysis. However, qualitative research methods, such as discourse analysis, are now appearing more frequently in psychological literature. As you might imagine, many researchers try to incorporate the strengths of both qualitative and quantitative data in their work, and there are examples of this in the core studies.

Core study	Qualitative data	Quantitative data
Milgram (obedience)	Nervous laughter and sweating was observed	65% went up to 450v 100% went to 300v
Piliavin et al. (subway Samaritan)	Comments elicited from passengers by observers (e.g. 'It's for a man to help him')	In cane (ill) condition, victim was helped spontaneously on 62/65 trials (drunk = 19/38)
Loftus and Palmer (eyewitness testimony)		Study 1 – speed estimate was measured as an average per condition Study 2 – 16/50 subjects in 'smashed' condition reported seeing broken glass, compared with 6/50 in control condition
Savage-Rumbaugh et al. (ape language)	The authors report that bonobos learned symbol use by modelling and observation, whereas the common chimpanzees had to be trained (instrumentally conditioned) to use symbols	Mulika's vocabulary tests showed she understood 42 symbols
Samuel and Bryant (conservation)		DV was measured as an average number of errors out of 12 per condition
Bandura et al. (aggression)		Children's aggressive behaviour was recorded using categories, recording at 5-second intervals for 20 minutes in stage three
Freud (Little Hans)	Study is largely qualitative (e.g. the description of Hans's fantasy of the two giraffes)	

(Continued)

Core study	Qualitative data	Quantitative data
Dement and Kleitman (dreaming)		Out of 191 REM awakenings, 152 dream recalls were recorded. Out of 160 NREM awakenings, only 11 dream recalls were recorded
Sperry (split-brains)	Subjects could not name an object placed in their left hand out of their view	
Rosenhan (sane in insane places)	The behaviour of patients was judged to be due to their 'pathology' rather than considered normal given the environment (e.g. 'Patient engages in writing behaviour' was recorded about the diary keeping as if it were an abnormal behaviour)	In the follow-up study, 10% of the research hospital's normal intake were suspected of being pseudopatients by two members of the hospital staff
Thigpen and Cleckley (multiple personality disorder)	As this is a case report of therapeutic sessions, any episode described by the researchers is going to give qualitative data	Psychometric test scores (e.g. IQ scores and memory function scores) and EEG scores
Griffiths (gambling)	The quotes from the regular gamblers show how they were thinking irrationally (e.g. 'I'm losing heavily here...[the machine's] not giving me the numbers I want. I've just taken a quid off it so it wants its money back'	Regular gamblers made 14% irrational comments in total, compared with approximately 2.5% for the non-regular gamblers

Examples of qualitative and quantitative data from the core studies

Implications of the core studies – are the findings useful?

A final issue that we would like you to consider here is the usefulness of psychological research. This seems very important to us, because psychology should be useful. If research does not help to explain why we think, feel and behave as we do, nor give us ideas for how we might think, feel and behave in different ways that will lead us to live happier and more fulfilled lives, then there does not seem to be much point in it!

So, are the core studies useful? The questions we need to ask are: useful for what, and to whom? Findings may be useful to psychologists in that they help to explain or predict behaviour, or generally useful for helping to explain behaviours and solve problems in the real world.

On the one hand, then, studies can be considered useful to psychology itself by further-ing our understanding of human behaviour or experience. A study or theory may also be highly generative, that is, it leads to a great deal of further research, both testing and refining the conclusions drawn in a particular area of study, and this makes it useful within psychology as a discipline. Examples of work which has been highly generative are Freud's theory of psychosexual development, and Piaget's theory of cognitive development. It follows that studies which contribute to the debate in a particular area are also useful to psychology. For example, Samuel and Bryant's work contributes to the debate concerning children's cognitive development by providing support for the sequence of Piaget's stages, but also suggesting refinements to the timing of the stages, as their work suggests that Piaget underestimated young children's abilities.

On the other hand, usefulness can be assessed by asking: are the conclusions/findings from the study of any use in helping to solve problems in the real world? The table below considers some examples of the real-life applications of findings from the core studies.

Study	Applications in real life
Samuel and Bryant/Piaget (conservation/cognitive development)	Understanding cognitive development in children can inform teachers about what is appropriate to teach at what stage in a child's development, and how to teach it (interactive learning environment that enables child to move from stage to stage when they are ready).
Loftus and Palmer (eyewitness testimony)	If memory is reconstructive in nature and can be altered by the use of leading questions, then we must take great care about how we question people on whose memory we rely – most importantly, witnesses to crimes, whose testimony in a court of law may be important evidence.

(Continued)

395

Study	Applications in real life
Griffiths (gambling)	Griffiths considers that a form of cognitive behaviour modification based on the thinking aloud method might be used in the rehabilitation of problem gamblers. Griffiths calls this 'audio playback therapy'.
Rosenhan (sane in insane places)	This work by Rosenhan was one of a number of studies that have resulted in the development of more valid and reliable diagnostic criteria for mental illnesses.

The usefulness of the core studies can also be considered in relation to the methods and issues. The usefulness of a study will be reduced if:

● the study is low in ecological validity and therefore findings cannot be generalised easily to a real-life setting;

● the study is reductionist and ignores other important factors or variables which affect behaviour;

● the findings of the study are not valid (e.g. if demand characteristics could have affected the findings, or if it is possible that other extraneous variables have confounded the results);

● sample biases mean the findings are not generalisable to a broad population.

Doing the core studies exam

Remember, there are **two** exams for OCR AS level psychology:

● The **core studies** exam, which will test the material covered in this book. This exam is 2 hours long and counts for 70 per cent of the AS marks.
● The **psychological investigations** exam, for which you will find some of the information in this book on research methods useful, and for which you will prepare and practise in lessons with your teacher. This exam lasts 1 hour and counts for 30 per cent of the AS marks.

Always keep in mind that the examiners are your friends! Their aim is to enable you to show them what you know and what you can do – they are not trying to catch you out. To help you, the exams will follow a structure, and you need to know what this is if you are to be fully prepared. Here we will look at the structure of the core studies examination only, as that is the focus of this book.

Preparing for the core studies exam   **7**

The structure of the exam

The core studies exam is in three sections. Below is a summary table, followed by detailed descriptions of the three sections, with examples.

Section A	Made up of 15 compulsory, short questions on all aspects of the core studies, and the methods, issues, approaches and perspectives	Carries 60 of the 120 marks available
Section B	More in-depth questions, on a specific core study (You will choose **one** of two given studies to write about – you will be asked to write in detail about some aspects of the study, and to relate the study to some of the issues and themes)	Carries 36 of the 120 marks available
Section C	In-depth questions, focusing on the approaches and perspectives and how they relate to the 15 core studies	Carries 24 of the 120 marks available

Section A

(*You must answer* **all** *parts of all questions 1 to 15.*)

All questions in Section A are **compulsory**. There are 15 questions in this section, worth a possible 60 of the 120 marks available on this paper.

Questions in Section A may be in two parts (with 2 marks for each part) or one part (for a total of 4 marks). Below are two examples of each type of question:

1.
   - Describe the sample used in the study by Milgram on obedience. [2]
   - Identify **one** ethical concern raised by Milgram's study and explain how the breaking of this guideline might be justified in this study. [2]

2.
   - Give one assumption of the behaviourist approach. [2]
   - Give one criticism of the behaviourist approach. [2]

3. Briefly explain why Samuel and Bryant carried out their study on cognitive development. [4]

4. The study by Bandura, Ross and Ross on the imitation of aggression used a number of experimental controls. Identify two of the controls used in the study and explain what they were used to control for in the study. [4]

397

Section B

(*You must complete* **all** *parts of question 16.*)

In Section B there is **one compulsory** question, in six parts. Section B is worth 36 of the 120 marks on this exam paper.

In the Section B question you will be asked to write about **one** core study, from a choice of two given studies, and you will answer questions about one or more of the following: aims; research method; location; sample; controls used; data-gathering methods; types of data gathered; results; and conclusions. You will be asked to write about the advantages/ disadvantages of some of these, as used in the study you have chosen to write about.

You will also be asked to suggest changes that might be made to some aspects of your chosen study and to consider what effects these changes might have, for example on the outcome of the study or on the validity of the findings.

Copies of these tables are provided on the CD-ROM.

> **Revision activity**
> To help you prepare for the questions which might ask you to suggest changes to the location, sample, method, procedure and data-gathering method, copy and complete the following three tables.

Researcher(s)	Location used	Suggested alternative location(s)	Possible effects of this change of location on the results and validity of the study
Milgram (obedience)	Laboratory-based study at Yale University	Downtown industrial area	
Piliavin et al. (subway Samaritan)	Carriage in a New York subway train	In the subway station rather than on the train. In a large shopping centre. On the street	
Griffiths (gambling)	Amusement arcade	At a racetrack, with regular and non-regular gamblers on horse races	
Dement and Kleitman (dreaming)	Sleep laboratory on a university campus	In the subjects' own homes (natural setting)	

How could the location be different? What effect might a different location have on the study's findings?

Researcher(s)	Sample used	Suggested alternative sample	Possible effects of this change of sample on the results and validity of the study
Milgram (obedience)	40 males, aged 20–50, range of jobs, volunteers, New Haven area		
Piliavin et al. (subway Samaritan)	4,450 subjects, male and female, black and white, on the New York subway		
Griffiths (gambling)	60 gamblers – 30 regular gamblers and 30 non-regular gamblers		
Dement and Kleitman (dreaming)	9 adults (7 male, 2 female)		
Maguire et al. (taxi drivers' brains)	16 right-handed male London taxi drivers and 50 healthy, right-handed men who did not drive taxis		
Loftus and Palmer (eyewitness testimony)	University students, first 45 of them and then a further 150		

How could the sample be different? What effect might a different sample have on the results of the study?

399

Researcher(s)	Research and data-gathering method	Aim	How this study could be carried out as a survey/ questionnaire/ self-report data-gathering methods	How changing to a self-report/survey method might affect the results and validity of the study
Milgram (obedience)	Laboratory-based study, observing how far a participant would go on the shock generator	To investigate how far participants would obey a malevolent authority figure instructing them to act against their conscience		
Piliavin et al. (subway Samaritan)	Field experiment using covert observation to record responses to staged incidents	To investigate whether an ill person who collapsed would get more help than a drunk person in the same situation		
Rosenhan (being sane in insane places)	Field experiment using participant observation, carried out covertly by the pseudopatients in hospital wards	To find out how patients on a psychiatric ward were treated, and to see if a person faking symptoms could be spotted		
Bandura et al. (aggression)	Laboratory experiment, covertly observing aggressive behaviour displayed in stage three	Do children learn to be aggressive by imitation?		

Making changes to the procedure/data-gathering method – How could the aim of laboratory and field experiments using observational methods be investigated using a survey/questionnaire/self-report methods?

Section C

(*You must answer* **either** *all parts of questions 17* **or** *all parts of question 18.*)

In Section C there will be a choice: you have to answer all parts of **one** of two questions in this section. Section C is worth 24 of the 120 marks available on this paper.

The questions in Section C will commonly relate the studies to the approaches and perspectives (social/individual differences/cognitive/developmental/physiological approach, and the behaviourist/psychodynamic perspective).

This question will be in four parts (a, b, c, d) and will generally require you to know the assumptions and criticisms (strengths and limitations) of the approaches and perspectives, and how these relate to the core studies, and to the topics studied in the core studies.

Here is an example of a question from Section C:

1.
    (a) Outline one assumption of the psychodynamic perspective in psychology. [2]
    (b) Describe how the psychodynamic perspective might explain mental disorders such as phobias. [4]
    (c) Describe one similarity and one difference between the study by Freud (Little Hans) and any other study of abnormal behaviour. [6]
    (d) Discuss the strengths and limitations of the psychodynamic perspective, using examples from any study involving this perspective. [12]

Revision activity

In order to prepare for the 'similarity/difference between studies' style of question (see (c) in the example above), you should carry out the following activity.

Get 15 index cards and write the researcher's name and a key word for each study on the cards, one study per card. You will also need a coin to toss.

Turn the 15 cards over on the table and shuffle them round. Working with a study buddy, pick a study card from the shuffled set. Then toss the coin. Heads means you have to identify a way the study on the card you picked is the same as another study from the same approach; tails means you have to identify a way the study is different from another study from the same approach.

Copy the table below – you will need 15 rows, one for each study.
Complete this table as you play the game and then use it as a revision aid.

There is a template for this 'similar to/different from' activity, along with a copy of the table, on the CD-ROM.

Study	Approach	Similar to...	Different from...:
Milgram (obedience)	Social	Piliavin et al.: Because both Piliavin et al. and Milgram carried out studies that required the participants to be deceived about the purpose of the study (Milgram) or about the nature of the 'emergency' (Piliavin et al.) Reicher and Haslam: Because both these studies had a volunteer sample	Reicher and Haslam: Because Reicher and Haslam carried out their study ethically, getting their participants' informed consent, whereas Milgram used deception in his study to conceal its aim Piliavin et al.: Because in Milgram's study the participants knew they were in a study, whereas the participants in Piliavin et al.'s study were not aware they were part of a study

To get the top band marks (10–12 marks) for (d) in Section C, you need to:

- write about at least two strengths and two weaknesses (if you were asked **only** for weaknesses or limitations, then you would offer at least four);

- have a good balance of strengths and weaknesses in your answer (when asked for both strengths and weaknesses);

- offer detailed and effective analysis, explaining each point clearly;

- provide an appropriate example from the study to support each point, illustrating the point being made;

- give an answer which is well structured and mostly grammatically correct, with only occasional spelling errors.

How can you make sure you get 12/12 here? One way might be to present each point, that is, each strength or weakness (limitation), using the model 'point, explain, example'. You should identify and explain your chosen strength or weakness (point and explain), then use an example from the study you have been given (or the study you have chosen, if there is a choice in the question) to illustrate the point you have made. Below is a question with a sample answer.

Discuss the strengths and limitations of the social approach using examples from Milgram's obedience study.

One strength of the social approach is that it identifies the way in which social influence, the behaviour of those around us, impacts on our behaviour. This is useful in explaining how people may behave in certain social situations, such as in crowds, or how they behave in the face of group pressure to conform. For example, in Milgram's study the impact of social influence can be seen in the high level of obedience to the authority figure, who prodded 65 per cent of the participants into carrying on shocking the learner with the shock generator up to 450v.

Another strength of the social approach is that it makes us question our own behaviour and challenges our belief that we are unique and fully in control of our own choices. If we are aware of this, we are in a good position to avoid falling under the influence of those who might have a negative influence on us, by choosing carefully those whom we want to have power over us. We need to use our democratic power wisely. Milgram's study shows us how good people might become easily integrated into a malevolent system, so we need to be prepared to monitor the system under which we live with a critical eye.

A limitation of the social approach is that it is difficult to provide evidence for social behaviour by carrying out research in the artificial setting of the laboratory. It is hard to measure social variables in the laboratory and this can lead to the study being low in ecological validity.

For example, the high level of obedience recorded in Milgram's laboratory-based study carried out at Yale University may have misled us about the extent to which people might obey in a real-life setting.

A further limitation or weakness of the social approach is that it does not provide us with hard-and-fast rules for behaviour. It does not take into account the individual variables that people bring to a situation, such as their personalities or moral strength. In Milgram's study, for example, 35 per cent of the participants did NOT go all the way to 450v, and called a halt to the study by refusing to go on. This shows us that social influence does not affect everyone in the same situation in the same way.

Don't worry if this looks very hard. You will get the hang of it if you practise writing up the strengths and weaknesses of all the approaches and perspectives, and illustrating them with each of the related studies.

> **Revision activity**
> Have a go at writing your own questions for this type of question:
>
> **Discuss the strengths and limitations of the xxxxxx approach, using examples from the yyyyyy study.**
>
> For xxxxxx, add in any of the five approaches (e.g. physiological).
>
> For yyyyyy, add any study that can be used to illustrate this approach (e.g. Dement and Kleitman).
>
> Then you can write the answers to your own questions!

And finally… doing exams can be loving exams…

Now you have worked your way through this final chapter, you should have a good idea of what it is you need to know about core studies, and have some ideas about how you can learn them and be prepared to write about them in your exam.

Being organised and prepared can take the stress out of exams and leave you with just enough of a buzz of arousal to really enjoy it and do your best on the day. We hope you found this book useful. Good luck!

Bibliography

Ahrens, S.R. (1954) 'Beiträge zur Entwicklung des Physiognoimie und Mimikerkenntnisse' (Contributions on the development of physiognomy and mimicry recognition), *Seitschrift für Experimentelle und Angewandte Psychologie*, 2, 412–54.

Aitchison, J. (1983) *The Articulate Mammal*, London: Hutchinson, 2nd edition.

Alexander, P.C. and Lupfer, S.L. (1987) 'Family characteristics and long-term consequences associated with sexual abuse', *Archives of Sexual Behaviour*, 16, 235–45.

Allen, V.L. and Levine, J.M. (1971) 'Social pressures and personal influence', *Journal of Experimental Social Psychology*, 7, 122–4.

Allport, F.H. (1955) *Theories of Perception and the Concept of Structure*, New York: Wiley.

Allport, G.W. (1954) *The Nature of Prejudice*, Wokingham: Addison-Wesley.

Anderson, J. (1995) *Learning and Memory: An Integrated Approach*, Chichester: Wiley.

Andreassi, J.L. (2006) *Psychophysiology: Human Behavior and Physiological Response*, Oxford: Routledge.

Ardrey, R. (1966) *The Territorial Imperative*, New York: Dell.

Arendt, H. (1965) *Eichmann in Jerusalem: A report on the banality of evil*, New York: Viking.

Aronson, E. (1976) *The Social Animal*, San Francisco: W.H. Freeman & Co.

Aronson, E. (1994) *The Social Animal*, New York: W.H. Freeman & Co., 7th edition.

Aronson, E. and Osherow, N. (1980) 'Co-operation, prosocial behaviour and academic performance: Experiments in the desegregated classroom' in L. Bickman (ed.), *Applied Social Psychology Annual*, Vol. 1, Beverly Hills, CA: Sage Publications.

Aronson, E., Wilson, T.D. and Akert, R.M. (1997) *Social Psychology*, New York: Longman, 3rd edition.

Asch, S.E. (1951) 'Effect of group pressure upon the modification and distortion of judgements' in H. Guetzkow (ed.), *Groups, Leadership and Men*, Pittsburg, PA: Carnegie Press.

Aschoff, J. (1979) 'Circadian rhythms: General features and endocrinological aspects' in

D.T. Krieger (ed.), *Endocrine Rhythms*, New York: Raven Press.

Aserinsky, E. and Kleitman, N. (1955) 'Two types of ocular motility occurring in sleep', *Journal of Applied Physiology*, 8, 1, 1–10.

Aserinsky, E. and Kleitman, N. (1953) 'Regularly occurring periods of eye motility and concomitant phenomena during sleep', *Science*, 118, 273–4.

Atkinson, R.C. and Shiffrin, R.M. (1968) 'Human memory: a proposed system and its control processes' in K.W. Spence and J.T. Spence (eds), *The Psychology of Learning and Motivation*, Vol. 2, London: Academic Press.

Atkinson, R.C. and Shiffrin, R.M. (1971) 'The control of short-term memory', *Scientific American*, 224, 82–90.

Atkinson, R.L., Atkinson, R.C., Smith, E.E. and Bem, D.J. (1993) *Introduction to Psychology*, New York: Harcourt Brace Jovanovich, 11th edition.

Ax, A.F. (1953) 'The physiological differentiation between fear and anger in humans', *Psychosomatic Medicine*, 15, 433–42.

Ayers, I. (1991) Fair driving: Gender and race discrimination in retail car negotiations, *Harvard Law Review*, 104.

Baddeley, A. (2000) 'The episodic buffer: A new component of working memory?', *Trends in Cognitive Sciences*, 4, no.11, 417–23.

Baddeley, A.D. and Hitch, G.J. (1974) 'Working memory' in G.H. Bower (ed.), *The Psychology of Learning and Motivation*, Vol. 8, London: Academic Press.

Bailey, A., Le Couteur, A., Gottesman, I., Bolton, P., Simonoff, E., Yuzda, E. and Rutter, M. (1995) 'Autism as a strongly genetic disorder: evidence from a British twin study', *Psychological Medicine*, Jan, 25, no.1, 63–77.

Baird, G., Simonoff, E., Pickles, A., Chandler, S., Loucas, T., Meldrum, D. and Charman, T. (2006) 'Prevalence of disorders of the autism spectrum in a population cohort of children in South Thames: The Special Needs and Autism Project (SNAP)', *The Lancet*, 368, no.9531, 210–15.

Bandura, A., Ross, D. and Ross, S.A. (1961) *Transmission of Aggression through Imitation of Aggressive Models*.

Bandura, A. (1977) 'Self-efficacy: toward a unifying theory of behavioural change', *Psychological Review*, 84, 191–215.

Bandura, A. (1977) *Social Learning Theory*, Englewood Cliffs, NJ: Prentice Hall.

Banyard, P. and Grayson, A. (1996) *Introducing Psychological Research*, Basingstoke: Macmillan Press.

Banyard, P. and Grayson, A. (2000) *Introducing Psychological Research*, Basingstoke: Palgrave Macmillan.

Bard, B. and Sachs, J. (1977) 'Language acquisition patterns in two normal children of deaf parents', paper presented to the 2nd Annual Boston University Conference on Language Acquisition, October 1977, cited in J.G. de Villiers and P.A. de Villiers (1978) *Early Language*, London: Fontana.

Baron-Cohen, S. (2005) 'The neuropsychology of autism and pervasive developmental disorders – the extreme male brain theory: an expert interview with Simon Baron-Cohen, PhD, MPhil', *Medscape Psychiatry and Mental Health*, 10, no.2, available at: http://www.medscape.com/viewarticle/518449

Baron-Cohen, S. (2002) 'The extreme-male-brain theory of autism', available at: http://www.autism-researchcentre.com/docs/papers/1999_BC_extrememalebrain.pdf

Baron-Cohen, S. (1999) 'The extreme-male-brain theory of autism' in Tager-Flusberg, H. (ed.) *Neurodevelopmental Disorders*, Cambridge, MA: MIT Press.

Baron-Cohen, S. (1989) 'Perceptual role-taking and protodeclarative pointing in autism', *British Journal of Developmental Psychology*, 7, 113–27.

Baron-Cohen, S. and Bolton, P. (1993) *Autism: the facts*, Oxford: Oxford University Press.

Baron-Cohen, S., Cosmides, L. and Tooby, J. (1997) *Mindblindness: An Essay on Autism and Theory of Mind*, Cambridge, MA: MIT Press.

Baron-Cohen, S., Leslie, A.M. and Frith, U. (1985) 'Does the autistic child have a theory of mind?', *Cognition*, 21, 37–46.

Barrett, M.D. (1986) 'Early semantic representations and early word usage', in S.A. Kuczaj and M.D. Barrett (eds), *The Development of Word Meaning*, New York: Springer Verlag.

Bartlett, F.C. (1932) *Remembering: A study in experimental and social psychology*, Cambridge: Cambridge University Press.

Bates, E., Bretherton, I. and Snyder, L. (1988) *From First Words to Grammar: Individual differences and dissociable mechanisms*, Cambridge: Cambridge University Press.

Batson, C.D. (1991) 'The altruism question: toward a social-psychological answer', Hillsdale, NJ: Erlbaum.

Bee, H. (1992) *The Developing Child*, New York: HarperCollins.

Bee, H. (1995) *The Growing Child*, New York: HarperCollins.

Berne, E. (1964) *Games People Play*, London: Penguin.

Blakemore, C. (1988) *The Mind Machine*, London: BBC Books.

Bliss, E.L. (1983) 'Multiple personalities, related disorders, and hypnosis', *American Journal of Clinical Hypnosis*, 26, 114–23.

Bower, G.H., Black, J.B. and Turner, T.J. (1979) 'Scripts in memory for text', *Cognitive Psychology*, 11, 177–220.

Bower, T.G.R. (1971) 'The object in the world of the infant', *Scientific American*, 225, 38–47.

Bowlby, J. (1951) *Maternal Care and Mental Health*, Geneva: World Health Organisation.

Bowlby, J. (1953) *Childcare and the Growth of Love*, London: Penguin.

Bowler, D.M. (1992) 'Theory of mind in Asperger Syndrome', *Journal of Child Psychology and Psychiatry*, 33, 877–93.

British Gambling Prevalence Survey (1999), http://www.gamblingcommission.gov.uk/Client/detail.asp?ContentId=288

British Psychological Society (1993), www.bps.org.uk

Broadbent, D.E. (1958) *Perception and Communication*, Oxford: Pergamon.

Brown, G.L., Goodwin, F.K., Ballenger, J.C., Goyer, P.F. and Major, L.F. (1979) 'Aggression in human correlates with cerebrospinal fluid amine metabolites', *Psychiatry Research*, 1, 131–9.

Brown, R. (1973) *A First Language*, Cambridge, MA: Harvard University Press.

Brown, R. (1986) *Social Psychology*, New York: The Free Press, 2nd edition.

Brown, R. (1995) *Prejudice: Its Social Psychology*, Oxford: Blackwell.

Bruner, J.S. and Goodman, C.C. (1947) 'Value and need as organising factors in perception', *Journal of Abnormal and Social Psychology*, 42, 33–44.

Burnstein, E., Crandall, C. and Kitayama, S. (1994) 'Some neoDarwinian decision rules for altruism: Weighing cues for inclusive fitness as a function of the biological importance of the decision', *Journal of Personality and Social Psychology*, 67, 773–89.

Burt, C. (1912) 'The evidence for the concept of intelligence', *British Journal of Educational Psychology*, 25, 158–77.

Burt, C. (1966) 'The examination at eleven plus', *British Journal of Educational Studies*, 7, 99–117.

Buss, A.H. (1966) *Psychopathology*, New York: Wiley.

Buss, A.H. (1966) 'Instrumentality of aggression, feedback and frustration as determinants of physical aggression', *Journal of Personality and Social Psychology*, 3, 153–62.

Butterworth, G. and Harris, M. (1994) *Principles of Developmental Psychology*, Lawrence Erlbaum Associates Ltd.

Campbell, R., Baron-Cohen, S. and Walker, J. (1995) 'Do people with autism show a face advantage in recognition of familiar faces and their parts? A test of central coherence theory', unpublished ms, Goldsmiths College, University of London.

Cannon, W.B. (1927) 'The James-Lange theory of emotions: A critical examination and an alternative', *American Journal of Psychology*, 39, 106–24.

Cannon, W.B. (1929) *Bodily Changes in Pain, Hunger, Fear and Rage*, New York: Appleton-Century-Crofts.

Carey, S. (1978) 'The child as word learner' in M. Halle, J. Bresnan and G. Miller (eds), *Linguistic Theory and Psychological Reality*, Cambridge, MA: MIT Press.

Carlson, N.R. (1986) *Physiology of Behaviour*, London: Allyn and Bacon, 3rd edition.

Carter, R. (1998) *Mapping the Mind*, London: Weidenfeld & Nicolson.

Cave, S. (2002) *Classification and Diagnosis of Psychological Abnormality*, London: Routledge.

Chomsky, N. (1965) *Aspects of the Theory of Syntax*, Cambridge, MA: MIT Press.

Chomsky, N. (1968) *Language and Mind*, New York: Harcourt Brace Jovanovich.

Chun, M. and Phelps, E. (1999) 'Memory deficits for implicit contextual information in amnesic subjects with hippocampal damage', *Nature Neuroscience*, 2, no.9, 844–7.

Clark, K. and Clark, M. (1947) 'Racial identification and preference in Negro children' in T.M. Newcombe and E.L. Hartley (eds), *Readings in Social Psychology*, New York: Holt, 169–78.

Clarke, A.M. and Clarke, A.D.B. (1976) *Early Experience: Myth and Evidence*, London: Open Books.

Cohen, J.D., Perlstein, W.M., Braver, T.S., Nystrom, L.E., Noll, D.C., Jonides, J. and Smith, E.E. (1997) 'Temporal dynamics of brain activation during a working memory task', *Nature*, 386, 604–8.

Corney, W.J. and Cummings, W.T. (1985) 'Gambling behaviour and information processing biases', *Journal of Gambling Studies*, 1, no.2, 111–18.

Craik, F. and Lockhart, R. (1972) 'Levels of processing', *Journal of Verbal Learning and Verbal Behaviour*, 11, 671–84.

Crime and Justice Survey (2003) available at: http://www.homeoffice.gov.uk/rds/offending_survey.html

Crutchfield, R.S. (1962) cited in R. Gross (1992) *Psychology: The Science of Mind and Behaviour*, London: Hodder & Stoughton, 2nd edition.

Curtiss, S. (1977) *Genie: A psycholinguistic study of a modern-day 'wild child'*, London: Academic Press.

Dabbs, J.M., Carr, T.S., Frady, R.L. and Riad, J.K. (1995) 'Testosterone, crime and misbehaviour among 692 male prison inmates', *Personality and Individual Differences*, 18, 627–33.

Damasio, A.R., Tranel, D. and Damasio, H. (1990) 'Individuals with sociopathic behaviour caused by frontal damage fail to respond autonomically to social stimuli', *Behavioural Brain Research*, 41, 81–94.

Darley, J.M. and Batson, C.D. (1973) 'From Jerusalem to Jericho: A study of situational and dispositional variables in helping behaviour', *Journal of Personality and Social Psychology*, 27, 100–8.

Darley, J.M. and Latané, B. (1968) 'Bystander intervention in emergencies: Diffusion of responsibility', *Journal of Personality and Social Psychology*, 8, 377–83.

Darley, J.M. and Latané, B. (1970) 'Norms and normative behaviour: field studies of social interdependence' in J. Macauley and L. Berkowitz (eds), *Altruism and Helping Behaviour*, New York: Academic Press.

Dasen, P. (1994) 'Culture and cognitive development from a Piagetian perspective' in W.J. Lonner and R.S. Malpass (eds), *Psychology and Culture*, Boston, MA: Allyn and Bacon.

Davison, G. and Neale, J. (1996) *Abnormal Psychology*, New York: Wiley, 6th edition.

Dawkins, R. (1976) *The Selfish Gene*, Oxford: Oxford University Press.

Dement, W. (1960) 'The effect of dream deprivation', *Science*, 131, 1705–7.

Diamond, M.C. (1988) *Enriching Heredity*, New York: The Free Press.

Diamond, M.C., Krech, D. and Rosenzweig, M.R. (1964) 'The effects of an enriched environment on the rat cerebral cortex', *Journal of Comparative Neurology*, 123, 111–19.

Diamond, M.C., Connor, J.R., Orenberg, E.K., Bissell, M., Yost, M. and Krueger, A. (1980) 'Environmental influences on serotonin and cyclic nucleotides in rat cerebral cortex', *Science*, 210, 652–4.

Diamond, S., Baldwin, R. and Diamond, R. (1963) *Inhibition and Choice*, New York: Harper & Row.

Diener, E. (1979) 'Deindividuation, self-awareness and disinhibition', *Journal of Personality and Social Psychology*, 37, 1160–71.

Diener, E. (1980) 'Deindividuation: The absence of self-awareness and self-regulation in group members' in P.B. Paulus (ed.), *Psychology of Group Influence*, Hillsdale, NJ: Lawrence Erlbaum.

Diener, E., Fraser, S.C., Beaman, A.L. and Kelem, R.T. (1976) 'Effects of deindividuation variables on stealing among Halloween trick-or-treaters', *Journal of Personality and Social Psychology*, 33, 178–83.

Dobson, C.B., Hardy, M., Heyes, S., Humphreys, A. and Humphreys, P. (1993) *Understanding Psychology*, London: Weidenfeld & Nicolson.

Dodd, M.L., Klos, K.J., Bower, J.H., Geda, Y.E., Josephs, K.A. and Ahlskog, J.E. (2005) 'Pathological gambling caused by drugs used to treat Parkinson's disease', *Archives of Neurology*, 62, 1377–81. Published online 11 July 2005 (doi:10.1001/archneur.62.9.noc50009).

Dollard, J., Doob, L., Miller, N., Mowrer, O.H. and Sears, R.R. (1939) *Frustration and Aggression*, New Haven, CT: Yale University Press.

Donaldson, M. (1978) *Children's Minds*, London: Fontana.

Dougherty, M.J. (2000) 'The genetics of autism', available at: http://www.actionbioscience.org/genomic/dougherty.html#Primer

Dunn, J. (1988) *The Beginnings of Social Understanding*, Oxford: Blackwell.

Dunn, J. and Kendrick, C. (1979) 'Interaction between young siblings in the context of family relationships' in M. Lewis and L.A. Rosenblum (eds), *The Child and its Family*, New York: Plenum Press.

Dunn, J. and Munn, P. (1985) 'Becoming a family member: family conflict and the development of social understanding in the first year', *Child Development*, 50, 306–18.

Dunn, J. and Plomin, R. (1990) *Separate Lives: Why siblings are so different*, New York: Basic Books.

Dunn, J., Kendrick, C. and MacNamee, R. (1981) 'The reaction of first-born children to the birth of a sibling: mothers' reports', *Journal of Child Psychology and Psychiatry*, 22, 1–18.

Durkin, K. (1995) *Developmental Social Psychology: From Infancy to Old Age*, Oxford: Blackwell.

Dutton, D.C. and Aron, A.P. (1974) 'Some evidence for heightened sexual attraction under conditions of high anxiety', *Journal of Personality & Social Psychology*, 30, 510–17.

Eagly, A.H. (1987) *Sex Differences in Social Behaviour: A social-role interpretation*, Hillsdale, NJ: Erlbaum.

Eagly, A.H. and Crowley, M. (1986) 'Gender and helping behaviour: A meta-analytic review of the social psychological literature', *Psychological Bulletin*, 100, 283–308.

Eichelman, B. (1993) 'Bridges from the animal laboratory to the study of violent or criminal individuals' in S. Hodgins (ed.), *Mental Disorder and Crime*, Newbury Park, CA: Sage, 194–207.

Eisen, S.A., Slutske, W.S., Lyons, M.J., Lassman, J., Xian, H., Toomey, R., Chantarujikapong, S. and Tsuang, M.T. (2001) 'The genetics of pathological gambling', *Seminars in Clinical Neuropsychiatry*, July, 6, no.3, 195–204.

Ekmon, P. (1992) 'An argument for basic emotions', *Cognition and Emotion*, 6, 169–200.

Engle, J. (1996) 'Introduction to temporal lobe epilepsy', *Epilepsy Research*, 26, 141–50.

Eriksson, P.S., Perfilieva, E., Bjork-Eriksson, T., Alborn, A.M., Nordborg, C., Peterson, D.A. and Gage, F.H. (1998) 'Neurogenesis in the adult human hippocampus', *Nature Medicine*, November, 4, no.11, 1313–17.

Exploring Autism (2002) 'What is autism?', available at: http://www.exploringautism.org/autism/index.htm

Eysenck, H.J. (1947) *Dimensions of Personality*, London: Routledge and Kegan Paul.

Eysenck, H.J. (1952) 'The effects of psychotherapy: An evaluation', *Journal of Consulting Psychology*, 16, 319–24.

Eysenck, H.J. (1970) *Crime and Personality*, London: Paladin.

Eysenck, H.J. (1973) *The Inequality of Man*, London: Temple Smith.

Eysenck, H.J. and Gudjoinsson, G.H. (1989) *The Causes and Cures of Criminality*, New York: Plenum.

Eysenck, M.W. (2004) *Psychology: An International Perspective*, London: Psychology Press.

Family Expenditure Survey 2000–2001, www.statistics.gov.uk/StatBase/Source.asp?vlnk=1385&More=Y - 33k -

Fantz, R.L. (1961) 'The origin of form perception', *Scientific American*, 204, 66–72.

Festinger, L., Pepitone, A. and Newcomb, T. (1952) 'Some consequences of deindividuation in a group', *Journal of Abnormal and Social Psychology*, 47, 382–9.

Finkelhor, D. (1979) *Sexually Victimised Children*, New York: Free Press.

Fisher, S. (1993) 'The pull of the fruit machine: a sociological typology of young players', *Sociological Review*, 41, 446–74.

Fiske, S.T. and Taylor, S.E. (1991) *Social Cognition*, New York: McGraw-Hill, 2nd edition.

Flavell, J.H. (1985) *Cognitive Development*, London: Prentice Hall.

Freud, A. and Dann, S. (1951) 'An experiment in group upbringing', *Psychoanalytic Study of the Child*, 6, 127–68.

Freud, S. (1909) *Analysis of a Phobia in a Five-year-old Boy*, in *The Pelican Freud Library* (1977) Vol. 8, Case Histories 1.

Freud, S. (1930) *Civilisation and its Discontents*, London: Hogarth Press.

Freud, S. (1905/1977) *Three Essays on the Theory of Sexuality*, Pelican Freud Library, Harmondsworth: Penguin.

Frith, U. (1989) *Autism: Explaining the Enigma*, Oxford: Basil Blackwell.

Frith, U. (1990) *Autism*, Oxford: Blackwell.

Frith, U. (2002) *Autism: Explaining the Enigma*, Oxford: Blackwell.

Frith, U. (1993) 'Autism', *Scientific American*, 268, no.66, 108–14.

Gardner, R.A. and Gardner, B.T. (1969) 'Teaching Sign Language to a Chimpanzee'. *Science*, 165, 664–72.

Gazzaniga, M.S., LeDoux, J.E. and Wilson, D.H. (1977) 'Language, praxis and the right hemisphere: Clues to some mechanisms of consciousness', *Neurology*, 27, 1144–7.

Gerard, H. and Miller, N. (1975) *School Desegregation*, cited in R. Brown (1986) *Social Psychology*, New York: The Free Press, 2nd edition.

Gergen, K.J., Gergen, M.M. and Barton, W. (1973) 'Deviance in the dark', *Psychology Today*, 7, 129–30.

Geschwind, N. and Levitsky, W. (1968) 'Human brain: left-right asymmetries in temporal speech region', *Science*, 161, 186–7.

Ghuman, P.A.S. (1982) in Eysenck, M.W. (2004) *Psychology: An International Perspective*, Psychology Press.

Giddens, A. (1997) *Sociology*, Abingdon: Polity Press, 3rd edition.

Gilbert, G.M. (1951) 'Stereotype persistence and change among college students', *Journal of Abnormal and Social Psychology*, 46, 245–54.

Gluhbegovic, N. and Williams, T.H. (1980) *The Human Brain: A Photographic Atlas*, Hagerstown, MD: Harper & Row.

Goldfarb, W. (1943) 'The effects of early institutional care on adolescent personality', *Journal of Experimental Education*, 12, 106–29.

Gopnik, A., Meltzoff, A.N. and Kuhl, P.K. (1999) *The Scientist in the Crib: What Early Learning Tells*

Us About the Mind, New York: HarperCollins Publishers.

Gould, E., Reeves, A.J., Fallah, M., Tanapat, P., Gross, C.G. and Fuchs, E. (1999) 'Hippocampal neurogenesis in adult Old World primates', *Proceedings of the National Academy of Sciences of the United States of America*, 27 April, 96, no.9, 5263–7.

Gregory, R. (1977) *Eye and Brain*, London: Weidenfeld & Nicolson.

Gross, R. (1992) *Psychology: Science of Mind and Behaviour*, London: Hodder & Stoughton, 2nd edition.

Gross, R. (2005) *Psychology: The Science of Mind and Behaviour*, London: Hodder Arnold, 3rd edition.

Gross, R. (1999) *Key Studies in Psychology*, London: Hodder & Stoughton, 3rd edition.

Gunter, B. and McAleer, J. (1990) *Children and Television*, London: Routledge.

Gupta, R. and Derevensky, J. (1997) 'Familial and social influences on juvenile gambling behavior', *Journal of Gambling Studies*, 13, no.3, 179–92.

Gwinner, E. (1986) 'Circannual rhythms in the control of avian rhythms', *Advances in the Study of Behaviour*, 16, 191–228.

Haney, C., Banks, C. and Zimbardo, P. (1973) 'A study of prisoners and guards in a simulated prison', *Naval Research Reviews*, 30, no.9, 4–17.

Happé, F. (1994) 'An advanced test of theory of mind: Understanding of story characters' thoughts and feelings by able autistic, mentally handicapped, and normal children and adults', *Journal of Autism and Developmental Disorders*, 24, 129–54.

Happé, F.G.E. (1997) 'Central coherence and theory of mind in autism: Reading homographs in context', *British Journal of Developmental Psychology*, 15, no.1, 1–12.

Harris, J. (1990) *Early Language Development*, London: Routledge.

Harris, M., Jones, D., Brookes, S. and Grant, J. (1986) 'Relations between the non-verbal context of maternal speech and rate of language development', *British Journal of Developmental Psychology*, 4, 261–8.

Harris, P.L. (1988) *Children and Emotion: the Development of Psychological Understanding*, Oxford: Blackwell.

Harris, P.L. and Muncer, A. (1988) 'Autistic children's understanding of beliefs and desires', paper presented at the British Psychological Society Developmental Section Conference, Coleg Harlech, Wales.

Hartmann, E. (1973) *The Functions of Sleep*, New Haven: Yale University.

Hartmann, E. (1984) *The Nightmare*, New York: Basic Books.

Hatzfeld, J. (2005) *Machete Season: The Killers in Rwanda Speak*, Straus and Giroux: New York.

Hauri, P. (1979) 'What can insomniacs teach us about the functions of sleep?' in R. Drucker-Colin, M. Shkurovich and M.B. Sterman (eds), *The Functions of Sleep*, New York: Academic, 251–71.

Hawkes, N., *The Times*, London, 27 January 1999, reported in *Psychology Review*, February 2000, 6, no.3.

Hayes, K.H. and Hayes, C. (1951) 'Intellectual development of a house-raised chimpanzee', *Proceedings of the American Philosophical Society*, 95, 105–9.

Hayes, N. (1993) *Principles of Social Psychology*, Hove: Psychology Press.

Hayes, N. (1994) *Foundations of Psychology: An Introductory Text*, Thomson Learning.

Heider, F. (1958) *The Psychology of Interpersonal Relations*, New York: Wiley.

Heim, A. (1970) *Intelligence and Personality*, Harmondsworth: Penguin.

Henslin, J.M. (1967) in Reith, G. (1999) *The Age of Chance: Gambling in Western Culture*, Abingdon: Routledge.

Hetherington, E.M. and Parke, R.D. (1986) *Child Psychology: A Contemporary View*, New York: McGraw-Hill, 3rd edition.

Hetherington, E.M. and Parke, R.D. (1987) *Child Psychology: A Contemporary Viewpoint*, New York: McGraw-Hill.

Hicks, R.E. (1975) 'Intrahemispheric response competition between vocal and unimanual performance in normal adult human males', *Journal of Comparative and Physiological Psychology*, 89, 50–60.

Hinde, R.A. (1987) *Individuals, Relationships and Culture: Links between Ethology and the Social Sciences*, Cambridge: Cambridge University Press.

Hinton, P.R. (2000) *Stereotypes, Cognition and Culture*, Hove: Psychology Press.

Hobbes, T. (1986) *Leviathan*, Harmondsworth: Penguin Press (original work published in 1651).

Hobsbawm, E. (1995) *Age of Extremes: The short twentieth century 1914–1991*, London: Abacus.

Hockett, C.F. (1959) 'Animal "languages" and human language', *Human Biology*, 31, 32–9.

Hodges, J. and Tizard, B. (1989) 'Social and family relationships of ex-institutional adolescents', *Journal of Child Psychology and Psychiatry*, 30, no. 1, 77–97.

Hofling, K.C., Brotzman, E., Dalrymple, S., Graves, N. and Pieces, C.M. (1966) 'An experimental study in the nurse–physician relationship', *Journal of Nervous and Mental Disorders*, 143, 171–80.

Hohmann, G.W. (1966) 'Some effects of spinal cord lesions on experienced emotional feelings', *Psychophysiology*, 3, 143–56.

Hopper, A., Ciorciari, J., Johnson, G., Spensley, J., Sergejew, A. and Stough, C. (2002) 'EEG coherence and dissociative identity disorder: Comparing EEG coherence in DID hosts, alters, controls and acted alters', *Journal of Trauma and Dissociation*, 3, 75–88.

Horn, J.M. (1983) 'The Texas adoption project: Adopted children and their intellectual resemblance to biological and adoptive parents', *Child Development*, 54, 268–75.

Horne, J. (1988) *Why We Sleep: The functions of sleep in humans and other mammals*, Oxford: Oxford University Press.

Horne, J.A. and Minard, A. (1985) 'Sleep and sleepiness following a behaviourally "active" day', *Ergonomics*, 28, 567–75.

Hovland, C.I. and Sears, R.R. (1940) 'Minor studies in aggression: 6. Correlation of lynchings with economic indices', *Journal of Psychology*, 9, 301–10.

Hubel, D.H. and Wiesel, T.N. (1979) 'Brain mechanisms of vision', *Scientific American*, 241, no.3, 150–62.

Huesmann, L.R. and Eron, L.D. (1984) 'Cognitive processes and the persistence of aggressive behaviour', *Aggressive Behaviour*, 10, 243–51.

Huesmann, L.R. and Eron, L.D. (1986) *Television and the Aggressive Child: A cross-national comparison*, Hillsdale, NJ: Erlbaum.

Hughes, M. (1975) *Egocentrism in Preschool Children*, unpublished Ph.D. thesis, University of Edinburgh.

Huston, T.L., Ruggiero, M., Conner, R. and Geis, G. (1981) 'Bystander intervention into crime: A study based on naturally-occurring episodes', *Social Psychology Quarterly*, 44, 14–23.

Ineichen, B., Harrison, G. and Morgan, H.G. (1984) 'Psychiatric hospital admissions in Bristol: 1. Geographical and ethnic factors', *British Journal of Psychiatry*, 145, 600–4.

Jackson, J.L., Calhoun, K.S., Amick, A.E., Maddever, H.M. and Habif, V.L. (1990) 'Young adult women who report childhood intrafamilial sexual abuse: Subsequent adjustment', *Archives of Sexual Behaviour*, 19, 211–21.

Jackson, P. (1995) *Dear Uncle Go: Male Homosexuality in Thailand*, Bangkok: Bua Luang Books.

Jacobs, B., Schall, M. and Scheibel, A.B. (1993) 'A quantitative dendritic analysis of Wernicke's area in human. II. Gender, hemispheric, and environmental change, *Journal of Comparative Neurology*, 327, 97–111.

Jacobs, P.A., Brunton, M. and Melville, M.M. (1965) 'Aggressive behaviour, mental abnormality and the XYY male', *Nature*, 208, 1351–2.

Jarrad, L.E. (1995) 'What does the hippocampus really do?', *Behavioural Brain Research*, 71, no.1–2, 1–10.

James, W. (1984) 'What is an emotion?', *Mind*, 19, 188–205.

Jenness, A. (1932) 'The role of discussion in changing opinion regarding matter of fact', *Journal of Abnormal and Social Psychology*, 27, 279–96.

Jensen, A.R. (1969) 'How much can we boost IQ and scholastic achievement?', *Harvard Educational Review*, 39, 1–123.

Johnson, R.D. and Downing, L.E. (1979) 'Deindividuation and valence of cues: Effects on prosocial and antisocial behaviour', *Journal of Personality and Social Psychology*, 37, 1532–8.

Jones, E. (1953–7) *Sigmund Freud: Life and Work*, New York: Basic Books, 3 vols.

Jones, E.E. and Sigall, H. (1971) 'The bogus pipeline: A new paradigm for measuring affect and attitude', *Psychological Bulletin*, 76, 349–64.

Jones, R.K. (1966) 'Observations on stammering after localized cerebral injury', *Journal of Neurology, Neurosurgery and Psychiatry*, 29, 192–5.

Kahney, H. (1993) *Problem Solving Current Issues*, Buckingham: Open University Press, 2nd edition.

Kalat, J.W. (1988) *Biological Psychology*, Belmont: Wadsworth.

Kamin, L. (1974) *The Science and Politics of IQ*, Harmondsworth: Penguin.

Kanner, L. (1943) 'Autistic disturbances of affective contact', *Nervous Child*, 2, 217–50.

Kanner, L. and Eisenberg, L. (1955) 'Notes of the follow-up studies of autistic children' in P. Hoch and J. Zubin (eds), *Psychopathology of Childhood*, New York: Grune and Stratton.

Karau, S.J. and Williams, K.D. (1993) 'Social loafing: A meta-analytic review and theoretical integration', *Journal of Personality and Social Psychology*, 65, 681–706.

Karlins, M., Coffman, T.L. and Walters, G. (1969) 'On the fading of social stereotypes: Studies in three generations of college students', *Journal of Personality and Social Psychology*, 13, 1–16.

Katz, D. and Braly, K.W. (1933) 'Racial stereotypes of 100 college students', *Journal of Abnormal and Social Psychology*, 28, 280–90.

Kaufman, L. and Rock, I. (1962) 'The moon illusion', *Science*, 136, 1023–31.

Kelley, H.H. (1973) 'The process of causal attribution', *American Psychologist*, 28, 107–28.

Kellogg, W.N. and Kellogg, L.A. (1933) *The Ape and the Child*, New York: McGraw-Hill.

Kelman, H.C. (1958) 'Compliance, identification and internalisation: Three processes of attitude change', *Journal of Conflict Resolution*, 2, 51–60.

Kelman, H.C. and Hovland, C.I. (1953) 'Reinstatement of the communication in delayed measurement of opinion change', *Journal of Abnormal and Social Psychology*, 48, 327–35.

Kilham, W. and Mann, L. (1974) 'Levels of destructive obedience as a function of transmitter and executant roles in the Milgram obedience paradigm', *Journal of Personality and Social Psychology*, 29, 696–702.

Kimura, D. (1973a) 'Manual activity during speaking – I. Right handers', *Neuropsychologia*, 11, 45–50.

Kimura, D. (1973b) 'Manual activity during speaking – II. Left handers', *Neuropsychologia*, 11, 51–5.

Kinsborne, M. (1972) 'Eye and head turning indicates cerebral lateralisation', *Science*, 176, 539–41.

Kline, P. and Storey, R. (1977) 'A factor analytic study of the oral character', *British Journal of Social and Clinical Psychology*, 16, no.3, 317–28.

Kolb, B. and Wishaw, I.Q. (1990) *Fundamentals of Neuropsychology*, New York: W.H. Freeman, 3rd edition.

La Pière, R.T. (1934) 'Attitudes vs actions', *Social Forces*, 13, 230–7.

Ladouceur, R., Gaboury, A., Bujold, A., Lachance, N. and Tremblay, S. (1991) 'Ecological validity in laboratory studies of videopoker gaming', *Journal of Gambling Studies*, 7, 109–16.

Ladouceur, R., Gaboury, A., Dumont, M. and Rochette, P. (1988) 'Gambling: Relationships between the frequency of wins and irrational thinking', *Journal of Psychology*, 122, 409–14.

Lahey, B.B. (1983) *Psychology: An introduction*, Dubuque, IA: William C. Brown & Co.

Langer, E.J. (1975) 'The illusion of control', *Journal of Personality and Social Psychology*, 32, no.2, 311–28.

Latané, B. and Darley, J.M. (1968) 'Group inhibition of bystander intervention', *Journal of Personality and Social Psychology*, 10, 215–21.

Latané, B. and Darley, J.M. (1970) *The Unresponsive Bystander: Why doesn't he help?*, Englewood Cliffs, NJ: Prentice Hall.

Latané, B. and Rodin, J. (1969) 'A lady in distress: Inhibiting effects of friends and strangers on bystander intervention', *Journal of Experimental Social Psychology*, 5, 189–202.

Le Bon, G. (1895) *The Crowd: a study of the popular mind*, London: T. Fisher Unwin.

LeDoux, J., Wilson, D.H. and Gazzaniga, M. (1977) 'A divided mind', *Annals of Neurology*, 2, 417–21.

Lenneberg, E. (1967) *Biological Foundations of Language*, New York: Wiley.

Lewis, D.O., Pincus, J.H., Bard, B. *et al.* (1988) 'Neuropsychiatric, psycho-educational, and family characteristics of 14 juveniles condemned to death in the United States', *American Journal of Psychiatry*, 154, 584–9.

Liebert, R.M. and Baron, R.A. (1972) 'Some immediate effects of televised violence on children's behaviour', *Developmental Psychology*, 6, 469–75.

Lintern, F., Williams, L. and Hill, A. (2003) *Psychology AS for OCR*, Oxford: Heinemann.

Littlewood, R. and Lipsedge, M. (1989) *Aliens and Alienists: Ethnic Minorities and Psychiatry*, London: Unwin Hyman.

Llewellyn, D.J. (2003) Available at: http://www.risk-taking.co.uk/intro.htm

Loew, C.A. (1967) 'Acquisition of a hostile attitude and its relationship to aggressive behaviour', *Journal of Personality and Social Psychology*, 5, 335–41.

Loftus, E.F. (1996) *Eyewitness Testimony*, Cambridge, MA: Harvard University Press.

Loftus, E.F. and Burns, H.J. (1982) 'Mental shock can produce retrograde amnesia', *Memory and Cognition*, 10, 318–23.

Loftus, E.F. and Zanni, G. (1975) 'Eyewitness Testimony: The influence of the wording of a question', *Bulletin of the Psychonomic Society*, Vol 5(1), 86–88.

Lorenz, K. (1950) 'The comparative method in studying innate behaviour patterns', *Symposium of the Society of Experimental Biology*, 4, 221–68.

Lucas, A., Morley, R., Cole, T.J., Lister, G. and Leeson-Payne, C. (1992) 'Breast milk and subsequent intelligence quotient in children born pre-term', *The Lancet*, 399, 261–4.

Maccoby, E.E. and Jacklin, C.N. (1974) *The Psychology of Sex Differences*, Stanford, CA: Stanford University Press.

Malinowski, B. (1927) *Sex and Repression in Savage Society*, New York: Harcourt Brace Jovanovitch.

Mantell, D.M. (1971) 'The potential for violence in Germany', *Journal of Social Issues*, 27, 101–12.

Maranon, G. (1924) 'Contribution à l'étude de l'action émotive de l'adrénaline', *Revue Française d'Endocrinologie*, 2, 301–25.

McGarrigle, J. and Donaldson, M. (1974) 'Conservation accidents', *Cognition*, 3, 341–50.

McGovern, D. and Cope, R. (1987) 'The compulsory detention of males of different ethnic groups, with special reference to offender patients', *British Journal of Psychiatry*, 150, 505–12.

Mead, M. (1928) *Coming of Age in Samoa*, Harmondsworth: Penguin.

Meadows, S. (1993) *The Child as a Thinker*, London: Routledge.

Meeus, W.H.J. and Raaijmakers, Q.A.W. (1986) 'Administrative obedience: Carrying out orders to use psychological-administrative violence', *European Journal of Social Psychology*, 16, 311–24.

Mesulam, M.M. (1981) 'Dissociative states with abnormal temporal lobe EEG: Multiple personality and the illusion of possession', *Archives of Neurology*, 38, 176–81.

Milgram, S. (1963) 'Behavioural study of obedience', *Journal of Abnormal and Social Psychology*, 67, 371–8.

Milgram, S. (1974) *Obedience to Authority*, New York: Harper Torchbooks.

Miller, G. (1956) 'The magical number seven, plus or minus two: some limits on our capacity for processing information', *Psychological Review*, 63, 81–97.

Mirescu, C., Peters, J.D., Noiman, L. and Gould, E. (2006) 'Sleep deprivation inhibits adult neurogenesis in the hippocampus by elevating glucocorticoids', *Proceedings of the National Academy of Sciences of the United States of America*, 103, no.50, 19170–5.

Moffitt, T.E. (1988) 'Neuropsychology and self-reported early delinquency in an unselected birth cohort', in T.E. Moffitt and S.A. Mednick (eds), *Biological Contributions to Crime Causation*, New York: Martinus Nijhoff, 93–120.

Moghaddam, F.M., Taylor, D.M. and Wright, S.C. (1993) *Social Psychology in Cross-Cultural Perspective*, New York: W.H. Freeman and Co.

Morris, R. (1994) 'Three sexes and four sexualities: redressing the discourses on gender and sexuality in contemporary Thailand', *Positions*, 2, no.1, 15–43.

Mullen, B. (1986) 'Atrocity as a function of lynch mob composition: A self-attention perspective', *Personality and Social Psychology Bulletin*, 12, 187–97.

Murdock, B.B. (1962) 'The serial position effect of free recall', *Journal of Experimental Psychology*, 64, 482–88.

413

National Autistic Society, 'Autism: what is it?', available at: http://www.nas.org.uk/nas/jsp/polopoly.jsp?d=211

Needleman, H.L., Schell, A., Bellinger, D., Leviton, A. and Allred, E. (1990) 'Lead-associated intellectual deficit', *New England Journal of Medicine*, 322, 83–8.

Nelson, K. (1973) 'Structure and strategy in learning to talk', *Monographs of the Society for Research in Child Development*, 38 (one and two).

Oliver, K. (2001) *Applying Skills to Psychology*, London: Hodder & Stoughton.

Olton, D.S. and Papas, B.C. (1979) 'Spatial memory and hippocampal function', *Neuropsychologia*, 17, 669–82.

Olton, D.S., Becker, J.T. and Handelman, G.H. (1979) 'Hippocampus, space and memory', *Behavioral and Brain Sciences*, 2, 313–65.

Olton, D.S., Collison, C. and Werz, M.A. (1977) 'Spatial memory and radial arm maze performance of rats', *Learning and Motivation*, 8, 289–314.

Olweus, D. (1980) 'Familial and temperamental determinants of aggressive behaviour in adolescent boys. A causal analysis', *Developmental Psychology*, 16, 644–66.

Orne, M.T. (1962) 'On the social psychology of the psychological experiment, with particular reference to demand characteristics and their implications', *American Psychologist*, 17, 776–83.

Orne, M.T. and Holland, C.C. (1968) 'On the ecological validity of laboratory deceptions', *International Journal of Psychiatry*, 6, 282–93, 766.

Ornstein, R. (1986) *The Physiology of Conscious-ness*, Harmondsworth: Penguin, 2nd edition.

Ozonoff, S., Pennington, B.E. and Rogers, S.J. (1991) 'Executive function deficits in high functioning autistic children: Relationship to the theory of mind', *Journal of Child Psychology and Psychiatry*, 32, 1081–1106.

Pavlov, I.P. (1927) *Conditioned Reflexes*, London: Oxford University Press.

Perner, J. (1991) *Understanding the Representational Mind*, Cambridge, MA: Bradford Books/MIT Press.

Perner, J., Leekam, S. and Wimmer, H. (1987) 'Three year olds' difficulty in understanding false belief: cognitive limitation, lack of knowledge or pragmatic misunderstanding?', *British Journal of Developmental Psychology*, 5, 125–37.

Pervin, L.A. (1984) *Personality*, New York: John Wiley, 4th edition.

Piaget, J. and Inhelder, B. (1956) *The Child's Conception of Space*, London: RKP.

Piliavin, I.M., Rodin, J.A. and Piliavin, J.A. (1969) *Good Samaritanism, an Underground Phenomenon?*, Journal of Personality and Social Psychology, 13, no.4, 289–99.

Piliavin, I.M., Piliavin, J.A. and Rodin, J. (1975) 'Costs, diffusion and the stigmatised victim', *Journal of Personality and Social Psychology*, 32, 429–38.

Piliavin, J.A., Dovidio, J.F., Gaertner, S. and Clark III, R.D. (1981) *Emergency Intervention*, New York: Academic Press.

Plomin, R. (ed.), DeFries, J., McClearn, G. and Rutter, M. (1997) *Behavioral Genetics*, New York: W.H. Freeman and Co.

Prince, M. (1909) *The Dissociation of a Personality*, New York: Longmans.

Putnam, F.W., Post, R.M. and Guroff, J.J. (1983) '100 cases of multiple personality disorder', paper presented at the annual meeting of the American Psychiatric Association, New York.

Rasmussen, T. and Milner, B. (1977) 'The role of early left-brain injury in determining lateralisation of cerebral speech functions', *Annals of the New York Academy of Sciences*, 299, 355–69.

Rehm, J., Steinleitner, M. and Lilli, W. (1987) 'Wearing uniforms and aggression. A field experiment', *European Journal of Social Psychology*, 17, 357–60.

Richter, C.P. (1922) 'A behaviouristic study of the activity of the rat', *Comparative Psychology Monographs*, 1, 1–55.

Ringelmann, M. (1913) 'Recherches sur les moteurs animés: Travail de l'homme', *Annales de l'Institut National Argonomique*, 2e série, tome 12, 1–40.

Rivers, W.H.R. (1901) 'Vision' in A.C. Haddon (ed.), *Reports of the Cambridge Anthropological Expedition to the Torres Straits*, Vol. 2, Part 1, Cambridge: Cambridge University Press.

Rose, S.A. and Blank, M. (1974) 'The potency of context in children's cognition: an illustration through conservation', *Child Development*, 45, 499–502.

Rosenhan, D.L. and Seligman, M.E.P. (1989) *Abnormal Psychology*, New York: Norton, 2nd edition.

Rosenzweig, M.R. (1984) 'Experience, memory and the brain', *American Psychologist*, 39, 365–76.

Ross, L. and Nisbett, R.E. (1991) *The Person and the Situation*, New York: McGraw-Hill.

Rumbaugh, D.M. (1977) *Language Learning by a Chimpanzee: The Lana Project*, New York: Academic Press.

Russell, J. and Roberts, C. (2001) *Angles on Psychological Research*, Cheltenham: Nelson Thornes.

Rutter, M. (1981) *Maternal Deprivation Reassessed*, Harmondsworth: Penguin, 2nd edition.

Sacks, O. (1985) 'The twins' in *The Man Who Mistook his Wife for a Hat and Other Clinical Tales*, New York: Harper & Row.

Sacks, O. (1995) *An Anthropologist on Mars*, London: Picador.

Saks, E.R. (1992) 'Multiple personality disorder and criminal responsibility', *U.C. Davis Law Review*, 25, 383–461.

Sapir, E. (1929) 'The status of linguistics as a science', *Language*, 5, 207–14.

Savage-Rumbaugh, S. (1988) 'A new look at ape language: comprehension of vocal speech and syntax', *Nebraska Symposium on Motivation*, 35, 201–55.

Savage-Rumbaugh, E.S. (1986) *Ape Language: From conditioned responses to symbols*, New York: Columbia University Press.

Savage-Rumbaugh, E.S. and Rumbaugh, D. (1979) 'Symbolization, language and chimpanzees: A theoretical reevaluation based on initial language acquisition processes in four young Pan troglogdytes', *Brain and Language*, 6: 265–300.

Savage-Rumbaugh, S. and Lewin, R. (1994) *Kanzi – The Ape at the Brink of the Human Mind*, London: Doubleday.

Schachter, S. (1964) 'The interaction of cognitive and physiological determinants of emotional state' in L. Berkowitz (ed.), *Advances in Experimental Social Psychology*, Vol. 1, New York: Academic Press.

Schaffer, H.R. (1971) *The Growth of Sociability*, Harmondsworth: Penguin.

Schaffer, H.R. and Emmerson, P.E. (1964) 'The development of social attachments in infancy',

Monographs of Social Research in Child Development, 29, no.94.

Schreiber, F.R. (1973) *Sybil*, Harmondsworth: Penguin.

Searle, A. (1999) *Introducing Research and Data in Psychology*, London: Routledge.

Sears, D.O. (1986) 'College sophomores in the laboratory: Influences of a narrow data base on social psychology's view of human nature', *Journal of Personality and Social Psychology*, 51, no.3, 515–30.

Sears, D.O. (1988) 'Symbolic racism' in P. Katz and D. Taylor (eds), *Eliminating Racism. Profiles in Controversy*, New York: Plenum, 53–84.

Seashore, R.H. and Eckerson, L.D. (1940) 'The measurement of individual differences in general English vocabularies', *Journal of Educational Psychology*, 31, 14–38.

Segall, M.H., Campbell, D.T. and Herskovits, M.J. (1963) 'Cultural differences in the perception of geometric illusions', *Science*, 139, 769–71.

Segall, M.H., Dasen, P.R., Berry, J.W. and Poortinga, Y.H. (1999) *Human Behaviour in Global Perspective: An Introduction to Cross-Cultural Psychology*, Needham Heights, MA: Allyn and Bacon, 2nd edition.

Seligman, M.E.P. (1975) *Helplessness: on Depression, Development and Death*, San Francisco: W.H. Freeman & Co.

Shallice, T. (1982) 'Specific impairments of planning', *Philosophical Transactions of the Royal Society of London*, B298, 199–209.

Shallice, T. and Warrington, E.K. (1970) 'Independent functioning of verbal memory stores: a neuropsychological study', *Quarterly Journal of Experimental Psychology*, 22, 261–73.

Sheehan, W., Sewall, B. and Thurber, S. (2005) 'Dissociative identity disorder and temporal lobe involvement: Replication and a cautionary note', available at: http://www.priory.com/psych/did.htm

Sheridan, C.L. and King, K.G. (1972) 'Obedience to authority with an authentic victim', *Proceedings of the 80th Annual Convention of the American Psychological Association*, 7, 165–6.

Sherif, M. (1966) *Group Conflict and Co-operation: Their social psychology*, London: RKP.

Shields, J. (1962) *Monozygotic Twins Brought Up Apart and Brought Together*, London: Oxford University Press.

Shotland, R.L. and Straw, M.K. (1976) 'Bystander response to an assault: When a man attacks a woman', *Journal of Personality and Social Psychology*, 34, 990–9.

Sigman, M., Mundy, P., Sherman, T. and Ungerer, J.A. (1986) 'Social interaction of autistic, mentally retarded and normal children and their caregivers', *Journal of Child Psychology and Psychiatry*, 27, 647–55.

Sime, J.D. (1983) 'Affiliative behaviour during escape to building exits', *Journal of Environmental Psychology*, 3, 21–41.

Sizemore, C.C. (1978) *I'm Eve*, New York: Jove.

Sizemore, C.C. and Pittillo, E.S. (1977) *I'm Eve*, New York: Doubleday.

Skinner, B.F. (1938) *The Behaviour of Organisms*, New York: Appleton-Century-Crofts.

Skinner, B.F. (1957) *Verbal Behaviour*, New York: Appleton-Century-Crofts.

Slobin, D.I. (1975) 'On the nature of talk to children' in E.H. Lenneberg and E. Lenneberg (eds), *Infant Development*, Hove: Lawrence Erlbaum Associates Ltd.

Smith, P. and Cowie, H. (1988) *Understanding Children's Development*, Oxford: Blackwell.

Spanos, N.P., Weekes, J.R. and Bertrand, L.D. (1985) 'Multiple personality: A social psychological perspective', *Journal of Abnormal Psychology*, 94, 362–76.

Spearman, C. (1904) 'General intelligence, objectively determined and measured', *American Journal of Psychology*, 15, 201–93.

Sperling, G. (1960) 'The information available in brief visual presentation', *Psychological Monographs*, 74, no.498.

Sperling, G. (1963) 'The information available in brief visual presentation', *Psychological Monographs*, 74.

Springer, S.P. and Deutsch, G. (eds) (1993) *Left Brain/Right Brain*, New York: W.H. Freeman & Co., 4th edition.

Stang, D.J. (1973) 'Conformity, ability and self-esteem', *Representative Research in Social Psychology*, 3, 97–103.

Stern, D. (1977) *The First Relationship: Infant and Mother*, London: Fontana.

Stirling, J.D. and Hellewell, J.S.E. (1999) *Psychopathology*, London: Routledge.

Storr, A. (1989) *Freud*, Oxford: Oxford University Press.

Szasz, T.S. (1960) 'The myth of mental illness', *American Psychologist*, 15, 113–18.

Tajfel, H. (1970) 'Experiments in intergroup discrimination', *Scientific American*, 223, 96–102.

Tajfel, H. (1982) *Social Identity and Intergroup Relations*, Cambridge: Cambridge University Press.

Tajfel, H. and Turner, J. (1979) 'An integrative theory of intergroup conflict' in G.W. Austin and S. Worchel (eds), *The Social Psychology of Intergroup Relations*, Monterey, California: Brooks Cole.

Tajfel, H. and Turner, J.C. (1986) 'The social identity theory of Intergroup Behaviour' in S. Worchel and W. Austin (eds), *Psychology of Intergroup Relations*, Chicago: Nelson-Hall.

Terman, L.M. (1916) *The Measurement of Intelligence*, Boston: Houghton Mifflin.

Terrace, H.S., Petitto, L.A., Sanders, R.J. and Bever, T.G. (1979) 'Can an ape create a sentence?', *Science*, 206, 891–902.

Thibaut, J.W. and Kelley, H.H. (1959) *The Social Psychology of Groups*, New York: Wiley.

Thigpen, Corbett, H. and Cleckley, Harvey M. (1957) *The Three Faces of Eve*, n.p.: Secker & Warburg.

Tizard, B. and Hodges, J. (1978) 'The effects of early institutional rearing on the development of eight-year-old children', *Journal of Child Psychology and Psychiatry*, 19, 99–118.

Tizard, B. and Rees, J. (1974) 'A comparison of the effects of adoption, restoration to the natural mother and continued institutionalisation on the cognitive development of four-year-old children', *Child Development*, 45, 92–9.

Tulving, E. (1972) 'Episodic and semantic memory' in E. Tulving and W. Donaldson (eds), *Organisation of Memory*, London: Academic Press.

Turnbull, C.M. (1961) *The Forest People*, New York: Simon & Schuster.

Turner, J.C. (1985) 'Social categorization and the self-concept: a social cognitive theory of group behaviour' in E.J. Lawler (ed.), *Advances in Group Processes: theory and research*, Vol. 2, Greenwich, CT: JAI Press, 77–122.

Turner, J.C. (1982) 'Towards a cognitive redefinition of the social group' in H. Tajfel (ed.), *Social*

Identity and Intergroup Relations, Cambridge: Cambridge University Press.

University of Iowa (2006) 'Study finds pathological gambling runs in families', *Science Daily*, 16 March (retrieved 2 December 2007).

Valins, S. (1966) 'Cognitive effects of false heart-rate feedback', *Journal of Personality and Social Psychology*, 4, 400–8.

Wagenaar, W.A. (1988) *Paradoxes of Gambling Behavior*, Hillsdale, NJ: Erlbaum.

Walker, M.B. (1992) 'Irrational thinking among slot machine players', *Journal of Gambling Studies*, 8, no.3, 245–61.

Walker, M.B. (1989) 'Some problems with the concept of "gambling addiction": Should theories of addiction be generalized to include excessive gambling?', *Journal of Gambling Studies*, 5, no.3, 179–200.

Watson, J.B. and Rayner, R. (1920) 'Conditioned emotional reactions', *Journal of Experimental Psychology*, 3, 1–14.

Watson, R.I. (1973) 'Investigation into deindividuation using a cross-cultural survey technique', *Journal of Personality and Social Psychology*, 25, 342–5.

Wechsler, D. (1958) *The Measurement and Appraisal of Adult Intelligence*, Baltimore: Williams and Wilkins, 4th edition.

Weiner, B. (1992) *Human Motivation: Metaphors, theories and research*, Newbury Park, CA: Sage.

Whyte, W.F. (1943) *Street Corner Society*, Chicago: University of Chicago Press.

Wicker, A.W. (1969) 'Attitudes versus actions: The relationship between verbal and overt behavioural responses to attitude objects', *Journal of Social Issues*, 25, 41–78.

Wilde Astington, J. (1994) *The Child's Discovery of the Mind*, London: Fontana Press.

Williams, K., Harkins, S. and Latané, B. (1981) 'Identifiability as a deterrent to social loafing: Two cheering experiments', *Journal of Personality and Social Psychology*, 40, 303–11.

Williams, T.M. (ed.) (1986) *The Impact of Television: A national experiment in three communities*, New York: Academic Press.

Wimmer, H. and Perner, J. (1983) 'Beliefs about beliefs: representation and constraining function of wrong beliefs in young children's understanding of deception', *Cognition*, 13, 103–28.

Witkin, H.A., Mednick, S.A., Schulsinger, F., Bakkestrom, E., Christansen, K.O., Goodenough, D.R., Hirschhorn, K., Lundsteen, C., Owen, D.R., Philips, J., Rubin, D.B. and Stocking, M. (1976) 'Criminality in XYY and XXY men: the elevated crime rate of XYY males is not related to aggression', *Science*, 193, 547–55.

Zimbardo, P.G. (1969/1970) 'The human choice: Individuation, reason and order versus deindividuation, impulse and chaos' in W.J. Arnold and D. Levine (eds), *Nebraska Symposium on Motivation*, Lincoln: University of Nebraska Press.

Zimbardo, P.G. (2007) *The Lucifer Effect*, London: Random House.

Zimbardo, P.G. (2006) 'On rethinking the psychology of tyranny: The BBC prison experiment', *British Journal of Social Psychology*, 45, 47–53.

Zuckerman, M. (1994) *Behavioural Expressions and Biosocial Bases of Sensation Seeking*, Cambridge: Cambridge University Press.

Zuckerman, M. (1950), www.risktaking.co.uk

Index

Index

Index

Index